INTRODUCTION TO
CRIMINAL JUSTICE
SECOND EDITION

ROBERT M. BOHM

PROFESSOR
DEPARTMENT OF CRIMINAL JUSTICE
AND LEGAL STUDIES
UNIVERSITY OF CENTRAL FLORIDA
ORLANDO, FLORIDA

KEITH N. HALEY

DEAN/PROFESSOR
SCHOOL OF CRIMINAL JUSTICE
TIFFIN UNIVERSITY
TIFFIN, OHIO

**Glencoe
McGraw-Hill**

New York, New York   Columbus, Ohio   Woodland Hills, California   Peoria, Illinois

Library of Congress Cataloging-in-Publication

Bohm, Robert M.
Introduction to criminal justice/ Robert M. Bohm, Keith N. Haley.
--2nd ed.
Includes bibliographical references and index.
ISBN 0-02-802823-6 (alk. paper). -- ISBN 0-02-802824-4 (alk. paper)
1. Criminal justice, Administration or --United States. 2. Crime--United States.
3. Criminal law--United States. I. Haley, Keith N. II. TITLE.
HV9950.B63   1998
364.973--DC21   98–24208
                                                                      CIP

Glencoe/McGraw-Hill

A Division of The McGraw-Hill Companies

Introduction to Criminal Justice, 2nd edition
Student Text

Send all inquiries to:
Glencoe/McGraw-Hill
936 Eastwind Drive
Westerville, OH 43081

ISBN 0-02-802823-6
ISBN 0-02-802830-9
ISBN 0-02-805063-0

Printed in the United States of America.

3 4 5 6 7 8 9 10 027 05 04 03 02 01 00 99

Brief Contents

Expanded Contents

3 Explaining Crime 63

4 The Rule of Law 105

5 History and Structure of American Law Enforcement 145

7 The Administration of Justice 223

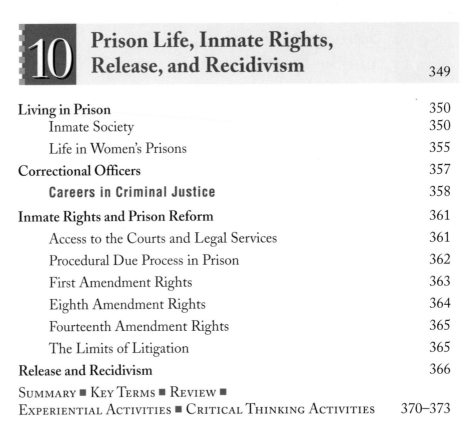

12 Juvenile Justice   423

13 Understanding and Predicting the Future of Criminal Justice   463

The *Introduction to Criminal Justice* Learning System

This book was designed for you to help you learn. You will learn more if you use a learning system. *Introduction to Criminal Justice*, second edition, uses the following integrated learning system:

1. **Concept Preview**—The chapter opener introduces the key concepts to be learned.

2. **Concept Development**—The chapter text explains concepts in a structured, visual format.

3. **Concept Reinforcement**—In-text examples, graphics, and special features enhance and strengthen your learning.

4. **Concept Review and Application**—End-of-chapter exercises and activities encourage you to apply what you learned.

1. Concept Preview

Chapter objectives alert you to the major concepts to learn. Turn the objectives into questions, and, as you read the chapter, look for the answers to the questions.

A **chapter outline** introduces the topics that will be discussed. Scan the outline to familiarize yourself with the subject matter.

The **opening photograph** sets the stage for the chapter content and provides a visual connection to the chapter.

2. Concept Development

The **heading structure** shows the relationship among the topics in a section and breaks the material into easily digestible segments of information. Scan the headings to locate the information that will help you answer the questions you formed from the chapter objectives.

Key terms are defined when introduced and are printed in boldface to make them easy to find.

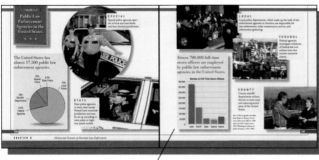

Important concepts and data are depicted in **visual format** to make them easier to understand.

Key Terms are also defined in the margin to make it easy for you to learn them.

3. Concept Reinforcement

Policy implications alert you to the issues facing criminal justice professionals.

Examples help you understand the concepts being presented.

Special features reinforce and enhance your understanding of the concepts presented.

4. Concept Review and Application

The **Summary by Chapter Objectives** sums up the chapter's major themes. The summary is organized by chapter objectives and provides you with general answers to the questions you posed when you began the chapter.

The **Key Terms** listing consolidates the criminal justice vocabulary presented in the chapter. If you can't remember what a term means, the page reference alerts you to the location of its definition in the chapter.

The **Questions for Review** reexamine key points presented in the chapter. These questions test your knowledge of the chapter concepts and can help you review for exams.

The **Experiential Activities** offer opportunities for you to broaden your understanding of the material presented, prepare yourself to participate in classroom discussions, and enhance your performance on exams. An Internet project encourages you to take advantage of this important technology.

The **Critical Thinking Exercises** encourage you to apply the concepts you have learned. Each scenario provides you the opportunity to analyze a situation, using the knowledge you have gained from the chapter, and to then propose a solution, evaluate a proposal, or make a decision.

Additional Study and Tutorial Resources

To assist you in learning and applying criminal justice concepts, Glencoe provides several resources in addition to the textbook. A print *Study Guide* and a *Tutorial With Simulation Applications* CD-ROM are available for purchase. The Glencoe *Introduction to Criminal Justice,* Second Edition, Study Center Web Site is available to you free of charge.

Tutorial With Simulation Applications CD-ROM

This *Tutorial With Simulation Applications CD-ROM* is a **comprehensive interactive study tool** designed to assist you in learning and applying concepts. It contains a visual tutorial of major concepts, followed by reinforcement exercises, followed by simulation applications:

- **Interactive Content Tutorial**
  This visually oriented tutorial covers all concepts in the textbook. Chapter content is divided into sections followed immediately by reinforcement and review questions.

- **26 Application Simulations**
  Chapter concepts and issues are explored and applied through application simulations, which pose real-world situations to which you are asked to respond. You receive immediate feedback regarding the appropriateness of your choices.

- **HyperChallenge Chapter Review Game**
  An innovative chapter review program called HyperChallenge is designed along the lines of "Jeopardy." New game boards are created every time you start a new game to help you prepare for tests and quizzes.

- **Glencoe CJ Online.** If you have access to the Internet, clicking on this button will start up a browser and connect to the *Glencoe Introduction to Criminal Justice, Second Edition, Study Center Web Site.* At that site you will find current events material, links to CJ sites, a CJ bulletin board, and multiple reinforcement and assessment tools.

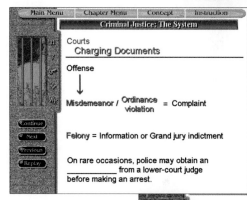

Glencoe Introduction to Criminal Justice, Second Edition, Study Center Web Site

This unique study center site contains a wealth of current event material and multiple reinforcement and assessment tools. Visit it at: **www.glencoe.com/ps/cj/intro.** Here is what you will find:

What's New

Links to newly posted articles/information and criminal justice related Web sites appear on each chapter resources page. Updated regularly.

Chapter Resources

In the News
New articles and information are correlated by textbook chapter section headings.

CJ Web Links
Relevant annotated Web links are organized by textbook section headings.

CJ Weblinks by Topic
All Web site links are grouped by topic.

Knowledge Checkpoint

Test your grasp of concepts through a variety of interactive reinforcement tools:

- Practice Tests
- Ehomework
- Crossword Puzzle
- Concentration Game
- Interactive Exercise

CJ Bulletin Board

You can post comments on criminal justice topics and view the comments of others on current events and issues.

Electronic Library

A link to Elibrary, a powerful online library, is available on a special subscription basis.

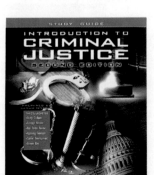

Study Guide

The print *Study Guide* is designed to assist you in reviewing and learning the course material. It contains the following sections:

- Study Outline
- Concept Review
- Key Terms Review
- Applying Concepts
- Career Development

Student Success in Criminal Justice

If you have just purchased this book for the introductory criminal justice course, congratulations! You have taken the first step toward a first-rate criminal justice education. However, it is not enough to own this book, you must read and study it and take advantage of the many learning aids we and your instructor provide. If you follow the strategies we outline, we are confident that you will be successful in this course. Not only will you earn a superior grade, but you will gain a broad and comprehensive understanding of criminal justice. That knowledge will serve you well as a strong foundation for other, more specialized courses in criminal justice and the social sciences.

The book is divided into 13 chapters and is organized to provide a logical approach to understanding the operation of criminal justice in the United States. We assume that you have little more than a popular, media-informed, largely erroneous knowledge of the subject. The first chapter contains important background information for topics presented elsewhere in the book. It presents a brief overview of the entire criminal justice response to crime; that is, the stages of the process from the commission of a crime through the law enforcement response and the administration of justice (courts and prosecution) to corrections. We recommend that you familiarize yourself with the basic elements of this process as soon as possible. This knowledge will help you understand how the different parts of the process fit together. This chapter also provides a detailed description of the costs of criminal justice in the United States—a subject that concerns nearly everyone—and introduces the aforementioned principal theme of the book: myths about crime and criminal justice.

Chapters 2, 3, and 4 furnish the context for understanding criminal justice in the United States. A critical understanding of criminal justice requires a critical understanding of the context in which it operates. The second chapter examines the nature of crime and its consequences, focusing on definitions, measurement, costs, fear, and victims. Chapter 3 surveys theories or explanations of crime and delinquency, their policy implications, and their problems. We believe that criminal justice policies should be based on well-supported and compelling theories of crime. All too often they are not. Finally, Chapter 4 addresses criminal law and its application. The purpose of criminal justice is to enforce criminal law. Much of Chapter 4 is devoted to procedural law, which deals with the rights afforded people accused of crimes.

The next seven chapters examine in detail what was briefly described in Chapter 1: the components and the oper-

ation of criminal justice in the United States. Chapters 5 and 6 cover law enforcement; Chapters 7 and 8, the administration of justice (courts and prosecution); and Chapters 9, 10, and 11, corrections. Chapter 12 is devoted to juvenile justice, and Chapter 13 explores the future of criminal justice.

Why Study Criminal Justice?

No one has to tell you how important criminal justice is in the United States today. The ways individuals and society respond to crime are commonplace in our daily lives. We cannot escape them. We fear crime. We distrust strangers. We avoid going to certain places, especially at night. We carry mace and whistles. We lock our car doors, as well as the doors to our homes. We have burglar alarms installed. We buy theft insurance. We own guns for protection. We keep ferocious dogs. We hire people to protect us. We participate in neighborhood watches. We travel in groups.

We also find crime and reactions to it fascinating. We read about them in newspapers, magazines, and books. We are enthralled by portrayals of them on television and in the movies. Unfortunately, crime victimizes too many of us, including the perpetrators themselves, whose lives, like those of their victims, are likely to be forever diminished because of their crimes.

Criminal justice is a response to crime, but unlike the personal responses listed above, criminal justice is a formal response by agents of local, state, and federal governments.

Many of you are probably interested in joining the millions of citizens with careers in criminal justice. An important purpose of this book is to enable you to make an informed decision about whether to pursue a career in criminal justice. For example, it is important to know that for more than two and one-half centuries, criminal justice officials in the United States have tried to significantly reduce crime, or at least the fear of crime. By nearly all available measures, they have not succeeded. There are many reasons for this failure and plenty of blame to go around. We believe that a major reason for the sad state of modern criminal justice is that many criminal justice personnel, particularly law enforcement and correctional officers, lack postsecondary education. We are convinced that a good postsecondary education in criminal justice, and in the liberal arts generally, can significantly improve the performance of most criminal justice officials.

The need for postsecondary criminal justice education becomes more evident everyday. For one thing, old types of crime disappear (it is no longer a crime for adults to consume alcohol), and new forms of crime emerge to befuddle the best efforts of those charged with dealing with crime. Police officers of the nineteenth century could not have imagined, nor dealt with, sophisticated computer crimes, and today's law enforcement officers (most of whom also lack the expertise to deal with computer crimes) rarely get calls about horse thieves. We are certain that criminal justice personnel who have criminal justice degrees and have used this book as directed, and then go to work in the field, will be better at their jobs for using it.

This book, however, is not just for students interested in careers in criminal justice. It is also for students who want to learn more about this important social institution. Knowledge of criminal justice is vital to a free and democratic people. All citizens need to know their legal rights and responsibilities. Also, the better informed citizens are, the better able they are to protect themselves. A major theme of this book is that much of what the public "knows" about criminal justice in the United States is myth—that is, simply wrong or significantly misunderstood. Consequently, in addition to presenting current and accurate information about criminal justice in the United States and standard and generally accepted interpretations of historical and modern developments, this book "sets the record straight" in areas where, we believe, many people are being misled. With an education in criminal justice, you will feel more comfortable and better equipped to participate in criminal justice policy formulation. You will also be more effective in solving problems in your community. More generally, a good criminal justice education will help you develop the critical thinking skills you need to be a constructive participant in a democratic nation and to have greater control over your own destiny.

How to Study Criminal Justice

As promised, here is a detailed and, we believe, foolproof strategy for succeeding in your introductory criminal justice course. (The strategy can also be applied successfully in other courses.) Before beginning, however, it is important to emphasize three qualities that are important in the learning process and that we cannot teach you: *desire, commitment, and perseverance.* If you are unwilling to apply those three qualities to your study of criminal justice, we cannot guarantee success.

Criminal justice, like any other course, builds in stages. As previously noted, information presented in later chapters often assumes knowledge of information introduced in earlier chapters. You cannot afford to fall behind and then expect to catch up in one massive cramming session.

To get off to a good start, prepare yourself before the course begins by setting learning goals, organizing your time, studying your syllabus, and examining your own learning style.

Set Learning Goals for Yourself

The purpose of setting goals is to understand exactly what you plan to accomplish. Ask yourself what you want out of this course. Is it a specific grade? Perhaps you need an A or a B to keep up your grade average. Perhaps you need a certain body of knowledge from this course to get into a higher level course. Perhaps you need a specific set of skills. You may be taking this course to meet a requirement for your job, to attain a personal career goal, or simply to satisfy your curiosity about the subject. Be forewarned, however: if you set your goals too low, you are likely to achieve only those low goals. For example, if you are not interested in the course but are taking it only because it is required of all majors, you should not be disappointed if you earn less than an A or a B.

Organize Your Time

Now that you have set your goals, you need to organize your time to accomplish them. Time management allows you to meet your goals and still have time for activities. It helps you work smarter, not just harder. As a rule of thumb, for every class hour, allow two study hours. If an exam is coming up, allow more study time. Plan to study when you are most alert. You will retain information longer if you study on a regular basis, rather than during one or two cramming sessions. Either before or after a study session, have some fun! Timely breaks from studying enhance the learning process.

Study Your Syllabus

Usually the course syllabus is available on the first day of class, but sometimes it is available sooner. If you can get a copy early, you will be that much ahead. The syllabus is your map for navigating the course. It should define the goals or objectives of the course, specify the textbook and supporting materials to be used, and explain course requirements, including the method or formula for determining final grades. The syllabus will also include a course schedule indicating when particular topics will be covered, what material needs to be read for each class, and when tests will be given. Other useful information on a course syllabus may include the instructor's name, office location, phone number, and office hours and, perhaps, the types of extra credit or special projects you may complete. Keep the syllabus in your notebook or organizer at all times. Review it at the beginning of each class and study session so you will know what course material will be covered and what you will be expected to know. Write down important due dates and test dates on your calendar.

Eight-Step Study Plan to Maximize Your Learning

This plan is based on research that shows that people learn—and remember—best when they have repeated exposure to the same material. This technique not only helps you learn better but can also reduce anxiety by allowing you to become familiar with material step by step. You will go over material at least six times before you take an exam.

Step 1: Use a Reading Strategy

In most cases, you will be asked to read material before each class. The SQ3R (Survey, Question, Read, Recite, and Review) method can help you get the most out of the material in every chapter of your book. Reading the material before class will acquaint you with the subject matter, arouse your interest in the subject, and help you know what questions to ask in class.

Survey By surveying an assignment, you are preparing yourself for a more thorough reading of the material.

Read the Chapter Title, the Chapter Objectives, and the Chapter Outline What topics does the chapter cover? What are the learning objectives? Do you already know something about the subject?

Read the Summary by Chapter Objectives This will give you an overview of what is covered in the chapter.

Look for Key Terms Key terms are the names for or words associated with the important concepts covered in the chapter. Key terms are printed in boldface type in the text. Definitions of the key terms appear in the margins near the text in which they are introduced.

Question Turn the chapter objectives into questions. For example, if the objective is, "Identify institutions of social control and explain what makes criminal justice an institution of social control," turn it into a question by asking yourself, "What are institutions of social control and why is criminal justice an institution of social control?" Look for the answers to your questions as you read the chapter. By beginning the study of a chapter with questions, you will be more motivated to read the chapter to find the answers. To make sure your answers are correct, consult the summary at the end of the chapter.

You can also write a question mark in pencil in the margin next to any material you don't understand as you read the chapter. Your goal is to answer all your questions and erase the question marks before you take an exam.

Read Before you begin a thorough reading of the material, make sure that you are rested and alert and that your reading area is well-lighted and ventilated. This will not only make

your reading time more efficient but help you understand what you read.

Skim the Material Generally, you will need to read material more than once before you really understand it. Start by skimming, or reading straight through, the material. Do not expect to understand everything at once. You are getting the big picture and becoming familiar with the material.

Read, Highlight, Outline The second time, read more slowly. Take time to study explanations and examples. Highlight key terms, important concepts, numbered lists, or other items that will help you understand the material. Most students use colored highlighting markers for this step. Put question marks in pencil in the margin beside any points or concepts you don't understand.

Outline the chapter in your notebook. By writing the concepts and definitions into your notebook, you are using your tactile sense to reinforce your learning and to remember better what you read. Be sure you state concepts and definitions accurately. You can use brief phrases or take more extensive notes for your outline, depending on the material.

Apply What You Read In criminal justice, as in other courses, you must be able to apply what you read. The experiential activities and critical thinking exercises at the end of each chapter allow you to do this. Complete those activities and exercises when you have finished studying the chapter.

Recite In this step, you do a self-check of what you have learned in reading the chapter. Go back to the questions you formed from the chapter objectives and see if you can answer them. Also, see if you can answer the Questions for Review

Study Plan

1. Use a Reading Strategy
2. Combine Learning Styles in Class
3. Review Class Notes
4. Reread the Text
5. Get Help if Necessary
6. Study Creatively for Tests
7. Develop Test-Taking Strategies
8. Review Your Results

at the end of each chapter. Try explaining the material to a friend so that he or she understands it. These exercises will reveal your strengths and weaknesses.

Review Now go back and review the entire chapter. Erase any question marks that you have answered. If you still don't understand something, put a Post-it by it or mark it in your text. These items are the questions you can ask in class.

Step 2: Combine Learning Styles in Class

Think of the time you spend in class as your opportunity to learn by listening and participating. You are combining visual, aural, and tactile learning styles in one experience.

Attendance: More Than Just Showing Up
Your attitude is a critical element. Attend class *ready to learn.* That means being prepared by having read and reread the assignment, having your questions ready, and having your note-taking materials organized.

Because criminal justice, like other courses, builds in stages, it is important for you to attend every class. You cannot ask questions if you are not there. And you may miss handouts, explanations, or key points that often are included on a test.

One final note. If you cannot attend a class, call the instructor or a classmate to find out what you have missed. You do not want to show up the next day and find out the instructor is giving a test!

Attention: Active Listening and Learning
During most classes, you spend more time listening than you do reading, writing, or speaking. Learning by listening, however, calls for you to become an *active listener* and to participate in the class. This means you come to class prepared, you focus on the subject, you concentrate on what the instructor or other students are saying, and you ask questions. Block out distractions such as street noises or people walking by the classroom.

Participation
In reading the material before class, you will have made a list of questions. If those questions are not answered in class, then ask your instructor to answer them. If the instructor makes a point you do not understand, jot it down and ask him or her to explain it as soon as you can.

Note Taking
Why take notes? We forget nearly 60 percent of what we hear within one hour after we hear it. Memory is highly unreliable. This is why taking notes during class is so important.

Note taking involves both listening and writing at the same time. You must learn not to concentrate too much on one and forget the other. Follow these tips for taking good notes.

Listen for and Record Main Ideas You do not need to write down everything your instructor or other students say. By reading your assignment before class, you will know what the main topics are. Listen for those topics when your instructor goes over the material in class, then take notes on what he or she says about them. If the instructor emphasizes the importance of a topic for a test, be sure to make a note of this information as well (for example, "This section really important for exam"). If you think you have missed a point, either ask your instructor to repeat or rephrase it right away, or mark the point with a question mark and ask your instructor about it later.

Use Outline Style and Abbreviations Set up your notes in outline style, and use phrases instead of complete sentences. Use abbreviations of symbols whenever possible (& for *and*, *w* for *with*, and so on). This technique will help you write faster to keep up with the instructor.

Step 3: Review Class Notes

Listening and taking notes are critical steps in learning, but reviewing your notes is equally important. Remember: Repetition reinforces learning. The more times you go over material, the better you learn it.

Fill in the Blanks
As soon as possible after a class, review your notes to fill in any missing information. Make sure you do it the same day. Sometimes you may be able to recall the missing information. If you can't, check your textbook or ask to see another student's notes to obtain what you need. Spell out important abbreviations that you may not recognize later.

Highlight Important Information
Marking different types of information helps organize your notes. You want to find what you need when you need it. Try these suggestions for highlighting your notes.

1. Use different colored highlighting pens to mark key terms, important Supreme Court decisions, and other kinds of information. Then, you will know that green, for example, always indicates key terms; blue indicates Supreme Court decisions; and so on. This method will help you find specific information quickly and easily.

2. Write a heading such as "Costs of Criminal Justice" at the beginning of each key topic. These headings can either correspond to those in the chapter, or you may make up your own headings to help you remember key information.

Step 4: Reread the Text

After reviewing your notes, you are ready to reread the chapter to fix the concepts in your mind.

Read for Details

- Go over the key points and main ideas carefully. Make sure you understand them thoroughly and can explain them to someone in your own words.
- Review the Chapter Objectives (that you have turned into questions) and the Questions for Review. Make sure you can answer all the questions and that you understand your answers.

Mark Your Text

- Highlight any important terms or concepts you may have missed in your previous reading.
- Highlight any Myth/Fact boxes, FYIs, or figures you feel are important to remember.
- Erase any question marks in the margin that represent questions you have answered.
- Use Post-it notes to mark anything of which you are still unsure. Ask questions about those points in the next class, talk them over with other students, or make an appointment to meet with your instructor to discuss your questions.

Step 5: Get Help if Necessary

What if you have read the material, taken notes, and asked questions, and you still do not understand the mater-

ial? You can get further help. As soon as it becomes apparent that you need some help, ask for it. If you wait until the semester is nearly over, it may be too late. Here are several sources of help.

Your Instructors   Most instructors are willing to spend extra time with students who need help. Find out what your instructor's office hours are and schedule an appointment to go over the material in more detail. You may need several sessions. Remember to take notes during those sessions.

Study Groups   Join a study group in your class, or start your own. What one person does not learn, another does. Study groups take advantage of each member's expertise. You can often learn best by listening and talking to others in such groups. Chances are that, together, you will be able to master the material better than any one of you could alone. This is an example of power in numbers.

Learning Labs   Many schools have learning labs that offer individual instruction or tutoring for students who are having trouble with course material. Ask your instructor or classmates for information about the learning labs in your college or university.

Private Tutors   You might consider getting help from a private tutor if you can afford the fee. Although this route will cost you more, it may take only a few sessions to help you understand the material and keep up with the class. Check with your instructor about the availability of private tutors.

Step 6: Study Creatively for Tests

If you have read your assignments, attended class, taken notes and reviewed them, answered the Questions for Review, and completed the Experiential Activities and Critical Thinking Exercises, then you have been studying for tests all along. This kind of preparation means less stress when test time comes around.

Review: Bringing It All Together   You should enter all exam dates on your calendar so that you know well in advance when to prepare for a test. If you plan extra time for study during the week, you will not have to cram the night before the test.

During that week, bring together all your textbook notes, all your handouts, and other study materials. Reread them, paying particular attention to anything you marked that the instructor emphasized or that you had trouble understanding.

In addition to studying the Summary by Chapter Objectives, Key Terms, and Questions for Review at the end of each chapter, it is a good idea to make a summary sheet of your own that lists all the major points and other information that will be covered on the test. If you have quizzes or tests you have already taken, review them as well.

Focus on the material you either missed or did not do well on before.

Do not hesitate to ask the instructor for information about the test, in particular:

- The types of test items he or she will use (multiple-choice, true-false, matching, fill-in-the-blanks, short answer, essay)
- What material, if any, will be emphasized, and what material, if any, will not be included
- How much time you will have to take the test

Step 7: Test-Taking Strategies

No matter how well you prepare for a test, you will feel some anxiety just before and even during the exam. This is natural—*everybody* feels this way. The guidelines in this section will help you manage your anxiety so that you can do your best.

Before the Test: Get Ready   Use this checklist to help you prepare the night before or a few hours before an exam.

- Gather supplies: unless instructed otherwise, at least 2 sharpened pencils with good erasers, a watch for timing yourself, and other items if you need them (such as a blue book for essay exams).
- If the test is in your first class, get up at least an hour before the exam to make sure you will be fully awake.
- Eat well before the test, but avoid having a heavy meal, which can make you sleepy.
- Arrive early to review your notes and study materials. Remember: luck favors the prepared!

During the Test: Go for It!   Memorize these strategies to help you during the exam.

- Follow the directions. Listen carefully to the instructor's directions and read the printed directions carefully. Ask questions if the directions are unclear.
- Preview the test. Take a few minutes to look over the entire test. This will give you an idea of how much time to allot to each of the components.
- Do the easier sections first. If you get stumped on a question, skip it for now. You can come back to it later. Finish with the harder sections.
- Go back over the test. If you finish ahead of time, double-check your work and look for careless errors. Make sure your writing is legible if you are taking an essay exam or an exam that requires short answers. Make sure that your name and other information the instructor requires are on the test papers.

Step 8: Reviewing Your Results

Never throw away any of your quizzes or tests. Tests give you direct feedback on your progress in the course. Whether the test is a weekly quiz or a mid-term, do not just look at the grade and put the paper in your file or notebook. Use the results of each quiz or test to help you achieve your goals.

Learn From Your Successes   First review the test for those questions you answered correctly. Ask yourself the following questions:

- What are my strongest areas? You will know which topics to spend less time studying for the next exam.
- What types of items did I find easiest to answer (multiple-choice, true-false, etc.)? You might want to start with these types of items on the next exam, giving you more time to work on the harder items.

Learn From Your Mistakes   Look over your errors, and ask yourself these questions:

- What types of items did I miss? Is there a pattern (for instance, true-false items, Supreme Court decisions)?
- Did I misunderstand any items? Was it clear to me what each item was asking for?
- Were my mistakes the result of carelessness? Did I read the items incorrectly or miss details? Did I lose track of time? Was I so engrossed in a test section that I forgot to allow myself enough time to get through the entire test at least once?

Look back through the textbook, your notes, class handouts, and other study materials to help you understand how and why you made the mistakes you did. Ask your instructor or classmates to go over your test with you until you know exactly why you missed the items. Evaluating your errors can show you where you need help and what to watch out for in the next test.

Refine Your Action Plan: The Learning Spiral
You can think of the eight-step action plan as an upward spiral. Each time you travel a full cycle of the plan, you accumulate more knowledge and experience. You go one turn higher on the spiral.

Use your test feedback and classroom work to help you refine your plan. Perhaps you need to spend more time reading the textbook or reviewing key terms. Perhaps you did not allow enough time for study during the week. Or you might need extra help from your instructor, your classmates, or tutors. Make adjustments in your plan as you tackle the next part of the course.

Acknowledgments

This book, like any book, is the product of a collaborative effort. We would like to acknowledge and thank the many people who helped to make both the first and this second edition possible. First, our thanks go to Kevin I. Minor and H. Preston Elrod, both at Eastern Kentucky University, for their significant contributions to the chapters on corrections and the juvenile justice system, respectively. We would also like to thank the following colleagues for their substantial help with revisions: James R. Acker, State University of New York at Albany (Chapter 4: The Rule of Law), John O. Smykla, University of Alabama (Chapter 11: Community Corrections), and Donna M. Bishop, University of Central Florida (Chapter 12: Juvenile Justice). In addition, for their insightful reviews, criticisms, helpful suggestions, and information, we would like to thank these colleagues:

Brandon Applegate
University of Central Florida

Richard L. Ashbaugh
Clackamas Community College

Gregg Barak
Eastern Michigan University

Michael Barrett
Ashland University

Denny Bebout
Central Ohio Technical College

Anita Blowers
University of North Carolina at Charlotte

Robert J. Boyer
Luzerne County Community College

William D. Burrell
Probation Services Division State of New Jersey

Michael Cain
Coastal Bend Community College

Vincent J. Capozzella
Jefferson Community College

Jonathan Cella
Central Texas Community College

Charles Chastain
University of Arkansas at Little Rock

Daryl Cullison
Columbus State Community College

Vicky Dorworth
Montgomery College

Joyce K. Dozier
Wilmington College

Mary Ann Eastep
University of Central Florida

John W. Flickinger
Tiffin University

Kenneth A. Frayer
Schoolcraft College-Radcliff

David O. Friedrichs
University of Scranton

Gary Green
Minot State University

Alex Greenberg
Niagara County Community College

Bob Hale
Southeastern Louisiana University

David O. Harding
Ohio University at Chillicothe

Stuart Henry
Eastern Michigan University

Joseph Hogan
Central Texas College

Thomas E. Holdren
Muskingum Technical College

Michael Hooper
Pennsylvania State University at Harrisburg

James L. Hudson
Clark State Community College

W. Richard Janikowski
University of Memphis

Lamar Jordan
Southern Utah University

Don Knueve
Defiance College

Peter C. Kratcoski
Kent State University

Gregory C. Leavitt
Green River Community College

Vivian Lord
University of North Carolina at Charlotte

Karol Lucken
University of Central Florida

Richard Lumb
University of Northern Michigan

Kathleen Maguire
Hindelang Criminal Justice Research Center

Bradley Martin
University of Findlay

Richard M. Martin
Elgin Community College

Dale Mooso
San Antonio College

James Newman
Rio Hondo College

Sarah Nordin
Solano Community College

Les Obert
Casper College

Nancy Oesch
Florida Metropolitan University

Mary Carolyn Purtill
San Joaquin Delta College

Joseph B. Sanborn, Jr.
University of Central Florida

Martin D. Schwartz
Ohio University

Lance Selva
Middle Tennessee State University

James E. Smith
West Valley College

Jeffrey B. Spelman
North Central Technical College

Gene Stephens
University of South Carolina

James Stinchcomb
Miami-Dade Community College

William L. Tafoya
University of Illinois at Chicago

Roger D. Turner
Shelby State Community College

Ronald E. Vogel
California State University at Long Beach

Robert R. Wiggins
Cedarville College

Harold Williamson
Northeastern Louisiana University

Finally, we would like to express our appreciation to our publishing team at Glencoe/McGraw-Hill, whose vision, guidance, and support helped bring this project to fruition.

Thanks also to our families and friends for their understanding and patience over the several years we have worked on this project.

About the Authors

Robert M. Bohm is a Professor of Criminal Justice and Legal Studies at the University of Central Florida in Orlando. He has also been a faculty member in the Departments of Criminal Justice at the University of North Carolina at Charlotte (1989–1995) and at Jacksonville State University in Alabama (1979–1989). In 1973–1974, he worked for the Jackson County Department of Corrections in Kansas City, Missouri, first as a corrections officer and later as an instructor/counselor in the Model Inmate Employment Program, a Law Enforcement Assistance Administration sponsored work-release project. He received his Ph.D. in Criminology from Florida State University in 1980. He has published more than three dozen journal articles and book chapters in the areas of criminal justice and criminology. Besides being the first edition co-author of *Introduction to Criminal Justice* (Glencoe/McGraw-Hill, 1997), he is the editor of *The Death Penalty in America: Current Research* (Anderson, 1991), the author of *A Primer in Crime and Delinquency* (Wadsworth, 1997) and *Deathquest: An Inquiry into the Theory and Practice of Capital Punishment in the United States* (Anderson, 1999), and an editor (with James R. Acker and Charles S. Lanier) of *America's Experiment with Capital Punishment: Reflections on the Past, Present, and Future of the Ultimate Sanction* (Carolina Academic Press, 1998). He has been active in the American Society of Criminology, the Southern Criminal Justice Association, and especially the Academy of Criminal Justice Sciences, having served as Trustee-at-Large (1987–90), Second Vice-President (1990–91), First Vice-President (1991–92), and President (1992–93). In 1989, he was selected as the Outstanding Educator of the Year by the Southern Criminal Justice Association.

Keith N. Haley is the Dean of the School of Criminal Justice at Tiffin University in Tiffin, Ohio. He has also served in the following positions: Coordinator of the Criminal Justice Program at Collin County Community College in Texas; Executive Director of the Ohio Peace Officer Training Council, the state's law enforcement standards and training commission; Chairman of the Criminal Justice Department at the University of Cincinnati, which offers B.S., M.S., and Ph.D. degrees in criminal justice; police officer in Dayton, Ohio; Community School Director in Springfield, Ohio; Director of the Criminal Justice Program at Redlands Community College in Oklahoma; and electronics repairman and NCO in the U.S. Marines. Haley holds a B.S. in Education from Wright State University and an M.S. in Criminal Justice from Michigan State University. Haley has written or co-authored several books, including *How to Take a Test and Score With Memory Power* (Imprint Publications, 1977) and *Crime and Punishment in the Lone Star State* (McGraw-Hill Custom, 1997), as well as many articles and papers. He has also served as a consultant to many public service, business, and industrial organizations. Mr. Haley is also active in the affairs of the Academy of Criminal Justice Sciences and is the 1998–99 chair of the Academy's Membership Committee.

Dedication

To Linda Taconis, with love.
—Robert M. Bohm

To my wife, Shelby, and daughter, Jill, with love.
—Keith N. Haley

1 Crime and Justice in the United States

CHAPTER OBJECTIVES

After completing this chapter, you should be able to:

1 Describe how the type of crime routinely presented by the media compares with crime routinely committed.

2 Identify institutions of social control and explain what makes criminal justice an institution of social control.

3 Summarize how the criminal justice system responds to crime.

4 Explain why criminal justice in the United States is sometimes considered a nonsystem.

5 Describe the costs of criminal justice in the United States and compare those costs among federal, state, and local governments.

6 Explain how myths about crime and criminal justice affect the criminal justice system.

Criminal Justice: The System

Criminal justice in the United States is administered by a loose confederation of more than 50,000 agencies of federal, state, and local governments. Those agencies consist of the police, the courts, and corrections. Together, they are commonly referred to as the *criminal justice system*. Although there are differences in the ways the criminal justice system operates in different jurisdictions, there are also similarities. The term **jurisdiction,** as used here, means a politically defined geographical area (for example, a city, a county, a state, or a nation).

The following paragraphs will provide a brief overview of a typical criminal justice response to criminal behavior. Figure 1-2 on pages 8–9 is a graphic representation of the process. It includes the variations for petty offenses, misdemeanors, felonies, and juvenile offenses. A more detailed examination of the criminal justice response to crime and delinquency will be provided in later chapters of this book.

Police

The criminal justice response to crime begins when a crime is reported to the police or, far less often, when the police themselves discover that a crime has been committed. Sometimes solving the crime is easy—the victim or a witness knows the perpetrator, or where to find him or her. Often, an arrest supported by witness statements and crime scene evidence is sufficient to close a case, especially with a less serious crime. More often, though, the police must conduct an in-depth investigation to determine what happened in a particular crime. Even when the police start with a known crime or a cooperative victim or witness, the investigation can be lengthy and difficult.

If police investigation of the crime is successful, a suspect is arrested. An **arrest** is the seizing and detaining of a person by lawful authority. After an arrest has been made, the suspect is brought to the station house to be booked. **Booking** is the administrative recording of the arrest. It typically involves entering the suspect's name, the charge, and perhaps the suspect's fingerprints or photograph in the police blotter.

Courts

Soon after a suspect has been arrested and booked, a prosecutor reviews the facts of the case and the available evidence. Sometimes a prosecutor reviews a case before arrest. The prosecutor decides whether to charge the suspect with a crime or crimes. If no charges are filed, the suspect must be released.

Charging Documents There are three principal kinds of charging documents:

1. A complaint
2. An information
3. A grand jury indictment

If the offense is a **misdemeanor** (a less serious crime) or an **ordinance violation** (usually the violation of a law of a city or town), then in many jurisdictions the prosecutor prepares a complaint. A **complaint** is a charging document specifying that an offense has been committed by a person or persons named or described. If the offense is a **felony** (a relatively serious

Jurisdiction A politically defined geographical area.

Arrest The seizing and detaining of a person by lawful authority.

Booking The administrative recording of an arrest. Typically, the suspect's name, the charge, and perhaps the suspect's fingerprints or photograph are entered in the police blotter.

Misdemeanor A less serious crime generally punishable by a fine or by incarceration for not more than one year.

Ordinance violation Usually, the violation of a law of a city or town.

Complaint A charging document specifying that an offense has been committed by a person or persons named or described.

Suspects who remain in custody must be brought before a judge for an initial appearance without unnecessary delay.

offense punishable by death or by confinement in a prison for more than one year), an information is used in about half the states. A grand jury indictment is used in the other half. An **information** outlines the formal charge or charges, the law or laws that have been violated, and the evidence to support the charge or charges. A **grand jury indictment** is a written accusation by a grand jury that one or more persons have committed a crime. (Grand juries will be described later in this discussion.) On rare occasions, police may obtain an arrest warrant from a lower-court judge before making an arrest. An **arrest warrant** is a written order directing law enforcement officers to arrest a person. The charge or charges against a suspect are specified on the warrant. Thus, an arrest warrant may also be considered a type of charging document.

Pretrial Stages After the charge or charges have been filed, the suspect, who is now the **defendant,** is brought before a lower-court judge for an initial appearance. At the **initial appearance** the defendant is given formal notice of the charge or charges against him or her and advised of his or her constitutional rights (for example, the right to counsel). In the case of a misdemeanor or an ordinance violation, a **summary trial** (an immediate trial without a jury) may be held. In the case of a felony, a hearing is held to determine whether the defendant should be released or whether there is probable cause to hold the defendant for a preliminary hearing. **Probable cause** is a standard of proof that requires trustworthy evidence sufficient to make a reasonable person believe that, more likely than not, the proposed action is justified. If the suspect is to be held for a preliminary hearing, bail is set if the judge believes release on bail is appropriate. **Bail,** usually a monetary guarantee deposited with the court, is meant to ensure that the defendant will appear at a later stage in the criminal justice process.

Felony A relatively serious offense punishable by death or by confinement in a prison for more than one year.

Information A document that outlines the formal charge(s) against a suspect, the law(s) that have been violated, and the evidence to support the charge(s).

Grand jury indictment A written accusation by a grand jury that one or more persons have committed a crime.

Arrest warrant A written order directing law enforcement officers to arrest a person.

Defendant A person against whom a legal action is brought, a warrant is issued, or an indictment is found.

Initial appearance A pretrial stage in which a defendant is brought before a lower court to be given notice of the charge(s) and advised of her or his constitutional rights.

Summary trial An immediate trial without a jury.

Probable cause A standard of proof that requires evidence sufficient to make a reasonable person believe that, more likely than not, the proposed action is justified.

Bail Usually, a monetary guarantee deposited with the court to ensure that suspects or defendants will appear at a later stage in the criminal justice process.

Crime and Justice in the United States

FIGURE 1–2

Overview of the Criminal Justice System

The Criminal Justice System

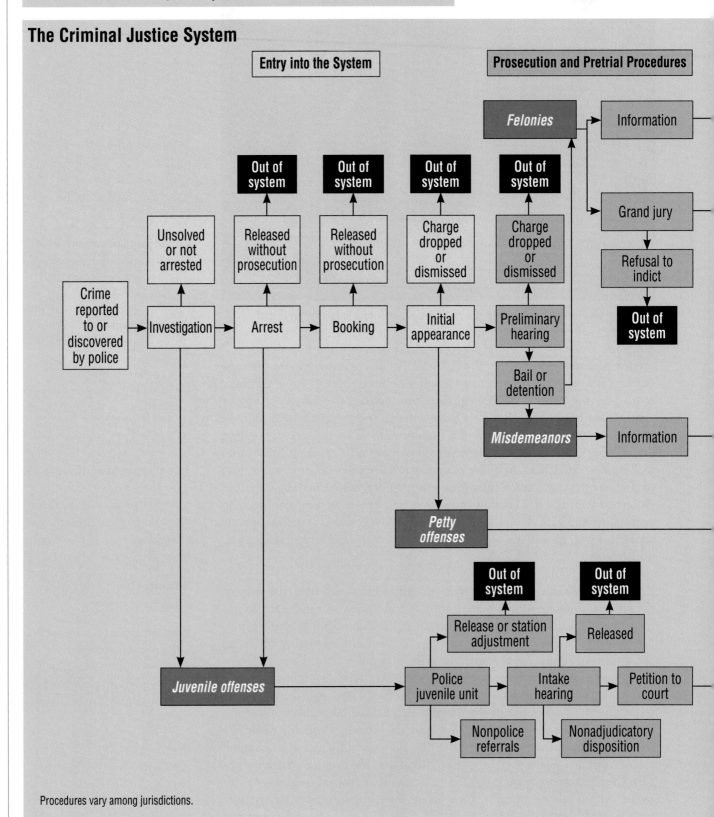

Entry into the System

Prosecution and Pretrial Procedures

Procedures vary among jurisdictions.

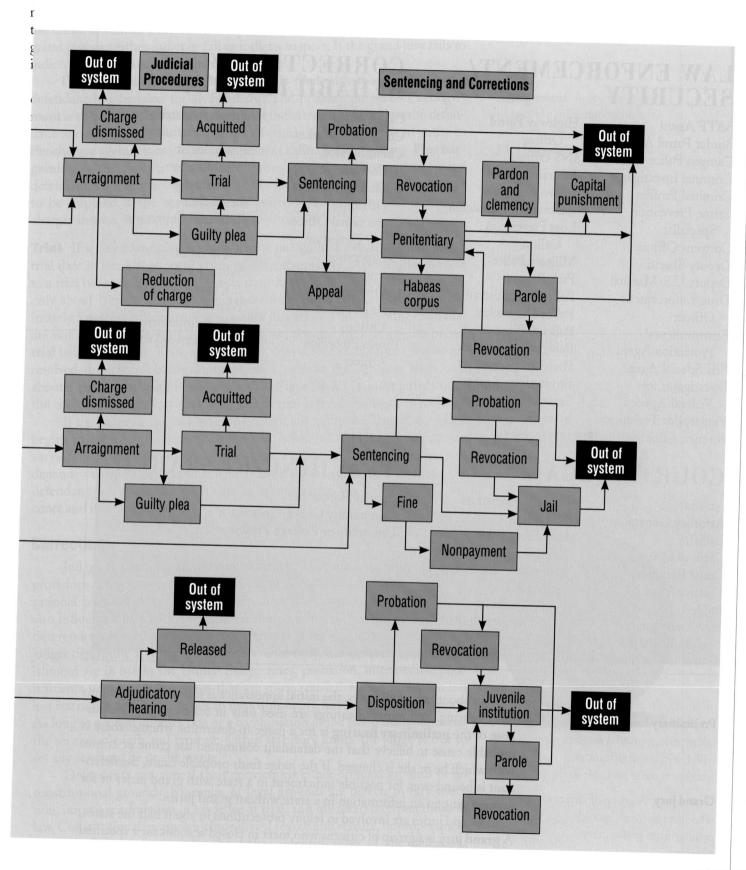

22

2 Crime and Its Consequences

CHAPTER OBJECTIVES

After completing this chapter, you should be able to:

1 Distinguish between a social definition and a legal definition of crime and summarize the problems with each.

2 List the technical and ideal elements of a crime.

3 Identify some of the legal defenses or legal excuses for criminal responsibility.

4 Explain why crime and delinquency statistics are unreliable.

5 Identify the two major sources of crime statistics in the United States.

6 Describe the principal finding of the national crime victimization surveys.

7 Summarize the general finding of self-report crime surveys.

8 Identify the costs of crime.

9 Describe the extent of fear of crime in the United States and the characteristics of people most likely to fear crime.

10 List the characteristics of people who are the most likely and the least likely to be victims of crime.

Definitions of Crime

Crime is from the Latin *crimen,* meaning "accusation" or "fault."

The object of criminal justice in the United States is to prevent and control crime. Thus, to understand criminal justice, it is necessary to understand crime. An appropriate definition of crime, however, remains one of the most critical unresolved issues in criminal justice today. One problem is that many dangerous and harmful behaviors are not defined as crimes, while many less dangerous and less harmful behaviors are. Ultimately, which among many relatively dangerous and harmful behaviors are considered crimes depends on how crime is defined. We begin, then, by examining how crime is defined and the problems with defining what is a crime.

Social Definitions

The broadest definitions of crime are social definitions. A typical social definition of crime is behavior that violates the norms of society—or, more simply, antisocial behavior. A **norm** is any standard or rule regarding what human beings should or should not think, say, or do under given circumstances. Because social definitions of crime are broad, they are less likely than narrower definitions to exclude behaviors that ought to be included. Nevertheless, there are several problems with social definitions of crime.

First, norms vary from group to group within a single society. There is no uniform definition of antisocial behavior. Take, for example, the acts involved in gambling, prostitution, abortion, and homosexual behavior. As current public debates indicate, there is much controversy in the United States over whether those acts should be crimes. Even with acts about which there seems to be a consensus, like murder and rape, there is no agreement on what constitutes such acts. For example, if a patient dies from a disease contracted from a doctor who did not wash his or her hands before examining the patient, has the doctor committed murder? Or, if a man has forcible sexual intercourse with a woman against her will but, before the act, at the woman's request, puts on a condom so that the woman will not get a sexually transmitted disease, has the man committed rape? Those examples illustrate the difficulty of determining what, in fact, constitutes antisocial behavior, let alone crime.

Second, norms are always subject to interpretation. Each norm's meaning has a history. Consider abortion, for example. For some people, abortion is the killing of a fetus or a human being. For other people, abortion is not killing because, for them, human life begins at birth and not at conception. For the latter group, the abortion issue concerns women's freedom to control their own bodies. For the former group, abortion constitutes an injustice to the helpless.

Third, norms change from time to time and from place to place. For example, the consumption of alcohol was prohibited in the United States during the 1920s and early 1930s but is only regulated today. Until the passage of the Harrison Act, in 1914, it was legal in the United States to use opiates such as opium, heroin, and morphine without a doctor's

Norm Any standard or rule regarding what human beings should or should not think, say, or do under given circumstances.

More and more states are legalizing casino gambling as a means of generating income.

Following are some examples of behaviors that in the early 1990s were prohibited by criminal law (and may still be):

- In Massachusetts, shaving your whiskers while driving.
- Walking down the street with your shoelaces untied in Maine.
- Securing a giraffe to a telephone pole in Atlanta.
- Gargling in public in Louisiana.
- In Nebraska, sneezing in public.
- Serving ice cream on cherry pie in Kansas.
- In Gary, Indiana, entering a theater within four hours of eating garlic.
- Fishing in your pajamas in Chicago.
- In Indiana, shooting open a can of food.
- Setting a fire under a mule in Ohio.
- In Florida, breaking more than three dishes a day.[1]

prescription. Such use is prohibited today. Casino gambling is allowed in some states but forbidden in other states. Prostitution is legal in a few counties in Nevada, but illegal in the rest of the United States. Prior to the mid-1970s, a husband could rape his wife with impunity in all but a handful of states. Today, laws in every state prohibit a husband from raping or assaulting his wife.

A Legal Definition

In an attempt to avoid the problems with social definitions of crime, a legal definition of crime is used in criminal justice in the United States. A typical **legal definition of crime** is *an intentional violation of the criminal law or penal code, committed without defense or excuse and penalized by the state.* The major advantage of a legal definition of crime, at least on the surface, is that it is narrower and less ambiguous than a social definition of crime. If a behavior violates the criminal law, then by definition it is a crime. However, although a legal definition eliminates some of the problems with social definitions of crime, a legal definition of crime has problems of its own.

First, some behaviors prohibited by the criminal law arguably should not be. This problem of **overcriminalization** arises primarily in the area of so-called victimless crimes. Lists of victimless crimes typically include gambling, prostitution involving consenting adults, homosexual acts between consenting adults, and the use of some illegal drugs, such as marijuana. Ultimately, whether those acts should or should not be prohibited by criminal law depends on whether they are truly victimless—an issue we will not debate here.

Legal definition of crime According to a typical legal definition, crime is an intentional violation of the criminal law or penal code, committed without defense or excuse and penalized by the state.

Overcriminalization The prohibition by the criminal law of some behaviors that arguably should not be prohibited.

Ever since criminal sanctions were established for illegal drug use, some have argued for decriminalization by elimination or reduction of criminal penalties for possession or distribution of certain drugs.

Nonenforcement The failure to routinely enforce prohibitions against certain behaviors.

A second problem with a legal definition of crime is that for some behaviors prohibited by the criminal law, the law is not routinely enforced. **Nonenforcement** is common for many white-collar and government crimes. It is also common for blue laws, which require stores and other commercial establishments to be closed on Sundays. Many jurisdictions in the United States have blue laws, or they did until recently. The principal problem with the nonenforcement of prohibitions is that it causes disrespect for the law. People come to believe that because criminal laws are not routinely enforced, there is no need to routinely obey them.

Undercriminalization The failure to prohibit some behaviors that arguably should be prohibited.

A third problem with a legal definition of crime is the problem of **undercriminalization.** That is, some behaviors that arguably should be prohibited by the criminal law are not. Have you ever said to yourself that there ought to be a law against whatever it is you are upset about? Of course, most of the daily frustrations that people claim ought to be crimes probably should not be. Some people argue, however, that some very harmful and destructive actions or inactions that are not criminal should be. Examples include the government's allowing employers (generally through the nonenforcement of laws) to maintain unsafe working conditions that cause employee deaths and injuries, and corporations' intentional production of potentially hazardous products to maximize profits.[2]

Elements of Crime

A legal definition of crime is the basis of criminal justice in the United States. The legal definition of crime provided earlier in this chapter, however, is only a general definition. It does not specify all the elements necessary to make a behavior a crime. Technically and ideally, a crime has not been committed unless all seven of the following elements are present:[3]

1. Harm	**5.** Causation
2. Legality	**6.** Concurrence
3. *Actus reus*	**7.** Punishment
4. *Mens rea*	

It is only in a technical and ideal sense that all seven elements must be present. In actual practice, a behavior is often considered a crime when one or more of the elements is absent. We will examine each of the seven elements in turn, indicating exceptions to the technical and ideal where relevant.

Harm For crime to occur, there must be an external consequence, or **harm.** A mental or emotional state is not enough. Thus, thinking about committing a crime or being angry enough to commit a crime, without acting on the thought or the anger, is not a crime. The harm may be physical or verbal. Physically striking another person without legal justification is an example of an act that does physical harm. An example of an act that does verbal harm is a threat to strike another person, whether or not the threat is carried out. Writing something false about another person that dishonors or injures that person is a physical harm called **libel.** The spoken equivalent of libel is called **slander.**

> **Harm** The external consequence required to make an action a crime.
> **Libel** The writing of something false about another person that dishonors or injures that person.
> **Slander** The spoken equivalent of libel.

Whether the legal element of harm is present in all crimes is sometimes questioned. Some crimes, such as gambling, prostitution, and homosexuality, have come to be called "victimless crimes" by those who argue that only those people involved in these behaviors are harmed, if at all. Other people maintain that the participants, their families, and the moral fabric of society are jeopardized by such behavior. In short, there is considerable debate as to whether so-called victimless crimes really are harmless.

Legality The element of legality has two aspects. First, the harm must be legally forbidden for a behavior to be a crime. Thus, violations of union rules, school rules, religious rules, or any rules other than those of a political jurisdiction may be "wrong," but they are not crimes unless they are also prohibited by criminal law. Second, a criminal law must not be retroactive, or *ex post facto.* An *ex post facto* **law** (1) declares criminal an act that was not illegal when it was committed, (2) increases the punishment for a crime after it is committed, or (3) alters the rules of evidence in a particular case after the crime is committed. The first meaning is the most common. The United States Constitution (Article I, Section 10.1) forbids *ex post facto* laws.

> **Legality** The requirement (1) that a harm must be legally forbidden for the behavior to be a crime and (2) that the law must not be retroactive.
> ***Ex post facto* law** A law that (1) declares criminal an act that was not illegal when it was committed, (2) increases the punishment for a crime after it is committed, or (3) alters the rules of evidence in a particular case after the crime is committed.
> ***Actus reus*** Criminal conduct—specifically, intentional or criminally negligent (reckless) action or inaction that causes harm.

Actus reus The Latin term ***actus reus*** refers to criminal conduct—specifically, intentional or criminally negligent (reckless) action or inaction that causes harm. It is important to emphasize that crime involves not only things people do but also things they do not do. In other words, if people do not act in situations where the law requires them to act, they are committing crimes.

Mens rea Criminal intent; a guilty state of mind.

Negligence The failure to take reasonable precautions to prevent harm.

Duress Force or coercion as an excuse for committing a crime.

Juvenile delinquency A special category of offense created for young offenders, usually those between 7 and 18 years of age.

For example, parents are legally required to provide their children with adequate food, clothing, and shelter. If parents fail to provide those necessities—that is, if they fail to act when the law requires them to—they are committing a crime.

Mens rea The Latin term **mens rea** refers to criminal intent or a guilty state of mind. It is the mental aspect of a crime. Ideally, criminal conduct is limited to intentional or purposeful action or inaction and not to accidents. In practice, however, reckless actions or *negligence* may be criminal. **Negligence** is the failure to take reasonable precautions to prevent harm.

In some cases, offenders lack the capacity (sometimes called competence) to form *mens rea*. If they do not have that capacity, they are not to be held responsible for their criminal conduct. If they have a diminished capacity to form *mens rea,* they are to be held less than fully responsible. In other cases, offenders who have the capacity to form *mens rea* are not held responsible for their crimes, or are held less responsible for them, either because they did not have *mens rea* when they acted or because there were extenuating circumstances when they did act with *mens rea.*

Legal Defenses for Criminal Responsibility In the United States, an offender is not considered responsible or is considered less responsible for an offense if he or she, for example, (1) acted under duress, (2) was underage, (3) was insane, (4) acted in self-defense or in defense of a third party, (5) was entrapped, or (6) acted out of necessity. Those conditions are legal defenses or legal excuses for criminal responsibility.

If a person did not want to commit a crime but was forced or coerced to do so against his or her will, he or she committed the crime under **duress** and is generally excluded from criminal liability. Suppose that an intruder held a gun to the head of a loved one and threatened to kill that person if you did not rob a local convenience store and return immediately to give the intruder the money. If you committed the robbery to save the life of your loved one, you would probably not be held legally responsible for the crime, because you committed it under duress. There were extenuating circumstances when you acted with *mens rea.* To prevent all offenders from claiming duress, the burden of proof is placed on the defendant.

Another legal excuse or legal defense against criminal responsibility is being underage. Although the age at which a person is considered legally responsible for his or her actions varies by jurisdiction, in most American jurisdictions a child under the age of 7 is not held responsible for a crime. It is assumed that a child under 7 years of age does not have the capacity to form *mens rea.* A child under 7 years of age is considered a *legal infant* or of *legal nonage.* Such a child is protected by the criminal law but not subject to it. Thus, if a 6-year-old child picks up a shotgun and shoots his or her parent, the child is unlikely to be charged with a crime. On the other hand, if a parent abuses a child, the criminal law protects the child by holding the abusive parent responsible for his or her actions.

In most developed countries children under 18 years of age are not considered entirely responsible for their criminal acts. It is assumed that their capacity to form *mens rea* is not fully developed. A special category of offense called **juvenile delinquency** has been created for those children. In most

American jurisdictions, the upper age limit for juvenile delinquency is 18. The lower limit is usually 7. The criminal law treats anyone beyond the age of 18 as an adult. However, the upper age limit of juvenile delinquency is lower in some jurisdictions and sometimes varies with the sex of the offender. In some jurisdictions there is a legal borderland between the ages of 16 and 18. An offender in that age range may be treated as a juvenile or as an adult, depending on the severity of the offense. In some cases, an offense is considered heinous enough for a court to certify a juvenile, regardless of age, as an adult and to treat him or her accordingly. The subject of juvenile delinquency will be discussed more fully in Chapter 12.

A third legal defense or legal excuse from criminal responsibility is insanity. **Insanity** is a legal term, not a medical one. It refers to mental or psychological impairment or retardation. Like many of the other legal defenses or excuses, an insanity defense rests on the assumption that someone who is insane at the time of a crime lacks the capacity, or has diminished capacity, to form *mens rea*. Thus, that person either should not be held responsible or should be held less responsible for crime.

In most western European nations, legal insanity is determined solely by the judgment and testimony of medical experts. British and American law, by contrast, provide guidelines for judges, juries, and medical experts to follow in determining whether or not a defendant is legally insane. The oldest—and, until recently, the most popular—of those guidelines is the M'Naghten rule, which was first used in an English trial in 1843.

Under the M'Naghten rule:

> [E]very man is to be presumed to be sane, and . . . to establish a defense on the ground of insanity, it must be clearly proved that, at the time of the committing of the act, the party accused was laboring under such a defect of reason, from disease of the mind, as not to know the nature and quality of the act he was doing; or if he did know it, that he did not know he was doing what was wrong.[4]

In short, according to the M'Naghten rule, a person is legally insane if, at the time of the commission of the act, he or she (1) did not know the nature and quality of the act or (2) did not know that the act was wrong. The burden of proof is on the defendant.

One problem with the M'Naghten rule is the difficulty of determining what a person's state of mind was at the time of the commission of the criminal act. The rule has also been criticized for its ambiguity. What is a "defect of reason," and by whose standards is the act a product of defective reason? Does "disease of the mind" refer to organic diseases, nonorganic diseases, or both? What does it mean to "know" the nature and quality of the act? Does it mean an intellectual awareness, an emotional appreciation, or both? Does "wrong" mean legally wrong, morally wrong, or both?

Perhaps the most serious problem with the M'Naghten rule is that it does not address the situation of a defendant who knew the difference between right and wrong but nevertheless was unable to control his or her actions. To remedy that problem, some states have adopted the *irresistible-impulse* or *control* test and use it in conjunction with the M'Naghten rule. In those states a defense against criminal conviction on grounds of insanity is

Insanity Mental or psychological impairment or retardation as a defense against a criminal charge.

Daniel M'Naghten was acquitted of the murder of a person he had mistaken for his real target, Sir Robert Peel, then the Prime Minister of Great Britain. M'Naghten claimed that he was delusional at the time of the killing.

In a 1994 trial in Virginia, attorneys for Lorena Bobbitt, who had sliced off her husband's penis with a kitchen knife while he was sleeping, successfully used the *irresistible-impulse* defense against charges of malicious wounding. She was acquitted of the crime.

first made by using the M'Naghten rule. If the conditions of M'Naghten are met, the irresistible-impulse or control test is applied. If it is determined that the defendant knew that he or she was doing wrong at the time of the commission of the criminal act but nevertheless could not control his or her behavior, the defendant is entitled to an acquittal on the grounds of insanity. The major problem with the irresistible-impulse or control test is distinguishing reliably between behavior that is uncontrollable and behavior that is simply uncontrolled.

Since 1980, the test for insanity used by most states has been the *substantial-capacity* test of the American Law Institute's Model Penal Code. Under that test, a defendant is not to be found guilty of a crime "if at the time of such conduct as a result of mental disease or defect he lacks substantial capacity either to appreciate the criminality of his conduct or to conform his conduct to the requirements of law." By using the term *substantial capacity*, the test does not require that a defendant be completely unable to distinguish right from wrong. The test has been criticized for its use of the ambiguous terms *substantial capacity* and *appreciate*. It also does not resolve the problem of determining whether behavior is uncontrollable or uncontrolled.

Following the public uproar over the 1982 acquittal of John Hinckley, the would-be assassin of President Ronald Reagan, on the grounds that he was legally insane, several states enacted "guilty but insane" or "guilty but mentally ill" laws. Defendants who are found guilty but insane generally receive sentences that include psychiatric treatment until they are cured. Then they are placed in the general prison population to serve the remainder of their sentences.

The difficulty of applying tests of insanity in legal proceedings is suggested by the different outcomes in England and the United States. In England, 33-50 percent of homicide offenders are classified as legally insane. In the United States, only 2-4 percent of homicide offenders are so classified.

A fourth legal defense or legal excuse from criminal responsibility is self-defense or the defense of a third party. Generally, people are relieved of criminal responsibility if they use only the amount of force reasonably necessary to defend themselves or others against an apparent threat of unlawful and immediate violence. When it comes to the protection of property, however, the use of force is much more limited. Deadly force is not allowed, but nondeadly force may be used to protect one's property. The reason people are not held legally responsible for acting in self-defense or in defense of a third party is that they do not act with *mens rea*.

Entrapment is a fifth legal defense or legal excuse from criminal responsibility. People are generally considered either not responsible or less responsible for their crimes if they were entrapped, or induced into committing them, by a law enforcement officer or by someone acting as an agent for a law enforcement officer, such as an informer or an undercover agent. A successful entrapment defense, however, requires proof that the law enforcement officer or his or her agent instigated the crime or created the intent to commit the crime in the mind of a person who was not already predisposed to committing it. Thus, it is not entrapment if a law enforcement officer merely affords someone an opportunity to commit a crime, as, for example, when an undercover agent poses as a drug addict and purchases drugs from a drug dealer.

Entrapment A legal defense against criminal responsibility when a law enforcement officer or his or her agent has induced to commit a crime someone who was not already predisposed to committing it.

The final legal defense or legal excuse from criminal responsibility to be discussed here is necessity. A **necessity defense** can be used when a crime has been committed to prevent a greater or more serious crime. In such a situation, there are extenuating circumstances, even though the act was committed with *mens rea*. Although it is rarely used, the necessity defense has been invoked occasionally, especially in cases of "political" crimes. The necessity defense was used successfully by Amy Carter (daughter of former President Jimmy Carter), Jerry Rubin, and other activists who were charged with trespassing for protesting apartheid on the property of the South African embassy in Washington, D.C. The court agreed with the protesters that apartheid was a greater crime than trespassing. Interestingly, the law does not recognize economic necessity as a defense against or an excuse from criminal responsibility. Therefore, the unemployed and hungry thief who steals groceries cannot successfully employ the necessity defense.

Necessity defense A legal defense against criminal responsibility that is used when a crime has been committed to prevent a greater or more serious crime.

Causation A fifth ideal legal element of crime is causation, or a causal relationship between the legally forbidden harm and the *actus reus*. In other words, the criminal act must lead directly to the harm without a long delay. In a recent case in Georgia, for example, a father was accused of murdering

Mala in se Wrong in themselves. A description applied to crimes that are characterized by universality and timelessness.

Mala prohibita Offenses that are illegal because laws define them as such. They lack universality and timelessness.

his baby daughter. The murder charges were dropped, however, because too much time had passed between the night the 3-1/2-month-old girl was shaken into a coma and her death 18 months later. Because of Georgia's year-and-a-day rule, the father was not charged with murder, but he still faced a charge of cruelty to children, which in Georgia carries a maximum sentence of 20 years. The purpose of the requirement of causation is to prevent people from facing the threat of criminal charges the rest of their lives.

Concurrence Ideally, for any behavior to be considered a crime, there must be concurrence between the *actus reus* and the *mens rea*. In other words, the criminal conduct and the criminal intent must occur together. For example, suppose you call someone to repair your broken washing machine, and that person comes to your home, fixes your washing machine, and on the way out takes your television set. The repair person cannot be found guilty of entering your home illegally (trespass) because that was not his or her initial intent. However, the repair person can be found guilty of stealing your television set.

Punishment The last of the ideal legal elements of a crime is punishment. For a behavior to be considered a crime, there must be a statutory provision for punishment or at least the threat of punishment. Without the threat of punishment, a law is unenforceable and is therefore not a criminal law.

Degrees or Categories of Crime

Crimes can be classified according to the degree or severity of the offense, according to the nature of the acts prohibited, or on some other basis, such as a statistical reporting scheme. One way crimes are distinguished by degree or severity of the offense is by dividing them into *felonies* and *misdemeanors*. The only way to determine whether a crime is a felony or misdemeanor is by knowing the legislated punishment. Consequently, a felony in one jurisdiction might be a misdemeanor in another jurisdiction, and vice versa. Generally, a felony, as noted in Chapter 1, is a relatively serious offense punishable by death, a fine, or confinement in a state or federal prison for more than one year. A misdemeanor, on the other hand, is any lesser crime that is not a felony. Misdemeanors are usually punishable by no more than a $1,000 fine and one year of incarceration, generally in a county or city jail.

Another way of categorizing crimes is to distinguish between offenses that are *mala in se* and offenses that are *mala prohibita*. Crimes *mala in se* are "wrong in themselves." They are characterized by universality and timelessness. That is, they are crimes everywhere and have been crimes at all times. Examples are murder and rape. Crimes *mala prohibita* are offenses that are illegal because laws define them as such. They lack universality and timelessness. Examples are trespassing, gambling, and prostitution.

For statistical reporting purposes, crimes are frequently classified as *crimes against the person* or *violent crimes* (for example, murder, rape, assault), *crimes against property* or *property crime* (for instance, burglary, larceny, auto theft), and *crimes against public decency, public order, and public justice* or *public order crimes* (for example, drunkenness, disorderly conduct, vagrancy).

Figure 2–1 is a list of selected crimes and their definitions, grouped by type. The selection, placement, and definition of the crimes are somewhat arbitrary. There are many different types of crime, and some crimes can be

CHAPTER 2   *Crime and Its Consequences*

FIGURE 2–1

Types and Definitions of Selected Crimes

Violent Crimes	Crimes that involve force or threat of force.
Murder	The unlawful killing of another human being with malice aforethought.
Manslaughter	The unlawful killing of another human being without malice aforethought.
Aggravated assault	An assault committed (1) with the intention of committing some additional crime, (2) with peculiar outrage or atrocity, or (3) with a dangerous or deadly weapon.
Forcible rape	The act of having sexual intercourse with a woman, by force and against her will.
Robbery	Theft from a person, accompanied by violence, threat of violence, or putting the person in fear.
Kidnapping	The unlawful taking and carrying away of a human being by force and against his or her will.
Property Crimes	Crimes that involve taking money or property, but usually without force or threat of force.
Larceny	The unlawful taking and carrying away of another person's property with the intent of depriving the owner of that property.
Burglary	Entering a building or occupied structure to commit a crime therein.
Embezzlement	The willful taking or converting to one's own use another person's money or property, which was lawfully acquired by the wrongdoer by reason of some office, employment, or position of trust.
Arson	Purposely setting fire to a house or other building.
Extortion/blackmail	The obtaining of property from another by wrongful use of actual or threatened force, violence, or fear, or under color of official right.
Receiving stolen property	Knowingly accepting, buying, or concealing goods which were illegally obtained by another person.
Fraud	The false representation of a matter of fact, whether by words or by conduct, by false or misleading allegations, or by concealment of that which should have been disclosed, which deceives and is intended to deceive, and causes legal harm.
Forgery	The fraudulent making of a false writing having apparent legal significance.
Counterfeiting	Under federal law, falsely making, forging, or altering any obligation or other security of the United States, with intent to defraud.
"Morals" Offenses	Violations of virtue in sexual conduct (for example, fornication, seduction, prostitution, adultery, illicit cohabitation, sodomy, bigamy, and incest).
Public Order Offenses	Violations that constitute a threat to public safety or peace (for example, disorderly conduct, loitering, unlawful assembly, drug offenses, driving while intoxicated).
Offenses Against the Government	Crimes motivated by the desire to effect social change or to rebel against perceived unfair laws and governments (for example, treason, sedition, hindering apprehension or prosecution of a felon, perjury, and bribery).
Offenses by Government	Harms inflicted upon people by their own governments or the governments of others (for example, genocide and torture, police brutality, civil rights violations, and political bribe taking).
Hate Crimes	Criminal offenses committed against a person, property, or society which are motivated, in whole or in part, by the offender's bias against a race, a religion, an ethnic/national origin group, or a sexual-orientation group.
Organized Crimes	Unlawful acts of members of highly organized and disciplined associations engaged in supplying illegal goods and services, such as gambling, prostitution, loansharking, narcotics, and labor racketeering.
White-Collar and Corporate Crimes	Generally nonviolent offenses committed for financial gain by means of deception by entrepreneurs and other professionals who utilize their special occupational skills and opportunities (for example, environmental pollution, manufacture and sale of unsafe products, price fixing, price gouging, and deceptive advertising).
Occupational Crimes	Offenses committed through opportunities created in the course of a legal business or profession and crimes committed by professionals, such as lawyers and doctors, acting in their professional capacities.
"Victimless" Crimes	Offenses involving a willing and private exchange of goods or services that are in strong demand but are illegal (for example, gambling, prostitution, drug law violations, and homosexual acts between consenting adults).

Dark figure of crime The number of crimes not officially recorded by the police.

Crime index An estimate of crimes committed.

FIGURE 2–2

Dark Figure of Crime

True Amount of Crime
(entire circle)

placed in more than one category. Legal definitions of crime vary among jurisdictions and frequently list numerous degrees, conditions, and qualifications. A good source of legal crime definitions is *Black's Law Dictionary.*

Measurement of Crime

Many people who read the daily newspaper or watch the nightly news on television believe that crime is the most pressing problem in the United States. But is it? How do you know how much crime is committed? How do you know if crime is, in fact, increasing or decreasing? Besides what you learn from the media, perhaps you have been the victim of crime or know someone who has been. Although that information is important, it does not indicate whether your experience with crime or the experience of someone you know is typical. The fact is that what we and the media know about crime, by and large, is based on statistics supplied by government agencies.

Crime Statistics

The difficulty in relying on crime statistics to measure the prevalence of crime is that "statistics about crime and delinquency are probably the most unreliable and most difficult of all social statistics."[6] In other words, "it is impossible to determine with accuracy the amount of crime [or delinquency] in any given jurisdiction at any particular time."[7] Why? There are several reasons. First, "some behavior is labeled . . . 'crime' by one observer but not by another."[8] If a behavior is not labeled a crime, it is not counted. On the other hand, if a behavior is wrongly labeled a crime, then it may be wrongly counted as a crime. Both situations contribute to the inaccuracy of crime statistics. Second, a large proportion of crimes are undetected. Crimes that are not detected obviously cannot be counted. Third, some crimes may not be reported to the police. If they are not reported to the police, they are unlikely to be counted. Fourth, crimes that are reported to the police may not be officially recorded by them, for various reasons (to be discussed later), or may be inaccurately recorded. Crimes that are not officially recorded by the police are called the **dark figure of crime** (see Figure 2–2).

For all of the foregoing reasons, any record of crimes—such as "offenses known to the police," arrests, convictions, or commitments to prison—can be considered at most a **crime index,** or an estimate of crimes committed. Unfortunately, no index or estimate of crimes is a reliable indicator of the actual amount of crime. The indexes or estimates vary independently of the true amount of crime, whatever that may be. Figure 2–2 portrays one possible relationship of a crime index to the dark figure of crime and the true amount of crime. It shows how great a discrepancy there can be between the index and the actual amount of crime.

Adding to the confusion is the reality that any index of crime varies with changes in police practices, court policies, and public opinion—to name just three factors. Suppose, for example, that a large city is hosting a major convention and city leaders want to make a good impression on visitors. The mayor asks the police chief to order officers to "sweep" the streets of prostitutes. As a result of that police policy, there is a dramatic increase in arrests for prostitution and in the index measuring prostitution. Does the increase in the index mean that the true amount of prostitution increased in the city? The answer is that we do not know and, for that matter, can never know. All we do know is that the index measuring prostitution increased as a result of police practices.

Thus, despite what some government agencies or the media may suggest, we do not know, nor can we ever know, the true amount of crime. For the same reasons, we can never know for sure whether crime is increasing, decreasing, or remaining at the same level. The sophisticated student of crime knows only that indexes of crime are imperfect estimates that vary widely. Those variations, which are independent of variations in the true amount of crime, depend on such things as police practices, court policies, and public opinion. Therefore, comparisons of crime measures are an especially dubious exercise. Criminal justice officials and professors routinely compare crime measures in different jurisdictions and in different jurisdictions at different times. What they are doing, though they rarely acknowledge it, even when they are aware of it, is comparing indexes or estimates of crime. Although such comparisons tell us nothing about differences in true amounts of crime, they do provide insights into police practices, court policies, and public opinion.

Probably the best index of crime—that is, the least inaccurate!—is **offenses known to the police.** That index, which is reported in the FBI's uniform crime reports (to be discussed later), is composed of crimes that are both reported to and recorded by the police. The reason it is an inaccurate measure of the true amount of crime is that the number of offenses known to the police is always much smaller than the number of crimes actually committed. One reason is that victims do not report all crimes to the police. There are many reasons for the nonreporting of crimes:[9]

1. "Victims may consider the crime insignificant and not worth reporting."
2. "They may hope to avoid embarrassing the offender, who may be a relative, school friend, or fellow employee."
3. "They may wish to avoid the publicity which might result if the crime were reported."
4. "They might have agreed to the crime, as in gambling offenses and some sexual offenses."
5. "They may wish to avoid the inconvenience of calling the police, [filling out a report, appearing in court, and so on]."
6. "They may be intimidated by [or afraid of] the offender."
7. "They may [dislike] the police or [be] opposed to the punitive policies of the legal system."
8. "They may feel that the police are so inefficient that they will be unable to catch the offender even if the offense is reported."

Another reason the number of offenses known to the police is necessarily much smaller than the number of crimes actually committed is that the police do not always officially record the crimes that are reported to them. In practice, police officers often use their discretion to handle informally an incident reported to them; that is, they do not make an official report of the incident. Or they may exercise discretion in enforcing the law (for instance, by not arresting the customer in a case of prostitution). The law is often vague, and officers may not know the law or how to enforce it. Still another reason is that

Offenses known to the police
A crime index, reported in the FBI's uniform crime reports, composed of crimes that are both reported to and recorded by the police.

According to the national crime victimization surveys for 1973 through 1994, only about 35 percent of crimes, on average, are reported to the police. In 1994 the average for personal crimes of violence reported to the police was about 42 percent.

Crime and Its Consequences   **CHAPTER 2**

FIGURE 2–3

Indexes of Crime

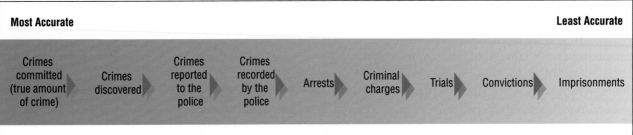

Most Accurate | Least Accurate

Crimes committed (true amount of crime) → Crimes discovered → Crimes reported to the police → Crimes recorded by the police → Arrests → Criminal charges → Trials → Convictions → Imprisonments

The further away from the initial commission of a crime, the more inaccurate crime indexes are as measures of the true amount of crime.

some police officers feel they are too busy to fill out and file police reports. Also, some officers, feeling an obligation to protect the reputations of their cities or being pressured by politicians to "get the crime rate down," may manipulate statistics to show a decrease in crime.[10]

Additionally, the number of offenses included in the index is much smaller than the actual number of crimes because of the way crimes are counted. For the FBI's uniform crime reports, when more than one crime is committed during a crime event, only the most serious is counted for statistical purposes. The seriousness of the crime is determined by the maximum legal penalty associated with it. Thus, for example, if a robber holds up ten people in a tavern, takes their money, shoots and kills the bartender, and makes a getaway in a stolen car, only one crime, the murder, is counted for statistical purposes. However, the offender could legally be charged with several different crimes. (The practice of counting only the most serious offense in a multiple-crime event is being changed with the implementation of the National Incident-Based Reporting System, which will be discussed later in this chapter.)

Despite the problems in recording crime events, *offenses known to the police* is a more accurate index of crime than arrest statistics, charging statistics, trial statistics, conviction statistics, sentencing statistics, or imprisonment statistics. As shown in Figure 2–3 above, the further a crime index is from the initial commission of crime, the more inaccurate it is as a measure of the true amount of crime.

Crime Rates

Crime rate A measure of the incidence of crime expressed as the number of crimes per unit of population or some other base.

When crime indexes are compared, rarely are total numbers of crimes used. Instead, crime is typically reported as rates. A **crime rate** is expressed as the number of crimes per unit of population or some other base. Crime rates are used instead of total numbers because they are more comparable. For example, suppose you wanted to compare the crime of murder in the United States for the years 1960 and 1996. There were 9,110 murders and nonnegligent manslaughters reported to and recorded by the police in 1960; there were 19,645 murders and nonnegligent manslaughters reported to and recorded by the police in 1996. According to those data, the total number of murders and nonnegligent manslaughters reported to and recorded by the police in 1996 was a little more than twice the number for 1960, an increase of about 116 percent. Although this information may be helpful, it ignores the substantial increase in the population of the United States—and thus in the number of potential murderers and potential murder victims—between 1960 and 1996.

A better comparison—though, of course, not an accurate one—would be a comparison that takes into account the different population sizes. To enable such a comparison, a population base, such as "per 100,000 people" is arbitrarily chosen. Then the total number of murders and nonnegligent manslaughters for a particular year is divided by the total population of the United States for the same year. The result is multiplied by 100,000. When those calculations are made for the years 1960 and 1996, the rate of murders and nonnegligent manslaughters is 5.1 per 100,000 people for 1960 and 7.4 per 100,000 people for 1996 (see Figure 2–4). According to those figures, the rate of murder and nonnegligent manslaughter in 1996 was a little more than 1.45 times the rate in 1960, an increase of about 45 percent. Thus, although both sets of data show that murders and nonnegligent manslaughters reported to and recorded by the police increased between 1960 and 1996, the increase is not nearly as great when the increase in the size of the population is taken into account. Crime rates provide a more accurate indication of increases or decreases in crime indexes than do total numbers of crimes. Remember, however, that what are being compared are indexes and not true amounts.

A variety of factors indirectly related to crime can affect crime rates. For example, burglary rates might increase, not because there are more burglaries, but because more things are insured, and insurance companies require police reports before they will reimburse their policyholders. Changing demographic characteristics of the population can also have an effect. For example, because of the post–World War II baby boom (1945–1964), between 1963

Florida's crime rate dropped 1.7% from 1995 to 1996, according to the Florida Department of Law Enforcement (FDLE). Using that statistic, state officials claimed success for the state's emphases on imprisonment and juvenile crime. However, the FDLE report failed to mention that 20 Florida police agencies had not submitted crime reports for 1996. Rather than exclude those 20 agencies from the analysis, the FDLE instead recorded no crimes for the 348,231 residents of those 20 jurisdictions. If the FDLE had used numbers only from those agencies that reported, its calculation of the Florida crime rate would have been 0.2% higher in 1996 than it was in 1995, not 1.7% lower.[11]

FIGURE 2–4

Calculating Crime Rates

1960

$$\frac{9{,}110 \text{ murders \& nonnegligent manslaughters}}{179{,}323{,}175 \text{ (1960 U.S. population)}} \times 100{,}000 = 5.1 \text{ per } 100{,}000 \text{ people}$$

1996

$$\frac{19{,}645 \text{ murders \& nonnegligent manslaughters}}{265{,}284{,}000 \text{ (1996 U.S. population)}} \times 100{,}000 = 7.4 \text{ per } 100{,}000 \text{ people}$$

Uniform crime reports A collection of crime statistics and other law enforcement information gathered under a voluntary national program administered by the FBI.

Eight index crimes The Part I offenses in the FBI's uniform crime reports. They are (1) murder and nonnegligent manslaughter, (2) forcible rape, (3) robbery, (4) aggravated assault, (5) burglary, (6) larceny-theft, (7) motor vehicle theft, and (8) arson, which was added in 1979.

and 1988 there were more people in the age group most prone to committing recorded crime (18- to 24-year-olds). All other things being equal, higher crime rates would be expected between 1963 and 1988 simply because there were more people in the age group that commits the most recorded crime. By the same token, a decrease in crime rates might be expected after 1988, all other things being equal, because the baby boom generation is no longer at those crime-prone ages. However, an increase in crime might be expected when their children reach the age range 18 to 24.

Urbanization is another factor, especially with regard to violent crime. Violent crime is primarily a big-city phenomenon. Thus, violent crime rates might increase as more of the population moves from rural to urban areas or as what were once rural areas become more urban.

Uniform Crime Reports (UCR)

One of the primary sources of crime statistics in the United States is the **uniform crime reports.** The uniform crime reports (UCR) are a collection of crime statistics and other law enforcement information published annually under the title *Crime in the United States.* They are the result of a voluntary national program begun in the 1920s by the International Association of Chiefs of Police.[13] The program was turned over to the FBI in 1930 by the Attorney General, whose office Congress had authorized to serve as the national clearinghouse for crime-related statistics. Today more than 16,000 city, county, and state law enforcement agencies are active in the program; they represent more than 95 percent of the United States population.[14]

The uniform crime reports include two major indexes: (1) offenses known to the police, discussed earlier, and (2) statistics about persons arrested. The section on offenses known to the police, or offenses reported to the police, provides information about the **eight index crimes,** or Part I offenses:

1. Murder and nonnegligent manslaughter
2. Forcible rape
3. Robbery
4. Aggravated assault
5. Burglary
6. Larceny-theft
7. Motor vehicle theft
8. Arson (added in 1979)

The first four offenses are considered violent offenses; the last four are considered property offenses. According to the UCR, in 1996 nearly 13.5 million index offenses were reported to the police.

The other major crime index in the uniform crime reports is based on arrest statistics.

MYTH

When the media report that crime has increased or decreased from one year to the next, they are generally referring to increases or decreases in the true amount of crime.

FACT

What the media are usually referring to when they report that "crime" has increased or decreased from one year to the next is an increase or decrease in the aggregate rate of the eight index crimes (that is, the "crime index total"), not the rates of other crimes or the true amount of crime.

Arrest data are provided for the eight index crimes, as well as 21 other crimes and status offenses. The 21 other crimes and status offenses are referred to as Part II offenses. A **status offense** is an act that is illegal for a juvenile but would not be a crime if committed by an adult (such as truancy or running away from home). Figure 2–5 lists the 21 other crimes and status offenses (Part II offenses) in the FBI's uniform crime reports.

According to the UCR, law enforcement agencies made about 15 million arrests for violations of Part I and Part II offenses nationwide in 1996.[15] The offenses for which the most arrests were made in 1996 (approximately 1.5 million arrests each) were drug abuse violations, larceny-theft, and driving under the influence.[16] The second largest number of arrests (about 1.3 million) was for simple assault.[17] Arrestees generally were young (45 percent were under 25 years of age), male (79 percent), and white (67 percent).[18] The index crime for which women were most frequently arrested was larceny-theft, which accounted for 74 percent of all female arrests for index offenses and 16 percent of all female arrests. More than half the female larceny-theft arrestees were under 25.[19]

Status offense An act that is illegal for a juvenile but would not be a crime if committed by an adult.

FIGURE 2–5

Part I and Part II Offenses of the FBI's Uniform Crime Reports

Part I Offenses—Index Crimes		Part II Offenses
1. Murder and nonnegligent manslaughter		1. Other assaults (simple)
2. Forcible rape		2. Forgery and counterfeiting
3. Robbery	**Violent Crime**	3. Fraud
4. Aggravated assault		4. Embezzlement
		5. Stolen property: buying, receiving, possessing
5. Burglary—breaking or entering		6. Vandalism
6. Larceny–theft		7. Weapons: carrying, possessing, etc.
7. Motor vehicle theft	**Property Crime**	8. Prostitution and commercialized vice
8. Arson		9. Sex offenses
		10. Drug abuse violations
		11. Gambling
		12. Offenses against the family and children
		13. Driving under the influence
		14. Liquor laws
		15. Drunkenness
		16. Disorderly conduct
		17. Vagrancy
		18. All other offenses
		19. Suspicion
		20. Curfew and loitering laws
		21. Runaway

Crime index offenses cleared
The number of offenses for which at least one person has been arrested, charged with the commission of the offense, and turned over to the court for prosecution.

In addition to statistics on offenses known to the police and persons arrested, the uniform crime reports include statistics on crime index offenses cleared by the police. **Crime index offenses cleared** (also called *clearance rates* or *percent cleared by arrest*) is a rough index of police performance in solving crimes. According to the UCR, an offense that is cleared is one for which "at least one person is arrested, charged with the commission of the offense, and turned over to the court for prosecution."[20] The arrest of one person may clear several crimes, or one offense may be cleared by the arrest of several people. Clearances recorded in one year may be for offenses committed in previous years. Clearance rates remain remarkably stable from year to year. Generally, the police are able to clear about 70 percent of murders and nonnegligent manslaughters, 50 percent of forcible rapes, 25 percent of robberies, 60 percent of aggravated assaults, 15 percent of burglaries, 20 percent of larceny-thefts, 15 percent of motor vehicle thefts, and 15 percent of acts of arson.[21] Annually, the police are able to clear about 20 percent of all index offenses (22 percent in 1996).[22]

The uniform crime reports also provide statistics about law enforcement personnel, such as the number of full-time sworn officers in a particular jurisdiction and the number of law enforcement officers killed in the line of duty.

The 1996 edition of the uniform crime reports includes for the first time data reported on crimes motivated by bias against individuals on account of race, religion, sexual orientation, or ethnicity. The UCR has designated these as hate crimes or bias crimes. In 1996, crimes against persons made up 69 percent of the 10,702 hate crime offenses reported; crimes against property accounted for the remaining 31 percent.[23] Of the crimes against persons, intimidation accounted for about 56 percent; simple assault, 24 percent; aggravated assault, 20 percent; and murder and rape, less than 1 percent each.[24] Of all the hate crimes reported, 63 percent were motivated by racial bias, 14 percent by religious bias, 12 percent by sexual-orientation bias, and 11 percent by ethnic bias.[25]

Finally, in recent editions of the uniform crime reports, special sections have been devoted to topical studies. The 1996 special section, entitled "Drugs in America: 1980–1995," presents a relatively detailed examination of the national drug arrest trends during that period. Data are provided for drug arrests by drug type (heroin/cocaine, marijuana, synthetic, or other), region of the country, type of arrest (sale/manufacture or possession), age (adult or juvenile), race, and gender. Among other things, the data show that since 1980, arrests for all drug types have increased steadily and substantially, reaching their highest level in 1995.[26]

National Incident-Based Reporting System (NIBRS)

In 1982, a joint task force of the Bureau of Justice Statistics (BJS) and the Federal Bureau of Investigation (FBI) was created to study and recommend ways to improve the quality of information contained in the uniform crime reports.[27] The result is the National Incident-Based Reporting System (NIBRS), which collected its first data in 1991. Under NIBRS, participating law enforcement authorities provide offense and arrest data on 22 broad categories of crime, covering 46 offenses (as compared to the 8 UCR index

offenses), and provide only arrest information on 11 other offenses (as compared to the 21 Part II UCR offenses) (see Figure 2–6).

Perhaps the greatest and most important difference between the NIBRS and the UCR is that the NIBRS contains more data on each crime, making it possible to examine crimes in much more detail. The NIBRS contains more than 50 different pieces of information about a crime, divided into six segments, or categories. It is hoped that the increased amount of information in the NIBRS will provide the basis for a much greater understanding of crime and its causes (or at least of crime reporting and recording behavior) than is possible with the data from the UCR. Figure 2–7on page 42 lists the NIBRS data elements.

The BJS and the FBI hope that eventually the NIBRS will replace the UCR as the source of official FBI crime counts. As of May 1997, only slightly more than 5 percent of the U.S. population was represented by NIBRS reporting agencies (as compared with 95% for the UCR). So far, the biggest impediment to implementation of the NIBRS is that it is a "paperless"

FIGURE 2–6

The National Incident-Based Reporting System

Group A Offenses	Group B Offenses
Arson	Bad checks
Assault offenses	Curfew/loitering/vagrancy
Bribery	Disorderly conduct
Burglary/breaking and entering	Driving under the influence
Counterfeiting/forgery	Drunkenness
Destruction/damage/vandalism	Liquor law violations
Drug/narcotic offenses	Nonviolent family offenses
Embezzlement	Peeping Tom
Extortion/blackmail	Runaways
Fraud offenses	Trespassing
Gambling offenses	All other offenses
Homicide offenses	
Kidnapping/abduction	
Larceny/theft offenses	
Motor vehicle theft	
Pornography/obscene material	
Prostitution offenses	
Robbery	
Sex offenses, forcible	
Sex offenses, nonforcible	
Stolen property offenses	
Weapons law violations	

repeated assaults as one victimization. The UCR counts crimes reported by people and businesses that the NCVS doesn't reach. Unlike the UCR, the NCVS relies on random samplings of victims and their memories of things that may have happened months ago, both of which are subject to some degree of error. Other problems with the NCVS are interviewers who may be biased or who may cheat, and respondents who may lie or exaggerate, or may respond without understanding the questions.

Differences in the data sources help explain the differences in the trends indicated by the NCVS and the UCR. For example, in one year (1990), NCVS respondents indicated that they had experienced about 50 percent more crimes, on average, than were recorded by the FBI. However, the differences varied by offense. The smallest difference between the two indexes for that year was for motor vehicle theft (20 percent). The largest difference was for burglary (67 percent). The smaller difference for motor vehicle theft was probably due to insurance companies requiring a police report before reimbursing policyholders for their losses.

Sometimes overall changes in the two indexes differ. For example, between 1984 and 1985, the total number of crimes in the UCR increased 4.6 percent, while the total number of crimes in the NCVS decreased 1.9 percent. The difference probably stems from the difference in what the two indexes measure. Thus, between 1984 and 1985, there was an apparent increase in the number of crimes reported to and recorded by the police, but an apparent decrease in the number of crimes to which people said they had been subjected. Figure 2–8 on page 45 displays the trends in four measures or indexes of serious violent crime. Remember that serious violent crimes include murder, rape, robbery, and aggravated assault.

Self-Report Crime Surveys

Self-report crime surveys
Surveys in which subjects are asked whether they have committed crimes.

Whereas other tallies of crime rely on summary police reports, incident-based reports, or victim interviews, **self-report crime surveys** ask selected subjects whether they have committed crimes. Self-report crime surveys, like all crime measures, are indexes of crime; they are not accurate measures of the true amount of crime. To date, most self-report crime surveys conducted in the United States have been administered to schoolchildren, especially high school students. Examples of such nationwide self-report crimes survey efforts are the National Youth Survey, begun in 1975, and the effort to ascertain the levels of smoking, drinking, and illicit drug use among secondary school students, begun by the National Institute on Drug Abuse in 1975 (see Figure 2–9 on pages 46–47).

MYTH   FACT

Criminal activity is concentrated among certain groups of people.

Early self-report crime surveys of adults found an enormous amount of hidden crime in the United States. They found that more than 90 percent of all Americans had committed crimes for which they could have been imprisoned.

FIGURE 2–8

Four Measures of Serious Violent Crime

Offenses in Millions

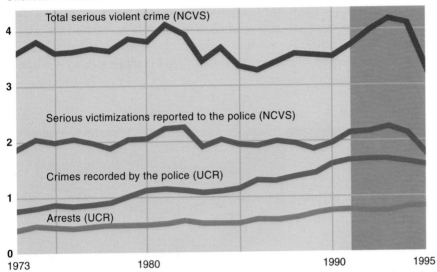

Note: Serious violent crimes include murder, rape, robbery, and aggravated assault. The light beige area indicates that because of changes made to the victimization survey, data prior to 1992 are adjusted to make them comparable to data collected under the redesigned methodology.

Total serious violent crime (NCVS): The number of murders recorded by police plus the number of rapes, robberies, and aggravated assaults from the victimization survey, whether or not they were reported to the police.

Serious victimizations reported to the police (NCVS): The number of murders recorded by police plus the number of rapes, robberies, and aggravated assaults that victims said were reported to the police, as measured by the victimization survey.

Crimes recorded by the police (UCR): The number of murders, forcible rapes, robberies, and aggravated assaults in the Uniform Crime Reports of the FBI, excluding those that involved victims under age 12.

Arrests (UCR): The number of persons arrested for murder, forcible rape, robbery, or aggravated assault as reported by law enforcement agencies to the FBI.

Source: Michael R. Rand, James P. Lynch, and David Cantor, "Criminal Victimization, 1973–95," U.S. Department of Justice, Office of Justice Programs, Bureau of Justice Statistics (Washington: GPO, April 1997), p. 2, Figure 2.

Earlier self-report crime surveys of adults interestingly enough found an enormous amount of hidden crime in the United States. Those self-report crime surveys indicated that more than 90 percent of all Americans had committed crimes for which they could have been found guilty and imprisoned.[32] This is not to say that all Americans are murderers, thieves, or rapists, for they are not, but only that crime serious enough to warrant an individual's imprisonment is more widespread among the U.S. population than many people might think. Moreover, it is unlikely to think that the pervasiveness of crime in the population has lessened significantly since the earlier self-report crime surveys were conducted.

One lesson that can be learned from the aforementioned survey findings is that most people are better described as representing a continuum, that is, as having committed more crime or less crime, rather than simply being described as criminal or noncriminal. In society, there are probably few "angels," that is, people who have never committed a crime. Likewise, there are probably few criminals whose whole lives are totally oriented toward the commission of crimes. It probably makes more sense for us, then, to talk about relative degrees of criminality, rather than to talk about all-encompassing criminality or its absence.

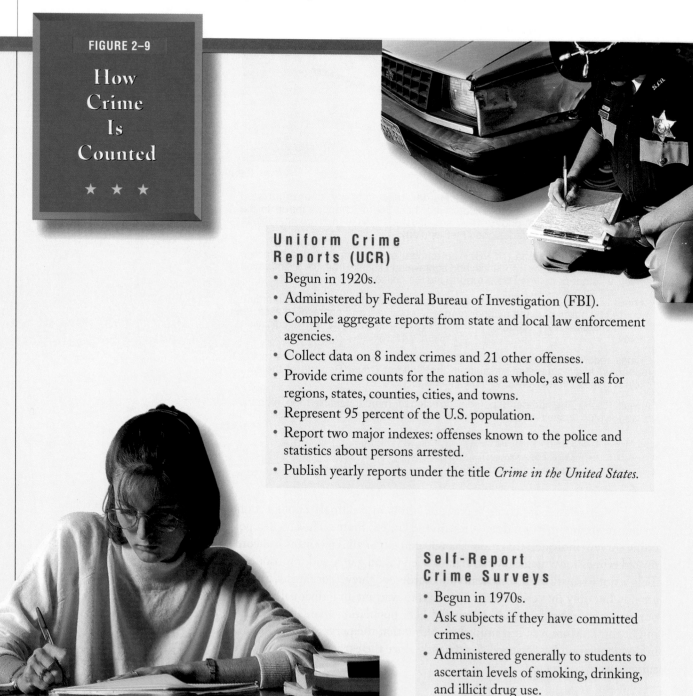

FIGURE 2-9

How Crime Is Counted

★ ★ ★

Uniform Crime Reports (UCR)

- Begun in 1920s.
- Administered by Federal Bureau of Investigation (FBI).
- Compile aggregate reports from state and local law enforcement agencies.
- Collect data on 8 index crimes and 21 other offenses.
- Provide crime counts for the nation as a whole, as well as for regions, states, counties, cities, and towns.
- Represent 95 percent of the U.S. population.
- Report two major indexes: offenses known to the police and statistics about persons arrested.
- Publish yearly reports under the title *Crime in the United States*.

Self-Report Crime Surveys

- Begun in 1970s.
- Ask subjects if they have committed crimes.
- Administered generally to students to ascertain levels of smoking, drinking, and illicit drug use.

One of the criticisms of the National Youth Survey, and a problem with many self-report crime surveys, is that it asks about less serious offenses, such as cutting classes, disobeying parents, and stealing items worth less than $5, while omitting questions about serious crimes, such as robbery, burglary, and sexual assault. Self-report crime surveys also suffer from all the problems of other surveys, problems that were described in the last subsection—they produce different results from other surveys, and they are not an accurate measure of crime.

National Crime Victimization Surveys (NCVS)

- Begun in 1972.
- Compile data from interviews with victims of crime.
- Collect data from nationally representative sample of approximately 50,000 households and all household members at least 12 years of age.
- Provide information about victims, offenders, and crimes.
- Estimate the proportion of each crime type reported to law enforcement and summarize the victims' reasons for reporting or not reporting crimes to the police.
- Publish yearly reports under the title *Criminal Victimization in the United States*.
- Administered by Bureau of Justice Statistics (BJS).

National Incident-Based Reporting System (NIBRS)

- Begun in 1991 as a redesign of UCR to provide more comprehensive and detailed crime statistics.
- Collects information on each criminal incident in 22 broad categories of crime, covering 46 offenses.
- Collects data through computerized records-management systems.
- Reports data on victim-offender relationship, type and location of the incident, type of weapon used, type of injury sustained by the victim, and sex, age, and race of offender and victim.
- Currently represents slightly more than 5 percent of the U.S. population.
- Administered by BJS and FBI.

The $19.6 billion cost to victims of crimes reported in the 1994 national crime victimization survey is less than one-tenth as great as the annual losses of victims of corporate crimes, estimated at $200 billion.[35] The crime of price-fixing, in which competing companies explicitly agree to keep prices artificially high to maximize profits, is estimated by itself to cost consumers about $60 billion a year.[37]

Costs of Crime

According to data from the national crime victimization survey, in 1994 the total economic loss to victims of crime in the United States was $19.6 billion.[33] Figure 2–10 shows the breakdown of this amount among categories of personal and property crimes. The total includes losses from property theft or damage, cash losses, medical expenses, and income lost from work because of injuries, police and court-related activities, or time spent repairing or replacing property.[34] It does not include the cost of the criminal justice process (described in Chapter 1), increased insurance premiums, security devices bought for protection, losses to businesses (which are substantial), or corporate crime.[36]

Until recently, the national crime victimization surveys provided the best estimates of the costs of crime. Those cost estimates, however, are deficient in two ways. First, they include only a limited number of personal and property crimes. And, as noted previously, they do not include the cost of the criminal justice process, increased insurance premiums, security devices bought for protection, losses to businesses, or corporate crime. Second, they report estimates only of relatively short-term and tangible costs. They do not include long-term and intangible costs associated with pain, suffering, and reduced quality of life.

To compensate for the deficiencies of the NCVS, a recent study was sponsored by the National Institute of Justice.[38] In addition to the more

FIGURE 2–10

Total Economic Loss to Victims of Personal and Property Crimes, 1994

Type of Crime	Gross Loss (in millions of dollars)
All crimes	19,587
Personal crimes	**1,865**
Crimes of violence	1,771
Rape/sexual assault	97
Robbery	743
Assault	931
Purse snatching	38
Pocket picking	56
Property crimes	**17,722**
Household burglary	4,608
Motor vehicle theft	7,229
Thefts	5,886

Note: Detail may not add to total shown because of rounding.

Source: *Criminal Victimization in the United States, 1994*, p. 74, Table 82.

standard cost estimates in the NCVS, the new study estimated long-term costs as well as the intangible costs of pain, suffering, and reduced quality of life. Intangible costs were calculated in a number of ways. For example, the costs of pain, suffering, and reduced quality of life for nonfatal injuries were estimated by analyzing jury awards to crime and burn victims. Only the portion of the jury award intended to compensate the victim for pain, suffering, and reduced quality of life was used; punitive damages were excluded from the estimates.

Furthermore, although the new study includes only "street crimes" and "domestic crime," it expands on the crime categories and information included in the NCVS by (1) including crimes committed against people under the age of 12, (2) using better information on domestic violence and sexual assault, (3) more fully accounting for repeat victimizations, and (4) including child abuse and drunk driving. Excluded from the new study are crimes committed against business and government, personal fraud, white-collar crime, child neglect, and most "victimless" crimes, including drug offenses.

The new study estimates that the annual tangible cost of personal and property crime—including medical costs, lost earnings, and public program costs related to victim assistance—is $105 billion, or more than $400 per U.S. resident. When the intangible costs of pain, suffering, and reduced quality of life are added, the annual cost increases to an estimated $450 billion, or about $1,800 per U.S. resident. Figure 2–11 shows how the $450 billion is divided into specific costs of crime.

Violent crime (including drunk driving and arson) accounts for $426 billion of the total, while property crime accounts for the remaining $24 billion. The study found that violence against children accounts for more than 20 percent of all tangible costs and more than 35 percent of all costs (including pain, suffering, and reduced quality of life).

FYI

Between 1980 and 1997, the United States spent about $290 billion on federal, state, and local antidrug efforts. That is more than the federal government spent on medical research into cancer, heart disease, or AIDS. In 1996 alone, the federal government spent an estimated $13.7 billion to combat drugs. About two-thirds of all money spent has gone to interdiction and to overseas programs to eliminate drug production.[39]

FIGURE 2–11

Annual Cost of Crime in the United States

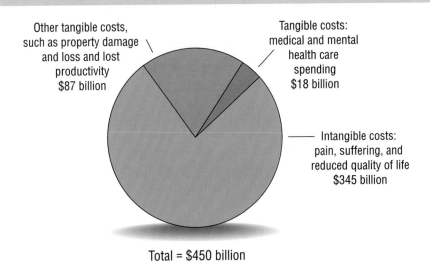

Other tangible costs, such as property damage and loss and lost productivity $87 billion

Tangible costs: medical and mental health care spending $18 billion

Intangible costs: pain, suffering, and reduced quality of life $345 billion

Total = $450 billion

Source: Ted R. Miller, Mark A. Cohen, and Brian Wiersema, *Victim Costs and Consequences: A New Look*, U.S. Department of Justice, National Institute of Justice Research Report (Washington: GPO, February 1996), p. 17.

Crime and Its Consequences   **CHAPTER 2**

Of the crimes included in the study, rape has the highest annual victim costs, at $127 billion a year (excluding child sexual abuse). Second is assault, with victim costs of $93 billion a year, followed by murder (excluding arson and drunk driving deaths), at $71 billion annually. Drunk driving (including fatalities) is next at $61 billion a year, and child abuse is estimated to cost $56 billion annually.

Among the tangible costs of crime excluded from the new study are the costs of the criminal justice process and private security expenditures. Omitted also are the intangible costs of fear of crime, a fear that makes people prisoners in their own homes, divides people, and destroys communities.

Fear of Crime

A by-product of crime, beyond actual physical or material loss, is fear. For many crime victims, it is the most burdensome and lasting consequence of their victimizations. However, fear of crime is also contagious. One does not have to be a victim of violent crime to be fearful of violent crime. In fact, research shows that people who have heard about other people's victimizations are nearly as fearful as the people who have been victimized themselves.[40]

What People Fear

Fear of crime, especially violent crime, is widespread. For example, a recent public opinion poll found that 80 percent of Americans are "concerned . . . about becoming a victim of crime"; 29.4 percent are "somewhat concerned" and 50.6 percent are "very concerned."[41] When Americans are asked specifically what they fear, surveys show the following categories:[42]

- 40 percent worry about sexual assault, either against themselves or against a family member.
- 40 percent are concerned about burglaries when they are not home.
- 30 percent worry about being attacked while driving their cars.
- 30 percent worry about being mugged.
- 25 percent worry about being beaten up, knifed, or shot.
- 25 percent worry about burglaries when they are home.
- 20 percent worry about being murdered.

It is interesting to note that no more than 40 percent of Americans are fearful of any specific type of crime, though 80 percent of Americans are fearful of crime in general. Those survey results suggest that there is a greater fear of being a crime victim in general—that is, a greater abstract fear of crime—than there is of being the victim of a specific crime.

When and Where People Fear

Fear of violent crime is greatest at night when a person is alone and away from home. Although only 9 percent of Americans feel unsafe and insecure in their own homes at night, 38 percent of them are afraid to walk alone

at night in some areas within a mile of their homes.[44] Those figures have remained about the same for the past decade.[45]

It is interesting that in 1997 "only" 46 percent of the public felt that crime in their areas had been increasing in the past year, compared with 54 percent who felt that way in 1992. (In 1997, 32 percent believed crime in their areas had been decreasing, 20 percent thought it was the same, and 2 percent had no opinion.)[46] During times when people have perceived that the amount of crime in their areas was decreasing, their fear of crime has remained relatively stable, again pointing to an abstract fear of crime.

Who Fears Crime

Fear of criminal victimization is neither evenly distributed across the population nor commensurate with the statistical probability of being the victim of crime. Recent surveys reveal some of the differences in the public's fear of crime.[47] Among those differences are the following:

- **Gender** Females are more fearful than males.
- **Race/Ethnicity** Nonwhites, especially Hispanics and blacks, are more fearful than whites.
- **Age** People 30 years old and older are slightly more fearful than people less than 30 years old.
- **Religion** Jews are more fearful than either Protestants or Catholics.
- **Community** People living in urban areas are more fearful than people living in suburban or rural areas.
- **Region** Among those people most concerned, Easterners and Southerners (in that order) are more fearful than Westerners and Midwesterners. (Overall concern about crime does not differ greatly by region of the country.)
- **Education** A person's concern about being a crime victim is slightly lower the higher the level of education. Those people most concerned are likely to be only high school graduates or less.
- **Income** Fear of crime victimization declines with increasing family income. (People whose family income is $50,000 or more are less fearful of crime than people whose family income is less than $50,000.)

According to a report released February 6, 1997, by the Centers for Disease Control and Prevention, the United States had the highest rate of childhood homicide out of the world's 26 richest countries. The United States accounted for 73 percent of murders of children 14 and younger in the industrialized countries surveyed. The United States also led in the rate of firearm-related deaths among children.[48]

It is important to stress that the preceding descriptions of the kinds of people who are most and least fearful of crime in general do not address the specific types of crimes that people fear. Also, the descriptions are generalizations. As with all generalizations, there are exceptions or qualifications. In a recent study of fear of seven types of criminal victimization, four exceptions to or qualifications of the preceding general descriptions were revealed.[49] First, although females are generally more fearful of crime than are males, their greater fear applies only to sexual assault and other personal violent crimes. Females are no more fearful than males of having their homes burglarized. Second, although people 30 years old and older are slightly more fearful in general than people less than 30 years old, younger people are more fearful than older people of sexual assault and burglary. For nonsexual violent

Crime and Its Consequences **CHAPTER 2**

offenses, there are no age differences. Third, Hispanics and blacks are more fearful than whites only of sexual assault of themselves or someone in their household and of being murdered. Fourth, only fear of being beaten, knifed, or shot and fear of getting mugged increase with the level of urbanization of the community in which people live.

As noted previously, the groups that are the most fearful of crime are not necessarily those with the highest rates of victimization. For example, elderly women, the demographic group most afraid of crime, are the least likely to be victimized.[50] More generally, women and older people are more fearful of crime than are men and younger people, even though women and older persons are less likely to be victims of crime.[51]

MYTH

The people most fearful of crime are the people most vulnerable to crime.

FACT

The people most fearful of crime are not necessarily members of groups with the highest rates of victimization. For example, the demographic group most afraid of crime, elderly women, is the least likely to be victimized.

Fear of crime has many detrimental consequences. It makes people feel vulnerable and isolated, it reduces a person's general sense of well-being, it motivates people to buy safety devices with money that otherwise could be used to improve their quality of life, and it also contributes to neighborhood decline and the crime problem. As Wesley Skogan explains:

Fear . . . can work in conjunction with other factors to stimulate more rapid neighborhood decline. Together, the spread of fear and other local problems provide a form of positive feedback that can further increase levels of crime. These feedback processes include (1) physical and psychological withdrawal from community life; (2) a weakening of the informal social control processes that inhibit crime and disorder; (3) a decline in the organizational life and mobilization capacity of the neighborhood; (4) deteriorating business conditions; (5) the importation and domestic production of delinquency and deviance; and (6) further dramatic changes in the composition of the population. At the end lies a stage characterized by demographic collapse.[52]

Victims of Crime

Findings from the 1995 NCVS, the latest statistics available, reveal that in 1995 a total of 38.4 million crimes were attempted or completed against U.S. residents aged 12 or older—approximately 10 million personal crimes (rape and sexual assault, robbery, aggravated and simple assault, pocket picking, and purse snatching) and nearly 28.5 million property crimes (household burglary, motor vehicle theft, and other thefts).[53] Of the approximately 10 million personal crimes, 9.6 million were violent.[54] However, in 71 percent of all violent crimes, the crime was attempted or threatened but not completed.[55] Still, in about 25 percent of the violent crimes, a victim was injured.[56]

Victimization Trends

As noted previously, data from pre-1993 victimization surveys are not directly comparable with data from post-1993 surveys because of the redesign of the survey. However, in this section, meaningful comparisons between pre- and post-1993 data are made by means of adjustments of the pre-1993 data to take into account the survey design changes. Of course, comparisons using only post-1993 survey data needed no adjustments.

From 1994 through 1995, the victimization rate for personal crimes (per 1,000 persons 12 or older or per 1,000 households) decreased 13 percent, while the victimization rate for property crimes fell about 9 percent.[57] The victimization rate for violent crimes declined 12.4 percent during that period—the largest single-year decrease ever measured by the victimization survey.[58]

Figure 2–12 on page 54 displays trends in violent and property crime rates from 1973 through 1995. The top graph shows that although 1973–1995 violent crime victimization rates varied, they stayed within a relatively narrow range, and the rate in 1994 was about the same as in 1973. (As noted previously, there was a historic drop in the rate in 1995 compared with 1994.) The bottom graph illustrates that unlike violent crime rates, property crime rates declined steadily during the period.

Who the Victims Are

Although each year millions of people are victimized by crime, victimization—like the fear of crime—is not spread evenly throughout the population. Certain types of people are much more likely to be crime victims. For example, a recent Justice Department study discovered that the most common victims of violent crime in the United States are children 12–17 years of age.[60] The study found that in 1992, children in that age range were the victims of 23 percent of all violent crimes, even though they make up only about 10 percent of the U.S. population. Children 12–17 were raped, robbed, and beaten twice as often as young adults and five times more often than adults 35 and older. The vast majority of violent crimes committed against those children were assaults (83 percent in 1992). Most of the assaults (56 percent) did not involve weapons or serious injury. Two-thirds of the victims were attacked by someone 12 to 20 years of age. The 1.5 million crimes committed against children 12–17 in 1992 were 23 percent more than in 1987.

MYTH

Adults are more likely to be raped than are children.

FACT

Girls younger than 18 are the victims of more than half the rapes reported to police, even though the younger the rape victim, the less likely the crime is to be reported to the police. Girls younger than 18 make up about 25 percent of the U.S. female population. In 1992, girls younger than 12 were the victims in 16 percent of rapes reported to the police. Moreover, the younger the victim, the more likely that the attacker is a relative or acquaintance.[61]

The relationship between the viewing of violence on television and the violence in society is a hotly debated topic. However, television violence may have more to do with fear of crime than it does with actual violent behavior. George Gerbner, a professor and dean emeritus at the Annenberg School for Communication at the University of Pennsylvania, has studied the subject for more than 20 years. He says, "The contribution of television to the committing of violence is relatively minor, maybe 5 percent. Whereas the contribution of television to the perception of violence is much higher. People are almost paralyzed by fear." From his research, Gerbner has concluded that heavy television viewers tend to suffer from what he calls the "mean world syndrome." Heavy viewers are more likely than light viewers to overestimate their chances of encountering violence, to believe that their neighborhoods are unsafe, and to assume that crime is rising, whether or not it actually is. They are also more likely to buy guns for protection.[62]

FIGURE 2–12

Trends in Violent and Property Crime Rates

Violent crime rates, 1973–95 (with adjustments based on the redesign of the National Crime Victimization Survey)

Victimization rate per 1,000 persons age 12 or older

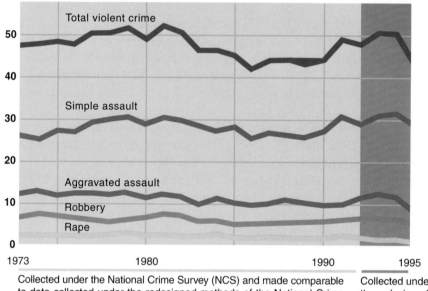

Collected under the National Crime Survey (NCS) and made comparable to data collected under the redesigned methods of the National Crime Victimization Survey (NCVS)

Collected under the redesigned NCVS

Property crime rates, 1973–95 (with adjustments based on the redesign of the National Crime Victimization Survey)

Victimization rate per 1,000 persons age 12 or older

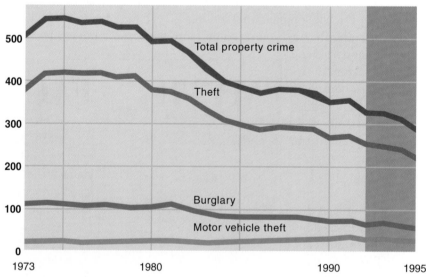

The light beige area identifies data collected under the National Crime Survey of BJS and then adjusted to be comparable to data collected beginning in 1992 under the redesigned methodology of the National Crime Victimization Survey of BJS.

Source: Michael R. Rand, James P. Lynch, and David Cantor, *Criminal Victimization, 1973–95,* U.S. Department of Justice, Office of Justice Programs, Bureau of Justice Statistics (Washington: GPO, April 1997), p. 1, Figure 1, and p. 4, Figure 5.

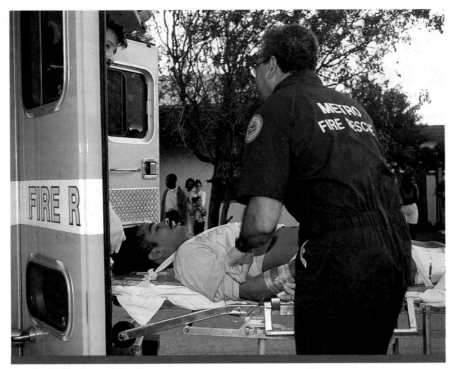

Young, economically disadvantaged black males are the most likely victims of personal violent crime.

Data from the 1995 national crime victimization survey provide an even more detailed picture of criminal victimization in the United States. According to the survey, the most likely victims of personal violent crimes—such as rape/sexual assault, robbery, and other assaults—are poor, young (12–19 years old) black or Hispanic males living in urban areas of the West.[63] The same characteristics describe the most likely victims of personal theft as well, except that personal theft victims are more likely to reside in the Northeast than in the West.[64]

The most likely victims of household property crimes—such as burglary, motor vehicle theft, and other thefts—are households headed by blacks or Hispanics, renters, and households with incomes of $75,000 or more (although households with incomes less than $7,500 are more than 1.5 times as likely to be burglary victims).[65] Households in urban areas of the West are more likely to be victims of household property crimes than are households in rural or suburban areas or other regions of the country.[66]

The group least likely to experience either lethal or nonlethal forms of criminal victimization is persons aged 65 or older. Among the elderly, however, males, blacks, divorced or separated persons, urban residents, and renters are more likely than other elderly persons to be victims of crime.[67] Furthermore, when members of this group are victimized, they are more likely than younger people to be harmed by strangers and to sustain grievous injuries.

ADDITIONAL READING

Barak, Gregg (ed.). *Crimes by the Capitalist State: An Introduction to State Criminality.* New York: State University of New York Press, 1991.

Coleman, James W. *The Criminal Elite: The Sociology of White Collar Crime,* 4th ed. New York: St. Martin's, 1998.

Green, Gary S. *Occupational Crime,* 2d ed. Chicago: Nelson-Hall, 1995.

Reiman, Jeffrey J. *The Rich Get Richer and the Poor Get Prison,* 4th ed. Boston: Allyn & Bacon, 1995.

Simon, David R. *Elite Deviance,* 5th ed. Boston: Allyn & Bacon, 1996.

ENDNOTES

1. Sheryl Lindsell-Roberts, *Loony Laws and Silly Statutes* (New York: Sterling, 1994).

2. For additional examples and further discussion of this issue, see Robert M. Bohm, "Some Relationships That Arguably Should Be Criminal Although They Are Not: On the Political Economy of Crime," pp. 3–29 in K. D. Tunnell (ed.), *Political Crime in Contemporary America: A Critical Approach* (New York: Garland, 1993); Gregg Barak (ed.), *Crimes by the Capitalist State: An Introduction to State Criminality* (New York: State University of New York Press, 1991); Gregg Barak and Robert M. Bohm, "The Crimes of the Homeless or the Crime of Homelessness? On the Dialectics of Criminalization, Decriminalization, and Victimization," *Contemporary Crises,* Vol. 13, 1989, pp. 275–88; James W. Coleman, *The Criminal Elite: The Sociology of White Collar Crime,* 4th ed. (New York: St. Martin's, 1998); Gary S. Green, *Occupational Crime,* 2d ed. (Chicago: Nelson-Hall, 1996); David R. Simon, *Elite Deviance,* 5th ed. (Boston: Allyn and Bacon, 1996).

3. These elements and the discussion that follows are based on material from Edwin H. Sutherland and Donald R. Cressey, *Criminology,* 9th ed. (Philadelphia: J. B. Lippincott, 1974), pp. 13–15.

4. *M'Naghten's Case,* 8 Eng. Rep. 718 (1843).

5. Herbert Modlin, "Crime and Insanity," *Firing Line,* May 25, 1984.

6. Sutherland and Cressey, op. cit., p. 25.

7. Ibid. The remainder of the discussion in this section is based on material from the aforementioned source, pp. 25–30.

8. Ibid.

9. Ibid., pp. 27–28.

10. D. Seidman and M. Couzens, "Getting the Crime Rate Down: Political Pressure and Crime Reporting," *Law and Human Behavior,* Vol. 8, 1974, pp. 327–42. See also L. DeFleur, "Biasing Influences on Drug Arrest Records: Implications for Deviance Research," *American Sociological Review,* Vol. 40, 1975, pp. 88–103; W. L. Selke and H. E. Pepinsky, "The Politics of Police Reporting in Indianapolis, 1948-1978," *Law and Human Behavior,* Vol. 6, 1982, pp. 327–42.

11. "Crime Drop: More Fiction Than Fact?" *The Orlando Sentinel,* May 11, 1997, p. B-1.

12. Darrell Steffensmeir, "Is the Crime Rate Really Falling? An 'Aging' U.S. Population and Its Effect on the Nation's Crime Rate, 1980–1984," *Journal of Research in Crime and Delinquency,* Vol. 24, 1987, pp. 23–48.

13. Federal Bureau of Investigation, *Crime in the United States 1996,* U.S. Department of Justice (Washington: GPO, 1997).

14. Ibid.

15. Ibid.

16. Ibid.

17. Ibid.

18. Ibid., p. 214.

19. Ibid.

20. Ibid., p. 203.

21. Ibid., p. 204.

22. Ibid., p. 203.

23. Federal Bureau of Investigation, op. cit., pp. 58–59.

24. Ibid.

25. Ibid.

26. Ibid., pp. 280–84.

27. Unless indicated otherwise, all information in this section is from Brian A. Reaves, "Using NIBRS Data to Analyze Violent Crime," U.S. Department of Justice, *Bureau of Justice Statistics Technical Report* (Washington: GPO, October 1993).

28. Ibid., pp. 14 and 36; "Violent Crimes Plummet 7%— Drop Biggest in 35 Years," *The Orlando Sentinel,* June 2, 1997, p. A-4; "FBI Report: Crime Rate Still Falling," *The Orlando Sentinel,* October 5, 1997, p. A-3.

29. "Crime Drop," op. cit.

30. U.S. Department of Justice, "Implementing the National Incident-Based Reporting System: A Project Status Report," (Washington: GPO, July 1997).

31. U.S. Department of Justice, Office of Justice Programs, Bureau of Justice Statistics, Criminal Victimization in the United States, 1994 (Annapolis, MD: Bureau of Justice Statistics Clearinghouse, 1997).

32. See, for example, J. S. Wallerstein and C. J. Wylie, "Our Law–Abiding Lawbreakers," *Probation,* Vol. 25, 1947, pp. 107–12; I. Silver, Introduction to *The Challenge of Crime in a*

Free Society (New York: Avon, 1968). See also C. Tittle, W. Villemez, and D. Smith, "The Myth of Social Class and Criminality," *American Sociological Review,* Vol. 43, 1978, pp. 643–56. Juvenile delinquency is also widespread. See, for example, Jerald Bachman, Lloyd Johnston, and Patrick O'Malley, *Monitoring the Future* (Ann Arbor: University of Michigan, Institute for Social Research, 1992); Martin Gold, "Undetected Delinquent Behavior," *Journal of Research in Crime and Delinquency,* Vol. 3, 1966, pp. 27–46; Martin Gold, *Delinquent Behavior in an American City* (Belmont, CA: Brooks/Cole, 1970); Maynard Erickson and LaMar Empey, "Court Records, Undetected Delinquency, and Decision-Making," *Journal of Criminal Law, Criminology, and Police Science,* Vol. 54, 1963, pp. 446–69; James Short and F. Ivan Nye, "Extent of Unrecorded Delinquency," *Journal of Criminal Law, Criminology, and Police Science,* Vol. 49, 1958, pp. 296–302.

33. *Criminal Victimization in the United States, 1994,* p. 74, Table 82.

34. U.S. Department of Justice, Office of Justice Programs, Bureau of Justice Statistics, *Criminal Victimization in the United States, 1992* (Annapolis, MD: Bureau of Justice Statistics Clearinghouse, 1994), p. 148.

35. Simon, op. cit., p. 93.

36. Ibid.

37. Ibid., p. 104.

38. Ted R. Miller, Mark A. Cohen, and Brian Wiersema, "Victim Costs and Consequences: A New Look," U.S. Department of Justice, National Institute of Justice Report (Washington: GPO, February 1996).

39. Michael Griffin, "Drug War Strategies Are Not Poles Apart," *The Orlando Sentinel,* October 29, 1996, p. A-1.

40. Wesley Skogan, "Fear of Crime and Neighborhood Change," in Albert J. Reiss, Jr., and Michael Tonry (eds.), *Communities and Crime,* Vol. 8 of *Crime and Justice: A Review of Research* (Chicago: The University of Chicago Press, 1986).

41. *Sourcebook of Criminal Justice Statistics Online,* June 1997, p. 156, Table 2.37 (1995 data).

42. Kathleen Maguire and Ann L. Pastore (eds.), *Sourcebook of Criminal Justice Statistics 1993,* U.S. Department of Justice, Bureau of Justice Statistics (Washington: GPO, 1994), p. 182, Table 2.30; Bahram Haghighi and Jon Sorensen, "America's Fear of Crime," in Timothy J. Flanagan and Dennis R. Longmire (eds.), *Americans View Crime and Justice: A National Public Opinion Survey* (Thousand Oaks, CA: Sage, 1996), p. 22, Table 2.1.

43. "Mean Dogs Catch Blame for Bite Rise," *The Orlando Sentinel,* May 30, 1997, p. A-5.

44. Kathleen Maguire and Ann L. Pastore (eds.), *Sourcebook of Criminal Justice Statistics 1996,* U.S. Department of Justice, Bureau of Justice Statistics (Washington: GPO, 1997), p. 134, Table 2.29.

45. Ibid.

46. Ibid., Table 2.28.

47. Ibid., Tables 2.30, 2.31, and 2.32; Kathleen Maguire and Ann L. Pastore (eds.), *Sourcebook of Criminal Justice Statistics 1994,* U.S. Department of Justice, Bureau of Justice Statistics (Washington: GPO, 1995) (from draft data); Haghighi and Sorensen, op. cit., p. 19.

48. Elizabeth Kolbert, "Aggression in Kids Linked to TV Violence: Experts Say Connection Isn't Cause," *The Charlotte (NC) Observer,* December 18, 1994, p. 18A.

49. Haghighi and Sorensen, op. cit., pp. 26–27.

50. Wesley Skogan and Michael G. Maxwell, *Coping With Crime: Individual and Neighborhood Reactions* (Beverly Hills, CA: Sage, 1981).

51. Haghighi and Sorensen, op. cit., p. 19.

52. Skogan, "Fear of Crime and Neighborhood Change," op. cit., p. 215.

53. *Facts on File: World News Digest with Index,* Vol. 57, No. 2936, March 13, 1997, p. 170.

54. Bruce M. Taylor, "Changes in Criminal Victimization, 1994–95," U.S. Department of Justice, Bureau of Justice Statistics (Washington: GPO, April 1997), p. 2, Table 1.

55. Ibid.

56. Ibid.

57. Ibid.

58. Ibid. Taylor, op cit.

59. Ibid.; Michael R. Rand, James P. Lynch, and David Cantor, "Criminal Victimization, 1973–95," U.S. Department of Justice, Office of Justice Programs, Bureau of Justice Statistics (Washington: GPO, April 1997), p. 1.

60. "Clinton Asks for Money to Aid the Victims of Gang Violence," *The Orlando Sentinel,* October 27, 1996, p. A-3.

61. Robert Davis, "Young People Victimized the Most, Study Says," *USA Today,* July 18, 1994, p. 3A.

62. Patrick A. Langan and Caroline Wolf Harlow, "Child Rape Victims, 1992," U.S. Department of Justice, Bureau of Justice Statistics, *Crime Data Brief* (Washington: GPO, June 1994).

63. Taylor, op. cit., p. 3, Table 2.

64. Ibid.

65. Ibid., p. 4, Table 3.

66. Ibid.

67. U.S. Department of Justice, Bureau of Justice Statistics, "Elderly Crime Victims," *Selected Findings From BJS* (Annapolis, MD: Bureau of Justice Statistics Clearinghouse, 1994).

3 Explaining Crime

CHAPTER OBJECTIVES

After completing this chapter, you should be able to:

1 Define *criminological theory* and explain why it is important to study.

2 State the causes of crime, according to classical and neoclassical criminologists, and the policy implications of those theories.

3 Identify the basic difference between classical and positivist theories of crime causation.

4 Describe the basis of biological theories of crime causation, as well as their policy implications.

5 Describe how psychological theories explain the causes of crime and how those theories are applied.

6 Relate sociological theories of crime causation and their policy implications.

7 Distinguish major differences among classical, positivist, and critical theories of crime causation.

8 Describe how critical theorists would explain the causes of crime and how they would address them through policy.

Introduction to Criminological Theory

A theory is an explanation that tells why or how things are related to each other. A theory of crime explains why or how a certain thing or certain things are related to criminal behavior. For example, some theories assume that crime is a part of human nature, that human beings are born evil. In those theories, human nature is the thing explained in relation to crime. Other theories assume that crime is caused by biological things (for example, chromosome abnormalities, hormone imbalances), psychological things (for example, below-normal intelligence, satisfaction of basic needs), sociological things (for example, social disorganization, inadequate socialization), economic things (for example, unemployment, economic inequality); or some combination of all four kinds of things.

Criminological theory is important because most of what is done in criminal justice is based on theory, whether we or the people who implement policies based on the theory know it or not. Thus, criminal justice policies, whether new strategies of policing or new forms of punishment, are logical products of criminological theories. However, more often than not, criminal justice policies are initiated simply because they seem to make sense. What policy makers and the public sometimes do not understand is that one reason the policies make sense is that they are usually based on theories that are popular with, but unrecognized by, policy makers and the public.

The failure to understand the theoretical basis of criminal justice policies leads to at least two undesirable consequences. First, if criminal justice policy makers do not know the theory or theories on which their proposed policies are based, then they will be unaware of the problems that are likely to undermine the success of the policies. Much time and money could be saved if criminal justice policies were based on a thorough theoretical understanding. Second, criminal justice policies invariably intrude on people's lives. If people's lives are going to be disrupted by criminal justice policies, it seems only fair that there be very good reasons for the disruption.

Technically, criminological theory refers not only to explanations of criminal behavior but also to explanations of police behavior and the behavior of attorneys, prosecutors, judges, correctional personnel, victims, and other actors in the criminal justice process. However, in this chapter, our focus is on theories of crime causation. Figure 3–1 on pages 66–67 outlines the crime causation theories presented in this chapter.

Classical and Neoclassical Approaches to Explaining Crime

The causes of crime have long been the subject of much speculation, theorizing, research, and debate among scholars and the public. Each theory of crime has been influenced by the religious, philosophical, political, economic, social, and scientific trends of the time. One of the earliest secular approaches to explaining the causes of crime was the classical theory, developed in Europe at a time of profound social and intellectual change. Before classical theory, crime was generally equated with sin and was considered "the work of the devil."

Classical Theory

Classical theory is a product of the Enlightenment, or the Age of Reason, a period of history that began in the early 1500s and lasted until the late 1700s. The Enlightenment thinkers, including members of the classical school of criminology, promoted a new, scientific view of the world. In so doing, they rejected the then-dominant religious view of the world, which was based on revelation and the authority of the Church. The Enlightenment thinkers assumed that human beings could understand the world through science—the human capacity to observe and to reason. Moreover, they believed that if people could understand the world and its functioning, they could change it. The Enlightenment thinkers rejected the belief that either the nature of the world or the behavior of the people in it was divinely ordained or determined.

Instead, the Enlightenment thinkers believed that people exercise *free will,* or the ability to choose any course of action, for which they are completely responsible. Human behavior was considered motivated by a *hedonistic rationality,* in which a person weighs the potential pleasure of an action against the possible pain associated with it. In that view, human beings commit crime because they rationally calculate that the crime will give them more pleasure than pain.

The classicists, as Enlightenment thinkers, were concerned with protecting the rights of humankind from the corruption and excesses of the existing legal institutions. Horrible and severe punishments were common both before and during the Enlightenment. For example, in England during the eighteenth century, more than 200 offenses carried the death penalty including stealing turnips, associating with gypsies, cutting down a tree, and picking pockets. Barbarous punishments were not the only problem. At the time, crime was rampant, yet types of crime were poorly defined. What we today call *due process of law* was either absent or ignored. Torture was employed routinely to extract confessions. Judgeships were typically sold to wealthy persons by the sovereign, and judges had almost total discretion. Consequently, there was little consistency in the application of the law or in the punishments imposed.

It was within that historical context that Cesare Beccaria, perhaps the best known of the classical criminologists, wrote and published anonymously in 1764 his truly revolutionary work, *An Essay on Crimes and Punishments (Dei Delitti e delle Pene).* His book is generally acknowledged to have had an enormous practical influence on the establishment of a more humane system of criminal law and procedure.[1] In the book, Beccaria sets forth most of what we now call classical criminological theory.

According to Beccaria, the only justified rationale for laws and punishments is the principle of **utility,** that is, "the greatest happiness shared by the greatest number."[2] The basis of society, as well as the origin of punishments and the right to punish, is the **social contract.** The social contract is an

Classical theory A product of the Enlightenment, based on the assumption that people exercise free will and are thus completely responsible for their actions. In classical theory, human behavior, including criminal behavior, is motivated by a hedonistic rationality, in which actors weigh the potential pleasure of an action against the possible pain associated with it.

Utility The principle that a policy should provide "the greatest happiness shared by the greatest number."

Social contract An imaginary agreement to sacrifice the minimum amount of liberty necessary to prevent anarchy and chaos.

FIGURE 3–1

Theories of Crime Causation

THEORIES	THEORISTS	CAUSES	POLICY IMPLICATIONS
Classical and Neoclassical			
	Beccaria	Free-willed individuals commit crime because they rationally calculate that crime will give them more pleasure than pain.	Deterrence: Establish social contract. Enact laws that are clear, simple, unbiased, and reflect the consensus of the population. Impose punishments that are proportionate to the crime, prompt, certain, public, necessary, the least possible in the given circumstances, and dictated by law, not judges' discretion. Educate the public. Eliminate corruption from the administration of justice. Reward virtue.
Positivist			
Biological	Lombroso, Sheldon	Biological inferiority causes people to commit crimes.	Isolate, sterilize, or execute offenders. For specific problems, brain surgery, chemical treatment, improved diets, and better mother and child health care.
Psychological			
Intelligence	Goddard	Mental inferiority (low IQ) causes people to commit crimes.	Isolate, sterilize, or execute offenders.
Psychoanalytic	Freud	Crime is a symptom of more deep-seated problems.	Provide psychotherapy or psychoanalysis.
Humanistic	Maslow, Halleck	Crime is a means by which individuals can satisfy their basic human needs (Maslow). Crime is an adaptation to helplessness caused by oppression (Halleck).	Help people satisfy their basic needs legally (Maslow). Eliminate sources of oppression. Provide legal ways of coping with feelings of helplessness caused by oppression; psychotherapy (Halleck).
Sociological			
Durkheim	Durkheim	Crime is a social fact. It is a "normal" aspect of society, although different types of societies should have greater or lesser degrees of it. Crime is also functional for society.	Contain crime within reasonable boundaries.
Chicago School	Park, Burgess, Shaw, McKay	Delinquency is caused by detachment from conventional groups, which is caused by social disorganization.	Organize and empower neighborhood residents.

FIGURE 3–1 (CONTINUED)

Theories of Crime Causation

THEORIES	THEORISTS	CAUSES	POLICY IMPLICATIONS
Positivist (continued)			
Sociological			
Anomie or strain	Merton, Cohen, Cloward, Ohlin	For Merton, it is the contradiction between cultural goals and the social structure's capacity to provide the institutionalized means to achieve those goals. For Cohen and gang delinquency, it is caused by an inability to conform to middle-class values and to achieve status among peers legally.	Reduce aspirations. Increase legitimate opportunities. Do both.
Learning	Tarde, Sutherland, Burgess, Akers, Jeffery	Crime is committed because it is positively reinforced, negatively reinforced, or imitated.	Provide law-abiding models. Regulate association. Eliminate crime's rewards. Reward law-abiding behavior. Punish criminal behavior effectively.
Control	Reiss, Toby, Nye, Reckless, Hirschi	Crime is a result of improper socialization.	Properly socialize children so that they develop self-control and a strong moral bond to society.
Critical			
Labeling	Lemert	Does not explain the initial cause of crime and delinquency (primary deviance); explains only secondary deviance with the acceptance of a criminal label.	Do not label. Employ radical nonintervention. Employ reintegrative shaming.
Conflict	Vold, Turk	Crime is caused by relative powerlessness.	Dominant groups give up power to subordinate groups. Dominant groups become more effective rulers and subordinate groups better subjects.
Radical	Quinney, Chambliss, Platt	Competition among wealthy people and among poor people as well as between rich and poor (the class struggle) and the practice of taking advantage of other people cause crime.	Define crime as a violation of basic human rights. Replace the criminal justice system with "popular" or "socialist" justice. Create a socialist society appreciative of human diversity.
British or Left Realism	Young	Directs attention to the fear and victimization experienced by working class individuals.	Employ police power to protect people living in working-class communities.
Peacemaking	Quinney, Pepinsky	Same as radical (different prescription for change).	Transform human beings so that they are able to experience empathy with those less fortunate and respond to other people's needs. Reduce hierarchical structures. Create communities of caring people. Champion universal social justice.
Feminist theory	Daly, Chesney-Lind, Simpson	Patriarchy (men's control over women's labor and sexuality) is the cause of crime.	Abolish patriarchal structures and relationships. Champion greater equality for women in all areas.

Special or **specific deterrence**
The prevention of individuals from committing crime again by punishing them.

General deterrence The prevention of people in general or society at large from engaging in crime by punishing specific individuals and making examples of them.

Cesare Beccaria, the best known of the classical criminologists, opposed the death penalty. In *An Essay on Crimes and Punishments,* he wrote:

The death penalty cannot be useful, because of the example of barbarity it gives men. . . . It seems to me absurd that the laws, which are an expression of the public will, which detest and punish homicide, should themselves commit it, and that to deter citizens from murder, they order a public one.[6]

Neoclassical theory
A modification of classical theory in which it was conceded that certain factors, such as insanity, might inhibit the exercise of free will.

imaginary agreement entered into by persons who sacrifice the minimum amount of their liberty necessary to prevent anarchy and chaos.

Beccaria believed that the only legitimate purpose of punishment is deterrence, both special and general.[3] **Special** or **specific deterrence** is the prevention of the punished persons from committing crime again. **General deterrence** is the use of the punishment of specific individuals to prevent people in general or society at large from engaging in crime. To be both effective and just, Beccaria argued, punishments must be "public, prompt, necessary, the least possible in the given circumstances, proportionate to the crime, dictated by the laws."[4] It is important to emphasize, however, that Beccaria promoted crime prevention over punishment.

In addition to the establishment of a social contract and the punishment of people who violate it, Beccaria recommended four other ways to prevent or to deter crime.[5] The first was to enact laws that are clear, simple, and unbiased and that reflect the consensus of the population. The second was to educate the public. Beccaria assumed that the more educated people are, the less likely they are to commit crimes. The third was to eliminate corruption from the administration of justice. Beccaria believed that if the people who dispense justice are themselves corrupt, people lose respect for the justice system and become more likely to commit crimes. The fourth was to reward virtue. Beccaria asserted that punishing crime is not enough; it is also important to reward law-abiding behavior. Such rewards might include public recognition of especially meritorious behavior or, perhaps, an annual tax deduction for people who have not been convicted of a crime.

The application of classical theory was supposed to make the criminal law fairer and easier to administer. To those ends, judges would not select sentences. They could only impose the sentences dictated by legislatures for specific crimes. All offenders would be treated alike, and similar crimes would be treated similarly. Individual differences among offenders and unique or mitigating circumstances about the crime would be ignored. A problem is that all offenders are not alike and similar crimes are not always as similar as they might appear on the surface. Should first offenders be treated the same as those who commit crime repeatedly? Should juveniles be treated the same as adults? Should the insane be treated the same as the sane? Should a crime of passion be treated the same as the intentional commission of a crime? The classical school's answer to all of those difficult questions would be a simple yes.

Despite those problems, Beccaria's ideas, as previously noted, were very influential. France, for example, adopted many of Beccaria's principles in its Code of 1791—in particular, the principle of equal punishments for the same crimes. However, because classical theory ignored both individual differences among offenders and mitigating circumstances, it was difficult to apply the law in practice. Because of that difficulty, as well as new developments in the emerging behavioral sciences, modifications of classical theory and its application were introduced in the early 1800s.

Neoclassical Theory

Several modifications of classical theory are collectively referred to as **neoclassical theory.** The main difference between the two has to do with classical theory's assumption about free will. In the neoclassical revision, it was conceded that certain factors, such as insanity, might inhibit the exercise of free will. Thus, the idea of premeditation was introduced as a measure of the degree of free will exercised. Also, mitigating circumstances were considered legitimate grounds for an argument of diminished responsibility.

Those modifications of classical theory had two practical effects on criminal justice policy. First, they provided a reason for nonlegal experts such as medical doctors to testify in court as to the degree of diminished responsibility of an offender. Second, offenders began to be sentenced to punishments that were considered rehabilitative. The idea was that certain environments, for example, environments free of vice and crime, were more conducive than others to the exercise of rational choice.

The reason we have placed so much emphasis on the classical school of criminology and its neoclassical revisions is that, together, they are essentially the model on which criminal justice in the United States is based today. During the past two decades, at least in part because the public frequently perceived as too lenient the sentences imposed by judges for certain crimes, such measures as legislatively imposed sentencing guidelines have limited the sentencing authority of judges in many jurisdictions. Public outrage over the decisions of other criminal justice officials has led to similar measures. For example, parole has been abolished in the federal jurisdiction and in some states because many people believe that parole boards release dangerous criminals from prison too soon.

The revival of classical and neoclassical theories during the past two decades, and the introduction of a more modern version called *rational choice theory,* are also probably a reaction to the allegation of some criminologists and public officials that criminologists have failed to discover the causes of crime. As a result of that belief, there has been a renewed effort to deter crimes by sentencing more offenders to prison for longer periods of time and, in many jurisdictions, by imposing capital punishment for heinous crimes. Ironically, one reason the theory of the classical school lost favor in the nineteenth century was the belief that punishment was not a particularly effective method of preventing or controlling crime.

Positivist Approaches to Explaining Crime

The theory of the positivist school of criminology grew out of positive philosophy and the logic and basic methodology of empirical and experimental science. Positive philosophy was an explicit rejection of the critical and "negative" philosophy of the Enlightenment thinkers. Among the founders of positivism was Auguste Comte, who has also been credited with founding sociology. Comte acknowledged that the Enlightenment thinkers had contributed to progress by helping to break up the old system and by paving the way for a new one.[8] However, Comte argued that the thought of the Enlightenment had outlived its usefulness and had become obstructive.

At about the same time that positivist philosophy was developing, experimentation with animals was becoming an increasingly accepted way of learning about human beings in physiology, medicine, psychology, and psychiatry. Human beings were beginning to appear to science as one of many

At the beginning of 1997, there were approximately 1.7 million people incarcerated in the United States. Nearly 1.1 million were in state prisons, about 100,000 were in federal prisons, and more than half a million were in local jails. Between 1980 and 1997, the state prison population increased 264 percent, the federal prison population 344 percent, and jail populations 184 percent. On December 31, 1996, one of every 118 men and one of every 1818 women were under the jurisdiction of state or federal correctional authorities.[7]

In the *Descent of Man* (1871), British naturalist Charles Darwin suggested that some people were "less highly evolved or developed than others," that some people "were nearer their apelike ancestors than others in traits, abilities, and dispositions."[9]

creatures, with no special connection to God. Human beings were beginning to be understood, not as free-willed, self-determining creatures who could do anything that they wanted to do, but rather as beings whose action was determined by biological and cultural factors.

Positivism was a major break with the classical and neoclassical theories that had preceded it. The following are key assumptions of the positivist school of thought:

1. Human behavior is determined and not a matter of free will. Consequently, positivists focus on cause-and-effect relationships.
2. Criminals are fundamentally different from noncriminals. Positivists search for such differences by scientific methods.
3. Social scientists (including criminologists) can be objective, or value-neutral, in their work.
4. Crime is frequently caused by multiple factors.
5. Society is based on consensus but not on a social contract.

As the social sciences developed and social scientists directed their attention to the problem of crime, they adopted, for the most part, those positivist assumptions. Thus, for example, theories of crime were (and continue to be) based on biological positivism, psychological positivism, sociological positivism, and so on. However, as theories based on positivist assumptions were developed, it became apparent to close observers that there were problems, not only with the theories, but with the positivist assumptions as well. We will briefly discuss five of those problems.[10] In subsequent subsections, we will also describe problems peculiar to specific positivist theories of crime causation.

The first problem with positivism is overprediction: positivist theories generally account for too much crime. They also do not explain exceptions well. For example, a positivist theory that suggests that crime is caused by poverty overpredicts because not all poor people commit crime. It also cannot explain adequately why many poor people do not commit crimes.

Second, positivist theories generally ignore the criminalization process, the process by which certain behaviors are made illegal. They separate the study of crime from a theory of the law and the state and take the legal definition of crime for granted. Ignored is the question why certain behaviors are defined as criminal while other, similar behaviors are not.

A third problem with positivism is its consensual worldview, the belief that most people agree about most things most of the time. Such a view ignores a multitude of fundamental conflicts of value and interest in society. It also tends to lead to a blind acceptance of the status quo.

A fourth problem is positivism's belief in determinism, the idea that choice of action is not free, but is determined by causes independent of a person's will. Positivists generally assume that humans only adapt or react, but humans also create. How else could we explain new social arrangements or ways of thinking? A belief in determinism allows positivists to present an absolute situation uncomplicated by the ability to choose.

Finally, a fifth problem with positivist theories is the belief in the ability of social scientists (criminologists) to be objective, or value-neutral, in their work. Positivists fail to recognize that to describe and evaluate such human actions as criminal behavior is fundamentally a moral endeavor and, therefore, subject to bias.

Biological Theories

Biological theories of crime causation are based on the beliefs that criminals are physiologically different from noncriminals and that structure determines function. In other words, criminals behave differently because, structurally, they are different. To test biological theories, efforts are made to demonstrate, through measurement and statistical analysis, that there are or are not significant structural differences between criminals and noncriminals.

The cause of crime, from this perspective, is **biological inferiority.** Biological inferiority in criminals is assumed to produce certain physical or genetic characteristics that distinguish criminals from noncriminals. It is important to emphasize that in these theories, the physical or genetic characteristics themselves are not the cause of crime but only the symptoms, or *stigmata,* of the more fundamental inferiority. Several different methodologies have been employed to detect physical differences between criminals and noncriminals. They are criminal anthropology, study of body types, and heredity studies, including family trees, statistical comparisons, twin studies, and adoption studies.

Criminal Anthropology **Criminal anthropology** is the study of "criminal" human beings. It is associated with the work of an Italian army doctor, and, later, university professor Cesare Lombroso.

Biological inferiority According to biological theories, a criminal's innate physiological makeup, which is assumed to produce certain physical or genetic characteristics that distinguish criminals from noncriminals.

Criminal Anthropology The study of "criminal" human beings.

Careers in Criminal Justice

CRIMINOLOGIST

Criminologists study causes of crime and motivations of criminals, often considering sociological and psychological factors. Their study also includes crime prevention, as well as the punishment and rehabilitation of offenders. Criminological study assists educators, lawmakers, criminal justice officials, policy makers, and others interested in resolving problems of crime and criminals. Criminologists often work closely with members of other professions, including psychologists, sociologists, statisticians, law enforcement officers, corrections officials, and the legal community.

Criminologists are employed for the most part in academia. Thousands, however, hold jobs in government agencies. Some criminologists work as consultants in the private sector. Most entry-level positions require a four-year degree, although the federal government recognizes education and experience in certifying applicants for entry-level positions. Earnings for criminologists depend on education, experience, and the work setting.

STATISTICIAN

A criminal justice statistician collects, analyzes, and presents numerical data that may be used for such purposes as predicting criminal behavior, assessing the nature of law enforcement problems, analyzing legal and social problems, or helping public officials make decisions and evaluate the results of new programs.

Approximately one-fourth of all criminal justice statisticians work for the federal government. Private consulting firms and universities that conduct criminal justice research also compete for the services of criminal justice statisticians. Entry-level jobs generally require a four-year degree with at least 15 semester hours of statistics or a combination of mathematics and statistics. Earnings vary, but statisticians who work in private industry generally earn higher salaries than those who work in academia or in government.

Lombroso's theory consisted of the following propositions:[11]

1. Criminals are, by birth, a distinct type.
2. That type can be recognized by physical characteristics, or *stigmata*, such as enormous jaws, high cheekbones, and insensitivity to pain.
3. The criminal type is clearly distinguished in a person with more than five stigmata, perhaps exists in a person with three to five stigmata, and does not necessarily exist in a person with fewer than three stigmata.
4. Physical stigmata do not cause crime; they only indicate an individual who is predisposed to crime. Such a person is either an **atavist**—that is, a reversion to a savage type—or a result of degeneration.
5. Because of their personal natures, such persons cannot desist from crime unless they experience very favorable lives.

Atavist A person who reverts to a savage type.

Lombroso's theory was popular in the United States until about 1915, although variations of his theory are still being taught today. The major problem with Lombroso's criminal anthropology is the assumption that certain physical characteristics are indicative of biological inferiority. Unless there is independent evidence to support that assumption, other than the association of the physical characteristics with criminality, then the result is circular reasoning. In other words, crime is caused by biological inferiority, which is itself indicated by the physical characteristics associated with criminality.

Body-Type Theory Body-type theory is an extension of Lombroso's criminal anthropology. William Sheldon, whose work in the 1940s was based on earlier work by Ernst Kretchmer in the 1920s, is perhaps the best known of the body-type theorists. According to Sheldon, human beings can be divided into three basic body types, or *somatotypes*, which correspond to three basic temperaments.[12] The three body types are the endomorphic (soft, fat), the mesomorphic (athletically built), and the ectomorphic (tall, skinny).

Sheldon argued that everyone has elements of all three types, but that one type usually predominates. In a study of 200 Boston delinquents between 1939 and 1949, Sheldon found that delinquents were more mesomorphic than nondelinquents, and that serious delinquents were more mesomorphic than less severe delinquents. Subsequent studies by the Gluecks in the 1950s and by Cortes in the 1970s also found an association between mesomorphy and delinquency.

The major criticism of body-type theory is that differences in behavior are indicative of the social selection process and not biological inferiority. In other words, delinquents are more likely to be mesomorphic than nondelinquents because, for example, mesomorphs are more likely to be selected for gang membership. Also, the finding that delinquents are more likely than nondelinquents to be mesomorphic contradicts, at least with regard to physique, the theory's general assumption that criminals (or delinquents) are biologically inferior.[13]

In any event, if one believes that crime is the product of biological inferiority, then the policy implications are limited. Either criminals are isolated from the rest of the population by imprisoning them, for example, or they are executed. If they are isolated, moreover, they may also need to be sterilized to ensure that they do not reproduce.

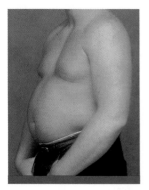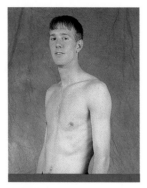

William Sheldon, a well-known body-type theorist, divided humans into three basic body types. Left: endomorphic (soft, fat); Center: mesomorphic (athletically built); Right: ectomorphic (tall, skinny).

Heredity Studies A variety of methods has been employed to test the proposition that criminals are genetically different from noncriminals. Perhaps the earliest method was the use of family trees, in which a family known to have many "criminals" was compared with a family free of "criminals."

However, a finding that criminality appears in successive generations does not prove that criminality is inherited or is the product of a hereditary defect. For example, the use of a fork in eating has been a trait of many families for generations, but that does not prove that the use of a fork is inherited. In short, the family tree method cannot adequately separate hereditary influences from environmental influences.

A second method used to test the proposition that crime is inherited or is the product of a hereditary defect is statistical comparison. The rationale is that if criminality exhibits the same degree of family resemblance as other, physical traits, such as eye or hair color, then criminality, like those other traits, must be inherited. Although there is some evidence to support the notion, statistical comparisons also fail to adequately separate hereditary influences from environmental influences.

A third, more sophisticated method of testing the proposition that crime is inherited or is the result of a hereditary defect is the use of twin studies. Heredity is assumed to be the same in identical twins because they are the product of a single egg. Heredity is assumed to be different in fraternal twins because they are the product of two eggs fertilized by two sperm. The logic of the method is that if there is greater similarity in behavior between identical twins than between fraternal twins, the behavior must be due to heredity, since environments are much the same. More than a half century of this methodology has revealed that identical twins are more likely to demonstrate concordance (both twins' having criminal records) than are fraternal twins, thus supporting the hereditary link. A problem with the twin studies, however, is the potential confounding of genetic and environmental influences. Identical twins tend to be treated more alike by others, spend much more time together, and have a greater sense of shared identity than do fraternal twins. All those factors are important environmental influences.

A fourth method, the most recent and most sophisticated method of examining the inheritability of criminality, is the adoption study. The first such study was conducted in the 1970s. In this method, the criminal records of adopted children (almost always boys) who were adopted at a relatively

FYI

The family tree method was used by both Dugdale (1875) and Estabrook (1916), who both compared the Jukes family with the Jonathan Edwards family. The Jukes family presumably had 7 murderers, 60 thieves, 50 prostitutes, and assorted other criminals. The Edwards family, on the other hand, presumably had no criminals but, instead, had Presidents of the United States, governors, Supreme Court justices, federal court justices, and assorted writers, preachers, and teachers. As it turns out, the Edwards family was not as crime-free as originally believed. Apparently, Jonathan Edwards's maternal grandmother had been divorced on grounds of adultery, a grandaunt had murdered her son, and a granduncle had murdered his sister.

ased on the analysis of thousands of DNA samples, preliminary findings of the Human Genome Diversity Project—the first worldwide survey of humankind—demonstrate the "generic unity that binds our diverse, polyglot species." The data show that "any two people, regardless of geography or ethnicity, share at least 99.99 percent of their genetic makeups." As for the 0.01 percent of the genome that makes people different, "it doesn't shake out along racial lines. . . . Instead, some 85 percent of human genetic diversity occurs within ethnic groups, not between them."[14]

Limbic system A structure surrounding the brain stem that, in part, controls the life functions of heartbeat, breathing, and sleep. It also is believed to moderate expressions of violence; such emotions as anger, rage, and fear; and sexual response.

early age are compared with the criminal records of both their biological parents and their adoptive parents (almost always fathers). The rationale is that if the criminal records of adopted boys are more like those of their biological fathers than like those of their adoptive fathers, the criminality of the adopted boys can be assumed to be the result of heredity.

The findings of the adoption studies reveal that the percentage of adoptees who are criminal is greater when the biological father has a criminal record than when the adoptive father has one. However, there also is an interactive effect. A greater percentage of adoptees have criminal records when both fathers have criminal records than when only one of them does. Like the twin studies, the adoption studies presumably demonstrate the influence of heredity but cannot adequately separate it from the influence of the environment. A problem with the adoption studies is the difficulty of interpreting the relative influences of heredity and environment, especially when the adoption does not take place shortly after birth or when, as is commonly the case, the adoption agency attempts to find an adoptive home that matches the biological home in family income and socioeconomic status.

If criminals are genetically different from noncriminals or the product of genetic defect, then the policy implications are the same as for other theories that propose that criminals are biologically inferior: isolate, sterilize, or execute. However, in the future, new technologies may make possible genetic engineering—that is, the removal or alteration of defective genes.

Other Areas of Biological Research Research on limbic system and brain chemical dysfunctions, endocrine abnormalities, and minimal brain damage are further attempts to link biological conditions to criminality. At least some unprovoked violent criminal behavior is believed to be caused by tumors and other destructive or inflammatory processes of the **limbic system**.[15] The limbic system (see Figure 3–2) is a structure surrounding the brain stem that, in part, controls the life functions of heartbeat, breathing, and sleep. It also is believed to moderate expressions of violence; such emotions as anger, rage, and fear; and sexual response. Surgical removal of the affected area sometimes eliminates expressions of violence. A problem with that type of intervention, however, is that it can cause unpredictable and undesirable behavior changes and, of course, is irreversible.

Some criminal behaviors are believed to be influenced by low levels of brain neurotransmitters (substances brain cells use to communicate).[16] For example, low levels of the brain neurotransmitter *serotonin* have been found in impulsive murderers and arsonists. Research is currently being conducted to determine whether low levels of another neurotransmitter, *norepinephrine*, are associated with compulsive gambling. Another interesting discovery in this area may help explain cocaine use. Apparently cocaine increases the level of the neurotransmitter *dopamine*, which activates the limbic system to produce pleasure. If such chemical deficiencies are linked to those behaviors, chemical treatment or improved diets might help. Neurotransmitters are products of the foods people eat.

Criminal behaviors have also been associated with endocrine, or hormone, abnormalities, especially those involving *testosterone* (a male sex hormone) and *progesterone* and *estrogen* (the female sex hormones).[17] For example, administering estrogen to male sex offenders has been found to reduce their sexual drives. A similar effect has been achieved by administering the drug

FIGURE 3–2

The Limbic System

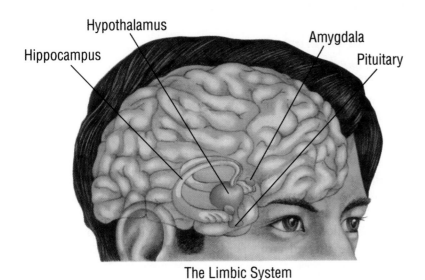

Hypothalamus

Hippocampus

Amygdala

Pituitary

The Limbic System

Some unprovoked violent criminal behavior is believed to be caused by brain tumors and other destructive processes of the limbic system.

Depo-Provera, which reduces testosterone levels. However, a problem with Depo-Provera is that it is successful only for male sex offenders who cannot control their sexual urges. It does not seem to work on offenders whose sex crimes are premeditated. Studies have also found a large number of crimes committed by females during the menstrual or premenstrual periods of the female hormonal cycle. Those periods are characterized by a change in the estrogen-progesterone ratio.

Research on minimal brain damage has found that it increases an individual's chances of being identified as delinquent.[19] Minimal brain damage is believed to be most commonly caused by nutritional or oxygen deficiencies during pregnancy, or during or shortly after birth, or by insufficient protein and sensory stimulation during a child's formative years. Because minimal brain damage is also strongly associated with lower socioeconomic status, social deprivation must be considered a crucial element in its occurrence.

To reduce minimal brain damage in the population, adequate prenatal medical care and nutrition must be provided to all expectant mothers. To minimize complications during birth, adequate medical assistance must be provided. Further reductions in minimal brain damage would require providing adequate protein and social and intellectual stimulation to developing infants and young children.

In sum, there are probably no positivist criminologists today who would argue that biology or genetics makes people criminals. Nor, for that matter, are there many criminologists today who would deny that biology has some influence on criminal behavior. The position held by most criminologists today is that criminal behavior is the product of a complex interaction between biology and environmental or social conditions. What is inherited is not criminal behavior, but rather the way in which the person responds to his

FYI

In 1996, California became the first state to require chemical castration of repeat child molesters. Under the law, molesters who commit a second crime against a child under 13 must receive weekly injections of the drug Depo-Provera. In 1997, Florida and Georgia passed similar legislation requiring repeat offenders to be chemically castrated, and Texas approved voluntary castration for repeat molesters. In all four states, offenders may choose surgical castration instead.[18]

or her environment. In short, biology or genetics gives an individual a predisposition, or a tendency, to behave in a certain way. Whether a person actually behaves in that way and whether that behavior is defined as a crime depend primarily on environmental or social conditions.

Psychological Theories

In this subsection, we will examine psychological theories of crime causation. We will begin with a description of the relationship between intelligence and criminality and delinquency and proceed to discussions of psychoanalytic and humanistic psychological theories. We reserve our discussion of learning or behavioral theories, which are also psychological theories, for the section under the more general heading of sociological theories.

Intelligence and Crime The idea that crime is the product primarily of people of low intelligence was popular in the United States between 1914 and around 1930. It received some attention again during the mid-1970s and in the mid-1990s. The belief requires only a slight shift in thinking from the idea that criminals are biologically inferior to the idea that they are mentally inferior.

In 1931, Edwin Sutherland reviewed approximately 350 studies on the relationship between intelligence and delinquency and criminality.[20] The studies reported the results of intelligence tests of about 175,000 criminals and delinquents. Sutherland concluded from the review that although intelligence may play a role in individual cases, given the selection that takes place in arrest, conviction, and imprisonment, the distribution of the intelligence scores of criminals and delinquents is very similar to the distribution of the intelligence scores of the general population.

For the next 40 years or so, the issue of the relationship between intelligence and crime and delinquency appeared resolved. However, in the mid-1970s, two studies were published that resurrected the debate.[21] Those studies found that IQ was an important predictor of both official and self-reported juvenile delinquency, as important as social class or race. Both studies acknowledged the findings of Sutherland's earlier review. Both also noted that a decreasing number of delinquents had been reported as being of below-normal intelligence over the years. However, in both studies, it was maintained that the difference in intelligence between delinquents and nondelinquents had never disappeared and had stabilized at about 8 IQ points. The studies failed to note, however, that the 8-point IQ difference found between delinquents and nondelinquents was generally within the normal range. The authors of the studies surmised that IQ influenced delinquency through its effect on school performance.

We cannot conclude with any degree of confidence that delinquents, as a group, are less intelligent than nondelinquents. We do know that most adult criminals are not of below-normal intelligence. Obviously, low-level intelligence cannot account for the dramatic increase in the crime rate over the last couple of decades, until recently, unless one is prepared to conclude that the population of offenders is getting less intelligent. Low-level intelligence certainly cannot account for complex white-collar and political crimes.

Nevertheless, to the degree, if any, that crime is caused by low-level intelligence, the policy implications are the same as for theories of biological inferiority: isolate, sterilize, or execute. Intelligence is believed to have a large genetic component.

Psychoanalytic Theories Psychoanalytic theories of crime causation are associated with the work of Sigmund Freud and his followers.[22] Freud did not theorize much about criminal behavior itself, but a theory of crime causation can be deduced from his more general theory of human behavior and its disorders. Had he contemplated the issue, Freud probably would have argued that crime, like other disorders, was a symptom of more deep-seated problems and that if the deep-seated problems could be resolved, the symptom of crime would go away.

Freud believed that some people who had unresolved deep-seated problems were psychopaths (sociologists call them *sociopaths*). **Psychopaths, sociopaths,** or **antisocial personalities** are characterized by no sense of guilt, no subjective conscience, and no sense of right and wrong. They have difficulty in forming relationships with other people; they cannot empathize with other people. Many criminal offenders are presumed to be psychopaths. Figure 3–3 provides an extended list of the characteristics of psychopaths.

The principal policy implication of considering crime symptomatic of deep-seated problems is to provide psychotherapy or psychoanalysis. *Psychoanalysis* is a procedure, first developed by Freud, that among other things, attempts to make patients conscious or aware of unconscious and deep-seated problems to resolve the symptoms associated with them.

Psychopaths, sociopaths, or **antisocial personalities**
Persons characterized by no sense of guilt, no subjective conscience, and no sense of right and wrong. They have difficulty in forming relationships with other people; they cannot empathize with other people.

FIGURE 3–3

Characteristics of the Psychopath

Characteristics of the Psychopath

1. Superficial charm and good "intelligence."
2. Absence of delusions and other signs of irrational "thinking."
3. Absence of "nervousness" or psychoneurotic manifestations.
4. Unreliability.
5. Untruthfulness and insincerity.
6. Lack of remorse or shame.
7. Inadequately motivated antisocial behavior.
8. Poor judgment and failure to learn by experience.
9. Pathologic egocentricity and incapacity for love.
10. General poverty in major affective reactions.
11. Specific loss of insight.
12. Unresponsiveness in general interpersonal relations.
13. Fantastic and uninviting behavior, with drink and sometimes without.
14. Suicide rarely carried out.
15. Sex life impersonal, trivial, and poorly integrated.
16. Failure to follow any life plan.

Source: From Hervey Cleckley's "The Mask of Sanity," *Institutions, Etc.: A Journal of Progressive Human Services*, Vol. 8, No. 9 (September 1985), p. 21. Reprinted by permission.

Methods used include a variety of projective tests (such as the interpretation of Rorschach inkblots), dream interpretation, and free association. Another policy implication that derives logically from Freudian theory is to provide people with legal outlets to sublimate or redirect their sexual and aggressive drives. (Freud believed that all human beings are born with those two drives and that those are the primary sources of human motivation.)

Psychoanalysis, and the psychoanalytic theory on which it is based, are components of a medical model of crime causation that has, to varying degrees, informed criminal justice policy in the United States for a century. The general conception of this medical model is that criminals are biologically or, especially, psychologically "sick" and in need of treatment.

Despite the enduring popularity of this theory, a number of problems have been identified with it. First, the bulk of the research on the issue suggests that most criminals are not psychologically disturbed or, at least, are no more disturbed than the rest of the population.[23]

Second, if a person who commits a crime has a psychological disturbance, that does not mean that the psychological disturbance causes the crime. Many people with psychological disturbances do not commit crimes, and many people without psychological disturbances do commit crimes.

Third, psychoanalytic theory generally ignores the environmental circumstances in which the problematic behavior occurs. The problem is considered a personal problem and not a social one.

Fourth, there are problems with psychoanalysis and other forms of psychotherapy. Psychotherapy rests on faith. Much of its theoretical structure is scientifically untestable. The emphasis of psychotherapy as an approach to rehabilitation is on the individual offender and not on the offender in interaction with the environment in which the criminal behavior occurs. The behaviors that are treated in psychotherapy are not criminal; they are the deep-seated problems. It is assumed that criminal behavior is symptomatic of those problems. That assumption may not be true. Many people who do not engage in crime have deep-seated problems, and many people who do not have those problems do engage in crime.

Humanistic Psychological Theory Humanistic psychological theory, as described here, refers primarily to the work of Abraham Maslow and Seymour Halleck. The theories of Maslow and Halleck are fundamentally psychoanalytic, but they are called humanistic because they assume that human beings are basically good even though they are sometimes influenced by society to act badly. By contrast, Freudian theory assumes that human beings are inherently bad, motivated by sexual and aggressive drives.

Maslow did not apply his theory to crime itself, so we must infer from Maslow's work what we think he would have said about the causes of crime had he addressed the subject. Maslow maintained that human beings are motivated by a need hierarchy (Figure 3–4) comprising five basic levels of needs:

1. Physiological (food, water, and procreational sex).
2. Safety (security; stability; freedom from fear, anxiety, chaos, etc.)
3. Belongingness and love (friendship, love, affection, acceptance).
4. Esteem (self-esteem and the esteem of others).
5. Self-actualization (being true to one's nature, becoming everything that one is capable of becoming).[24]

FIGURE 3-4

Maslow's Hierarchy of Needs

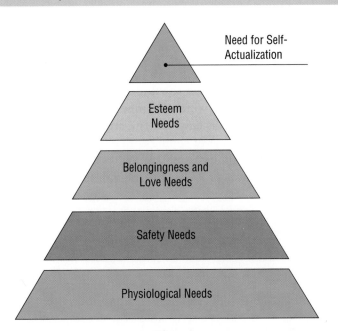

Source: Adapted from Clifton Williams and George P. Huber, *Human Behavior in Organizations,* 3d ed. (Cincinnati: South-Western Publishing Co., 1986).

According to Maslow, during a given period, a person's life is dominated by a particular need. It remains dominated by that need until the need has been relatively satisfied, at which time a new need emerges to dominate that person's life. From this view, crime may be understood as a means by which individuals satisfy their basic human needs. They choose crime because they cannot satisfy their needs legally or, for whatever reason, choose not to satisfy their needs legally. An obvious policy implication of the theory is to help people satisfy their basic human needs in legitimate ways. That may require governments to ensure adequate food, shelter, and medical care for those in need or to provide educational or vocational opportunities for those who are unable to obtain them. Those strategies are implied by several sociological theories as well. On a basic, interpersonal level, Maslow's theory might imply the need to make sympathetic listeners available to people who would benefit from sharing their problems.

Seymour L. Halleck views crime as one of several adaptations to the helplessness caused by oppression.[225] For Halleck, there are two general types of oppression, *objective* and *subjective.* Each has two subtypes. The subtypes of objective oppression are (a) social oppression (for example, oppression resulting from racial discrimination) and (b) the oppression that occurs in two-person interactions (for example, a parent's unfair restriction of the activities of a child). The subtypes of subjective oppression are (a) oppression from within (guilt) and (b) projected or misunderstood oppression (a person's feeling of being oppressed when, in fact, he or she is not).

For Halleck, the emotional experience of either type of oppression is helplessness, to which the person sometimes adapts by resorting to criminal behavior. Halleck suggests that the criminal adaptation is more likely when alternative adaptations, such as conformity, activism, or mental illness, are not possible or are blocked by other people. He also maintains that criminal behavior is sometimes chosen as an adaptation over other possible alternatives because it offers gratifications or psychological advantages that could not be achieved otherwise. Halleck's psychological advantages of crime are listed in Figure 3–5.

There are at least three crime policy implications of Halleck's theory. First, sources of social oppression should be eliminated wherever possible. Affirmative action programs, which attempt to rectify historic patterns of discrimination in such areas as employment, are an example of such efforts. Second, alternative, legal ways of coping with oppression must be provided. An example is the opportunity to file claims with the Equal Employment Opportunity Commission (EEOC) in individual cases of employment

FIGURE 3–5

Halleck's 14 Psychological Advantages of Crime

Psychological Advantages of Crime

1. The adaptational advantages of crime in changing one's environment are more desirable than illness or conformity.

2. Crime involves activity, and when man is engaged in motoric behavior, he feels less helpless.

3. However petty a criminal act may be, it carries with it a promise of change in a favorable direction.

4. During the planning and execution of a criminal act, the offender is a free man. (He is immune from the oppressive dictates of others.)

5. Crime offers the possibility of excitement.

6. Crime calls for the individual to maximize his faculties and talents which might otherwise lie dormant.

7. Crime can relieve feelings of inner oppression and stress.

8. Crime increases external stresses, which allows the individual to concentrate upon these threats to his equilibrium and temporarily allows him to abandon his chronic intrapsychic problems.

9. Once a person has convinced himself that the major pressures in his life come from without, there is less tendency to blame himself for this failure.

10. Adopting the criminal role provides an excellent rationalization for inadequacy.

11. Crime has a more esteemed social status than mental illness.

12. America has an ambivalent attitude toward crime. Although crime is regularly condemned, it is also glamorized.

13. Deviant behavior sometimes helps the criminal to form close and relatively nonoppressive relations with other criminals.

14. Crime can provide pleasure or gratify needs.

Source: Seymour L. Halleck, *Psychiatry and the Dilemmas of Crime* (New York: Harper and Row, 1967), pp. 76–80. Reprinted by permission.

discrimination. Third, psychotherapy should be provided for subjective oppressions. Psychotherapy could make the individual aware of oppressive sources of guilt or sources of misunderstood oppression so that the individual could better cope with them.

A major problem with the theories of Maslow and Halleck is that they do not go far enough. They do not identify and analyze the sources of need deprivation (Maslow) and of objective oppression (Halleck). In other words, neither Maslow nor Halleck asks the basic questions: Why can't people satisfy their basic needs legally, or why do they choose not to? Why don't societies ensure that basic needs can be satisfied legally so that the choice to satisfy them illegally makes no sense? Similarly, why does society so oppress many people, and why aren't more effective measures taken to greatly reduce that oppression?

Sociological Theories

Sociologists emphasize that human beings live in social groups and that those groups and the social structure they create (for example, political and economic systems) influence behavior. Most sociological theories of crime causation assume that a criminal's behavior is determined by his or her social environment, which includes families, friends, neighborhoods, and so on. Most sociological theories of crime explicitly reject the notion of the born criminal.

The Contributions of Durkheim Many of the sociological theories of crime causation have their roots in the work of the French sociologist Emile Durkheim. Durkheim rejected the idea that the world is simply the product of individual actions. His basic premise is that society is more than a simple aggregate of individuals; it is a reality *sui generis* (unique).[26] Rejecting the idea that social phenomena, such as crime, can be explained solely by the biology or psychology of individuals, Durkheim argued instead that society is not the direct reflection of the characteristics of its individual members, because individuals cannot always choose. For Durkheim, social laws and institutions are "social facts" that dominate individuals, and all people can do is submit to them. The coercion may be formal—for example, by means of law—or informal—for example, by means of peer pressure. Like Comte before him, Durkheim maintained that with the aid of positive science, all people can expect is to discover the direction or course of social laws so that they can adapt to them with the least amount of pain.

For Durkheim, crime, too, is a social fact. It is a normal aspect of society, although different types of societies should have greater or lesser degrees of it. The cause of crime for Durkheim is **anomie,** that is, the dissociation of the individual from the **collective conscience,** or the general sense of morality of the times. Not only did Durkheim believe that crime is a normal aspect of society, he also believed that crime is functional for society. He noted that crime marks the boundaries of morality. In other words, people would not know what acceptable behavior is if crime did not exist. Crime is also functional because it provides a means of achieving necessary social change through, for example, civil disobedience and, under certain circumstances, directly contributes to social change, as in the repeal of prohibition. Because Durkheim believed that crime was a normal social fact and was functional for

Anomie For Durkheim, the dissociation of the individual from the collective conscience.

Collective conscience The general sense of morality of the times.

Explaining Crime   **CHAPTER 3**

society, the policy he advocated was simply to contain crime within reasonable boundaries. Durkheim warned, however, that too much crime could destroy society.

The Theory of the Chicago School In the 1920s, members of the Department of Sociology at the University of Chicago tried to identify environmental factors associated with crime. Specifically, they attempted to uncover the relationship between a neighborhood's crime rate and the characteristics of the neighborhood. It was the first large-scale study of crime in the United States and was to serve as the basis for many future investigations into the causes of crime and delinquency.

The research of the **Chicago School** was based on a model taken from ecology, and as a result, that school is sometimes call the Chicago School of Human Ecology.[27] Ecology is a branch of biology in which the interrelationship of plants and animals is studied in their natural environment. Robert Park was the first of the Chicago theorists to propose this organic or biological analogy—that is, the similarity between the organization of plant and animal life in nature and the organization of human beings in societies.

Park and his colleagues described the growth of American cities like Chicago in ecological terms, saying growth occurs through a process of invasion, dominance, and succession.[28] That is, a cultural or ethnic group *invades* a territory occupied by another group and *dominates* that new territory until it is displaced, or *succeeded*, by another group and the cycle repeats itself.

This model of human ecology was used by other Chicago theorists, most notably Clifford R. Shaw and Henry D. McKay in their studies of juvenile delinquency in Chicago.[29] From the life histories of delinquents, Shaw and McKay confirmed that most of the delinquents were not much different from nondelinquents in their personality traits, physical condition, and intelligence.[30] However, Shaw and McKay did find that the areas of high delinquency were "socially disorganized." For the Chicago theorists, **social disorganization** is the condition in which the usual controls over delinquents are largely absent, delinquent behavior is often approved of by parents and neighbors, there are many opportunities for delinquent behavior, and there is little encouragement, training, or opportunity for legitimate employment.

In 1932, Shaw and his colleagues established the Chicago Area Project (CAP), which was designed to prevent delinquency through the organization and empowerment of neighborhood residents. Neighborhood centers, staffed and controlled by local residents, were established in six areas of Chicago. The centers had two primary functions. One was to coordinate community resources, such as schools, churches, labor unions, and industries, to solve community problems. The other function was to sponsor activity programs, such as scouting, summer camps, and sports leagues, to develop a positive interest by individuals in their own welfare and to unite citizens to solve their own problems. CAP operated continuously for 25 years, until Shaw's death in 1957. Evaluations of the project suggest that it had a negligible effect on delinquency.

One of the problems with the theory of the Chicago School is the presumption that social disorganization is a cause of delinquency. Both social disorganization and delinquency may be the product of other, more basic factors. For example, one factor that contributes to the decline of city neighborhoods is the decades-old practice of *redlining*, in which banks refuse to lend money in an area because of the race or ethnicity of the inhabitants. Though

Chicago School A group of sociologists at the University of Chicago who assumed in their research that delinquent behavior was a product of social disorganization.

Social disorganization The condition in which the usual controls over delinquents are largely absent, delinquent behavior is often approved of by parents and neighbors, there are many opportunities for delinquent behavior, and there is little encouragement, training, or opportunity for legitimate employment.

CHAPTER 3 *Explaining Crime*

From his analysis of the life histories of individual delinquents, Chicago sociologist Clifford Shaw discovered that many delinquent activities began as play activities at an early age.

illegal today, the practice continues. What usually happens in redlined areas is that neighborhood property values decline dramatically. Then land speculators and developers, typically in conjunction with political leaders, buy the land for urban renewal or gentrification and make fortunes in the process. In other words, political and economic elites may cause both social disorganization and delinquency—perhaps not intentionally, but by the conscious decisions they make about how a city will grow—making social disorganization appear to be the basic cause of delinquency.

Anomie or Strain Theory In an article published in 1938, Robert K. Merton observed that a major contradiction existed in the United States between cultural goals and the social structure.[31] He called the contradiction **anomie,** a concept first introduced by Durkheim. Specifically, Merton argued that in the United States the cultural goal of achieving wealth is deemed possible for all citizens, even though the social structure limits the legitimate "institutionalized means" available for obtaining the goal. For Merton, legitimate institutionalized means are the Protestant work ethic (hard work, education, and deferred gratification); illegitimate means are force and fraud. Because the social structure effectively limits the availability of legitimate institutionalized means, a *strain* is placed on people (hence the other name of the theory). Merton believed that strain could affect people in all social classes, but he acknowledged that it would most likely affect members of the lower class.

Merton proposed that individuals adapt to the problem of anomie or strain in one of several different ways: (1) conformity, (2) innovation, (3) ritualism, (4) retreatism, and (5) rebellion. Figure 3–6 on page 84 displays these different adaptations. According to Merton, most people adapt by conforming; they "play the game." Conformers pursue the cultural goal of wealth only through legitimate institutional means. Innovation is the adaptation at the root of most crime. After rejecting legitimate institutional means, innovators pursue the cultural goal of wealth through illegitimate means. Ritualism is the adaptation of the individual who "takes no chances," usually a member of

Anomie For Merton, the contradiction between the cultural goal of achieving wealth and the social structure's inability to provide legitimate institutional means for achieving the goal. For Cohen, it is caused by the inability of juveniles to achieve status among peers by socially acceptable means.

Explaining Crime   **CHAPTER 3**

FIGURE 3-6

Merton's Typology of Modes of Individual Adaptation

Modes of Adaptation	Culture Goals	Institutional Means
I. Conformity	+	+
II. Innovation	+	–
III. Ritualism	–	+
IV. Retreatism	–	–
V. Rebellion	±	±

Key: + signifies "acceptance," – signifies "rejection," and ± signifies "rejection of prevailing values and substitution of new values."

Source: Reprinted by permission of Macmillan Publishing Co., Inc., from *Social Theory and Social Structure,* by Robert K. Merton, Copyright © 1968, 1967, by Robert K. Merton.

the lower middle class. Ritualists do not actively pursue the cultural goal of wealth (they are willing to settle for less) but follow the legitimate institutional means anyway. Retreatists include alcoholics, drug addicts, psychotics, and other outcasts of society. Retreatists "drop out"; they do not pursue the cultural goal of wealth, so they do not employ legitimate institutional means. Last is the adaptation of rebellion. Rebels reject both the cultural goal of wealth and the legitimate institutional means of achieving it. They substitute both different goals and different means. Rebellion can also be a source of crime.

In summary, Merton believed that a source of some, but not all, crime and delinquency was anomie or strain, a disjunction or contradiction between the cultural goal of achieving wealth and the social structure's ability to provide legitimate institutional means of achieving the goal.

Beginning in the mid-1950s, concern developed over the problem of juvenile gangs. Albert K. Cohen adapted Merton's anomie or strain theory to his attempt to explain gang delinquency.[32] In attempting to explain such behavior, Cohen surmised that it was to gain status among peers. Thus, Cohen substituted the goal of status among peers for Merton's goal of achieving wealth.

For Cohen, anomie or strain is experienced by juveniles who are unable to achieve status among peers by socially acceptable means, such as family name and position in the community or academic or athletic achievement. In response to the strain, either they can conform to middle-class values (generated primarily through the public school) and resign themselves to their inferior status among their peers, or they can rebel and establish their own value structures by turning middle-class values on their head. Juveniles who rebel in this way tend to find each other and to form groups or gangs to validate and reinforce their new values. Like Merton, Cohen believed that anomie can affect juveniles of any social class but that it disproportionately affects juveniles from the lower class.

Richard Cloward and Lloyd Ohlin extended Merton's and Cohen's formulations of anomie theory by suggesting that not all gang delinquents adapt

The 1995 National Youth Gang Survey sponsored by the Office of Juvenile Justice and Delinquency Prevention revealed 23,388 youth gangs with a total of 664,906 members, operating in all 50 states. A youth gang is defined as "a group of youths . . . aged approximately 10 to 22 that . . . responsible persons in the community [were] willing to identify or classify as a 'gang.'" Motorcycle gangs, hate or ideology groups, prison gangs, and adult gangs are excluded from the survey.

to anomie in the same way. Cloward and Ohlin argue that the type of adaptation made by juvenile gang members depends on the *illegitimate opportunity structure* available to them.[33] They identified three delinquent subcultures: the criminal, the violent, and the retreatist. According to Cloward and Ohlin, if illegitimate opportunity is available to them, most delinquents will form *criminal* gangs to make money. However, if neither illegitimate nor legitimate opportunities to make money are available, delinquents often become frustrated and dissatisfied and form *violent* gangs to vent their anger. Finally, there are delinquents who, for whatever reason, are unable to adapt by joining either criminal or violent gangs. They *retreat* from society, as in Merton's retreatist adaptation, and become alcoholics and drug addicts.

The policy implications of anomie or strain theory are straightforward: reduce aspirations or increase legitimate opportunities or do both. Increasing legitimate opportunities, already a cornerstone of the black civil rights movement, struck a responsive chord as the 1960s began. Examples of this strategy are affirmative action employment programs, expansion of vocational education programs, and government grants that enable low-income students to attend college. Reducing aspirations (that is, desires to be wealthy), received little attention, however, because to attempt it would be to reject the "American dream," a principal source of motivation in a capitalist society.

According to Albert K. Cohen's version of anomie theory, juveniles who are unable to achieve status among their peers by socially acceptable means sometimes turn to gangs for social recognition.

Among the problems with the anomie theories of Merton, Cohen, and Cloward and Ohlin is their reliance on official statistics (police and court records) as measures of crime. Because these theorists relied on official statistics, their theories focus on lower-class crime and delinquency and ignore white-collar and government crimes.

Learning Theories Gabriel Tarde was one of the first theorists to believe that crime was something learned by normal people as they adapted to other people and the conditions of their environment. His theory was a product of his experience as a French lawyer and magistrate and was described in his book *Penal Philosophy*, published in 1890. Reflecting the state of knowledge about the learning process in his day, Tarde viewed all social phenomena as the product of imitation. Through **imitation** or **modeling,** a person can learn new responses, such as criminal behavior, by observing others, without performing any overt act or receiving direct reinforcement or reward.[35]

The first twentieth-century criminologist to forcefully argue that criminal behavior was learned was Edwin H. Sutherland. His theory of **differential association,** developed between 1934 and 1947, was that persons who become criminal do so because of contacts with criminal patterns and isolation from noncriminal patterns. Together with its more recent modifications, his theory remains one of the most influential theories of crime causation.[36] The nine propositions of Sutherland's theory are presented in Figure 3–7.

Imitation or **modeling** A means by which a person can learn new responses by observing others without performing any overt act or receiving direct reinforcement or reward.

Differential association Sutherland's theory that persons who become criminal do so because of contacts with criminal patterns and isolation from anticriminal patterns.

Explaining Crime   **CHAPTER 3**

FYI

When Robert Kennedy was Attorney General of the United States under his brother, President John F. Kennedy, he read and was impressed by Cloward and Ohlin's book *Delinquency and Opportunity: A Theory of Delinquent Gangs* (1960). Kennedy was so impressed that he asked Lloyd Ohlin to help shape a new federal policy on juvenile delinquency. That effort, based on anomie theory, produced the Juvenile Delinquency Prevention and Control Act of 1961. The act included a comprehensive action program to provide employment opportunities and work training, in combination with community organization and improved social services, to disadvantaged youths and their families.[34]

FIGURE 3–7

Sutherland's Propositions of Differential Association

Differential Association

1. Criminal behavior is learned.
2. Criminal behavior is learned in interaction with other persons in a process of communication.
3. The principal part of the learning of criminal behavior occurs within intimate personal groups.
4. When criminal behavior is learned, the learning includes (a) techniques of committing the crime, which are sometimes very complicated, sometimes very simple; (b) the specific direction of motives, drives, rationalizations, and attitudes.
5. The specific direction of motives and drives is learned from definitions of the legal codes as favorable and unfavorable.
6. A person becomes delinquent because of an excess of definitions favorable to violation of law over definitions unfavorable to violation of law. This is the principle of differential association.
7. Differential associations may vary in frequency, duration, priority, and intensity.
8. The process of learning criminal behavior by association with criminal and anticriminal patterns involves all of the mechanisms that are involved in any other learning.
9. While criminal behavior is an expression of general needs and values, it is not explained by those general needs and values, since noncriminal behavior is an expression of the same needs and values.

Source: Edwin H. Sutherland and Donald R. Cressey, *Criminology,* 9th ed. (Philadelphia: J. B. Lippincott, 1974), pp. 75–77. Reprinted by permission.

Borrowing a premise from the theory of the Chicago School, Sutherland maintained that differential associations would not produce criminality if it were not for *differential social organization.* In other words, the degree to which communities promote or inhibit criminal associations varies with the way or the degree to which they are organized (that is, the extent of *cultural conflict*).

Since its final formulation in 1947, modifications and additions have been made to Sutherland's theory as new developments in learning theory have emerged. For example, Daniel Glaser modified Sutherland's theory by introducing *role theory* and by arguing that criminal behavior could be learned by identifying with criminal roles and not just by associating with criminals.[37] Thus, a person could imitate the behavior of a drug dealer without actually having met one. Glaser obviously believed that the media had a greater influence on the learning of criminal behavior than Sutherland believed they had.

Robert L. Burgess and Ronald L. Akers, as well as C. Ray Jeffery, adapted the principles of *operant conditioning* and *behavior modification,* developed by the psychologist B. F. Skinner, and the principle of *modeling,* as developed by Albert Bandura, to the explanation of criminal behavior.

Burgess, Akers, and Jeffery integrated psychological concepts with sociological ones. Although they referred to their theories by different names, we will use the more general term *learning theory*.

Learning theory explains criminal behavior and its prevention with the concepts of *positive reinforcement, negative reinforcement, extinction, punishment,* and *modeling* or *imitation*. In this view, crime is committed because it is positively reinforced, negatively reinforced, or imitated. We described the imitation or modeling of criminal behavior in our earlier discussion of Tarde. Here we will focus on the other concepts.[38]

Positive reinforcement is the presentation of a stimulus that increases or maintains a response. The stimulus, or *reward,* can be either material, like money, or psychological, like pleasure. People steal (a response) because of the rewards—for example, the objects or money—that they receive. They use drugs (at least at first) because of the rewards, the pleasure, that the drugs give them.

Negative reinforcement is the removal or reduction of a stimulus whose removal or reduction increases or maintains a response. The stimulus in negative reinforcement is referred to as an *aversive stimulus*. Aversive stimuli, for most people, include pain and fear. Stealing may be negatively reinforced by removing or reducing the aversive stimuli of the fear and pain of poverty. For drug addicts, the use of drugs is negatively reinforced because the drugs remove or reduce the aversive stimulus of the pain of drug withdrawal. In short, both positive and negative reinforcement explain why a behavior, such as crime, is maintained or increases. Both types of reinforcement can simultaneously affect the same behavior. In other words, people may commit crime, in this view, both because the crime is rewarded and because it removes an aversive stimulus.

According to learning theory, criminal behavior is reduced, but not necessarily eliminated, through *extinction* or *punishment*. **Extinction** is a process in which behavior that previously was positively reinforced is no longer reinforced. In other words, the rewards have been removed. Thus, if burglars were to continually come up empty-handed in their quests—not to receive rewards for their efforts—they would no longer continue to commit burglary. **Punishment** is the presentation of an aversive stimulus to reduce a response. It is the principal method used in the United States, and in other countries, to prevent crime or, at least, reduce it. For example, one of the reasons offenders are imprisoned is to punish them for their crimes.

Among the policy implications of learning theory is to punish criminal behavior effectively, that is, according to learning theory principles. For a variety of reasons, punishment is not used effectively in criminal justice in the United States. For example, to employ punishment effectively, one must prevent escape. Escape is a natural reaction to the presentation of an aversive stimulus like imprisonment. In the United States, the chances of an offender's escaping punishment are great. Probation probably does not function as an aversive stimulus, and most offenders, especially first-time offenders, are not incarcerated.

To be effective, punishment must be applied consistently and immediately. As for immediacy, the process of criminal justice in the United States generally precludes punishment immediately after a criminal act is committed. The process is a slow and methodical one. Consistent application of punishment is rare because most criminal offenders are not caught.

Learning theory A theory that explains criminal behavior and its prevention with the concepts of positive reinforcement, negative reinforcement, extinction, punishment, and modeling or imitation.

Positive reinforcement The presentation of a stimulus that increases or maintains a response.

Negative reinforcement The removal or reduction of a stimulus whose removal or reduction increases or maintains a response.

Extinction A process in which behavior that previously was positively reinforced is no longer reinforced.

Punishment The presentation of an aversive stimulus to reduce a response.

Review and Applications

CHAPTER OBJECTIVE 1

Criminological theory is the explanation of the behavior of criminal offenders, as well as the behavior of police, attorneys, prosecutors, judges, correctional personnel, victims, and other actors in the criminal justice process. Learning criminological theory helps us to understand the basis of policies that are proposed and implemented to prevent and control crime.

CHAPTER OBJECTIVE 2

Classical and neoclassical criminologists theorize that human beings are free-willed individuals who commit crime when they rationally calculate that the crime will give them more pleasure than pain. In an effort to deter crime, classical criminologists advocate the following policies: (1) establish a social contract, (2) enact laws that are clear, simple, unbiased, and reflect the consensus of the population, (3) impose punishments that are proportionate to the crime, prompt, certain, public, necessary, the least possible in the given circumstances, and dictated by laws rather than by judges' discretion, (4) educate the public, (5) eliminate corruption from the administration of justice, and (6) reward virtue. Neoclassical criminologists modified the theory and introduced the concepts that mitigating circumstances might inhibit the exercise of free will and that punishment should be rehabilitative.

CHAPTER OBJECTIVE 3

Positivists reject the classical notion that individuals have free will and rationally choose to commit crime. Positivists assume, instead, that criminal behavior is determined by biological, psychological, and social factors.

CHAPTER OBJECTIVE 4

For biological positivists, the basic cause of crime is biological inferiority, which is indicated by physical or genetic characteristics that distinguish criminals from noncriminals. The policy implications of biological theories of crime causation include a choice of isolation, sterilization, or execution. For specific problems, biological theorists advocate brain surgery, chemical treatment, improved diets, and better mother and child care (before, during, and after birth).

CHAPTER OBJECTIVE 5

According to psychological theories of crime causation, crime results from individuals' mental or emotional disturbances, inability to empathize with others, inability to legally satisfy their basic needs, or oppressive circumstances of life. To combat crime, psychological positivists, like their biological counterparts, would isolate, sterilize, or execute offenders that were not amenable to treatment. For treatable offenders, psychotherapy or psychoanalysis may prove effective. Other policy implications are to help people satisfy their basic needs legally, to eliminate sources of oppression wherever possible, and to provide legal ways of coping with oppression.

CHAPTER OBJECTIVE 6

Sociological theories propose that crime is caused by *anomie,* or the dissociation of the individual from the *collective conscience,* or general sense of morality of the times; by *social disorganization;* by *anomie* resulting from a lack of opportunity to achieve aspirations; by the learning of criminal values and behaviors; and by the failure to properly socialize individuals. Among the policy implications of sociological theories of crime causation are containing crime within reasonable boundaries (because some crime is functional for society); organizing and empowering neighborhood residents; reducing aspirations, increasing legitimate opportunities, or doing both; providing law-abiding models, regulating associations, eliminating crime's rewards, rewarding law-abiding behavior, and punishing criminal behavior effectively; and properly socializing children so that they develop self-control and a strong moral bond to society.

CHAPTER OBJECTIVE 7

First, unlike classical theories, which assume that human beings have free will, and positivist theories, which assume that human beings are determined, critical theories assume that human beings are both determined and determining. Second, in contrast to both classical and positivist theories, which assume that society is characterized primarily by consensus over moral values, critical theories assume that society is characterized primarily by conflict over moral values. Finally, unlike positivist theorists, who assume that social scientists can be objective or value-neutral in their work, many critical theorists assume that everything they do is value-laden by virtue of their being human, that it is impossible to be objective.

CHAPTER OBJECTIVE 8

Depending on their perspective, critical theorists explain crime as the result of labeling and stigmatization; of relative powerlessness, the class struggle, and the practice of taking advantage of other people; or of patriarchy. Those who support labeling theory would address crime by, among other things, avoiding labeling people as criminals or by employing radical non-intervention or reintegrative shaming. Conflict theorists would address crime by having dominant groups give up some of their power to subordinate groups or having dominant groups become more effective rulers and subordinate groups better subjects. Radical theorists would define crime as a violation of basic human rights, replace the criminal justice system with popular or socialist justice, and (except for anarchists) would create a socialist society appreciative of human diversity. Left realists would use police power to protect people living in working-class communities. Peacemaking criminologists would transform human beings so that they were able to empathize with those less fortunate and respond to other people's needs, would reduce hierarchical structures, would create communities of caring people, and would champion universal social justice. Feminist theorists would address crime by eliminating patriarchal structures and relationships and promoting greater equality in all areas for women.

KEY TERMS

theory, p. 64
criminological theory, p. 64
classical theory, p. 65
utility, p. 65
social contract, p. 65
special or specific deterrence, p. 68
general deterrence, p. 68
neoclassical theory, p. 68
biological inferiority, p. 71
criminal anthropology, p. 71
atavist, p. 72
limbic system, p. 74
psychopaths, p. 77

sociopaths, p. 77
antisocial personalities, p. 77
anomie (Durkheim), p. 81
collective conscience, p. 81
Chicago School, p. 82
social disorganization, p. 82
anomie (Merton), p. 83
imitation or modeling, p. 85
differential association, p. 85
learning theory, p. 87
positive reinforcement, p. 87
negative reinforcement, p. 87
extinction, p. 87
punishment, p. 87

control theory, p. 88
labeling theory, p. 90
criminalization process, p. 90
conflict theory, p. 91
power differentials, p. 92
relative powerlessness, p. 92
radical theories, p. 93
class struggle, p. 94
left realists, p. 96
peacemaking criminology, p. 96
feminist theory, p. 96
patriarchy, p. 97

QUESTIONS FOR REVIEW

1. What are two undesirable consequences of the failure to understand the theoretical basis of criminal justice policies?

2. Before the Enlightenment and classical theory, what was generally believed to be the cause of crime?

3. Who was arguably the best known and most influential of the classical criminologists, and how did his ideas become known?

4. What is the difference between special or specific deterrence and general deterrence?

a. Which theory or theories of crime causation described in this chapter best explain the behavior of intentional speeders?

b. What crime prevention and correctional policies described in this chapter should be used with intentional speeders?

ADDITIONAL READING

Beccaria, Cesare. *On Crimes and Punishments.* Translated, with an introduction, by Harry Paolucci. Indianapolis: Bobbs-Merrill, 1975.

Bohm, Robert M. "Radical Criminology: An Explication." *Criminology,* Vol. 19 (1982), pp. 565–89.

Bohm, Robert M. *A Primer on Crime and Delinquency.* Belmont, CA: Wadsworth, 1997.

Currie, Elliott. *Confronting Crime: An American Challenge.* New York: Pantheon, 1985.

Daly, Kathleen and Meda Chesney-Lind. "Feminism and Criminology." *Justice Quarterly,* Vol. 5 (1988), pp. 497–538.

Davis, Nanette J. *Sociological Constructions of Deviance: Perspectives and Issues in the Field,* 2d ed. Dubuque, IA: Wm. C. Brown, 1980.

DeKeseredy, Walter S. and Martin D. Schwartz. *Contemporary Criminology.* Belmont, CA: Wadsworth, 1996.

Fishbein, Diana H. "Biological Perspectives in Criminology." *Criminology,* Vol. 28, (1990) pp. 27–72.

Gould, Stephen Jay. *The Mismeasure of Man.* New York: Norton, 1981.

Jones, David A. *History of Criminology.* Westport, CT: Greenwood, 1987.

Lynch, Michael J. and W. Byron Groves. *A Primer in Radical Criminology,* 2d ed. New York: Harrow and Heston, 1989.

Michalowski, Raymond J. *Order, Law, and Crime: An Introduction to Criminology.* New York: Random House, 1985.

Simpson, Sally S. "Feminist Theory, Crime, and Justice." *Criminology,* Vol. 27 (1989), pp. 605–31.

Sutherland, Edwin H. and Donald R. Cressey. *Criminology,* 9th ed. Philadelphia: J. B. Lippincott, 1974.

Taylor, Ian, Paul Walton, and Jock Young. *The New Criminology: For a Social Theory of Deviance.* New York: Harper and Row, 1974.

Vold, George B., Thomas J. Bernard, and Jeffrey B. Snipes. *Theoretical Criminology,* 4th ed. New York: Oxford, 1997.

Williams, Frank P. III and Marilyn D. McShane. *Criminological Theory: Selected Classic Readings,* 2d ed. Cincinnati: Anderson, 1998.

ENDNOTES

1. Cesare Beccaria, *An Essay on Crimes and Punishments,* trans., with introduction, by Harry Paolucci (Indianapolis: Bobbs-Merrill, 1975), p. ix.
2. Ibid., p. 8.
3. Ibid., p. 42.
4. Ibid., p. 99.
5. Beccaria, op. cit.
6. Ibid., p. 50.
7. Christopher J. Mumola and Allen J. Beck, "Prisoners in 1996," U.S. Department of Justice, Bureau of Justice Statistics Bulletin (Washington: GPO, 1997), p.1; Kathleen Maguire and Ann L. Pastore (eds.), *Sourcebook of Criminal Justice Statistics 1995,* U.S. Department of Justice, Bureau of Justice Statistics Bulletin (Washington: GPO, 1996), p. 548, Table 6.11. Calculations made from data in both sources.
8. See Irving M. Zeitlin, *Ideology and the Development of Sociological Theory,* 3d ed. (Englewood Cliffs, NJ: Prentice Hall, 1987).
9. George B. Vold, *Theoretical Criminology,* 4th ed. (New York: Oxford, 1997).
10. See Ian Taylor, Paul Walton, and Jock Young, *The New Criminology: For a Social Theory of Deviance* (New York: Harper and Row, 1974), pp. 24–32.
11. George B. Vold and Thomas J. Bernard, *Theoretical Criminology,* 3d ed. (New York: Oxford, 1986), p.48.
12. See William H. Sheldon, *Varieties of Delinquent Youth* (New York: Harper, 1949).
13. See Diana H. Fishbein, "Biological Perspectives in Criminology." *Criminology,* Vol. 28 (1990), pp. 27–72; Vold and Bernard, op. cit., pp. 87–92; Daniel J. Curran and Claire M. Renzetti, *Theories of Crime* (Boston: Allyn and Bacon, 1994), pp. 54–63; James Q. Wilson and Richard J. Herrnstein, *Crime and Human Nature* (New York: Simon & Schuster, 1985), pp. 75–81, 90–100.
14. Paul Salopek, "What's Next for Mankind?" *The Orlando Sentinel* (from the *Chicago Tribune*), (June 1, 1997), p. G-1.

15. See National Institute for Juvenile Justice and Delinquency Prevention, *Preventing Delinquency,* Vol.1. U.S. Department of Justice, OJJDP (Washington: GPO, 1977).

16. See Curran and Renzetti, op. cit., p. 78; Fishbein, op. cit., pp. 38, 47.

17. See Fishbein, ibid., pp. 48, 53; National Institute, op. cit.; Curran and Renzetti, ibid., pp. 73–77, 80–81.

18. "Wilson's Signature Makes Chemical Castration a Law," *The Orlando Sentinel,* September 18, 1996, p. A-10; "Florida Legislature 97," *The Orlando Sentinel,* May 4, 1997, p. A-22; "Texas OKs Voluntary Castration for Molesters," *The Orlando Sentinel,* May 21, 1997, p. A-16; "Drug Castrations May Be Years Away," *The Orlando Sentinel,* June 2, 1997, p. C-6.

19. See National Institute, op. cit., pp. 120–122; Vold and Bernard, op. cit., pp. 101–103.

20. Edwin H. Sutherland and Donald R. Cressey, *Criminology,* 9th ed. (Philadelphia: J. B. Lippincott, 1974), p. 152.

21. Robert Gordon, "Prevalence: The Rare Datum in Delinquency Measurement and Its Implications for the Theory of Delinquency," in Malcolm W. Klein (ed.), *The Juvenile Justice System* (Beverly Hills, CA: Sage, 1976), pp. 201–84; Travis Hirschi and Michael J. Hindelang, "Intelligence and Delinquency: A Revisionist Review," *American Sociological Review,* Vol. 42 (1977), pp. 572–87.

22. See Robert S. Woodworth and Mary R. Sheehan, *Contemporary Schools of Psychology,* 3d ed. (New York: The Ronald Press Co., 1964).

23. Walter Bromberg and Charles B. Thompson, "The Relation of Psychosis, Mental Defect, and Personality Types to Crime," *Journal of Criminal Law and Criminology,* Vol.28 (1937), pp. 70–89; Karl F. Schuessler and Donald R. Cressey, "Personality Characteristics of Criminals," *American Journal of Sociology,* Vol. 55 (1950), pp. 476–84; Gordon P. Waldo and Simon Dinitz, "Personality Attributes of the Criminal: An Analysis of Research Studies, 1950–1965," *Journal of Research in Crime and Delinquency,* Vol. 4 (1967), pp. 185–202; John Monahan and Henry J. Steadman, "Crime and Mental Disorder: An Epidemiological Approach," in Michael Tonry and Norval Morris (eds.), Crime and Justice, Vol. 4 (Chicago: University of Chicago Press, 1983).

24. Abraham H. Maslow, *Motivation and Personality,* 2d ed. (New York: Harper and Row, 1970).

25. Seymour L. Halleck, *Psychiatry and the Dilemmas of Crime* (New York: Harper and Row, 1967).

26. Emile Durkheim, *Rules of Sociological Method* (New York: Free Press, 1964).

27. Vold and Bernard, op. cit., p. 160.

28. Robert E. Park, Ernest Burgess, and Roderick D. McKenzie, *The City* (Chicago: University of Chicago Press, 1928).

29. Clifford R. Shaw, *Delinquency Areas* (Chicago: University of Chicago Press, 1929); Clifford R. Shaw and Henry D. McKay, *Social Factors in Juvenile Delinquency* (Chicago: University of Chicago Press, 1931); Clifford R. Shaw and Henry D. McKay, *Juvenile Delinquency and Urban Areas* (Chicago: University of Chicago Press, 1942).

30. Clifford R. Shaw, *The Jackroller* (Chicago: University of Chicago Press, 1930); Clifford R. Shaw, *The Natural History of a Delinquent Career* (Chicago: University of Chicago Press, 1931); Clifford R. Shaw, *Brothers in Crime* (Chicago: University of Chicago Press, 1938).

31. Robert K. Merton, "Social Structure and Anomie," *American Sociological Review,* Vol. 3 (1938), pp. 672–82.

32. Albert K. Cohen, *Delinquent Boys: The Culture of the Gang* (New York: Free Press, 1955).

33. Richard A Cloward and Lloyd E Ohlin, *Delinquency and Opportunity: A Theory of Delinquent Gangs* (New York: Free Press, 1960).

34. Vold and Bernard, op. cit., p. 201.

35. See, for example, Albert Bandura, *Social Learning Theory* (Englewood Cliffs, NJ: Prentice Hall, 1977).

36. See, for example, Edwin H. Sutherland and Donald R. Cressey, *Criminology,* 9th ed. (Philadelphia: J. B. Lippincott, 1974).

37. Daniel Glaser, "Criminality Theories and Behavioral Images," *American Journal of Sociology,* Vol. 61 (1956), pp. 433–44.

38. Definitions of learning theory concepts are from Howard Rachlin, *Introduction to Modern Behaviorism,* 2d ed. (San Francisco: W. H. Freeman, 1976).

39. Michael R. Gottfredson and Travis Hirschi, *A General Theory of Crime* (Stanford, CA: Stanford University Press, 1990).

40. Edwin Lemert, *Social Pathology: A Systematic Approach to the Theory of Sociopathic Behavior* (New York: McGraw-Hill, 1951).

41. See Edwin M. Schur, *Radical Nonintervention* (Englewood Cliffs, NJ: Prentice Hall, 1973).

42. Robert J. Lilly, Francis T. Cullen, and Richard A. Ball, *Criminological Theory: Context and Consequences* (Newbury Park, CA: Sage, 1989), pp. 131–135.

43. John Braithwaite, *Crime, Shame and Reintegration* (Cambridge: Cambridge University Press, 1989).

44. Vold and Bernard, op. cit., p. 256.

45. George B. Vold, *Theoretical Criminology* (New York: Oxford, 1958).

46. William J. Chambliss, "Functional and Conflict Theories of Crime: The Heritage of Emile Durkheim and Karl Marx," in W. J. Chambliss and M. Mankoff (eds.), *Whose Law, What Order?* (New York: Wiley, 1976), p. 9.

47. Tony Platt, "Prospects for a Radical Criminology in the USA," in I. Taylor et al. (eds.), *Critical Criminology* (Boston: Routledge & Kegan Paul, 1975), p. 103.

48. Ibid.; for a similar definition, see also Herman Schwendinger and Julia Schwendinger, "Defenders of Order or Guardians of Human Rights?" in I. Taylor et al. (eds.), *Critical Criminology,* pp. 113–46.

49. See, for example, Richard Kinsey, John Lea, and Jock Young, *Losing the Fight Against Crime* (London: Basil Blackwell, 1986); Roger Matthews and Jock Young (eds.), *Confronting Crime* (London: Sage, 1986).

50. Werner Einstadter and Stuart Henry, *Criminological Theory: An Analysis of Its Underlying Assumptions* (Fort Worth, TX: Harcourt Brace, 1995), p. 256.

51. Ibid., p. 257.

52. See Harold E. Pepinsky and Richard Quinney (eds.), *Criminology as Peacemaking* (Bloomington: Indiana University Press, 1991).

53. For two excellent reviews, see Kathleen Daly and Meda Chesney-Lind, "Feminism and Criminology," *Justice Quarterly,* Vol. 5 (1988), pp. 497–538; Sally S. Simpson, "Feminist Theory, Crime, and Justice," *Criminology,* Vol. 27 (1989), pp. 605–31.

54. See Einstadter and Henry, op. cit., p. 275.

55. Ibid.

56. Diane Craven, "Female Victims of Violent Crime," U.S. Department of Justice, Bureau of Justice Statistics Selected Findings (Washington: GPO, 1996).

4 The Rule of Law

Two Types of Law: Criminal Law and Civil Law

Criminal law One of two general types of law practiced in the United States (the other is civil law); "a formal means of social control [that uses] rules . . . interpreted [and enforced] by the courts . . . to set limits to the conduct of the citizens, to guide the officials, and to define . . . unacceptable behavior."

Penal code The criminal law of a political jurisdiction.

Tort A violation of the civil law.

Civil law One of two general types of law practiced in the United States (the other is criminal law); a means of resolving conflicts between individuals. It includes personal injury claims (torts), the law of contracts and property, and subjects such as administrative law and the regulation of public utilities.

As discussed in Chapter 2, the conventional, though not necessarily the best, definition of *crime* is "a violation of the criminal law." **Criminal law** is one of two general types of law practiced in the United States; the other is civil law. Criminal law is:

a formal means of social control [that] involves the use of rules that are interpreted, and are enforceable, by the courts of a political community. . . . The function of the rules is to set limits to the conduct of the citizens, to guide the officials (police and other administrators), and to define conditions of deviance or unacceptable behavior.[1]

The purpose of criminal justice is to enforce the criminal law.

A crime, as noted, is a violation of the criminal law, or of the **penal code** of a political jurisdiction. Although crime is committed against individuals, it is considered an offense against the state, that is, the political jurisdiction that enacted the law.[2] A **tort**, on the other hand, is a violation of the **civil law** and is considered a private matter between individuals. Civil law also includes the law of contracts and property and subjects such as administrative law and the regulation of public utilities.

For legal purposes, a particular act may be considered an offense against an individual or the state or both. It is either a tort or a crime or both, depending on how it is handled. For example, a person who has committed an act of assault may be charged with a crime. If that person is convicted of the crime, the criminal court may order the offender to be imprisoned in the county jail for six months and to pay a fine of $500. Both the jail sentence and the fine are punishments, with the fine going to the state treasury (in federal court to the national treasury). The criminal court could also order the offender to pay restitution to the victim. In that case, the offender would pay the victim a sum of money either directly or indirectly, through an intermediary. In addition, the victim may sue the offender in civil court for damages, such as medical expenses or wages lost because of injury. If the offender is found liable (responsible) for the damages because he or she has committed a tort (civil courts do not "convict"), the civil court may also order the offender to compensate the victim in the amount of $500 for damage to the victim's interests. The payment of compensation in the civil case is not punishment; it is for the purpose of "making the victim whole again."

Substantive vs. Procedural Law

There are two types of criminal law: substantive and procedural. **Substantive law** is the body of law that defines criminal offenses and their penalties. Substantive laws, which are found in the various penal codes, govern what people legally may and may not do in their relationships with other people. Examples of substantive laws are those that prohibit and penalize murder, rape, robbery, and other crimes. **Procedural law**, sometimes called *adjective* or *remedial* law, governs the ways in which the substantive laws are to be administered. It covers such subjects as the way suspects can legally be arrested, searched, interrogated, tried, and punished. In other words,

Substantive law The body of law that defines criminal offenses and their penalties.

Procedural law The body of law that governs the ways in which the substantive laws are to be administered; sometimes called *adjective* or *remedial* law.

procedural law is concerned with **due process of law**, or the rights of people suspected of or charged with crimes. The last part of this chapter is devoted to a detailed description of procedural law.

Ideal Characteristics of the Criminal Law

Legal scholars identify five features that all "good" criminal laws ideally ought to possess. To the extent that those features are absent in criminal laws, the laws can be considered "bad" laws, and bad laws do exist. The five ideal features of good criminal laws are (1) politicality, (2) specificity, (3) regularity, (4) uniformity, and (5) penal sanction (see Figure 4–1).[3]

Politicality **Politicality** refers to the legitimate source of criminal law. Only violations of rules made by the state (that is, the political jurisdiction that enacted the laws) are crimes. Violations of rules made by other institutions, such as families, churches, schools, and employers, may be "bad," "sinful," or "socially unacceptable," but they are not crimes because they were not prohibited by the state.

Specificity **Specificity** refers to the scope of criminal law. Although civil law may be general in scope, criminal law should provide strict definitions of specific acts. The point is illustrated by an old case in which a person stole an airplane but was found not guilty of violating a criminal law that prohibited the taking of "self-propelled vehicles." The judge ruled that at the time the law was enacted, *vehicles* did not include airplanes. Ideally, as the Court ruled in *Papachristou v. City of Jacksonville* (1972), a statute or ordinance "is void for vagueness . . . [if] it fails to give a person of ordinary intelligence fair notice that his contemplated conduct is forbidden."

Regularity **Regularity** is the applicability of the criminal law to all persons. Ideally, anyone who commits a crime is answerable for it, regardless of the person's social status. Thus, ideally, when criminal laws are created, they should apply not only to the women who violate them, but also to the men; not only to the poor, but also to the rich. In practice, however, this ideal feature of law has been violated. Georgia's pre-Civil War criminal laws, for example, provided for a dual system of crime and punishment, with one set of laws for "slaves and free persons of color" and another for all other persons.

FIGURE 4–1

Ideal Characteristics of Criminal Law

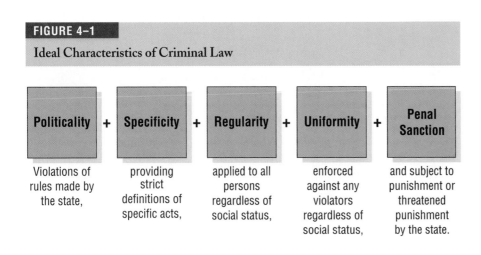

Politicality +	**Specificity** +	**Regularity** +	**Uniformity** +	**Penal Sanction**
Violations of rules made by the state,	providing strict definitions of specific acts,	applied to all persons regardless of social status,	enforced against any violators regardless of social status,	and subject to punishment or threatened punishment by the state.

Uniformity An ideal characteristic of criminal law: the enforcement of the laws against anyone who violates them, regardless of social status.

Penal sanction An ideal characteristic of criminal law: the principle that violators will be punished or at least threatened with punishment by the state.

Uniformity Uniformity refers to the way in which the criminal law should be enforced. Ideally, the law should be administered without regard for the social status of the persons who have committed crimes or are accused of committing crimes. Thus, when violated, criminal laws should be enforced against both young and old, both rich and poor, and so on. However, as is the case with regularity, the principle of uniformity is often violated because some people consider the strict enforcement of the law unjust in some cases. For example, juveniles who are caught misbehaving in violation of the criminal law are sometimes ignored or treated leniently through the exercise of police or judicial discretion.

Penal Sanction The last ideal feature of criminal law is **penal sanction,** the principle that violators will be punished, or at least threatened with punishment, by the state. Conventional wisdom suggests that there would be no point in enacting criminal laws if their violation were not responded to with punishment or threat of punishment. Most people assume that sanctionless criminal laws would be ignored. Because all criminal laws carry sanctions, the power of sanctionless laws can be left to philosophers to debate. Figure 4–2 shows the five general types of penal sanctions currently used in the United States, as well as the purpose and focus of each sanction. Combining different penal sanctions in the administration of justice is not uncommon.

Criminal Law as a Political Phenomenon

People sometimes forget that the criminal law is a political phenomenon, that it is created by human beings to regulate the behavior of other human beings. Some people, for example, view the criminal law as divinely inspired, something that should not be questioned or challenged.

FIGURE 4–2

Five General Types of Penal Sanctions

Type	Purpose	Focus
Punishment	Prevent undesired conduct. Provide retribution ("an eye for an eye").	Offending conduct
Restitution	Make the victim "whole again" by having the offender directly or indirectly pay the victim.	Crime victim
Compensation	Make the victim "whole again" by having the state pay for damages to the victim.	Crime victim
Regulation	Control future conduct toward the best interests of the community (e.g., making it a crime or traffic violation to operate a motor vehicle with a blood alcohol content higher than a specified level).	The entire community
Treatment or rehabilitation	Change the offender's behavior and, perhaps, personality.	Criminal offender

That viewpoint probably comes from a belief in the biblical story of Moses receiving the Ten Commandments from God on Mount Sinai. However, as critical theorists are quick to point out, the criminal law frequently promotes the interests of some groups over the interests of other groups. Thus, regardless of the law's source of inspiration, it is important to understand that what gets defined as criminal or delinquent behavior is the result of a political process in which rules are created to prohibit or to require certain behaviors. Nothing is criminal or delinquent in and of itself; only the response of the state makes it so.

Origins of Laws Formal, written laws are a relatively recent phenomenon in human existence. The first were created only about 5000 years ago. They emerged with the institutions of property, marriage, and government. "Stateless" societies apparently managed without them for two primary reasons. First, most stateless societies were governed by rigid customs that were strictly adhered to. Second, crimes of violence were considered private matters and were usually resolved through bloody personal revenge. Formal, written laws partially replaced customs when nation-states appeared, although customs often remained the force behind the laws. Formal laws also replaced customs with the advent of writing, which allowed recorded legislation to replace the recollections of elders and priests.

The first known written laws (approximately 3000 B.C.) have been found on clay tablets among the ruins

MYTH

Law makes people behave.

FACT

The existence of a law prohibiting a particular behavior does not prevent an individual from engaging in that behavior. Common sense suggests the implausibility of the notion. Ask yourself, if it were not for laws prohibiting murder, prostitution, or heroin use, for example, would you murder, engage in prostitution, or use heroin? Furthermore, how effective are speed limits in preventing you from exceeding them?

of Ur, one of the city-states of Sumeria. Attributed to King Urukagina of Lagash, the laws were truly enlightened for the times and attempted to free poor people from abuse by the rich and everybody from abuse by the priests. For example, one law forbade the high priest from coming into the garden of a poor mother and taking wood or fruit from her to pay taxes. Laws also cut burial fees to one-fifth of what they had been and forbade the clergy and high officials from sharing among themselves the cattle that were sacrificed to the gods. By 2800 B.C., the growth of trade had forced the city-states of Sumeria to merge into an empire governed by a single, all-powerful king.

Around 2200 B.C., a war settlement between the Sumerians and the Akkadians produced the Babylonian civilization. Babylonia's best-known king was Hammurabi (2123–2081 B.C.), who ruled for 43 years. Hammurabi is famous for the first great code of laws. The Code of Hammurabi, like the laws of Moses later, presumably was a gift from God. Hammurabi was said to have received it from the sun god, Shamash, about 2100 B.C. There was a

Generally, statutes and ordinances apply only in the particular jurisdiction in which they were enacted. A crime must be prosecuted in the jurisdiction in which it was committed, and it is generally held to have been committed in the jurisdiction in which it was completed or achieved its goal. Federal crimes violate federal statutes, and state crimes violate state statutes. A crime in one state may not be a crime in another state, but a violation of a federal statute is a crime if committed anywhere in the United States. When a certain behavior violates both federal and state statutes, and possibly local ordinances, as is the case with many drug law violations, there is overlapping jurisdiction. In such cases, there is frequently confusion over which jurisdiction has authority for the enforcement of the law and the prosecution of the crime.

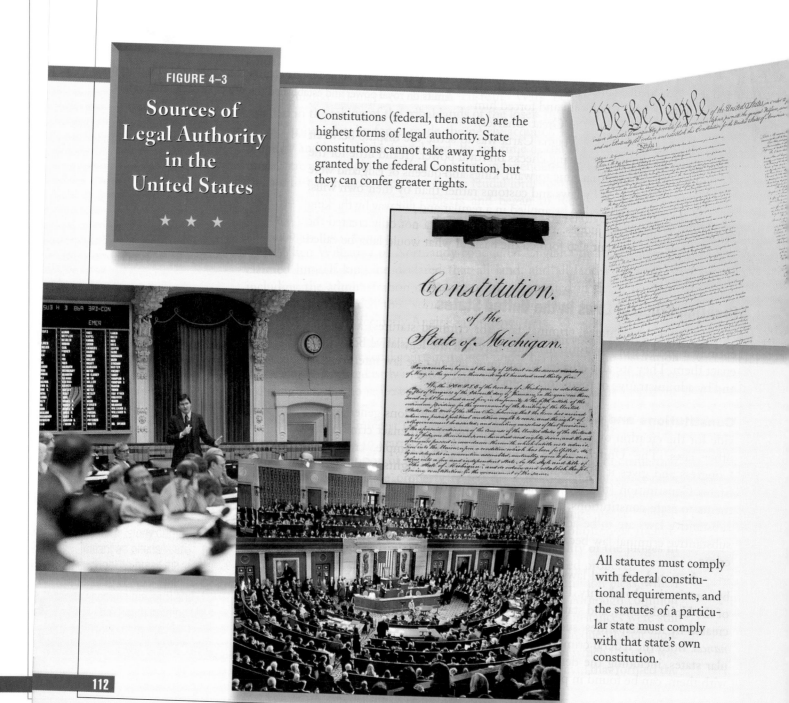

FIGURE 4–3

Sources of Legal Authority in the United States

★ ★ ★

Constitutions (federal, then state) are the highest forms of legal authority. State constitutions cannot take away rights granted by the federal Constitution, but they can confer greater rights.

Constitution of the State of Michigan.

All statutes must comply with federal constitutional requirements, and the statutes of a particular state must comply with that state's own constitution.

Common Law Common law, also called *case law,* is a by-product of decisions made by trial and appellate court judges, who produce case law whenever they render a decision in a particular case. The decision becomes a potential basis, or **precedent,** for deciding the outcomes of similar cases in the future. Although it is possible for the decision of any trial court judge to become a precedent, it is primarily the written decisions of appellate court judges that do. The reasons on which the decisions of appellate court judges are based are the only ones required to be in writing. This body of recorded decisions has become known as *common law.* Generally, whether a precedent is binding is determined by the court's location. (The different levels of courts in the United States will be described in detail in Chapter 7.)

Precedent A case that forms a potential basis for deciding the outcomes of similar cases in the future; a by-product of decisions made by trial and appellate court judges, who produce case law whenever they render a decision in a particular case.

Judicial decisions (common law or case law) interpret and apply both constitutional and statutory provisions and are indispensable to federal and state criminal law.

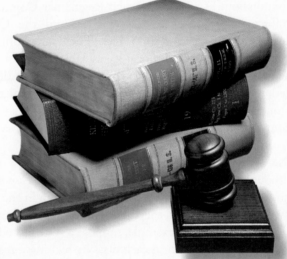

Local ordinances must be consistent with higher forms of law (constitutions, statutes). They can also result in criminal punishment (usually minor) if violated.

Violations of administrative or regulatory agency regulations and decisions can result in both civil and criminal sanctions.

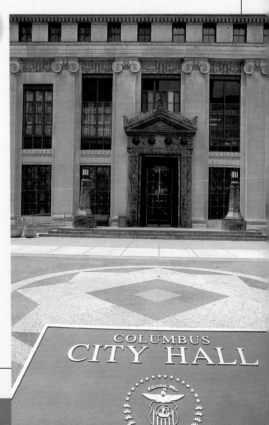

COLUMBUS
CITY HALL

Stare decisis The principle
of using precedents to guide
future decisions in court cases;
Latin for "to stand by decided
cases."

The principle of using precedents to guide future decisions in court cases is called *stare decisis* (Latin for "to stand by decided cases"). Much of the time spent by criminal lawyers in preparing for a case is devoted to finding legal precedents that support their arguments. The successful outcome of a case depends largely on the success of lawyers in that endeavor.

Although common law was an important source of criminal law in colonial America, that is no longer the case. Currently, what were originally common law crimes, as well as many new crimes, have been defined by statutes created by legislatures in nearly all states. There is no federal criminal common law. Nevertheless, as noted previously, common law or case law remains important for purposes of statutory interpretation.

Administrative or Regulatory Agency Decisions

Administrative or regulatory agencies are the products of statutes enacted by the lawmaking bodies of different jurisdictions. Those agencies create rules, regulate and supervise activities in their areas of responsibility, and render decisions that have the force of law. Examples of federal administrative or regulatory agencies are the Federal Trade Commission (FTC), the Federal Communications Commission (FCC), the Nuclear Regulatory Commission (NRC), the Drug Enforcement Administration (DEA), and the Occupational Safety and Health Administration (OSHA). There are administrative or regulatory agencies at the state and local levels as well. Although violations of many of the rules and regulations of such agencies are handled through civil law proceedings, some violations—especially habitual violations—may be addressed through criminal proceedings. Additionally, legislatures often enact criminal statutes based on the recommendations of regulatory agencies.

The Interdependency Among Sources of Legal Authority

Although federal and state criminal statutes are essentially independent of one another, and although almost all of the action in the enforcement of criminal laws is at the state level, there is an important interdependency among sources of legal authority. For example, suppose a state passed a law requiring teachers in public schools to begin each class by reciting a mandatory prayer. The law would probably be challenged as a violation of the *establishment clause* of the First Amendment to the U.S. Constitution, which states that "Congress shall make no law respecting an establishment of religion." The law would certainly be declared unconstitutional because it violated the U.S. Constitution. Provisions of the U.S. Constitution always take precedence over state statutes. However, if the state statute were not challenged, it would remain in effect in the particular state that enacted it. Figure 4–3 on pages 112–13 summarizes the relationships among the sources of legal authority in the United States.

Procedural Law: Rights of the Accused

Most of the procedural, or due-process rights, given to criminal suspects or defendants in the United States are found in the Bill of Rights, the first ten amendments to the United States Constitution. The Bill of Rights went into effect on December 15, 1791. Other procedural rights are found in

FIGURE 4–4

The 12 Provisions in the Bill of Rights Applicable to the Criminal Justice Process

Procedural Right	Amendment
1. Freedom from unreasonable searches and seizures	Fourth
2. Grand jury indictment in felony cases*	Fifth
3. No double jeopardy	Fifth
4. No compelled self-incrimination	Fifth
5. Speedy and public trial	Sixth
6. Impartial jury of the state and district where crime occurred	Sixth
7. Notice of nature and cause of accusation	Sixth
8. Confront opposing witnesses	Sixth
9. Compulsory process for obtaining favorable witnesses	Sixth
10. Counsel	Sixth
11. No excessive bail and fines*	Eighth
12. No cruel and unusual punishment	Eighth

* This right has not been incorporated and is not adhered to by the states.

state constitutions and federal and state statutes. Probably the best systematic collection of due-process rights is the *Federal Rules of Criminal Procedure.* Those rules apply only to federal crimes prosecuted in federal courts. Most states also have collections of rules regarding criminal procedures in state courts. Ohio, for example, has 60 such rules in its *Ohio Rules of Criminal Procedure.*

The Bill of Rights

The ink was barely dry on the new U.S. Constitution before critics attacked it for not protecting the rights of the people. The First Congress quickly proposed a set of 12 amendments and sent them to the states for ratification. By 1791, the states had ratified 10 of the amendments, which became known as the Bill of Rights. Although the Bill of Rights originally applied only to the national government, almost all of its provisions have also been applied to the states through a series of U.S. Supreme Court decisions. Figure 4–4 above lists the 12 provisions in the Bill of Rights that are applicable to the criminal justice process. Note that only two of the provisions—the prohibition against excessive bail and fines and the right to a grand jury indictment—are not yet applicable to the states.

The Fourteenth Amendment and Selective Incorporation of the Bill of Rights

The Fourteenth Amendment to the United States Constitution was finally ratified by the required three-fourths of all states in 1868, shortly after the conclusion of the Civil War. In part, the amendment reads as follows:

No State shall make or enforce any law which shall abridge the privileges or immunities of citizens of the United States, nor shall any State deprive any person of life, liberty, or property, without due process of law; nor deny to any person within its jurisdiction the equal protection of the laws.

One of the interesting and long-debated questions about the Fourteenth Amendment was whether its original purpose was to extend the procedural safeguards described in the Bill of Rights to people charged with crimes at the state level. Before the passage of the Fourteenth Amendment, the Bill of Rights applied only to people charged with federal crimes; individual states were not bound by its requirements. Some justices of the Supreme Court—for example, William Douglas (justice from 1939 to 1975), Hugo Black (justice from 1937 to 1971), and Frank Murphy (justice from 1940 to 1949)—believed that the Fourteenth Amendment was supposed to *incorporate* the Bill of Rights and make it applicable to the states. However, other justices, perhaps even a majority of them, did not. Thus, until the 1960s, the Supreme Court of the United States did not interpret the Fourteenth Amendment as incorporating the Bill of Rights.

There are at least three different explanations for the actions or, in this case, inactions of the Supreme Court.[7] First, there is little evidence that supporters of the Fourteenth Amendment intended it to incorporate the Bill of Rights. Second, by 1937 a series of court decisions had established the precedent that the due-process clause of the Fourteenth Amendment did not require states to follow trial procedures mandated at the federal level by provisions in the Bill of Rights. The Supreme Court had held that due process was not violated if procedures followed in state courts were otherwise fair. Third, there was the states' rights issue. Because the administration of justice is primarily a state and local responsibility, many people resented what appeared to be unwarranted interference by the federal government in state and local matters. Indeed, the Constitution, for the most part, leaves questions about policing and administering justice to the states, unless a state's procedure violates a fundamental principle of justice.

Regardless of the reason, it was not until the early 1960s that the Supreme Court, then headed by Chief Justice Earl Warren, began to selectively incorporate most of the procedural safeguards contained in the Bill of Rights, making them applicable to the states.

Thus, it took nearly 100 years after the ratification of the Fourteenth Amendment for suspects charged with crimes at the state level to be afforded most of the same due-process protections as people charged with crimes at the federal level. During the past 30 years, however, the composition of the Supreme Court has changed dramatically, and with the change in personnel, the Court's views of due-process rights have changed as well. Whereas the politically liberal Warren Court of the 1960s championed the rights of criminal suspects by extending procedural safeguards, the politically conservative Burger and Rehnquist Courts of the 1970s, 1980s, and 1990s have actively reversed or altered in other ways the work of the Warren Court.[8]

In the rest of this section, we will consider the procedural rights in the Bill of Rights, which are found in the Fourth, Fifth, Sixth, and Eighth Amendments to the U.S. Constitution.[9] Before we do, however, it is impor-

I n *Trop v. Dulles* (1958) Chief Justice Warren wrote that the protections of the Bill of Rights "must draw [their] meaning from evolving standards of decency that mark the progress of a maturing society."

CHAPTER 4   *The Rule of Law*

From left to right: Chief Justices Earl Warren, Warren Burger, and William Rehnquist. Whereas the politically liberal Warren Court of the 1960s championed the rights of criminal suspects by extending procedural safeguards, the politically conservative Burger and Rehnquist Courts of the 1970s, 1980s, and 1990s have actively reversed or altered in other ways the work of the Warren Court.

tant to emphasize that the specific interpretation of each of the procedural, or due-process, rights has evolved over time through dozens of Supreme Court and lower-court decisions, or precedents. In this introductory examination, we will limit our consideration of the legal development of those rights to what we believe are the most consequential cases, the landmark cases.

The Fourth Amendment

The Fourth Amendment reads as follows:

The right of the people to be secure in their persons, houses, papers, and effects, against unreasonable searches and seizures, shall not be violated, and no warrants shall issue, but upon probable cause, supported by oath or affirmation, and particularly describing the place to be searched, and the person or things to be seized.

The procedural rights in the Fourth Amendment influence the operation of criminal justice in the United States nearly every day. They concern the legality of searches and seizures and the question of what to do with evidence that is illegally obtained. **Searches** are explorations or inspections, by law enforcement officers, of homes, premises, vehicles, or persons, for the purpose of discovering evidence of crimes or persons who are accused of crimes. **Seizures** are the taking of persons or property into custody in response to violations of the criminal law.

According to the U.S. Supreme Court, the Fourth Amendment allows two kinds of searches and seizures: those made with a warrant and those made without a warrant. A **warrant** is a written order from a court directing law enforcement officers to conduct a search or to arrest a person. An **arrest** is the seizure of a person or the taking of a person into custody, either actual

Searches Explorations or inspections, by law enforcement officers, of homes, premises, vehicles, or persons, for the purpose of discovering evidence of crimes or persons who are accused of crimes.

Seizures The taking of persons or property into custody in response to violations of the criminal law.

Warrant A written order from a court directing law enforcement officers to conduct a search or to arrest a person.

Arrest The seizure of a person or the taking of a person into custody, either actual physical custody, as when a suspect is handcuffed by a police officer, or constructive custody, as when a person peacefully submits to a police officer's control.

physical custody, as when a suspect is handcuffed by a police officer, or constructive custody, as when a person peacefully submits to a police officer's control. An arrest can occur without an officer's physically touching a suspect.

The Fourth Amendment requires only that searches and seizures not be "unreasonable." Searches and seizures conducted with a legal warrant are generally considered reasonable. However, what is "reasonable" in warrantless searches remained vague for more than 100 years after the ratification of the amendment. It was not until a series of cases beginning in the 1960s that the Supreme Court began to provide a more precise definition of the term. Because the law concerning warrantless searches and seizures is complex, only a relatively brief and simplified overview will be provided here.

Searches and Seizures With a Warrant First, law enforcement officers must have *probable cause* before a judicial officer can legally issue a search or arrest warrant. Probable cause for a search warrant requires substantial and trustworthy evidence to support two conclusions: (1) that the specific objects to be searched for are connected with criminal activity and (2) that the objects will be found in the place to be searched. In nearly all jurisdictions, law enforcement officers seeking a search warrant must specify in a signed *affidavit,* a written and sworn declaration, the facts that establish probable cause. The facts in the affidavit are the basis for determining later whether or not there was probable cause to issue the warrant in the first place. Some jurisdictions allow sworn oral testimony to establish probable cause.

The Fourth Amendment requires that a search warrant contain a particular description of the place to be searched and the person or things to be seized. Thus, the warrant must be specific enough that a law enforcement officer executing it would know where to search and what objects to seize, even if the officer was not originally involved in the case. However, absolute technical accuracy in the description of the place to be searched is not necessary. It is required only that an officer executing a warrant can find, perhaps by asking questions of neighborhood residents, the place to be searched.

A warrant may also be issued for the search of a person or an automobile, rather than a place. A warrant to search a person should provide the person's name or at least a detailed description. A warrant to search an automobile should include either the car's license number or its make and the name of its owner.

Search warrants are required to be executed in a reasonable amount of time. For example, federal law requires that a search be conducted within 10 days after the warrant is issued. The federal government and nearly half of the states also have laws limiting the time of day during which search warrants may be executed. In those jurisdictions, searches may be conducted only during daytime hours unless there are special circumstances.

Generally, before law enforcement officers may enter a place to conduct a search, they must first announce that they are law enforcement officers, that they possess a warrant, and that they are there to execute it. The major exceptions to this requirement are situations in which it is likely that the evidence would be destroyed immediately on notification or in which notification would pose a threat to officers. However, if officers are refused entry after identifying themselves, they may then use force to gain entry, but only after they have given the occupant time to respond. In short, they

FYI

n *United States v. Mendenhall* (1980), the Supreme Court created the following test for determining whether an encounter constitutes a Fourth Amendment seizure: "A person has been 'seized' within the meaning of the Fourth Amendment only if, in view of all the circumstances surrounding the incident, a reasonable person would have believed that he was not free to leave."

CHAPTER 4   *The Rule of Law*

cannot legally yell, "Police officers," and immediately kick down the door. Finally, if in the course of conducting a legal search, law enforcement officers discover **contraband** (an illegal substance or object) or evidence of a crime not covered by the warrant, they may seize that contraband or evidence without getting a new warrant specifically covering it. Figure 4–5 on page 120 shows a sample search warrant and the supporting affidavit.

Arrests With a Warrant Most arrests are made without a warrant. It is only when law enforcement officers want to enter private premises to make an arrest that an arrest warrant is legally required. An arrest warrant is issued only if substantial and trustworthy evidence supports these two conclusions: (1) a violation of the law has been committed and (2) the person to be arrested committed the violation.

Searches and Seizures Without a Warrant In guaranteeing freedom from illegal searches and seizures, the Fourth Amendment protects a person's privacy. Under most circumstances, the amendment requires a warrant signed by a judge to authorize a search for and seizure of evidence of criminal activity. However, U.S. Supreme Court interpretations of the Fourth Amendment have permitted warrantless searches and seizures in some circumstances. A person is generally protected from searches and seizures without a warrant in places, such as home or office, where he or she has a legitimate right to privacy. That same protection, however, does not extend to all places where a person has a legitimate right to be. For example, the Supreme Court has permitted the stopping and searching of automobiles under certain circumstances and with probable cause. Several doctrines concerning search and seizure without a warrant have developed over time.

Before 1969, when law enforcement officers arrested a suspect, they could legally search, without a warrant, the entire premises surrounding the arrest. That kind of search is called a *search incident to arrest,* and like a search with a warrant, it required probable cause. Evidence obtained through a *search incident to arrest* was admissible as long as the arrest was legal.

In 1969, in the case of *Chimel v. California,* the Supreme Court limited the scope of *searches incident to an arrest.* The Court restricted the physical area in which officers could conduct a search to the area within the suspect's immediate control. The Court interpreted the area within the suspect's immediate control as an area near enough to the suspect to enable him or her to obtain a weapon or destroy evidence. The Court also ruled that it is permissible for officers, incident to an arrest, to protect themselves, to prevent a suspect's escape by searching the suspect for weapons, and to preserve evidence within the suspect's grabbing area.

The Supreme Court has continued to refine the scope of warrantless searches and seizures incident to an arrest. For example, in 1981, in *New York v. Belton,* the Court ruled that after police have made a lawful arrest of the occupant of an automobile, they may, incident to that arrest, search the automobile's entire passenger compartment and the contents of any containers found in that compartment. One year later, in *United States v. Ross,* the High Court clarified the *Belton* rule, saying that the scope of an automobile search incident to a lawful arrest under *Belton* does not include the car's trunk. Then, in 1991, in the case of *California v. Acevedo,* the Court ruled that police may

Contraband An illegal substance or object.

FYI

When the U.S. Supreme Court created its test for a Fourth Amendment seizure in *United States v. Mendenhall* (1980), the Court provided these examples of situations that might be construed as seizures, even if the person did not attempt to leave: (1) the threatening presence of several officers, (2) the display of a weapon by an officer, (3) some physical touching of the person, or (4) the use of language or a tone of voice that indicated that compliance with the officer's request might be compelled.

FIGURE 4–5

A Sample Search and Arrest Warrant

SEARCH AND ARREST WARRANT

THE STATE OF TEXAS § 155 E. Main Street
§ Dallas, Dallas County, Texas
COUNTY OF DALLAS §

THE STATE OF TEXAS to the Sheriff or any Peace Officer of Dallas County, Texas, or any Peace Officer of the State of Texas,

GREETINGS:

WHEREAS, the Affiant whose signature is affixed to the Affidavit appearing on the reverse hereof is a Peace Officer under the laws of Texas and did heretofore this day subscribed and swear to said Affidavit before me (which said affidavit is by this reference incorporated herein for all purposes), and whereas I find that the verified facts by Affiant in said Affidavit show that Affiant has probable cause for the belief he expresses therein and establishes the existence of proper grounds for the issuance of this Warrant:

NOW, THEREFORE, you are commanded to enter the s[u] described in said Affidavit and to there search for t described in said Affidavit and to seize the same an And, you are commanded to arrest and bring before and accused in said Affidavit. Herein fail not, but h this Warrant executed within three days, exclusive issuance and exclusive of the day of its execution w thereon, showing how you have executed the same.

ISSUED AT _11:35_ o'clock _A_ M., on this th
of _March_, 19_99_ to certify which w
day.

Sarah H. Solano
MAGISTRATE, DALLAS COUN[TY]

RETURN AND INVENTORY

THE STATE OF TEXAS §
§
COUNTY OF DALLAS §

The undersigned Affiant, being a Peace Officer und[er] and being duly sworn, on oath certifies that the forego[ing] hand on the day it was issued and that it was execute[d] of _____, 19____, by making the se[arch] therein and seizing during such search the following d[escribed] property:

_____
AFFIANT

SUBSCRIBED AND SWORN to before me, the unders[igned]
the_____day of_____, 19_[_]

_____
Notary Public in and for Dallas Cou[nty]

AFFIDAVIT FOR SEARCH WARRANT AND ARREST WARRANT

THE STATE OF TEXAS § 155 E. Main Street
§ City of Dallas, Dallas County, Texas
COUNTY OF DALLAS §

The undersigned Affiant, being a Peace Officer under the laws of Texas and being duly sworn, on oath makes the following statements and accusations:

1. There is in Dallas County, Texas, a suspected place and premises described and located as follows: A one story family dwelling, which is white in color, with a grey composition roof. The location of this residence is 155 E. Main Street, located in the City of Dallas, Dallas County, Texas.

2. There is at said suspected place and premises personal property concealed and kept in violation of the laws of Texas and described as follows: A CONTROLLED SUBSTANCE: TO WIT: Cocaine

3. Said suspected place and premises are in charge of and controlled by each of the following persons: A white male approximately 25 years of age, 5'10 in height, 160 pounds, with a mustache, black hair and brown eyes and other person or persons whose names, ages, and descriptions are unknown to the affiant.

4. It is the belief of Affiant, and he hereby charges and accuses, that: The above listed white male described in paragraph number 3 was in possession of an amount of cocaine located in the residence at 155 E. Main Street, located in the City of Dallas, Dallas County, Texas.

5. Affiant has probable cause for said belief by reason of the following facts: Affiant, Officer Smith, is employed by the City of Dallas Police Department and is currently assigned to the Narcotics Bureau.

I, the affiant, personally purchased an amount of cocaine from the suspect described in paragraph number 3 out of the aforementioned address at 155 E. Main Street, and that the affiant has been inside the above described residence within the last 24 hours, and personally observed the above described white male and other person, persons, whose names, ages, and identities, and descriptions are unknown to the affiant, in possession of and selling cocaine. Detective Jones purchased 0.3g of cocaine from the above described suspect for twenty dollars U.S. Currency. The cocaine was field tested by the affiant who knows due to his experience as a narcotics officer, what cocaine looks like and how it is packaged for resale.

I, the affiant, observed this on March 22, 1999.

Wherefore, Affiant asks for issuance of a warrant that will authorize him to search said suspected place and premises for said personal property and seize the same and to arrest each said described and accused person.

James C. Smith
AFFIANT

Subscribed and sworn to before me by said Affiant on this the _23rd_ day
of _March_, 19_99_.

Sarah H. Solano
MAGISTRATE, DALLAS COUNTY, TEXAS

search the trunk of a car in a warrantless search, even if not incident to an arrest, if they have probable cause to believe that contraband or another seizable object is in the trunk.

Other Supreme Court decisions have established principles governing when private areas may be searched incident to an arrest. In 1968, for instance, in the case of *Harris v. United States*, the Court established the *plain-view doctrine.* Under this doctrine, the police may seize an item—evidence or contraband—without a warrant if they are lawfully in a position to view the item and if it is immediately apparent that the item is evidence or contraband. In 1990, in the case of *Maryland v. Buie,* the Court addressed the issue of *protective sweeps.* The Court held that when a warrantless arrest takes place in a suspect's home, officers may make only a "cursory visual inspection" of areas that could harbor an accomplice or a person posing danger to them.

Even a warrantless search not incident to an arrest may be justified under the Supreme Court's *exigent-circumstances* doctrine. It permits police to make warrantless searches in exigent, or emergency, situations. Such situations could include a need to prevent the imminent destruction of evidence, a need to prevent harm to individuals, or the hot pursuit of suspects.

Frequently, law enforcement officers are not hampered by the warrant requirement, because suspects consent to a search. In other words, law enforcement officers who do not have enough evidence to obtain a search warrant, or who either cannot or do not want to take the time and trouble to obtain one, may simply ask a suspect whether they may conduct a search. If the suspect consents voluntarily, the search can be made legally. Law enforcement officers call this strategy "knock and talk." In 1973, in the case of *Schenckloth v. Bustamonte,* the Supreme Court upheld the legality of *consent searches.* The Court also ruled that officers do not have to tell suspects that they have a right to withhold consent.

It is not surprising that consent searches have become the most common type of searches performed by law enforcement officers. They are used frequently in traffic stops and drug interdiction efforts at airports and bus terminals. In the 1980s, as a new tool in the war on drugs, several police departments adopted programs in which officers boarded buses and asked passengers to consent to searches. The practice was challenged in a 1985 Florida case in which a bus passenger had consented to having his luggage searched. When the police found cocaine, the passenger was arrested and subsequently convicted. The Florida Supreme Court ruled that the search was unconstitutional. In 1991, the U.S. Supreme Court reversed the Florida Supreme Court (in *Florida v. Bostick*) and held that the search was not unconstitutional and that law enforcement officers may make such a search without a warrant or suspicion of a crime—as long as the passenger feels free to refuse the search.

Critics argue that, in most cases, consent searches cannot be truly voluntary, even when permission is granted, because most people are intimidated by the police and would have a hard time telling them no. Moreover, most people probably do not know that they may refuse a warrantless search except under the conditions described earlier.

Arrests Without a Warrant Officers may not enter a private home to make a warrantless arrest unless the offense is a serious one and there are exi-

nited States Supreme Court rulings often modify previous decisions. In *California v. Hodari D.* (1991), for example, the Court modified the plurality holding in *Mendenhall* (1980). In *Hodari D.,* the suspect ran from the police, and an officer pursued, thereby creating a circumstance in which a "reasonable person would have believed that she or he was not free to leave" or to disobey the officer's command to halt. There was no physical touching of the suspect. The Court held that in cases involving a "show of authority," as distinguished from physical touching, no "seizure" occurs unless and until the suspect yields or submits to the assertion of authority.

The Rule of Law   **CHAPTER 4**

Mere suspicion The standard of proof with the least certainty; a "gut feeling." With mere suspicion, a law enforcement officer cannot legally even stop a suspect.

Reasonable suspicion A standard of proof that is more than a gut feeling. It includes the ability to articulate reasons for the suspicion. With reasonable suspicion, a law enforcement officer is legally permitted to stop and frisk a suspect.

Frisking Conducting a search for weapons by lightly patting the outside of a suspect's clothing, feeling for hard objects that might be weapons.

The Fourth Amendment requires that a search warrant contain a particular description of the place to be searched and the objects or persons to be seized.

gent circumstances, such as the likely destruction of evidence or the hot pursuit of a felony suspect. This is the same *exigent-circumstances* doctrine that applies to warrantless searches and seizures.

A suspect who is arrested without a warrant and remains confined is entitled to have a judge determine whether there was probable cause for the arrest. Ordinarily, judges must make such a determination within 48 hours of arrest. The purpose of this proceeding is to ensure that the suspect's continuing custody is based on a judicial determination of probable cause and not merely on the police officer's judgment that probable cause supported an arrest.

Standards of Proof As mentioned previously and as specified in the Fourth Amendment, neither search nor arrest warrants can be issued legally unless law enforcement officers convince a judge that there is probable cause to believe that the specific items to be searched for are related to criminal activity and the items will be found in the place to be searched or that a violation of the law has been committed and the person to be arrested committed the violation. Probable cause is one among a number of standards of proof for various criminal justice activities. The amount of proof necessary depends on the activity in question. Figure 4–6 shows various standards of proof, along a continuum of certainty, and the criminal justice activities that correspond to them.

Toward one end of the continuum is the standard of proof with the least certainty: *mere suspicion*. **Mere suspicion** is equivalent to a "gut feeling." In other words, a law enforcement officer may have a feeling that something is amiss—an uncanny knack that some experienced law enforcement officers possess—but be unable to state exactly what it is. With only mere suspicion, law enforcement officers cannot legally even stop a suspect.

A standard of proof with greater certainty is *reasonable suspicion*. **Reasonable suspicion** is more than a gut feeling. It includes the ability to articulate reasons for the suspicion. For example, if a law enforcement officer observes a person in front of a bank wearing a heavy trenchcoat on a hot summer day, the officer might have a reasonable suspicion that something is amiss. The officer could state that idling in front of a bank while wearing a heavy trenchcoat on a hot summer day is suspect behavior. With reasonable suspicion, a law enforcement officer is legally permitted to stop and frisk a suspect. (*Terry v. Ohio*, 1968) **Frisking** a suspect means conducting a search for weapons by lightly patting the outside of a suspect's clothing, feeling for hard objects that might be weapons. Only if an officer feels something that may be a weapon may he or she search inside a pocket or an article of clothing. If evidence of a crime is discovered, the officer is permitted to make an arrest.

The standard of proof needed to conduct a search or to make an arrest is *probable cause*. The conventional

FIGURE 4–6

Standards of Proof and Criminal Justice Activities

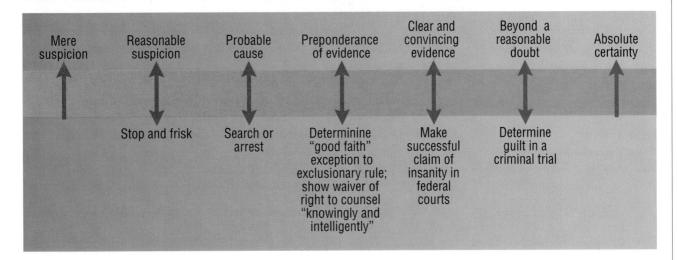

definition of **probable cause** is the amount of proof necessary for a reasonably intelligent person to suspect that a crime has been committed or that items connected with criminal activity can be found in a particular place. Although its meaning is not entirely clear—what is "reasonably intelligent"?—probable cause has a greater degree of certainty than reasonable suspicion. For probable cause, law enforcement officers must have some tangible evidence that a crime has been committed, but that evidence does not have to be admissible at trial. Such evidence might include a tip from a reliable informant or the pungent aroma of marijuana in the air.

The line between probable cause and reasonable suspicion, or even mere suspicion, is a fine one and a matter of interpretation. In practice, there are many gray areas. Consequently, criminal courts and the judicial officers who are authorized to approve search warrants have been given the responsibility of determining whether a standard of proof has been met in a particular situation. As noted, search warrants, for example, must generally be approved by a judicial officer before they can be executed. The way courts and judicial officers determine whether a standard of proof has been met will be discussed in detail in Chapter 7. Here we simply observe that one of the more frustrating aspects of criminal justice for much of the public is that offenders who are factually guilty of their crimes sometimes escape punishment because a judicial officer did not have probable cause to issue a warrant or a police officer did not have probable cause to make an arrest or reasonable suspicion to stop and frisk.

The next standard of proof along the continuum of legal certainty is *preponderance of evidence.* **Preponderance of evidence** is evidence that outweighs the opposing evidence, or sufficient evidence to overcome doubt or speculation. It is the standard of proof necessary to find a defendant liable in a civil lawsuit. This standard is also used in determining whether the *inevitable-discovery rule* applies. That is, the prosecution must prove by a preponderance of the evidence that evidence that actually was uncovered as a result of a constitutional violation would inevitably have been discovered

Probable cause The amount of proof necessary for a reasonably intelligent person to suspect that a crime has been committed or that items connected with criminal activity can be found in a particular place. It is the standard of proof needed to conduct a search or to make an arrest.

Preponderance of evidence Evidence that outweighs the opposing evidence, or sufficient evidence to overcome doubt or speculation.

Clear and convincing evidence
The standard of proof required in some civil cases and, in federal courts, the standard of proof necessary for a defendant to make a successful claim of insanity.

Beyond a reasonable doubt
The standard of proof necessary to find a defendant guilty in a criminal trial.

through lawful means, independently of the action constituting the violation. Finally, preponderance of evidence is the standard of proof by which the state must show in criminal proceedings that the right to counsel has been waived "knowingly and intelligently."

Next along the continuum of certainty is **clear and convincing evidence.** It is the standard of proof required in some civil cases and, in federal courts, the standard of proof necessary for a defendant to make a successful claim of insanity.

Of greater certainty still is proof **beyond a reasonable doubt,** the standard of proof necessary to find a defendant guilty in a criminal trial. Reasonable doubt is the amount of doubt about a defendant's guilt that a reasonable person might have after carefully examining all the evidence. In the case of *Sandoval v. California* (1994), the Supreme Court upheld the following definition of *reasonable doubt:*

> It is *not a mere possible doubt;* because everything relating to human affairs, and *depending on moral evidence,* is open to some possible or imaginary doubt. It is that state of the case which, after the entire comparison and consideration of all the evidence, leaves the minds of the jurors in that they connot say they feel an abiding conviction, *to a moral certainty,* of the truth of the charge. [Emphasis in original.]

Thus, to convict a criminal defendant in a jury trial, a juror must be convinced of guilt by this standard. What is considered reasonable varies, however, and reasonableness is thus a matter of interpretation. Therefore, the procedural laws in most jurisdictions require that 12 citizens all agree that a defendant is guilty beyond a reasonable doubt before that defendant can be convicted. No criminal justice activity requires absolute certainty as a standard of proof.

Exclusionary rule The rule that illegally seized evidence must be excluded from trials in federal courts.

The Exclusionary Rule The **exclusionary rule** was created by the Supreme Court in 1914 in the case of *Weeks v. United States.* In *Weeks,* the Supreme Court held that illegally seized evidence must be excluded from trials in federal courts. In 1961, the Warren Court extended the exclusionary rule to state courts in the case of *Mapp v. Ohio.* The exclusionary rule originally had three primary purposes: (1) to protect individual rights from police misconduct, (2) to prevent police misconduct, and (3) to maintain judicial integrity (for citizens to have faith in the administration of justice, courts should not admit evidence that is tainted by the illegal activities of other criminal justice officials). Today, however, the principal purpose of the exclusionary rule is to deter the police from violating people's Fourth Amendment rights.

MYTH

*M*any criminals escape punishment because of the exclusionary rule.

FACT

*V*ery few criminals escape punishment because of the exclusionary rule.

In practice, when suspects want to claim that incriminating evidence was obtained through an illegal search and seizure, that a confession was obtained without the required warnings or was involuntary, that an identification was made as a result of an invalid police lineup, or that evidence was in some other way illegally obtained, they attempt, through their attorneys, to show at a suppression hearing that the search and seizure, for example, violated the Fourth Amendment. If they are successful in their claims, the evidence that was obtained as a result of the illegal search and seizure will not be admitted at trial.

By the late 1970s, public opinion polls showed that Americans were becoming increasingly alarmed about the problem of crime and especially about what they perceived as the practice of allowing a substantial number of criminals to escape punishment because of legal technicalities. One legal technicality that received much of the public's scorn then was the exclusionary rule. In 1984, responding at least in part to public opinion, the Supreme Court, under Chief Justice Warren Burger, decided three cases that had the practical effect of weakening the exclusionary rule.

In two of the three cases, *United States v. Leon* and *Massachusetts v. Sheppard,* a *good-faith exception* to the *exclusionary rule* was recognized. The Court ruled that as long as the police act in good faith when they request a warrant, the evidence they collect may be used in court, even if the warrant is illegal or defective. In the *Leon* case, the judge's determination of probable cause turned out to be wrong. Prior to *Leon,* such an error by a judge would have been recognized as a violation of the Fourth Amendment, and the evidence seized with the warrant would have been excluded at trial. The Court reasoned that it was unfair to penalize law enforcement officers who conduct searches in which incriminating evidence is found, when those officers conduct the search in good faith that they have a legal warrant. In the *Sheppard* case, the judge had used the wrong form for the warrant. As in *Leon,* the Court reasoned that it was unfair to penalize law enforcement officers, and the public, just because there was a flaw in the warrant, when the officers had conducted a search in good faith and found incriminating evidence.

The third case, *Nix v. Williams,* established an *inevitable-discovery exception* to the *exclusionary rule.* The *Nix* case involved a murderer whom police had tricked into leading them to the hidden body of his victim. Before *Nix,* illegally seized evidence (in the *Nix* case, the body) had to be excluded from trial. In *Nix,* the Court held that evidence obtained in violation of a defendant's rights can be used at trial if the prosecution can show, by a preponderance of the evidence, that the information ultimately or inevitably would have been discovered by lawful means.

Of all the due-process guarantees in the Bill of Rights, those in the Fourth Amendment are the ones likely to require the most interpretation by the Supreme Court in the future. With advances in the technology of surveillance, the Court will have to determine the legality of increasingly more intrusive ways of gathering evidence. The star of a science fiction movie released several years ago was a police helicopter named *Blue Thunder.* The helicopter was able to hover silently outside apartment buildings, record what was being said inside the apartments, and take pictures of what was being done. Although the movie was science fiction, it will probably not be long before law enforcement has such equipment—if it does not have at least some of the equipment already. Will evidence obtained by means of the futuristic surveillance technology of *Blue Thunder* violate the Fourth Amendment prohibition against unreasonable searches and seizures? That decision will ultimately be made by the Supreme Court.

On March 1, 1995, in the case of *Arizona v. Evans,* the Supreme Court ruled that unlawful arrests based on computer errors do not always require the exclusion of evidence seized by police. In an Arizona case, the Court held that a good-faith exception to the exclusionary rule could be made as long as the illegal seizure of evidence was caused by the errors of court employees and not the police. In that case, a Phoenix man who had been stopped for a traffic violation was arrested because a computer record showed an outstanding arrest warrant for some traffic violations. In fact, the warrant had been dropped 17 days earlier, but the action had not been entered into the computer. After the arrest, marijuana was seized from the man's car, and he was arrested for illegal possession.

The Fifth Amendment

The Fifth Amendment reads as follows:

> No person shall be held to answer for a capital, or otherwise infamous crime, unless on a presentment or indictment of a grand jury, except in cases arising in the land or naval forces, or in the militia, when in actual service in time of war or public danger; nor shall any person be subject for the same offense to be twice put in jeopardy of life or limb; nor shall be compelled in any criminal case to be a witness against himself, nor be deprived of life, liberty, or property, without due process of law; nor shall private property be taken for public use without just compensation.

Right to Grand Jury Indictment and Protection Against Double Jeopardy As noted previously, the Fifth Amendment right to a grand jury indictment in felony cases, to be described in detail in Chapter 7, is one of the two Bill of Rights guarantees that has not yet been extended to the states (see *Hurtado v. California*, 1884). The Fifth Amendment protection against **double jeopardy**, on the other hand, has been (see *Benton v. Maryland*, 1969). The protection provides that no person shall "be subject for the same offense to be twice put in jeopardy of life or limb."

When most people think of double jeopardy, they probably think of the classic case in which a defendant cannot be retried for the same crime or a related crime after he or she has been acquitted by a jury. However, the protection against double jeopardy can apply even without an acquittal. Technically, it does not apply until jeopardy has attached. If a trial ends before jeopardy has attached, the prosecution has the right to retry the defendant for the same charge in a new trial. Thus, the key question is, When does jeopardy attach? In jury trials, jeopardy attaches when the entire jury has been selected and sworn in. In a bench trial (a trial before a judge without a jury), jeopardy attaches when the first witness has been sworn in. In cases that are resolved through a guilty plea, jeopardy attaches when the court unconditionally accepts the defendant's plea. Even after jeopardy has attached, however, the prosecution is generally not barred from retrying a defendant when a mistrial has been declared.

The theoretical rationale behind the protection against double jeopardy is that the state should have one and only one chance to convict a defendant charged with a crime. Otherwise, the state could endlessly harass its citizens, as sometimes happens in countries without this protection.

Protection Against Compelled Self-Incrimination Arguably, the most important procedural safeguard in the Fifth Amendment is the protection against compelled **self-incrimination.** The protection guarantees that in criminal cases, suspects or defendants cannot be forced to be witnesses against themselves. The protection is based on the belief that confessions may not be truthful if they are not made voluntarily. It also expresses an intolerance for certain methods used to extract confessions, even if the confessions ultimately prove to be reliable. A **confession** is an admission by a person accused of a crime that he or she committed the offense charged. According to the Supreme Court's **doctrine of fundamental fairness,** confessions are

---

Double jeopardy The trying of a defendant a second time for the same offense when jeopardy attached in the first trial and a mistrial was not declared.

Self-incrimination Being a witness against oneself. If forced, it is a violation of the Fifth Amendment.

Confession An admission by a person accused of a crime that he or she committed the offense charged.

Doctrine of fundamental fairness The rule that makes confessions inadmissible in criminal trials if they were obtained by means of either psychological manipulation or "third-degree" methods.

inadmissible in criminal trials if they were obtained by means of either psychological manipulation or "third-degree" methods—for example, beatings, subjection to unreasonably long periods of questioning, or other physical tactics.

Although the Fifth Amendment protection against compelled self-incrimination has long been observed in federal trials, it was not until the 1960s, in the case of *Malloy v. Hogan* (1964), that the Fifth Amendment protection against compelled self-incrimination was extended to trials in state courts. In *Miranda v. Arizona* (1966), the Court broadened the protection against compelled self-incrimination to cover nearly all custodial police interrogations. (Custodial police interrogations essentially mean questionings that take place after an arrest or the functional equivalent of an arrest; they may or may not take place at the police station.) In *Miranda,* the Court added that confessions obtained without suspects' being notified of their specific rights could not be admitted as evidence. Perhaps even more important, it established specific procedural safeguards that had to be followed to avoid violation of the protection against compelled self-incrimination. The court said:

> [P]rocedural safeguards must be employed to protect the privilege [against self-incrimination], and unless other fully effective means are adopted to notify the person of his right of silence and to assure that the exercise of the right will be scrupulously honored, the following measures are required. [The suspect] must be warned prior to any questioning (1) that he has the right to remain silent, (2) that anything he says can be used against him in a court of law, (3) that he has the right to the presence of an attorney, and (4) that if he cannot afford an attorney one will be appointed for him prior to any questioning if he so desires.

In the case of *Rhode Island v. Innis* (1980), the U.S. Supreme Court stated:

[T]he term "interrogation" under *Miranda* refers not only to express questioning, but also to any words or actions on the part of the police (other than those normally attendant to arrest and custody) that the police should know are reasonably likely to elicit an incriminating response from the suspect.

The first time the Supreme Court held that a coerced confession, brutally beaten out of the suspect, was inadmissible in a state trial was in 1936, in the case of *Brown v. Mississippi.* However, in the *Brown* case, the Court did not find that the coerced confession violated the Fifth Amendment protection against self-incrimination. Rather, the Court found that it violated the Fourteenth Amendment right to due process.

The Fifth Amendment protection against compelled self-incrimination applies to trial procedures as well as police interrogations.

However, if an individual being questioned is not yet in custody, the *Miranda* warnings do not have to be given. Also, volunteered confessions do not violate *Miranda* or the Fifth Amendment.

The Fifth Amendment protection against compelled self-incrimination has been weakened recently by the Supreme Court. For example, in *New York v. Quarles* (1984), the Supreme Court created a public-safety exception to the Fifth Amendment protection. Also, in *Arizona v. Fulminante* (1991), the Court ruled that improper use of a coerced confession is a harmless trial error if other evidence is strong enough to convict the defendant. The burden of proof is on the state to show that a coerced confession is harmless error. The case involved a defendant who had been sentenced to death for killing his 11-year-old stepdaughter. While in prison, the defendant confessed to an FBI informant after the informant promised to protect the defendant from other inmates. Prior to *Fulminante*, such a conviction would most likely have been reversed on appeal because of the use of the coerced confession.

The Fifth Amendment protection against compelled self-incrimination also applies to trial procedures. Not only do defendants have a right to refuse to answer any questions put to them by the prosecution during a trial (by "pleading the fifth"), but they also have the right not to take the witness stand in the first place. Moreover, the prosecution is forbidden to comment on the defendant's silence or refusal to take the witness stand. This protection rests on a basic legal principle: the government bears the burden of proof. Defendants are not obligated to help the government prove they committed a crime. In 1964 and 1965, those Fifth Amendment rights were extended to defendants being tried in state courts in the cases of *Malloy v. Hogan* and *Griffin v. California*, respectively.

The Sixth Amendment

The Sixth Amendment reads as follows:

> In all criminal prosecutions, the accused shall enjoy the right to a speedy and public trial, by an impartial jury of the State and district wherein the crime shall have been committed, which district shall have been previously ascertained by law, and to be informed of the nature and cause of the accusation; to be confronted with the witnesses against him; to have compulsory process for obtaining witnesses in his favor, and to have the assistance of counsel for his defense.

Right to a Speedy and Public Trial The Sixth Amendment right to a speedy and public trial applies directly to trials in federal courts. It was extended to trials in state courts in 1967, in the case of *Klopfer v. North Carolina* (right to a speedy trial), and in 1942, in the case of *In re Oliver* (right to a public trial). Delays in a trial can severely hamper a defendant's case if favorable witnesses have died, have moved and cannot be found, or have forgotten what they saw. Delays can also adversely affect defendants by forcing them to remain in jail for long periods of time while awaiting trial. A long wait in jail can be a very stressful and sometimes dangerous experience.

In determining what constitutes a speedy trial, the Supreme Court has created a balancing test that weighs both the defendant's and the prosecution's behavior (see *Barker v. Wingo*, 1972). Thus, the reason for the delay in a trial is critical. For example, a search for a missing witness would probably be considered an acceptable reason for delay. Court congestion, on the other hand, typically would not.

The acceptable length of delay in a trial also depends partly on the nature of the charge. In *Barker*, the Court held that "the delay that can be tolerated for an ordinary street crime is considerably less than for a serious, complex conspiracy charge." There has been great variation in the length of delay tolerated by specific courts. However, delays of less than five months have generally been considered acceptable, but delays of eight months or longer have not.

The Sixth Amendment right to a public trial means that a trial must be open to the public, but it need not be open to all who want to attend. Obviously, the number of people who can attend a trial depends on the size of the courtroom. The right would be violated only if the trial were held, for example, in a prison or in a closed judge's chambers against a defendant's wishes. Defendants have no right to a private trial.

A trial may be closed to the public if the defendant's right to a public trial is outweighed by "a compelling state interest." However, before a trial is closed, "the party seeking to close the hearing must advance an overriding interest that is likely to be prejudiced, the closure must be no broader than necessary to protect that interest, the trial court must consider reasonable alternatives to closing the proceeding, and it must make findings adequate to support the closure" (*Waller v. Georgia*, 1984). In some cases, parts of a trial may be closed—for example, to protect the identity of an undercover informant during his or her testimony.

Right to Impartial Jury of the State and District Wherein the Crime Shall Have Been Committed

The right to an impartial jury promises not only that a jury will be unbiased, but also that there will be a jury trial. As interpreted by the Supreme Court, this right means that defendants charged with felonies or with misdemeanors punishable by more than six months' imprisonment are entitled to be tried before a jury. The right was extended to the states in 1968, in the case of *Duncan v. Louisiana*. Most states also allow defendants to be tried by a jury for less serious misdemeanors, but states are not constitutionally required to do so.

For practical purposes, the right to an impartial jury is achieved by providing a representative jury, that is, a jury randomly selected from a fair cross-section of the community. However, whether members of such a jury will be impartial in a particular case is a question that defies an easy answer. Juries will be discussed more extensively in Chapter 7.

Finally, the Sixth Amendment guarantees the specific **venue,** or the place of trial. (Venue is also mentioned in the Constitution in Article III, Section 2: "Trial shall be held in the State where the said crimes shall have been committed. . . .") The venue of a trial must be geographically appropriate. Generally, a crime must be tried in the jurisdiction—the politically defined geographical area—in which it was committed. However, if a defense attorney believes that a client cannot get a fair trial in the appropriate venue because of adverse publicity or for some other reason, the attorney can ask the court for a change of venue. If the change of venue is granted, the trial will be moved to another location (within the state in cases of state law violations), where, presumably, the adverse publicity or other factors are not as great.

FYI

Federal courts are now regulated by the Speedy Trial Act of 1974, which specifies two separate time limits: one for the period between arrest and charging, and the other for the period between charging and trial. The act stipulates that, generally, a delay between arrest and charging (that is, the filing of an indictment or information) may be no more than 30 days, and a delay between charging and trial may be no more than 70 days. The act also specifies periods of delay that do not count—for example, delay due to the unavailability of an essential witness or continuances (that is, postponements) that serve "the ends of justice." If the delay, excluding periods of delay that do not count, is longer than the number of days allowed, the court must dismiss the charges. A dismissal *with prejudice,* which is given when there are no good reasons for the delay, prevents the reprosecution of the case. A dismissal *without prejudice* gives the prosecutor the option of prosecuting the case again.

Venue The place of the trial. It must be geographically appropriate.

Subpoena A written order issued by a court that requires a person to appear at a certain time and place to give testimony. It can also require that documents and objects be made available for examination by the court.

Right to Be Informed of the Nature and Cause of the Accusation The right to notice and a hearing is the very core of what is meant by due process. In *Twining v. New Jersey* (1908), for example, the Supreme Court held that "due process requires . . . that there shall be notice and opportunity for hearing given the parties. . . . [T]hese two fundamental conditions . . . seem to be universally prescribed in all systems of law established by civilized countries." The reason for the right is to prevent the practice, common in some countries, of holding suspects indefinitely without telling them why they are being held.

Right to Confront Opposing Witnesses The Sixth Amendment right to confront opposing witnesses was extended to trials in state courts in 1965, in the case of *Pointer v. Texas*. In essence, it means that defendants have a right to be present during their trials (otherwise, they could not confront opposing witnesses) and to cross-examine witnesses against them. However, the right to be present during the trial may be forfeited by a defendant's disruptive behavior. Thus, if a defendant continues to scream, use profanity, or refuse to sit quietly after being warned by the judge, the judge may have the defendant removed from the trial (see *Illinois v. Allen*, 1970).

Right to Compulsory Process for Obtaining Favorable Witnesses This right ensures a defendant the use of the subpoena power of the court to compel the testimony of any witnesses who may have information useful to the defense. A **subpoena** is a written order issued by a court that requires a person to appear at a certain time and place to give testimony. It can also require that documents and objects be made available for examination by the court. Even though the right to compulsory process for obtaining favorable witnesses was already applicable in many states because of its inclusion in state constitutions and laws, the Supreme Court officially extended it to state trials in 1967, in the case of *Washington v. Texas*.

Right to Counsel The Sixth Amendment right to privately retained and paid-for counsel has existed in federal courts since the ratification of the Bill of Rights. Criminal defendants in state courts did not gain the right until 1954. In the case of *Chandler v. Fretag*, the Supreme Court held that the right to a privately retained lawyer is "unqualified," that is, as long as a criminal defendant (or suspect) can afford to hire an attorney, he or she has the right to be represented by that attorney, not only at trial, but at any stage of the criminal justice process. But what if a criminal defendant were indigent, lacking the funds to hire an attorney? It was not until 1938, in the case of *Johnson v. Zerbst*, that the Supreme Court first extended the Sixth Amendment right to counsel to indigent defendants facing felony charges in federal trials. Until then, indigent defendants did without. Indigent defendants facing felony charges in state courts, for which imprisonment could be the result of conviction, had to wait another 25 years before the right to counsel was extended to them. That right was granted in the famous case of *Gideon v. Wainwright* (1963). Finally, in 1972, in the case of *Argersinger v. Hamlin*, the Court extended the Sixth Amendment right to counsel to defendants in misdemeanor trials in which a sentence to jail might result. Thus, as a result of those decisions, any person charged with a crime which could result in incar-

CHAPTER 4   *The Rule of Law*

ceration is entitled to legal representation. If the person cannot afford to hire an attorney, then the court is required to appoint one.

In other Supreme Court decisions, the Sixth Amendment right to counsel has been extended to indigents at additional *critical stages,* to be described in Chapter 7 and elsewhere in this book; and other circumstances in the administration of justice. Those include (by date of Supreme Court decision):

1. Arraignment, under most circumstances (*Hamilton v. Alabama,* 1961).

2. The plea bargaining process (*Carnley v. Cochran,* 1962).

3. Initial appearances where defendants may be compelled to make decisions that may later be formally used against them (*White v. Maryland,* 1963).

4. A first appeal that is a matter of right, that is, an appeal made available to all convicted defendants (*Douglas v. California,* 1963).

5. Questioning by law enforcement officers of suspects in police custody (*Escobedo v. Illinois,* 1964).

6. Proceedings after a grand jury indictment (*Massiah v. United States,* 1964).

7. Postindictment police lineups (*Gilbert v. California,* 1967).

8. Sentencing (*Mempa v. Rhay,* 1967).

9. Juvenile court proceedings in which children face possible institutional commitment (*In re Gault,* 1967).

10. Preliminary hearings (*Coleman v. Alabama,* 1970).

11. A psychiatric examination used by the prosecution to show that a murder defendant remains dangerous and should receive the death penalty (*Estelle v. Smith,* 1981).

To date, the Court has not extended the right to counsel to (1) preindictment lineups, (2) booking, (3) grand jury investigations, or (4) appeals after the first one.

The Sixth Amendment not only guarantees the right to counsel in the areas to which it has been extended, it also guarantees the right to the "effective assistance of counsel." However, it was not until 1984, in the case of *Strickland v. Washington,* that the Supreme Court first established standards to define "ineffective assistance of counsel." The Court ruled that two facts must be proven to show that counsel was ineffective: (1) that counsel's performance was "deficient," meaning that counsel was not a "reasonably competent attorney" or that his or her performance was below the standard commonly expected, and (2) that the deficiencies in the attorney's performance were prejudicial to the defense, meaning that there is a "reasonable probability that, but for the counsel's unprofessional errors, the result of the proceeding would have been different." In other words, not only must it be shown that an attorney was incompetent, it must also be shown that the incompetence led to the final result. Thus, if the defendant were clearly guilty of the crime with which he or she was charged, it would most likely be impossible to win a claim of "ineffective assistance of counsel."

Finally, the right to counsel may be waived, but only if the waiver is made "knowingly and intelligently." The burden of proof is on the state to show, by a preponderance of the evidence, that the waiver was made according to the aforementioned standards (see *Colorado v. Connelly*, 1986). Thus, the Sixth Amendment has also been interpreted to mean that defendants have the right to represent themselves, that is, to conduct the defense *pro se* (see *Faretta v. California*, 1975). However, if defendants choose to represent themselves, they cannot claim later, on appeal, that their defense suffered from ineffective assistance of counsel.

Careers in Criminal Justice

PARALEGAL

Paralegals, also called *legal assistants,* work directly under the supervision of lawyers. Paralegals perform many of the tasks lawyers perform, such as fact investigation, legal research, document preparation, file organization, and client correspondence.

Besides criminal law, paralegals may work in such areas as civil litigation, family law, corporate law, commercial law, and real estate law. Paralegals also work in the public sector, at the federal, state, and local levels. For example, many paralegals are employed by the courts, the prosecutor's office, and the public defender's office.

Employers generally require formal paralegal training. Most programs are completed in two years, although employers increasingly prefer graduates of four-year programs. Salaries vary with education and experience and whether employment is in the private sector or the public sector.

CRIMINAL DEFENSE AND PROSECUTING ATTORNEYS

Defense and prosecuting attorneys act as advocates and advisors to their respective clients. They represent their clients in criminal trials by presenting evidence that supports their positions in court and in plea negotiations.

Attorneys who work for state attorneys general, prosecutors, public defenders, and courts play a key role in the criminal justice process. At the federal level, attorneys investigate criminal cases for the Department of Justice. At all government levels, attorneys involved with criminal matters help establish enforcement procedures and argue criminal cases at trial.

To practice law in the courts of any state or other jurisdiction, a person must be licensed, or admitted to the bar of that jurisdiction, after passing a written bar examination. To qualify for the bar examination in most states, an applicant must complete college and graduate from a law school approved by the American Bar Association (ABA).

Salaries for criminal defense and prosecuting attorneys depend on academic and professional experience and the type, size, and location of the employer. Lawyers in private practice generally earn more than those in the public sector. Senior partners in some top firms specializing in criminal law have earned more than $1 million annually.

The Eight Amendment

The Eighth Amendment reads as follows:

Excessive bail shall not be required, nor excessive fines imposed, nor cruel and unusual punishments inflicted.

Protection Against Excessive Bail and Fines The Eighth Amendment protection against excessive bail and fines is the second Bill of Rights guarantee dealing directly with criminal justice that has not been extended to the states. (The first is the right to a grand jury indictment in felony cases.) However, there is a good possibility that the protection against excessive bail will be incorporated and made applicable to state-level criminal cases when the issue is finally brought before the Supreme Court.

In any event, it is important to note that the Eighth Amendment to the Constitution does not require that bail be granted to all suspects or defendants, only that the amount of bail not be excessive. What constitutes excessive bail is determined by several factors, including the nature and circumstances of the offense, the weight of evidence against the suspect or defendant, the character of the suspect or defendant, and the ability of the suspect or defendant to pay bail. The subject of bail will be discussed more fully in Chapter 7.

The Eighth Amendment also prohibits excessive fines. What is excessive depends on the seriousness of the crime. For example, in a conviction for illegal possession of a small amount of marijuana, a defendant's having to forfeit his or his home might be considered an excessive fine.

Protection Against Cruel and Unusual Punishment The final prohibition of the Eighth Amendment is against "cruel and unusual punishment." That prohibition was extended to trials in state courts in 1962, in *Robinson v. California*. Generally, discussions of this issue involve the practice of capital punishment, or the death penalty, which will be discussed in detail in Chapter 8. Here we will provide only a brief history of the definition of cruel and unusual punishment.

For approximately 120 years after the adoption of the Bill of Rights, the Supreme Court employed a fixed, historical meaning for "cruel and unusual punishment." In other words, the Court interpreted the concept's meaning in light of the practices that were authorized and were in use at the time the Eighth Amendment was adopted (1791). Thus, only the most barbarous punishments and tortures were prohibited. Capital punishment itself was not prohibited, because there was explicit reference to it in the Fifth Amendment and it was in use when the Eighth Amendment was adopted.

The Court, in *Wilkerson v. Utah* (1878), provided examples of punishments that were prohibited by the Eighth Amendment because they involved "torture" or "unnecessary cruelty." They included punishments in which the criminal "was embowelled alive, beheaded, and quartered." In another case, *In re Kemmler* (1890), the Court expanded the meaning of cruel and unusual punishment to include punishments that "involve torture or lingering death . . . something more than the mere extinguishment of life." The Court also provided some examples of punishments that would be prohibited under that standard: "burning at the stake, crucifixion, breaking on the wheel, or the like."

In 1910, in the noncapital case of *Weems v. United States,* the Supreme Court abandoned its fixed, historical definition of cruel and unusual punishment and created a new one. Weems was a U.S. government official in the

Philippines who was convicted of making two false accounting entries, amounting to 616 pesos.[10] He was sentenced to 15 years of hard labor and was forced to wear chains on his ankles and wrists. After completing his sentence, he was to be under surveillance for life, and he was to lose his voting rights as well. Weems argued that his punishment was disproportionate to his crime, and therefore, cruel and unusual.[11]

The Court agreed with Weems and, breaking with tradition, held "(1) that the meaning of the Eighth Amendment is not restricted to the intent of the Framers, (2) that the Eighth Amendment bars punishments that are excessive, and (3) that what is excessive is not fixed in time but changes with evolving social conditions."[12] Thus, the Court no longer interpreted the concept of cruel and unusual punishment in the context of punishments in use when the Eighth Amendment was adopted. Instead, it chose to interpret the concept in the context of "evolving social conditions."

The Court further clarified its position nearly 50 years later, in another noncapital case, *Trop v. Dulles* (1958). As punishment for desertion during World War II, Trop was stripped of his U.S. citizenship.[13] In reviewing the case on appeal, the Court ruled that the punishment was cruel and unusual because it was an affront to basic human dignity. Noting that the "dignity of man" was "the basic concept underlying the Eighth Amendment," the Court held that Trop's punishment exceeded "the limits of civilized standards." Referring to the earlier *Weems* case, the Court emphasized that "the limits of civilized standards . . . draws its meaning from the evolving standards of decency that mark the progress of a maturing society." Those "evolving standards of decency" are, in turn, determined by "objective indicators, such as the enactments of legislatures as expressions of 'the will of the people,' the decisions of juries, and the subjective moral judgments of members of the Supreme Court itself."[14] In short, it appears that a punishment enacted by a legislature and imposed by a judge or jury will *not* be considered cruel and unusual, as long as the U.S. Supreme Court determines that (1) it is not grossly disproportionate to the magnitude of the crime, (2) it has been imposed for the same offense in other jurisdictions, and (3) it has been imposed for other offenses in the same jurisdiction (see *Solem v. Helm*, 1983; *Harmelin v. Michigan*, 1991).

Protecting the Accused From Miscarriages of Justice

The legal system of the United States is unique in the world in the number of procedural rights that it provides people suspected or accused of crimes. The primary reason for procedural rights is to protect innocent people, as much as possible, from being arrested, charged, convicted, or punished for crimes they did not commit. One of the basic tenets of our legal system is that a person is considered innocent until proven guilty. However, even with arguably the most highly developed system of due-process rights in the world, people continue to be victims of miscarriages of justice.

Unfortunately, there is no official record of miscarriages of justice, so it is impossible to determine precisely how many actually occur each year. Nevertheless, in an effort to provide some idea of the extent of the problem, a study was conducted of wrongful convictions—miscarriages of justice at just one of the stages in the administration of justice.[15] In the study, *wrongful convictions* were defined as

> cases in which a person [is] convicted of a felony but later . . . found innocent beyond a reasonable doubt, generally due to a confession by the actual offender, evidence that had been available but was not sufficiently used at the time of conviction, new evidence that was not previously available, and other factors.[16]

The conclusions of the study were based on the findings of a survey. All attorneys general in the United States and its territories were surveyed, and in Ohio, all presiding judges of common pleas courts, all county prosecutors, all county public defenders, all county sheriffs, and the chiefs of police of seven major cities were also surveyed. The authors of the study conservatively estimated that approximately 0.5 percent of all felony convictions are in error.[17] In other words, of every 1,000 persons convicted of felonies in the United States, about 5 are probably innocent. The authors believe that the frequency of error is probably higher in less serious felonies and misdemeanors.[18]

Although an error rate of 0.5 percent may not seem high, consider that in 1996, a typical year, approximately 15 million people were arrested in the United States.[19] Assuming conservatively that 50 percent of all people arrested are convicted[20]—about 7.5 million convictions in 1996—then approximately 37,500 people were probably wrongfully convicted!

Eyewitness misidentification is the most important factor contributing to wrongful convictions.[21] The second and third most important contributing factors are police and prosecutorial errors, respectively. Overzealous police officers and prosecutors, convinced that a suspect or defendant is guilty, may prompt witnesses, suggest to witnesses what may have occurred at the time of the crime, conceal or fabricate evidence, or even commit perjury.[22] Another factor contributing to wrongful convictions is guilty pleas made "voluntarily" by innocent defendants.[23] Innocent defendants are more likely to plead guilty to crimes they did not commit when they are faced with multiple charges and when the probability of severe punishment is great.[24] They are also more likely to plead guilty to crimes they did not commit when they are mentally incompetent.[25]

When the charge is a less serious one, innocent people who are unable to post bail sometimes admit guilt to be released from jail immediately.[26] For many people, release from jail is more important than a minor criminal record. Besides, it is often difficult to prove one's innocence. (Remember, in the United States the prosecution is required to prove, beyond a reasonable doubt, that defendants are guilty. Defendants are not supposed to have to prove their innocence.) Problems faced by innocent people wrongly accused of crimes include inability to establish an alibi; identification by witnesses who swear they saw the defendant commit the crime (even though they are wrong); a lawyer who lacks the skill, time, or resources to mount a good defense; and a lawyer who is unconvinced of the defendant's innocence.[27] Inadequate legal representation is one of the most important factors in wrongful convictions in death penalty cases.[28]

The Rule of Law   CHAPTER 4

Other factors contributing to wrongful convictions are community pressures, especially in interracial and rape cases; false accusations; knowledge of a defendant's prior criminal record; judicial errors, bias, or neglect of duty; errors made by medical examiners and forensic experts; and errors in criminal record keeping and computerized information systems.[29] In short, numerous factors can cause wrongful convictions. And remember, the foregoing discussion addresses only wrongful convictions; it does not consider wrongful arrests or other miscarriages of justice.

Despite such miscarriages of justice, many people still resent the provision of procedural safeguards to criminal suspects. The accusation is frequently made that procedural rights protect criminals and penalize victims—that many criminals escape conviction and punishment because of procedural technicalities. For example, a driving force behind the good-faith and inevitable-discovery exceptions was the belief that a substantial number of criminal offenders escaped punishment because of the exclusionary rule. The available evidence, however, does not support the belief. One of the most thorough studies of the effect of the exclusionary rule was conducted by the National Institute of Justice (NIJ).[30] The NIJ study examined felony cases in California between 1976 and 1979—a period during which the American public was becoming increasingly alarmed about the problem of crime and especially about what was perceived as the practice of allowing a substantial number of criminals to escape punishment because of legal technicalities. The study found that only a tiny fraction (fewer than 0.5 percent) of the felony cases reaching the courts were dismissed because of the exclusionary rule. It is important to emphasize that the study examined only the cases that reached the courts. It excluded cases that prosecutors elected not to pursue to trial because they assumed that the exclusionary rule would make the cases impossible to win. However, other studies show that although there is some variation between jurisdictions, fewer than 1 percent of cases overall are dropped by prosecutors before trial because of search and seizure problems.[32] Interestingly, 71.5 percent of the California cases affected by the exclusionary rule involved drug charges. The problem in most of the drug cases was that in the absence of complaining witnesses, overaggressive law enforcement officers had to engage in illegal behavior to obtain evidence.

A study of the effect of the exclusionary rule at the federal level was conducted by the General Accounting Office (GAO).[33] The GAO examined 2,804 cases handled by 38 different U.S. attorneys in July and August of 1978. The GAO found results similar to those found by the NIJ in California. In only 1.3 percent of the nearly 3,000 cases was evidence excluded in the federal courts. Again, it is important to emphasize that the study included only cases that went to trial. However, as noted earlier, evidence shows that, overall, fewer than 1 percent of cases are dropped by prosecutors before trial because of search and seizure problems. It is important to understand, moreover, that having evidence excluded from trial does not necessarily mean that a case is impossible to win and that the defendant will escape punishment. A defendant may still be convicted on the basis of evidence that was not illegally obtained.

The *Miranda* mandates, like the exclusionary rule, are also viewed by many people as legal technicalities that allow guilty criminals to escape punishment. That view is fortified by Justice Byron White's dissent in *Miranda*: "In some unknown number of cases the rule will return a killer, a rapist or other criminal to the streets." No doubt, Justice White's warning is true, but the evidence suggests that only a very small percentage of cases are lost as a result of illegal confessions. In one large survey, for example, fewer than 1 percent of all cases were thrown out because of confessions illegally obtained.[34]

In another study of decisions made by the Indiana Court of Appeals or the Indiana Supreme Court from November 6, 1980, through August 1, 1986, the researchers found that in only 12 of 2,354 cases (0.51 percent) was a conviction overturned because of the failure of the police to correctly implement the *Miranda* safeguards.[35] In only 213 of the 2,354 cases (9 percent) was a claim even made about improper interrogation procedures by the police, and in 201 of those 213 cases, the conviction was affirmed by the appellate court, resulting in a reversal rate of 5.6 percent for the cases raising a *Miranda* question.[36]

The authors of that study speculated on possible reasons for the low rate of successful appeals. One was that the police routinely comply with the *Miranda* decision.[37] In fact, most police support *Miranda* and the other reforms because it makes them appear more professional. The second possible reason was that the police are able to solve most cases without having to question suspects.[38] Studies show that the *Miranda* warnings rarely stop suspects from confessing anyway. Many suspects attempt to clear themselves in the eyes of the police and end up incriminating themselves instead; other suspects simply do not understand that they have a right to remain silent.[39] Third, the police are able to evade *Miranda* by using more sophisticated strategies, such as skillfully suggesting that suspects volunteer confessions or casually talking with suspects in the back of squad cars.[41] And, fourth, prosecutors, knowing that they cannot win cases involving illegal interrogations, screen them out before trial or settle them through alternative means, such as plea bargaining.[42] However, as with the exclusionary rule, fewer than 1 percent of cases overall are dismissed or handled in other ways by prosecutors because of *Miranda*.[43] In short, the available evidence suggests that the effects of the exclusionary rule in both 4th and 5th Amendment contexts have been minor.[44]

MYTH

Many criminals escape punishment because of the Supreme Court's decision in Miranda v. Arizona.

FACT

Very few criminals escape punishment because of that decision.

4 Review and Applications

CHAPTER OBJECTIVE 1

There are two general types of law practiced in the United States—criminal and civil. Criminal law is a formal means of social control that involves the use of rules that are interpreted, and are enforceable, by the courts of a political community. The violation of a criminal law is a crime and is considered an offense against the state. Civil law is a means of resolving conflicts between individuals. The violation of a civil law is a tort—an injury, damage, or wrongful act—and is considered a private matter between individuals.

CHAPTER OBJECTIVE 2

There are two types of criminal law—substantive and procedural. Substantive law defines criminal offenses and their penalties. Procedural law specifies the ways in which substantive laws are administered. Procedural law is concerned with due process of law—the rights of people suspected of or charged with crimes.

CHAPTER OBJECTIVE 3

Ideally, "good" criminal law should possess five features: (1) politicality, (2) specificity, (3) regularity, (4) uniformity, and (5) penal sanction.

CHAPTER OBJECTIVE 4

Criminal law is the result of a political process in which rules are created by human beings to prohibit or regulate the behavior of other human beings. Formal, written laws are a relatively recent phenomenon; the first were created only about 5000 years ago.

CHAPTER OBJECTIVE 5

The criminal law of the United States is, for the most part, derived from the laws of England and is the product of constitutions and legislative bodies, common law, and administrative or regulatory agency rules and decisions.

CHAPTER OBJECTIVE 6

The courts, especially the U.S. Supreme Court, have selectively defined the procedural rights of persons accused of crimes as guaranteed by the U.S. Constitution. The procedural rights, or due-process rights, are found in the Fourth, Fifth, Sixth, and Eighth Amendments to the Constitution. Through its power of judicial review, the Supreme Court has overturned federal and state actions and has reversed some of its earlier decisions. Some Supreme Court decisions expanded the rights of accused persons; other decisions limited the actions of law enforcement personnel; still other decisions relaxed the limits that had been placed on the police. Interpretations by the Supreme Court are changeable because of changes in the Court's composition. As justices die or retire, new ones are appointed. New justices bring different legal views to the Court, and, over time, shift its position on some issues.

CHAPTER OBJECTIVE 7

The Fourth Amendment protects persons from unreasonable searches and seizures (including arrests). Under most circumstances, it requires that a judge issue a search warrant authorizing law officers to search for and seize evidence of criminal activity, but the warrant can be issued only when there is *probable cause.* In 1914, the Supreme Court adopted the *exclusionary rule,* which barred evidence seized illegally from being used in a criminal trial; in 1961, the rule was made applicable to the states. Subsequent Supreme Court decisions have narrowed the application of the exclusionary rule. The Fourth Amendment also protects persons from warrantless searches and seizures in places where they have a legitimate right to expect privacy. The protection, however, does not extend to every place where a person has a legitimate right to be. The Court has permitted stopping and searching an automobile when there is probable cause to believe the car is carrying something illegal.

CHAPTER OBJECTIVE 8

The Fifth Amendment provides many procedural protections, the most important of which is the protection against compelled self-incrimination. This protection was extended to most police custodial interrogations in the 1966 case of *Miranda v. Arizona*. According to *Miranda*, police custody is threatening and confessions obtained during custody can be admitted into evidence only if suspects have been (1) advised of their constitutional right to remain silent, (2) warned that what they say can be used against them in a trial, (3) informed of the right to have an attorney paid for by the state if they cannot afford one and to have the attorney present during interrogation, and (4) told of the right to terminate the interrogation at any time. Other due-process rights in the Fifth Amendment are the right to a grand jury indictment in felony cases (in federal court) and protection against double jeopardy.

CHAPTER OBJECTIVE 9

Many due-process rights are provided by the Sixth Amendment: the right to a speedy and public trial, the right to an impartial jury of the state and district where the crime occurred, the right to be informed of the nature and cause of the accusation, the right to confront opposing witnesses, the right to compulsory process for obtaining favorable witnesses, and the right to counsel. In the 1963 case of *Gideon v. Wainwright,* the Supreme Court extended the right to counsel to any poor state defendant charged with a felony.

CHAPTER OBJECTIVE 10

The Eighth Amendment protects against "cruel and unusual punishment." The Supreme Court has rarely ruled on this provision, generally approving a punishment as long as it has been enacted by a legislature, it has been imposed by a judge or jury, and the Court determines that (1) it is not grossly disproportionate to the magnitude of the crime, (2) it has been imposed for the same offense in other jurisdictions, and (3) it has been imposed for other offenses in the same jurisdiction. The Eighth Amendment also protects against excessive bail and fines, but those protections have not been made binding on state courts.

CHAPTER OBJECTIVE 11

The primary reason for procedural rights is to protect innocent people, as much as possible, from being arrested, charged, convicted, or punished for crimes they did not commit. However, even with arguably the most highly developed system of procedural, or due-process, rights in the world, people in the United States continue to be victims of miscarriages of justice.

KEY TERMS

criminal law, p. 106
penal code, p. 106
tort, p. 106
civil law, p. 106
substantive law, p. 106
procedural law, p. 106
due process of law, p. 107
politicality, p. 107
specificity, p. 107
regularity, p. 107
uniformity, p. 108
penal sanction, p. 108

precedent, p. 113
stare decisis, p. 114
searches, p. 117
seizures, p. 117
warrant, p. 117
arrest, p. 117
contraband, p. 119
mere suspicion, p. 122
reasonable suspicion, p. 122
frisking, p. 122
probable cause, p. 123
preponderance of evidence, p. 123

clear and convicting evidence, p. 124
beyond a reasonable doubt, p. 124
exclusionary rule, p. 124
double jeopardy, p. 126
self-incrimination, p. 126
confession, p. 126
doctrine of fundamental fairness, p. 126
venue, p. 129
subpoena, p. 130

The Rule of Law   CHAPTER 4

1. How does one know whether a particular offense is a *crime* or a *tort*?

2. How did the institution of the *eyre* contribute to the development of American criminal law?

3. What is the importance of the Magna Carta for American criminal law?

4. To what jurisdiction do federal and state criminal statutes (and local ordinances) apply?

5. What is *stare decisis*?

6. Why did it take nearly one hundred years after the ratification of the Fourteenth Amendment before suspects charged with crimes at the state level were afforded most of the same due-process protections as people charged with crimes at the federal level?

7. What are *searches* and *seizures*?

8. What is an *arrest*?

9. What two conclusions must be supported by substantial and trustworthy evidence before either a search warrant or an arrest warrant is issued? (The two conclusions are different for each type of warrant.)

10. In *Chimel v. California* (1969), what limitations did the Supreme Court place on searches incident to an arrest?

11. What is *probable cause*?

12. Today, what is the principal purpose of the exclusionary rule?

13. To what critical stages in the administration of justice has the Sixth Amendment right to counsel been extended, and to what critical stages has it not been extended?

14. What two conditions must be met to show that counsel was ineffective?

15. What are some of the factors that contribute to wrongful convictions?

16. Do many criminals escape conviction and punishment because of procedural technicalities, such as the exclusionary rule or the *Miranda* mandates?

1. By yourself or as part of a group, create a law. Choose a behavior that is currently not against the law in your community, and write a statute to prohibit it. Make sure that all five features of "good" criminal laws are included. (If this is a group exercise, decide by majority vote any issue for which there is not a consensus.) Critique the outcome.

2. Make an oral or written evaluation of the good-faith and inevitable-discovery exceptions to the exclusionary rule. Has the Supreme Court gone too far in modifying the exclusionary rule? Defend your answer.

3. **INTERNET** Access the topic "The Timetable of World Legal History" (at **www.wwlia.org/hist.htm**), which provides brief descriptions of important historical legal developments. (This web site also provides links to other sources of legal information.) Choose among the available topics (for instance, the actual text of the Magna Carta), and write a summary of the information you find.

Criminal Justice.

The exclusionary rule which provides that evidence obtained in violation of the search & seizure provisions shall be excluded → (1) IT is a rule that was framed by the courts / ② Prohibits the use of such evidence for any purpose. (Desregard 2).

The exclusionary rule as stated by the supreme court was Initially applicable to → the Federal courts but Not the states.

In recent times efforts have been made to modify the exclusionary rule - One of the arguments advanced ~~today~~ for modifying this rule is that police officers are more informed today & harsh methods for policing the police are no longer justifield.

In the case of Mapp - v - Ohio evidence was located after a search which the Ohio Authorities admitted was in violation of the federal constitution. this ruling made it mandatory that state officials comply with the minimum search & seizure Standards envnciated by the united Stated supreme court.

the Doctrine " Separate but Equal was Determined by the supreme court to be incapable of satisfying the constitution and was abandoned → case - Brown -v- Board of education.

Shortly before the civil war the supreme Declared that members of the made was the Dred Scott. -

plessy -v- Ferguson.

1. The sexual assault and murder of 7-year-old Megan Kanka in New Jersey on October 31, 1994, struck a national nerve. Megan was assaulted and killed by a neighbor, Jesse Timmendequas, who had twice been convicted of similar sex offenses and was on parole. In response to the crime and public uproar, the state of New Jersey enacted "Megan's Law." The law requires sex offenders, upon their release from prison, to register with New Jersey law enforcement authorities, who are to notify the public about the release. The public is to be provided with the offender's name, a recent photograph, a physical description, a list of the offenses for which he or she was convicted, and the offender's current address, place of employment or school, and automobile license plate number. The Supreme Court recently upheld Megan's Law.

   Currently, 39 states and the federal government have Megan's Laws that require sex offenders released from prison to register with local law enforcement authorities. Many of those laws, like New Jersey's, require that law enforcement officials use the information to notify schools and day care centers and, in some cases, the sex offender's neighbors. In 1997, California enacted a law allowing citizens access to a CD-ROM with detailed information on 64,000 sex offenders living in California who had committed a broad range of sex crimes since 1944.

   In 1996, President Clinton signed into law the Pam Lyncher Sexual Offender Tracking and Identification Act, which called for a national registry of sex offenders, to be completed by the end of 1998. The national registry will allow state officials to submit queries, such as the name of a job applicant at a day care center, and to determine whether the applicant is a registered sex offender in any of the participating states.

   a. Is Megan's Law a good law? (Consider the ideal characteristics of the criminal law.)
   b. Is Megan's Law fair to sex offenders who have served their prison sentences (that is, "paid their debt to society")?
   c. What rights does a sex offender have after being released from prison?
   d. What rights does a community have to protect itself from known sex offenders who have been released from prison?
   e. When the rights of an individual and the rights of a community conflict, whose rights should take precedence? Why?

2. In January 1998, the police in Cincinnati, Ohio, began using a special video camera to monitor activity on a "crime-ridden street corner." The camera, which cost $11,000, rotates, enabling it to observe activity in a 1,000 foot radius. It records 24 hours a day, and it can read a license plate number from more than a block away. To protect privacy, policy requires that all tapes be erased after 96 hours if they show no criminal activity. Residents of the area claim that the camera's presence has cleaned up the area by, among other things, scaring away drug dealers. Critics worry about government spying on residents. The city council is considering putting cameras in other parts of the city.

a. Should the city council have surveillance cameras installed in other parts of the city? Why or why not?

b. What legal or procedural issues should be considered before making a decision?

ADDITIONAL READING

Abraham, Henry J. *Freedom and the Court: Civil Rights and Liberties in the United States.* New York: Oxford University Press, 1977.

Alderman, Ellen and Caroline Kennedy. *In Our Defense: The Bill of Rights in Action.* New York: William Morrow, 1991.

Cox, Archibald. *The Court and the Constitution.* Boston: Houghton Mifflin, 1987.

Lewis, Anthony. *Gideon's Trumpet.* New York: Vintage, 1966.

Rembar, Charles. *The Law of the Land: The Evolution of Our Legal System.* New York: Simon and Schuster, 1980.

ENDNOTES

1. Jay A. Sigler, *Understanding Criminal Law* (Boston: Little, Brown, 1981), p. 3.
2. The discussion in the remainder of this section is based on material from Edwin H. Sutherland and Donald R. Cressey, *Criminology,* 9th ed. (Philadelphia: J. B. Lippincott, 1974), p. 8.
3. Ibid., pp. 4–8.
4. Most of the material in this section comes from Will Durant, *Our Oriental Heritage,* Part 1 of *The Story of Civilization* (New York: Simon & Schuster, 1954).
5. S. Francis Milsom, *The Historical Foundations of the Common Law* (London: Butterworths, 1969), p. 355.
6. Most of the material in this section comes from Raymond J. Michalowski, *Order, Law, and Crime: An Introduction to Criminology* (New York: Random House, 1985).
7. See Archibald Cox, *The Court and the Constitution* (Boston: Houghton Mifflin, 1987), pp. 239–49.
8. For an examination of the influence of the Burger and Rehnquist Courts on criminal procedure, see Mary Margaret Weddington and W. Richard Janikowski, "The Rehnquist Court: The Counter-Revolution That Wasn't: Part II, The Counter-Revolution That Is," *Criminal Justice Review,* Vol. 21, 1997, pp. 231–50.
9. In addition to the Supreme Court cases themselves, much of the information in the remainder of this chapter is from the following sources: John Ferdico, *Criminal Procedure for the Law Enforcement Officer* (St. Paul, MN: West, 1975); Yale Kamisar, Wayne R. LaFave, and Jerold H. Israel, *Modern Criminal Procedure,* 7th ed. (St. Paul, MN: West, 1990); Sanford H. Kadish and Monrad G. Paulsen, *Criminal Law and Its Processes,* 3d ed. (Boston: Little, Brown, 1975); Wayne R. LaFave and Jerold H. Israel, *Criminal Procedure* (St. Paul, MN: West, 1984, Supp. 1991); Jerold H. Israel and Wayne R. LaFave, *Criminal Procedure in a Nutshell* (St. Paul, MN: West, 1975); John M. Scheb and John M. Scheb II, *Criminal Law and Procedure,* 2d ed. (St. Paul, MN: West, 1994).

10. See Raymond Paternoster, *Capital Punishment in America* (New York: Lexington, 1991), p. 51.
11. Ibid.
12. Ibid., p. 52.
13. Ibid.
14. Ibid., p. 53.
15. C. Ronald Huff, Arye Rattner, and Edward Sagarin, "Guilty Until Proven Innocent: Wrongful Conviction and Public Policy," *Crime and Delinquency,* Vol. 32, 1986, pp. 518–44.
16. Ibid., p. 519.
17. Ibid., pp. 521–22.
18. Ibid., p. 523.
19. *Sourcebook of Criminal Justice Statistics Online* (www.albany.edu/sourcebook/), Table 4.1.
20. See Huff et al., op. cit., p. 523.
21. Ibid., p. 524.
22. Ibid., p. 528.
23. Ibid., p. 529.
24. Ibid.
25. Ibid., p. 533.
26. Ibid., p. 530.
27. Ibid.
28. Marcia Coyle, Fred Strasser, and Marianne Lavelle, "Fatal Defense," *The National Law Journal,* Vol. 12, 1990, pp. 30–44.
29. Huff et al., op. cit., pp. 530–33.
30. Samuel Walker, *Sense and Nonsense About Crime: A Policy Guide* (Monterey, CA: Brooks/Cole, 1985), pp. 94–97.
31. Michael L. Radelet, Hugo Adam Bedau, and Constance E. Putnam, *In Spite of Innocence* (Boston: Northeastern University Press, 1992).
32. F. Feeney, F. Dill, and A. Weir, *Arrests Without Conviction: How Often They Occur and Why* (Washington: U.S. Department of Justice, National Institute of Justice, 1983); P. Nardulli, "The Societal Cost of the Exclusionary Rule: An Empirical Assessment," *American Bar Foundation Research*

Journal, 1983, pp. 585–609; Report of the Comptroller General of the United States, *Impact of the Exclusionary Rule on Federal Criminal Prosecutions* (Washington: U.S. General Accounting Office, 1979); K. Brosi, *A Cross City Comparison of Felony Case Processing* (Washington: U.S. Department of Justice, Law Enforcement Assistance Administration, 1979); B. Forst, J. Lucianovic, and S. Cox, *What Happens After Arrest: A Court Perspective of Police Operations in the District of Columbia* (Washington: U.S. Department of Justice, Law Enforcement Assistance Administration, 1978).

33. Walker, op. cit.
34. Cited in Tamar Jacoby, "Fighting Crime by the Rules: Why Cops Like Miranda," *Newsweek,* July 18, 1988), p. 53.
35. Karen L. Guy and Robert G. Huckabee, "Going Free on a Technicality: Another Look at the Effect of the Miranda Decision on the Criminal Justice Process," *Criminal Justice Research Bulletin,* Vol. 4, 1988, pp. 1–3.

36. Ibid.
37. Ibid.
38. Ibid.
39. Jacoby, op. cit.
40. "DNA Evidence Clears Man Jailed 13 Years for Rape," *The Orlando Sentinel,* July 18, 1996, p. A–10; "Pardoned Man Not Bitter After 7-Year Prison Stay," *The Orlando Sentinel,* October 18, 1996, p. A–16.
41. Guy and Huckabee, op. cit.
42. Ibid.
43. Walker, op. cit.
44. For a different view, see Paul G. Cassell and Bret S. Hayman, "Police Interrogation in the 1990s: An Empirical Study of the Effects of *Miranda,*" *UCLA Law Review,* Vol. 43, 1996, pp. 839–931; and George C. Thomas, III, "Is *Miranda* a Real-World Failure? A Plea for More and Better Empirical Evidence," *UCLA Law Review,* Vol. 43, 1996, pp. 821–37.

5 History and Structure of American Law Enforcement

1991

CHAPTER OBJECTIVES

After completing this chapter, you should be able to:

1 Briefly describe the jurisdictional limitations of American law enforcement.

2 Trace the English origins of American law enforcement.

3 Discuss the early development of American law enforcement.

4 Describe the major developments that have occurred in policing in America.

5 Describe the structure of American law enforcement.

6 Discuss the development and growth of private security in the United States.

19 PCT 2554

ICE

The Limited Authority of American Law Enforcement

Jurisdiction The right or authority of a justice agency to act in regard to a particular subject matter, territory, or person.

The United States has almost 17,500 public law enforcement agencies at the federal, state, and local levels of government. The vast majority of those agencies, however, are local, serving municipalities, townships, villages, and counties. The authority of each agency—whether it is the FBI, a state highway patrol, or a city or county sheriff's department—is carefully limited by law. The territory within which an agency may operate is also restricted. The city police, for example, may not patrol or answer calls for service outside the city's boundaries unless cooperative pacts have been developed. **Jurisdiction,** which we have defined as a politically defined geographical area, also means the right or authority of a justice agency to act in regard to a particular subject matter, territory, or person. It includes the laws a particular police agency is permitted to enforce and the duties it is allowed to perform. The Oklahoma Highway Patrol, for example, has investigative and enforcement responsibilities only in traffic matters, while the Kentucky State Police have a broader jurisdiction, which includes the authority to conduct criminal investigations throughout the state. Each of the nearly two dozen major federal law enforcement agencies has a specific jurisdiction, although one criminal event may involve crimes that give several federal agencies concurrent jurisdiction. For example, in a bank robbery, if mail of any sort is taken, both the Postal Inspections Service and the FBI are likely to investigate the case.

Beyond the statutes that create and direct law enforcement agencies, the procedural law derived from U.S. Supreme Court decisions also imposes limitations on the authority of those agencies. Giving arrested suspects the familiar *Miranda* warnings before questioning is a good example of the Court's role in limiting the authority of the police. In addition, police civilian review boards, departmental policies and procedures, and civil liability suits against officers who have abused their authority curtail the power of the police in the United States.

The only police contact most citizens have is in a traffic situation in a local or state jurisdiction.

History and Structure of American Law Enforcement

Thus, there is a great difference between law enforcement with limited authority in a democratic nation operating under the rule of law and law enforcement in countries where the law is by decree and the police are simply a tool of those in power. Even in comparison with other democratic nations of the world, however, the United States has remarkably more police agencies that operate under far more restrictions on their authority. To understand the origin of those unique qualities of law enforcement in the United States, it is necessary to look first at the history of law enforcement in England, the nation that provided the model for most of American criminal justice.

English Roots

If you are the victim of a crime, you might expect that a uniformed patrol officer will respond quickly to your call and that a plainclothes detective will soon follow up on the investigation. Because there are thousands of police departments in local communities across the nation, you might also take for granted that the police handling your case are paid public servants employed by your city or county. Such was not always the case in the United States—nor in England, where the basic concepts of American law enforcement and criminal justice originated. The criminal justice system in England took hundreds of years to develop, but eventually the idea arose of a locally controlled uniformed police force with follow-up plainclothes investigators.

The Tithing System

Before the twelfth century in England, justice was primarily a private matter based on revenge and retribution.[1] Victims of a crime had to pursue perpetrators without assistance from the king or his agents. Disputes were often settled by blood feuds, in which families would wage war on each other.

By the twelfth century, a system of group protection had begun to develop. Often referred to as the **tithing system** or the frankpledge system, it afforded some improvements over past practices. Ten families, or a *tithing*, were required to become a group and agree to follow the law, keep the peace in their areas, and bring law violators to justice. Over even larger areas, ten tithings were grouped together to form a *hundred*, and one or several hundreds constituted a *shire*, which was similar to a modern American county. The shire was under the direction of the **shire reeve** (later called the *sheriff*), the forerunner of the American sheriff. The shire reeve received some assistance from elected constables at the town and village levels, who organized able-bodied citizens into **posses** to chase and apprehend offenders.[2] County law enforcement agencies in the United States still sometimes use posses to apprehend law violators.

The Constable-Watch System

The Statute of Winchester, passed in 1285, formalized the **constable-watch system** of protection. The statute provided for one man from each parish to be selected as **constable,** or chief peacekeeper. The statute further granted constables the power to draft citizens as watchmen, who were required to guard the city at night. Watchmen were not paid for their efforts and, as a result, were often found sleeping or in a pub rather than performing their duties. In addition, the statute required all male citizens between the

Tithing system A private self-help protection system in early medieval England in which a group of ten families, or a *tithing,* agreed to follow the law, keep the peace in their areas, and bring law violators to justice.

Shire reeve In medieval England, the chief law enforcement officer in a territorial area called a shire; later called the sheriff.

Posses Groups of able-bodied citizens of a community, called into service by a sheriff or constable to chase and apprehend offenders.

Constable-watch system A system of protection in early England in which citizens, under the direction of a constable, or chief peacekeeper, were required to guard the city and to pursue criminals.

Constable The peacekeeper in charge of protection in early English towns.

ages of 15 and 60 to maintain weapons and to join in the *hue and cry,* meaning to come to the aid of the constable or the watchman when either called for help. If they did not come when called, the male citizens were subject to criminal penalties for aiding the offender. This system of community law enforcement lasted well into the 1700s.

Two features of this system are worthy of note. First, the people were the police, and second, the organization of the protection system was local. These two ideas were transported to the American colonies centuries later.

The Bow Street Runners

In 1748, Henry Fielding, a London magistrate, founded a group of professional law enforcement agents to apprehend criminals and recover stolen property in the entertainment district of London, known as Bow Street, Covent Gardens. This publicly funded detective force, named the Bow Street Runners, was by far the most effective official law enforcement organization of its day. Efforts to duplicate it in other parts of London proved unsuccessful, but Fielding's work organizing the first British detective force and his writing addressing the shortcomings of the criminal justice system had a great deal of influence. They helped pave the way for a more professional and better-organized response to the crime problems that were dramatically increasing in London by the end of the eighteenth century.[3]

The London Metropolitan Police

Because of the Industrial Revolution, urban populations in cities like London swelled with an influx of people from the countryside looking for work in factories. A major result of this social transformation was that England began experiencing increasing poverty, public disorder, and crime. There was no clear consensus on what to do. Several efforts to establish a central police force for London had been opposed by people who believed that police of any kind were a throwback to the absolute power formerly wielded by English kings. Parliament eventually responded, in 1829, with the London Metropolitan Police Act. It created a 1000-officer police force with professional standards to replace the patchwork of community law enforcement systems then in use. Members of the London Police became known as "bobbies" or "peelers," after Robert Peel, the British Home Secretary who had prodded Parliament to create the police force.

The London Police were organized according to military rank and structure to ensure discipline and were under the command of two magistrates, who were later called commissioners. According to Peel, the main function of the police was to prevent crime without force, by preventive patrol of the community. Londoners, who resented such close scrutiny, did not at first welcome this police presence in the community. Eventually, though, the bobbies (the term was originally derogatory) showed that the police could have a positive effect on the quality of life in the community. Peel's military approach to policing, as well as some of his other principles, remain in effect today throughout the world. **Peel's Principles of Policing** are outlined in Figure 5–1.[4]

Peel's Principles of Policing A dozen standards proposed by Robert Peel, the author of the legislation resulting in the formation of the London Metropolitan Police Department. The standards are still applicable to today's law enforcement.

FIGURE 5–1

Robert Peel's Principles of Policing

1 The police must be stable, efficient, and organized along military lines.

2 The police must be under governmental control.

3 The absence of crime will best prove the efficiency of police.

4 The distribution of crime news is essential.

5 The deployment of police strength both by time and area is essential.

6 No quality is more indispensable to a policeman than a perfect command of temper; a quiet, determined manner has more effect than violent action.

7 Good appearance commands respect.

8 The securing and training of proper persons is at the root of efficiency.

9 Public security demands that every police officer be given a number.

10 Police headquarters should be centrally located and easily accessible to the people.

11 Policemen should be hired on a probationary basis.

12 Police records are necessary to the correct distribution of police strength.

The Development of American Law Enforcement

America has more police departments than any other nation in the world. The major reason for this is that local control is highly regarded in the United States. Thus, like many other services, police service is provided locally, even by small communities that can barely afford it. This practice is primarily responsible for the disparity in the quality of police personnel and service in the United States. The struggle to improve law enforcement in the nation began even before formal police departments came into existence.

Early American Law Enforcement

The chance for a better life, free of government intervention, was key in the decision of many colonists to cross the Atlantic and settle in the New World. American colonists from England brought with them the protection system with which they were familiar, if not completely satisfied. Boston established a night watch as early as 1634. Except for the military's intervention in major disturbances, the watch system, at least in the cities, was the means of preventing crime and apprehending criminals for the next two centuries. As in England, the people were the police and had very little authority

FYI

In Dutch-influenced New York in the seventeenth century, the first paid officers on the night watch were known as "leatherheads" because they wore leather helmets similar in appearance to the helmets worn by today's firefighters. That group was not known for its attention to duty and often spent entirely too much of its watch schedule inside.

149

to accomplish their charge on the watch. Citizens could pay for watch replacements, and often the worst of the lot ended up protecting the community. In fact, Boston and other cities would frequently deploy the most elderly citizens and would occasionally sentence minor offenders to serve on the watch.[5] Later, in rural and southern areas of the country, the office of sheriff was established, and the power of the posse was used to maintain order and apprehend offenders. In essence, two forms of protection began to evolve—the watch in the villages, towns, and cities and the sheriff in the rural areas, unincorporated areas, and counties. Communities in the North often had both systems.

Law Enforcement in the Cities

As had happened in England, the growth of the factory system lured people away from the farms to cities. Large groups of newcomers, sometimes immigrants from other countries, settled near factories. Factory workers put in long days, often in unsafe and unhealthy working conditions. Some workers organized strikes, seeking better working conditions, but the strikes were quickly put down. As the populations of cities swelled, living conditions in some areas became overcrowded and unhealthy.

Major episodes of urban violence occurred in the first half of the nineteenth century because of the social and economic changes transforming American cities. Racial and ethnic tensions often reached a boiling point, resulting in mob disturbances that lasted for days. A particular source of trouble were the drinking establishments located throughout working-class districts of cities. Regular heavy drinking led to fights, brawls, and even full-scale riots.

Unlike London, which organized its police force in 1829, American citizens resisted the formation of police departments, relying instead on the constable-watch system, whose members lit streetlights, patrolled the streets to maintain order, and arrested some suspicious people. Constables often had daytime duties, which included investigating health hazards, carrying out orders of the court, clearing the streets of debris, and apprehending criminals against whom complaints had been filed. Neither the night watch nor the constables tried to prevent or discover crime, nor did they wear any kind of uniform. This weak protection system was unable to contain the increasing lawlessness.

Municipal Police Forces In 1844, New York City combined its day and night watches to form the first paid, unified police force in the United States. Close ties developed between the police and local political leaders. As with the first police in London, citizens were suspicious of the constant vigil of police officers in their neighborhoods. Citizens had little respect for the New York police because they thought the unit was composed of political hacks appointed by local officials who wanted to control the police for their own gain. During the next several years, the struggle to control the police in New York built to a fever pitch.[6]

In 1853, the New York state legislature formed the Municipal Police Department, but within four years the force was so corrupt—from taking bribes to overlook crime—that the legislature decided to abolish it. It was replaced by the Metropolitan Police, which was administered by five commissioners

The citizens of Detroit, sick and tired of the torching of cars and vacant houses during Devil's Night each Halloween, have formed street patrols to prevent arson in their neighborhoods. The number of Devil's Night fires that plague Detroit has shrunk in most years since 1984. In that year, firefighters counted 810 fires. In 1997, with 35,000 volunteers patrolling the streets, they recorded 168 fires.

History and Structure of American Law Enforcement

By the early 1900s, most American cities had organized, uniformed police forces similar to the police force of Newport, Rhode Island, pictured here circa 1910.

appointed by the governor. The commissioners then selected a superintendent. Each commissioner was to oversee his colleagues on the commission as well as the superintendent and keep them honest. The new structure was an improvement, in the minds of the legislature, that would prevent corruption in the top level of the department. But when the Metropolitan Police Board called on Mayor Fernando Wood to abolish the Municipal Police, he refused. Even after New York's highest court upheld a decision to disband the Municipals, the mayor refused. The Metropolitans even tried to arrest Mayor Wood, but that failed attempt resulted in a pitched battle between the two police forces. When the National Guard was called in, Mayor Wood submitted to arrest but was immediately released on bail.

During the summer of 1857, the two police forces often fought over whether or not to arrest certain criminals. A particularly troubling practice was one police force's releasing from custody the criminals arrested by the other force. Lawbreakers operated freely during the dispute between the two police forces. Criminal gangs had a free hand to commit robberies and burglaries during most of the summer. The public became enraged over this neglect of duty and the increased danger on the streets of New York City. Only when another court order upheld the decision to disband the Municipal Police did Mayor Wood comply.

Following the course charted by New York City, other large cities in the United States soon established their own police departments. In 1855, Boston combined its day- and night-watch forces to form a city police department. By the end of the decade, police departments had been formed in many major cities east of the Mississippi. The duties of the officers did not vary substantially from the duties of those who had served on the watch. After the Civil War, however, peace officers began to take on the trappings of the police we recognize today. They began to wear uniforms, carry nightsticks, and even firearms, although many citizens resisted giving this much authority to the police.

Tangle of Politics and Policing Until the 1920s, in most cities of the United States, party politics prevented the development of professional police departments. Local political leaders understood that controlling the police was a means of maintaining their own political power and of allowing criminal friends and political allies to violate the law with impunity. In fact, in some cities, the police were clearly extensions of the local party machine, which attempted to dominate all activity in a community. If local politicians gave police applicants a job, it became the hired officers' job to get out the vote so that the politicians could keep theirs. The system was so corrupt in some cities that police officers bought their original positions, their promotions, and their special assignments. In collaboration with local politicians, but often on their own, the police were more than willing to ignore violations of the law if the lawbreakers gave them money, valuables, or privileges.

Law Enforcement in the States and on the Frontier

The development of law enforcement in the states and the frontier territories was often peculiar to the individual location. Without large population centers that required the control of disorderly crowds, law enforcement was more likely to respond to specific situations—for example, by rounding up cattle rustlers or capturing escaped slaves. Still, out of this kind of limited law enforcement activity, the basic organizational structure of police units with broader responsibilities was born.

Southern Slave Patrols In the South, the earliest form of policing was the plantation **slave patrols.**[7] Those patrols were created to enforce the infamous slave codes, the first of which was enacted by the South Carolina legislature in 1712. Eventually all the Southern colonies enacted slave codes. The slave codes protected the slaveholders' property rights in human beings, while holding slaves responsible for their crimes and other acts that were not crimes if committed by free persons. Under some slave codes, enslaved people could not hold meetings, leave the plantation without permission from the master, travel without a pass, learn to read and write, carry a firearm, trade, or gamble. Both the slave codes and the slave patrols were created in part because of a fear of bloody slave revolts, such as had already occurred in Virginia and other parts of the South.

Generally consisting of three men on horseback who covered a beat of 15 square miles, a slave patrol was responsible for catching runaway slaves, preventing slave uprisings, and maintaining discipline among the slaves. To maintain discipline, the patrols often whipped and terrorized black slaves

Slave patrols The earliest form of policing in the South. They were a product of the slave codes.

who were caught after dark without passes. The slave patrols also helped enforce the laws prohibiting literacy, trade, and gambling among slaves. Although the law required that all white males perform patrol services, the large plantation owners usually hired poor, landless whites to substitute for them. The slave patrols lasted until the end of the Civil War, in 1865. After the Civil War, the Ku Klux Klan served the purpose of controlling blacks just as the slave patrols had before the Civil War.

Frontier Law Enforcement In the remote and unpopulated areas of the nation, and particularly on the expanding frontier, justice was often in the hands of the people in a more direct way. Vigilantism was often the only way that people could maintain order and defend themselves against renegades and thugs.[8] Even when formal law enforcement procedures were provided by the sheriff or a marshal, courts in many communities were held only once or twice a year, leaving many cases unresolved. This idea of self-protection remains very popular in the South and the West, where firearms laws in many states permit people to carry loaded weapons in a vehicle, or even on their persons if they have completed a qualification and licensing procedure.

State Police Agencies Self-protection did not prove sufficient as populations and their accompanying problems increased. As early as 1823, mounted militia units in Texas protected American settlers in the territory. Called *rangers,* these mounted militia fought Native Americans and Mexican bandits. The Texas Rangers were officially formed in 1835, and the organization remains in existence today as an elite and effective unit of the Texas Department of Public Safety.[9]

The inefficiency and unwillingness of some sheriffs and constables to control crime, along with an emerging crime problem that exceeded the local community's ability to deal with it, prompted other states to form state law enforcement agencies. In 1905, Pennsylvania established the first modern state law enforcement organization with the authority to enforce the law statewide, an authority that made it unpopular in some communities, where enforcement of state laws had been decidedly lax.[10] The advent of the automobile and the addition of miles of state highways extended the authority of state police agencies. Some form of state law enforcement agency existed in every state by the 1930s.

Professionalism and Reform

You will recall that the people themselves were once the police, as they served on the watch. Being an adult citizen was about the only qualification. No training was required, and it was common practice for citizens who did not want to serve to hire replacements, sometimes hiring sentenced offenders. Because of the few services and the little order the watch provided, not much else seems to have been required. Even when

The Texas Rangers, organized in the early 1800s to fight Indians, patrol the Mexican border, and track down rustlers, were the first form of state police.

History and Structure of American Law Enforcement   **CHAPTER 5**

The Structure of American Law Enforcement

Describing American law enforcement and its structure is difficult because law enforcement agencies are so diverse (see Figure 5–2). To begin with, you must decide which law enforcement agency you are talking about. For example, Oklahoma Highway Patrol officers cruise the highways and back roads, enforcing traffic laws, investigating accidents, and assisting motorists over nearly endless miles of paved and unpaved routes. They do not ordinarily investigate criminal violations unless the violations are on state property. A sheriff and three deputies in rural Echols County, Georgia, in contrast, conduct

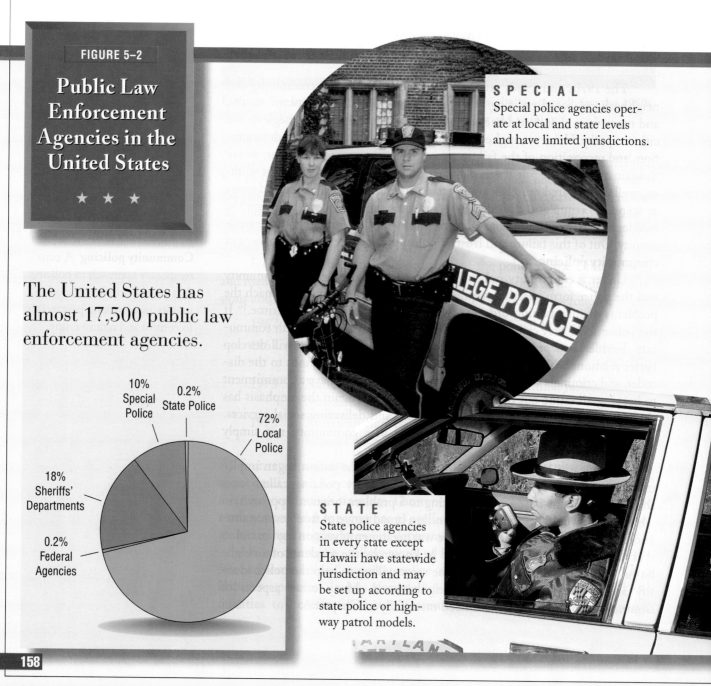

FIGURE 5–2

Public Law Enforcement Agencies in the United States

★ ★ ★

The United States has almost 17,500 public law enforcement agencies.

10% Special Police

0.2% State Police

72% Local Police

18% Sheriffs' Departments

0.2% Federal Agencies

SPECIAL
Special police agencies operate at local and state levels and have limited jurisdictions.

STATE
State police agencies in every state except Hawaii have statewide jurisdiction and may be set up according to state police or highway patrol models.

criminal investigations, serve subpoenas, and investigate accidents. In Alexis, Danvers, and Ogden, Illinois, only one employee, the chief of police, works in each department, and that person is responsible for all law enforcement, public order, and service duties. The 67 sworn law enforcement officers at the University of Texas in Austin are also a part of American law enforcement.[17]

Altogether, tens of thousands of law enforcement officers at the federal, state, county, and municipal levels protect life and property and serve their respective publics. They are employed by government, private enterprise, and quasi-governmental entities. Their responsibilities are specific and sometimes unique to the kind of organization that employs them. Examples of these organizations are airports, transit authorities, hospitals, and parks.

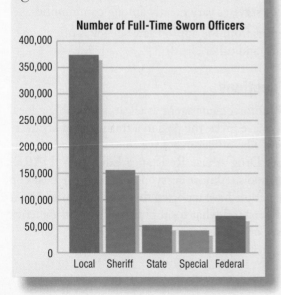

LOCAL
Local police departments, which make up the bulk of law enforcement agencies in America, are responsible for law enforcement, order maintenance, service, and information gathering.

FEDERAL
Federal agencies investigate violations of federal law and enforce laws that involve interstate crimes.

Almost 700,000 full-time sworn officers are employed by public law enforcement agencies in the United States.

Number of Full-Time Sworn Officers

Local	Sheriff	State	Special	Federal

(y-axis: 0, 50,000, 100,000, 150,000, 200,000, 250,000, 300,000, 350,000, 400,000)

COUNTY
County sheriffs' departments enforce the law in most rural and unincorporated areas of the United States.

Source: Data in graphs are taken from Brian A. Reaves, *Federal Law Enforcement Officers, 1996* and *Local Police Departments, 1993* (Washington: Bureau of Justice Statistics, 1997, 1996).

At the state level, there are highway patrols, bureaus of investigation, park rangers, watercraft officers, and other law enforcement agencies and personnel with limited jurisdictions. Colleges and universities employ police officers, and some of those forces are comparable to many medium-sized police departments in the United States.

At the federal level, there are about 50 law enforcement agencies. The Federal Bureau of Investigation (FBI), the U.S. Secret Service, and the Drug Enforcement Administration (DEA) are three of the better-known agencies. The U.S. Marshals Service, the Bureau of Alcohol, Tobacco, and Firearms, and the Customs Service are other federal law enforcement agencies, as are the Internal Revenue Service's Criminal Investigation Division, the White House Police, the Border Patrol, and nearly three dozen other agencies.

As the aforementioned list of law enforcement agencies suggests, explaining the law enforcement mandate in the United States and its execution is also difficult. The structure of police services in the United States is different from that in other countries of the world. France, Japan, and many other nations have only one police department. The United States has almost 17,500 public law enforcement agencies, and probably more when all the special police jurisdictions in the public sector are counted—for example, game protection agencies, water conservancies, and mental health institutions. Figure 5–2 summarizes the various law enforcement agencies in the United States.

We have already described law enforcement in America as fragmented, locally controlled, and limited in authority, but we need to add the terms *structurally* and *functionally different*. Virtually no two police agencies in America are structured alike or function in the same way. Police officers themselves are young and old; well-trained and ill-prepared; educated and uninformed; full-time and part-time; rural, urban, and suburban; generalists and specialists; paid and volunteer; and public and private. These differences lead to the following generalizations about law enforcement in the United States:

1. The quality of police services varies greatly among states and localities across the nation.

2. There is no consensus on professional standards for police personnel, equipment, and practices.

3. Expenditures for police services vary greatly among communities.

4. Obtaining police services from the appropriate agency is often confusing for crime victims and other clients.

Local Policing and Its Functions

If a person knows a law enforcement agent at all, it is probably a local police officer. The officer may have given the person a traffic ticket or investigated an automobile accident. The officer may have conducted a crime prevention survey. Children meet Drug Abuse Resistance Education (DARE) officers in public or private schools. Almost everyone has seen the beat cop drive by in a patrol car. Some people have reported thefts or burglaries, but it is doubtful that even they understand what local police officers in America really do, besides what they see on television and in movies.

Municipal Police Departments Municipal police departments come in all sizes, but most of them are small in the number of officers employed. The overwhelming majority of police departments in America employ fewer than 50 sworn officers. Figure 5–3 shows the number of sworn officers in local police agencies in the United States. As shown in Figure 5–3, approximately one-half of all local police departments in the United States employ fewer than 10 officers, and fewer than 1 percent employ more than 1,000 sworn personnel.

What are some of the characteristics of the sworn personnel who occupy the ranks of municipal police agencies in the United States? Most police officers are white males. In 1993, 75.2 percent of full-time sworn officers were white men. The larger the police agency, the more likely it is to employ minority officers. Women represented less than 9 percent of all sworn officers in the nation's local police departments in 1993. Figure 5–4 on page 162 provides a breakdown of police employment in local agencies by gender, race, and ethnicity.

FIGURE 5–3

Number of Sworn Personnel in Local Departments, 1993

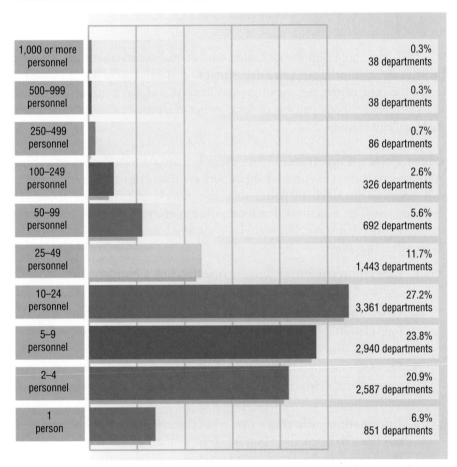

Category	Percent	Departments
1,000 or more personnel	0.3%	38 departments
500–999 personnel	0.3%	38 departments
250–499 personnel	0.7%	86 departments
100–249 personnel	2.6%	326 departments
50–99 personnel	5.6%	692 departments
25–49 personnel	11.7%	1,443 departments
10–24 personnel	27.2%	3,361 departments
5–9 personnel	23.8%	2,940 departments
2–4 personnel	20.9%	2,587 departments
1 person	6.9%	851 departments

Source: Brian Reaves, *State and Local Police Departments, 1993* (Washington: Bureau of Justice Statistics, 1996).

History and Structure of American Law Enforcement

CHAPTER 5

FIGURE 5-4

Characteristics of Local Full-Time Police Officers

Gender

Male
91.2%

Female
8.8%

Race/Ethnicity

White
80.9%

African American
11.3%

Hispanic
6.2%

Other
1.5%

Source: Brian Reaves, *State and Local Police Departments, 1993* (Washington: Bureau of Justice Statistics, 1996).

The first woman to have full police power (1905) was Lola Baldwin of Portland, Oregon. The first uniformed policewoman was Alice Stebbins Wells, who was hired by the Los Angeles Police Department in 1910. By 1916, sixteen other police departments had hired policewomen as a result of the success in Los Angeles.

A high school diploma or higher educational achievement was required by 86 percent of the local police departments of the nation in 1993. However, only 7 percent of the agencies required recruits to have a minimum of two years of college. Four percent of local police departments in 1993 required some college courses.[18]

Local Police Functions The local police are the workhorses of the law enforcement system in America. They perform many functions and tasks that will never be included in police detective novels or in movies about law enforcement. The functions that local police perform have been categorized in several different ways. One general grouping lists these four categories of local police functions:

1. **Law enforcement**—examples: investigating a burglary, arresting a car thief, serving a warrant, or testifying in court.

2. **Order maintenance or peacekeeping**—examples: breaking up a fight, holding back a crowd at a sporting event, or intervening in a domestic dispute before it gets violent.

3. **Service**—examples: taking people to the hospital, escorting funeral processions, delivering mail for city officials, or chasing bats out of a caller's house.

4. **Information gathering**—examples: determining neighborhood reactions to a proposed liquor license in the community, investigating a missing-child case, or investigating and reporting on a dangerous road condition.

Some police academies teach recruits the functions of a police officer through the use of the acronym *PEPPAS:*

P—Protect life and property (patrol a business district at night, keep citizens from a fire scene, or recover and return lost property).

E—Enforce the law (ensure traffic laws are obeyed, warn jaywalkers of the inherent danger, make out criminal complaints, or seize illegal weapons).

P—Prevent crime (give home security advice, patrol high-crime areas, or work as a DARE officer in schools).

P—Preserve the peace (disband disorderly groups, have a visible presence at sporting events, or intervene in neighbor conflicts).

A—Arrest violators (apprehend fleeing suspects, give citations to alcohol permit holders who sell to minors, or conduct drug raids).

S—Serve the public (give directions to travelers, deliver emergency messages, or administer first aid).

There are literally dozens of other functions that the police of a city, town, or village carry out, and much of the work falls into the category of helping out when no one else seems to be available. Because the police are on duty 24 hours a day in nearly every community, they are often called on to perform services that have nothing to do with law enforcement. That round-the-clock availability also significantly affects the structure, work life, and activity of a police agency.

MYTH   FACT

The police spend most of their time and resources apprehending law violators and combating crime.

Only about 10 percent of police time and resources are devoted to apprehending law violators and combating crime. Most of their time and resources are spent "keeping the peace," which means maintaining a police presence in the community, for example, by routine patrolling.

Organizational Structure How a police agency is structured depends on the size of the agency, the degree of specialization, the philosophy the leadership has chosen (such as community policing), the political context of the department (the form of municipal government), and the history and preferences of a particular community. Most medium-to-large police agencies are subdivided into patrol, criminal investigation, traffic, juvenile, and technical and support services. Subspecialties include robbery, gangs, training, bombs, property, victims' services, jail, and mounted patrol.

The Dallas (Texas) Police Department, with 2,841 sworn officers and 721 nonsworn employees, is large, sophisticated, and very specialized. For example, it has a separate detective unit for each major category of crime. Evidence technicians collect and preserve evidence during preliminary investigation of a crime. An entire contingent of officers is assigned to traffic regulation and enforcement duties. Bicycle patrol officers work the popular West End entertainment and restaurant section downtown. The Dallas

As you can see, the forms of municipal government vary in the amount of control citizens have over the municipality's leaders, the source of the executive authority of the chief of police, and the degree of insulation a chief of police has from interference by the executive head of the city (mayor or city manager) or the city council. Each form has advantages and disadvantages. At one time it was thought that city manager government was the system under which the police were most likely to develop professionally, be free of political meddling from city lawmakers, and be insulated from local corruption. Although many progressive and effective police departments operate under a city manager form of government, other municipal forms of government have records of both success and failure in local police effectiveness and integrity.

You have probably noticed from reading newspapers and listening to radio and television that chief executives of local police agencies have different titles, depending on the locale. Popular titles are chief of police (Kansas City), director of police (Dayton, Ohio), and commissioner (New York City).

County Law Enforcement

A substantial portion of law enforcement work in the United States is carried out by sheriffs' departments. In 1993, the nation had 3,085 sheriffs' departments, employing approximately 224,236 full-time personnel. Seventy percent of the personnel were sworn peace officers. Sheriffs frequently employ part-time personnel who work as special deputies, assisting with county fairs, traffic control, and other duties. Sheriffs' departments represent 18 percent of all the law enforcement departments in the United States, so there are good career opportunities within county law enforcement. The cost to provide county law enforcement in 1993 was $10.7 billion.[20]

Sheriffs' personnel are 83 percent white, 10 percent black, 6 percent Hispanic, and 1 percent other. Women make up 14.5 percent of the sworn personnel working for sheriffs' departments.[21] (See Figure 5–6.)

FIGURE 5–6

Characteristics of Sheriffs' Personnel, 1993

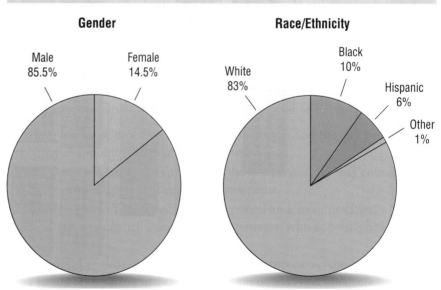

Source: Brian Reaves and Pheny Smith, *Sheriffs' Departments,* 1993 (Washington: Bureau of Justice Statistics, 1996).

As are most municipal police departments, most sheriffs' departments in America are small. Figure 5-7 shows the number of departments and their respective sizes. More than a dozen sheriffs' departments employ only the sheriff.

Sheriffs' departments often have employment qualifications similar to those of municipal police agencies. Ninety-three percent of sheriffs' departments require new officers to have a high school diploma, while 4 percent require some college, usually a two-year degree.

County Law Enforcement Functions The sheriff and department personnel perform functions that range from investigation to supervision of sentenced offenders. Even in the smallest departments, sheriffs are responsible for investigating crimes and enforcing the criminal and traffic laws of the state. They also perform many civil process services for the court, such as serving summonses, warrants, and various writs. In addition, they provide courtroom security and confine and transport prisoners. The larger the sheriff's department, the more confinement and corrections responsibilities it has. Sheriffs' departments frequently operate the county jail, which houses hundreds and even thousands of prisoners, depending on the particular

FIGURE 5-7

Number of Sworn Personnel in Sheriffs' Departments, 1993

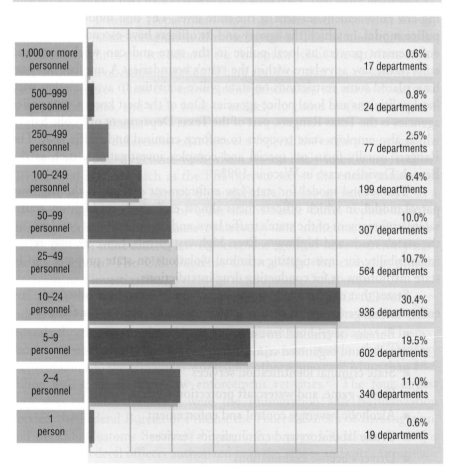

1,000 or more personnel	0.6% 17 departments
500–999 personnel	0.8% 24 departments
250–499 personnel	2.5% 77 departments
100–249 personnel	6.4% 199 departments
50–99 personnel	10.0% 307 departments
25–49 personnel	10.7% 564 departments
10–24 personnel	30.4% 936 departments
5–9 personnel	19.5% 602 departments
2–4 personnel	11.0% 340 departments
1 person	0.6% 19 departments

Source: Brian Reaves and Pheny Smith, *Sheriffs' Departments*, 1993 (Washington: Bureau of Justice Statistics, 1996).

History and Structure of American Law Enforcement

CHAPTER 5

FIGURE 5-8

Major Employers of Federal Officers Authorized to Make Arrests and Carry Firearms

Agency	Number of Full-Time Officers
Immigration and Naturalization Service	12,403
Federal Bureau of Prisons	11,329
Federal Bureau of Investigation	10,389
U.S. Customs Service	9,749
Internal Revenue Service	3,784
U.S. Postal Inspection Service	3,576
U.S. Secret Service	3,185
Drug Enforcement Administration	2,946
Administrative Office of the U.S. Courts	2,777
U.S. Marshals Service	2,650
National Park Service	2,148
Bureau of Alcohol, Tobacco and Firearms	1,869
U.S. Capitol Police	1,031
U.S. Fish and Wildlife Service	869
GSA-Federal Protective Service	643
U.S. Forest Service	619

Source: Brian A. Reaves, *Federal Law Enforcement Officers, 1996* (Washington: U.S. Bureau of Justice Statistics, December 1997) p. 2, Table 1.

American Private Security

Private security is a huge enterprise that complements public law enforcement in the United States. The Department of Labor's Bureau of Labor Statistics projects the continued growth of private security employment well into the 21st century. There may be as many as 1.8 million people now working in private security. Conservative estimates suggest that twice as many people work in private security as in public law enforcement. According to the National Association of Security Companies, the nation spends 73 percent more each year on private security than it does on public policing.[27]

A common way to subdivide private security employment is to classify the agencies and personnel as either contract or proprietary. **Contract security** companies offer protective services for a fee to people, agencies, and companies that do not employ their own security personnel or that need extra protection. A state university, for example, may employ private security officers to work at a football game. Contract security employees are not peace officers. **Proprietary security** agents and personnel provide protective

Contract security Protective services that a private security firm provides to people, agencies, and companies that do not employ their own security personnel or that need extra protection. Contract security employees are not peace officers.

Proprietary security In-house protective services that a security staff, not classified as sworn peace officers, provide for the entity that employs them.

Careers in Criminal Justice

FBI SPECIAL AGENT

FBI special agents investigate violations of federal laws. Their areas of concern include organized crime, white-collar crime, fraud, bribery, civil rights violations, bank robberies, extortion, kidnapping, air piracy, terrorism, and drug trafficking. A special agent must be a U.S. citizen between the ages of 23 and 37 and in excellent physical condition, must hold a four-year degree from an accredited college or university, must fulfill the additional requirements of one of four entry programs, and must complete a rigorous training program. In 1997, special agents entered service at Grade GS-10 on the federal government's general-schedule pay scale. Salaries vary by region of the country.

BORDER PATROL AGENT

Border Patrol agents enforce laws regulating the entry of aliens and products into the United States. They are employed by the Immigration and Naturalization Service (INS) of the U.S. Justice Department. Border Patrol agents must be U.S. citizens younger than 37 who are in good physical condition. In addition, an applicant must pass entry-level tests and a drug screening and must complete a training program. A bachelor's degree with the ability to speak Spanish or other languages is preferred. Border Patrol agents enter at the GS-5 or GS-7 grade, depending on their level of education.

---

services for the entity that employs them. They are not classified as sworn peace officers. For example, the Ford Motor Company employs its own security forces at its large manufacturing plants.

The services provided by the private security agencies of this nation are expected to cost $104 billion by the year 2000, substantially more than the $40 billion projected for public law enforcement.[28]

Reasons for Growth

A number of factors have stimulated the phenomenal growth of private security since the 1970s.

Declining Revenues for Public Policing In virtually all major cities and in state governments in the United States, the competition for limited funds to operate public services is fierce. Public police agencies have experienced their share of across-the-board government belt-tightening, and that has caused limitations and even freezes on the hiring of additional police officers. As a result, police departments have curtailed services no longer deemed critical. Often, businesses have filled the service gap by employing private security personnel.

The Intimate Nature of Crimes in the Workplace A business depends on a positive reputation to remain competitive. Widespread employee theft, embezzlement scandals, and substance abuse harm an organization's public image and may cause potential customers to question the quality of a company's products and services. By employing private security personnel to prevent and repress crime in their facilities, businesses can either hide the crimes that occur or minimize the negative publicity.

3. **INTERNET** Go to **www.officer.com** on the Internet and select two municipal police departments, one large and one small, and one county sheriff's department who list the agency's employment qualifications on their web page. Print out or copy the qualifications for later study. Then go to **www.career.com** on the Internet or to a major city newspaper's Help Wanted section and find the qualifications for a private security officer. Make a list of the similarities and differences between police and deputy sheriff qualifications and private security officer qualifications. Given your background and abilities, for which type of work would you be best suited? Why? Compile your findings in a two-page report and present it to the class.

CRITICAL THINKING EXERCISES

1. You live in a middle-class community of single-family homes close to the center of a midsize city. Over the past five years, everyone in your neighborhood has noted the rise in burglaries and many people feel that it is not safe to walk around the neighborhood after dark. You think that setting up a neighborhood watch would help lower the burglary rate and make people feel safer. Prepare an oral presentation of your ideas for a community meeting. Use the following questions as a guide.

   a. How would you go about organizing a night watch?

   b. How would you select volunteers?

   c. What training, if any, would volunteers have to have?

   d. How would you maintain interest and participation in the watch?

2. An off-duty police officer was seated in a restaurant when two men entered, drew guns, and robbed the cashier. The officer made no attempt to prevent the robbery or apprehend the robbers. Later the officer justified the conduct by stating that an officer, when off duty, is a private citizen with the same duties and rights of all private citizens. Do you agree? Explain.

ADDITIONAL READING

Bouza, Anthony V. *The Police Mystique: An Insider Looks at Cops, Crime, and the Criminal Justice System.* New York: Plenum, 1990.

Goldstein, Herman. *Problem-Oriented Policing.* New York: McGraw-Hill, 1990.

Gordon, Diana R. *The Justice Juggernaut: Fighting Street Crime, Controlling Citizens.* New Brunswick, NJ: Rutgers University Press, 1990.

Klockars, Carl B. *The Idea of Police.* Beverly Hills, CA: Sage, 1985.

Marx, Gary T. *Police Surveillance in America.* Berkeley: University of California Press, 1988.

Sparrow, Malcolm K., Mark H. Moore, and David M. Kennedy. *Beyond 911.* New York: Basic Books, 1990.

1. Material in this section was taken from T. A. Critchley, *A History of Police in England and Wales,* 2d ed. rev. (Montclair, NJ: Patterson Smith, 1972).

2. Ibid.

3. Patrick Pringle, *Hue and Cry: The Story of Henry and John Fielding and Their Bow Street Runners* (New York: William Morrow, 1965).

4. Material in this section was taken from A. C. Germann, F. Day, and R. Gallati, *Introduction to Law Enforcement and Criminal Justice* (Springfield, IL: Charles C. Thomas, 1962), pp. 54–55.

5. Edward Savage, *Police Records and Recollections, or Boston by Daylight and Gaslights for Two Hundred and Forty Years* (Boston: John P. Dale, 1873).

6. This material came from Carl Sifakis, *The Encyclopedia of American Crime* (New York: Smithmark, 1992), pp. 579–580.

7. Center for Research on Criminal Justice, *The Iron Fist and the Velvet Glove: An Analysis of the U.S. Police* (Berkeley, CA: Center for Research on Criminal Justice, 1975); Hubert Williams and Patrick V. Murphy, "The Evolving Strategy of Police: A Minority View," *Perspectives on Policing,* No. 13 (Washington: U.S. Department of Justice, January 1990).

8. Thad Sitton, *Texas High Sheriffs* (Austin: Texas Monthly Press, 1988).

9. Adrian N. Anderson, Ralph A. Wooster, David G. Armstrong, and Jeanie R. Stanley, *Texas and Texans,* (Glencoe/McGraw-Hill, 1993).

10. Bruce Smith, *Police Systems in the United States* (New York: Harper & Row, 1960), pp. 178–205.

11. *Our Police* (Cincinnati Police Division, 1984).

12. Gene Carte and Elaine Carte, *Police Reform in the United States: The Era of August Vollmer* (Berkeley: University of California Press, 1975).

13. Malcolm Sparrow, Mark Moore, and David Kennedy, *Beyond 911* (New York: Basic Books, 1990).

14. *Response Time Analysis: Executive Summary,* U.S. Department of Justice (Washington: GPO, 1978).

15. Samuel Walker, *The Police in America: An Introduction,* 2d ed. (New York: McGraw-Hill, 1992).

16. Robert C. Trojanowicz and Bonnie Bucqueroux, *Community Policing: A Contemporary Perspective* (Cincinnati: Anderson, 1989); Robert C. Trojanowicz and Bonnie Bucqueroux, *Community Policing: How to Get Started* (Cincinnati: Anderson 1994).

17. Federal Bureau of Investigation, *Crime in the United States, 1996* (Washington: GPO, 1997).

18. Brian A. Reaves, *Local Police Departments, 1993* (Washington: Bureau of Justice Statistics, 1996).

19. V. A. Leonard, *Police Organization and Management* (New York: Foundation Press, 1964).

20. Brian A. Reaves and Pheny Z. Smith, *Sheriff's Departments, 1993* (Washington: Bureau of Justice Statistics, 1996).

21. Ibid.

22. *Crime in the United States,* op. cit., p. 291, Table 76; Brian A. Reaves, *State and Local Police Departments, 1993* (Washington: Bureau of Justice Statistics, 1996).

23. Brian A. Reaves, *Federal Law Enforcement Officers, 1996* (Washington: Bureau of Justice Statistics, December 1997).

24. Ibid.

25. Kathleen Maguire and Ann L. Pastore (eds.), *Sourcebook of Criminal Justice Statistics 1996,* U. S. Department of Justice, Bureau of Justice Statistics (Washington: GPO, 1997), p. 14, Table 1.12.

26. Reaves, 1997, op. cit.

27. William Cunningham, John Strauchs, and Clifford Van Meter, *The Hallcrest Report II: Private Security Trends 1970–2000* (McLean, VA: Hallcrest Systems, 1990).

28. Ibid.

CHAPTER OUTLINE

6 Policing America: Culture, Conflict, and Decision Making

Policing in America

To successfully carry out the functions of law enforcement, order maintenance, service, and information gathering, the police must have the trust and cooperation of the public. The manner in which they carry out those functions, especially law enforcement and order maintenance, determines the community's respect for and trust in the police. Citizens who trust and respect the police are much more likely to help them carry out their functions; citizens who lack that trust and respect may rebel against the police in particular and government in general.

Public Attitudes Toward the Police

What do people think of the police? The answer depends on what and whom you ask. It also depends on people's prior experience with the police. Research shows that citizens who have experienced positive contacts with the police generally have positive attitudes toward the police.[1] Figure 6–1 reveals that, overall, 59 percent of the public has "a great deal" or "quite a lot" of confidence in the police, 30 percent has "some" confidence, and 11 percent has "very little" or "none." However, among nonwhites, only 45 percent have "a great deal" or "quite a lot" of confidence in the police, 35 percent have "some" confidence, and 20 percent have "very little" or "none." But what is it about the police that the public has or does not have confidence? To begin with, a majority of the public has confidence in the ability of the police to protect them from crime in general, to solve crime, and to prevent crime.

Protection From Crime Nearly three-quarters of the public (74%) have at least some confidence in the ability of the police to protect them from crime in general. As shown in the first panel of Figure 6–2, 30 percent of the public has "a great deal" of confidence, 44 percent has "some" confidence, 16 percent has "little" confidence, and 8 percent has "none at all." Among blacks, however, confidence in the police's ability to protect them from crime is decidedly lower. Only 18 percent of blacks have "a great deal" of confidence

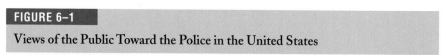

FIGURE 6–1

Views of the Public Toward the Police in the United States

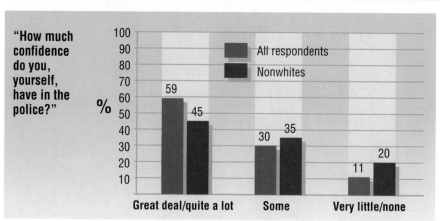

"How much confidence do you, yourself, have in the police?"

%

All respondents
Nonwhites

Great deal/quite a lot: 59 / 45
Some: 30 / 35
Very little/none: 11 / 20

Source: Kathleen Maguire and Ann L. Pastore (eds.), *Sourcebook of Criminal Justice Statistics 1996*, U.S. Department of Justice, Bureau of Justice Statistics (Washington: GPO, 1997), p. 119, Table 2.11.

FIGURE 6–2

Views of the Public Toward the Police in the United States

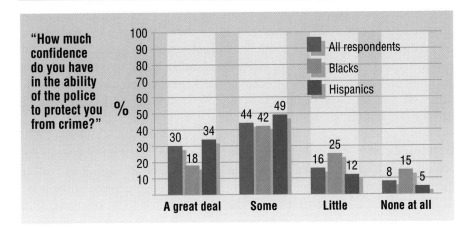

"How much confidence do you have in the ability of the police to protect you from crime?"

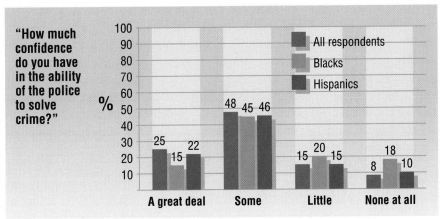

"How much confidence do you have in the ability of the police to solve crime?"

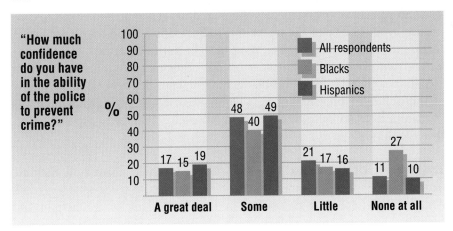

"How much confidence do you have in the ability of the police to prevent crime?"

Source: Kathleen Maguire and Ann L. Pastore (eds.), *Sourcebook of Criminal Justice Statistics 1996,* U.S. Department of Justice Statistics (Washington: GPO, 1997), p. 127, Table 2.22.

in the police's ability to protect them from crime, 42 percent have "some" confidence, 25 percent have "little" confidence, and 15 percent have "none at all." Among Hispanics, 34 percent have "a great deal" of confidence in the ability of the police to protect them from crime, 49 percent have "some" confidence, 12 percent have "little" confidence, and 5 percent have "none at all."

Policing America: Culture, Conflict, and Decision Making

The public, overall, is less confident in the police's ability to protect them from violent crime. Only one-half the public have either "a great deal" (20%) or "quite a lot" (30%) of confidence in the police's ability to protect them from violent crime; 39 percent have "not very much" confidence, and 9 percent have "none at all." Again, nonwhites have less confidence than the general public. When asked about the police's ability to protect them from violent crime, only 15 percent of nonwhites (and 16% of blacks) have "a great deal" of confidence, 25 percent (22% of blacks) have "quite a lot" of confidence, 45 percent (46% of blacks) have "not very much" confidence, and 13 percent (14% of blacks) have "none at all."[2]

Solving Crime The public as a whole has about as much confidence in the police's ability to solve crime as it does about the police's ability to protect them from crime in general. Seventy-three and one-half percent of the public have at least some confidence in the police's ability to solve crime; 25.5 percent have "a great deal" of confidence, 48 percent have "some" confidence, 15 percent have "little" confidence, and 8 percent have "none at all." As before, minorities have less confidence than the public as a whole. Among blacks, 15 percent have "a great deal" of confidence in the ability of the police to solve crime, 45 percent have "some" confidence, 20 percent have "little" confidence, and 18 percent have "none at all." Of Hispanics asked to rate their confidence in the ability of the police to solve crime, 22 percent have "a great deal" of confidence, 46 percent have "some" confidence, 15 percent have "little" confidence, and 10 percent have "none at all." (See the second panel of Figure 6–2.)

Preventing Crime The public as a whole is somewhat less confident about the ability of the police to prevent crime than it is about the ability of the police to protect them from crime in general and to solve crime. Only about 65 percent of the public have "a great deal" (17%) or "some" (48%) confidence in the ability of the police to prevent crime, 21 percent have "little" confidence, and 11 percent have "none at all." On this measure racial and ethnic differences are not as great as on the other measures. The only major exception is that 27 percent of blacks have no confidence at all in the ability of the police to prevent crime, whereas 9.5 percent of both whites and Hispanics have no confidence at all in the police's ability to prevent crime. (See the third panel of Figure 6–2.)

Treatment of Citizens People are also concerned about how they are treated by the police. Opinion polls show that nearly three-quarters of all Americans believe that the police in their communities are helpful and friendly. However, among blacks, only about 60 percent rate the police in their communities as being "excellent" or "pretty good" at being helpful and friendly; 29 percent rate them as only "fair" and 12 percent rate them as "poor."[3]

When asked whether or not the police in their communities treat people fairly, 63 percent of the general public rate the police as either "excellent" (20%) or "pretty good" (43%) on this measure, 24 percent rate them as "only fair," and 11 percent rate them as "poor." Among blacks, however, fewer than half (38%) rate the police as doing an "excellent" (9%) or "pretty good" (29%)

FIGURE 6-3

Views of the Public Toward the Police in the United States

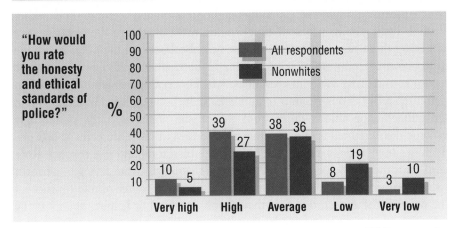

"How would you rate the honesty and ethical standards of police?"

Source: Kathleen Maguire and Ann L. Pastore (eds.), *Sourcebook of Criminal Justice Statistics 1996*, U.S. Department of Justice, Bureau of Justice Statistics (Washington: GPO, 1997), p. 126, Table 2.11.

job of treating people fairly, 36 percent rate them as "only fair," and 26 percent rate them as "poor."[4]

No treatment is as unfair as is police brutality. A majority of all Americans (60%) believe there is no police brutality in their areas. However, blacks are split on this issue: 45 percent of them think there is police brutality in their areas, while 46 percent do not.[5]

Honesty and Ethical Standards When asked to rate the honesty and ethical standards of the police, 10 percent of the general public rate the police as "very high" on this measure, 39 percent rate them as "high," 38 percent rate them as "average," 8 percent rate them as "low," and 3 percent rate them as "very low." Nonwhites rate the honesty and ethical standards of police lower: Only 5 percent rate the police as "very high," 27 percent rate them as "high," 36 percent rate them as "average," 19 percent rate them as "low," and 10 percent rate them as "very low." (See Figure 6–3.)

In sum, these data clearly show that the public as a whole has more respect for the police and their honesty and ethical standards than it does for a variety of other occupations.[6] Yet, the level of respect is not particularly high, nor is it uniform across races. While most of the public believes that the police do a pretty good job, it also believes there is much room for improvement.

The Roles of the Police

Our expectations of police behavior depend on where we live and when we consider the question. For example, we saw in the last chapter that Cincinnati wanted its police officers in the 1880s to be fleet-footed and honest. In Dallas, Miami, and New York City, citizens may expect police officers to have a working knowledge of Spanish. In Alaska, we would expect police officers to be self-reliant, enjoy the outdoors, and not mind working by themselves in lonely surroundings. In essence, what we expect from the police depends on how we view their role in society.

Role The rights and responsibilities associated with a particular position in society.

Role expectation The behavior and actions that people expect from a person in a particular role.

Role conflict The psychological stress and frustration that results from trying to perform two or more incompatible responsibilities.

A **role** consists of the rights and responsibilities associated with a particular position in society. A related concept is **role expectation,** the behavior and actions that people expect from a person in a particular role. Suppose, for example, that teenagers living in a wealthy neighborhood have been caught drinking alcohol. Their parents probably expect police officers to warn the young people and bring them home. In a less affluent neighborhood, on the other hand, the expectation of community residents might be that the police will arrest the teenagers and bring them into juvenile court. This example illustrates a problem that often arises in our attempt to understand the police role in America. When the public's expectations differ from the official police role, the public may become disenchanted and sometimes hostile toward law enforcement officers. Such negative feelings cause officers personal frustration and role conflict. **Role conflict** is the psychological strain and stress that results from trying to perform two or more incompatible responsibilities. A common source of role conflict for the police is the expectation that they should be social or helping agents at the same time they are expected to be control agents by arresting law violators.

What we expect from police officers, then, depends on how we view the police role—a role that has been described as complex, ambiguous, changing, and repressive. Obviously, not everyone views the role of the police in the same way, but a definition that includes the majority of perspectives is possible. The police:

1. Are community leaders in public safety. (By nature, this makes the work potentially dangerous.)
2. Possess broad discretion.
3. Solve sociological and technological problems for people on a short-term basis.
4. Occasionally serve in a hostile or dangerous environment.[7]

Police officers are expected to respond to traffic accidents.

Policing America: Culture, Conflict, and Decision Making

Think about some of the common situations in which police officers find themselves when people call and want something "fixed." One example would be an officer's response to freeway accidents where vehicles are overturned and burning and people are trapped inside. Such situations require leadership, informed and quick decisions, the solving of numerous immediate problems, and the use of extreme caution to prevent further injury to citizens or the police officer. Another example would be intervention in a long-running family dispute that has suddenly turned violent. Such a situation requires caution, quick thinking, and the solving of a number of problems in an effort to ensure the safety of all parties. Still another typical role of a police officer is to provide protection at protests and strikes. Those potentially volatile circumstances clearly illustrate the key elements of the police role. Of course, sometimes an officer's role may be simply to solve problems in the course of providing service, as when retrieving a citizen's dropped keys from below a sewer grate.

Characteristics of Police Work

Police work requires a combination of special characteristics. Personnel with the following qualities are best able to carry out the difficult service role mandated for law enforcement officers.

Quick Decision Making Sometimes police officers must make on-the-spot decisions about whether to use force, how to maneuver a patrol car, or whether to stop a suspect. Making the wrong decision can be fatal for the officer or the other person. All of the work in a lengthy investigation can be ruined by a single procedural law violation if an officer unintentionally makes a wrong decision.

The Independent Nature of Police Work The position of peace officer in all states in the United States is a position of honor and trust. After patrol officers attend roll call, stand inspection, check out their equipment, and depart into the streets in their patrol cars, they work virtually unsupervised until the end of their tour of duty.

Figure 6–4 on page 186 shows the Law Enforcement Officer's Code of Ethics, which was written as a guide for working police officers. It offers some professional direction in a line of work with many opportunities to go astray. The independent nature of police work increases the chances of malfeasance and corruption—topics to be discussed later in this chapter.

"Dirty Work" Most people agree that police work needs to be done. Most of us, however, do not want to do it, nor do we want to see it done. The reason is that much police work is distasteful—for example, dealing with people who have committed horrible acts and viewing mangled, broken, and decomposed bodies. The distasteful part of policing has been referred to as "dirty work."[8]

Danger Police officers in the United States spend a substantial amount of their time trying to resolve conflicts, frequently in hostile environments.[9]

FIGURE 6–4

Law Enforcement Officer Code of Ethics

The purpose of the Code of Ethics is to ensure that all peace officers are fully aware of their individual responsibility to maintain their own integrity and that of their agency. Every peace officer, during basic training, or at the time of appointment, shall be administered the [following] Code of Ethics.

As a law enforcement officer, my fundamental duty is to serve mankind; to safeguard lives and property; to protect the innocent against deception, the weak against oppression or intimidation, and the peaceful against violence or disorder; and to respect the constitutional rights of all men to liberty, equality, and justice.

I will keep my private life unsullied as an example to all; maintain courageous calm in the face of danger, scorn, or ridicule; develop self-restraint; and be constantly mindful of the welfare of others. Honest in thought and deed in both my personal and official life, I will be exemplary in obeying the laws of the land and the regulations of my department. Whatever I see or hear of a confidential nature or that is confided to me in my official capacity will be kept ever secret unless revelation is necessary in the performance of my duty. I will never act officiously or permit personal feelings, prejudices, animosities, or friendships to influence my decisions. With no compromise for crime and with relentless prosecution of criminals, I will enforce the law courteously and appropriately without fear or favor, malice or ill will, never employing unnecessary force or violence, and never accepting gratuities.

I recognize the badge of my office as a symbol of public faith, and I accept it as a public trust to be held so long as I am true to the ethics of the police service. I will constantly strive to achieve these objectives and ideals, dedicating myself to my chosen profession—law enforcement.

Canons

1. The primary responsibility of police officers and organizations is the protection of citizens by upholding the law and respecting the legally expressed will of the whole community and not a particular party or clique.

2. Police officers should be aware of the legal limits on their authority and the "genius of the American system," which limits the power of individuals, groups, and institutions.

3. Police officers are responsible for being familiar with the law and not only their responsibilities but also those of other public officials.

4. Police officers should be mindful of the importance of using the proper means to gain proper ends. Officers should not employ illegal means, nor should they disregard public safety or property to accomplish a goal.

5. Police officers will cooperate with other public officials in carrying out their duties. However, the officer shall be careful not to use his or her position in an improper or illegal manner when cooperating with other officials.

6. In their private lives, police officers will behave in such a manner that the public will "regard (the officer) as an example of stability, fidelity, and morality." It is necessary that police officers conduct themselves in a "decent and honorable" manner.

7. In their behavior toward members of the public, officers will provide service when possible, require compliance with the law, respond in a manner that inspires confidence and trust, and will be neither overbearing nor subservient.

8. When dealing with violators or making arrests, officers will follow the law; officers have no right to persecute individuals or punish them. And officers should behave in such a manner so the likelihood of the use of force is minimized.

9. Police officers should refuse to accept any gifts, favors, or gratuities that, from a public perspective, could influence the manner in which the officer discharges his or her duties.

10. Officers will present evidence in criminal cases impartially because the officer should be equally concerned with both the prosecution of criminals and the defense of innocent persons.

Source: Commission on Peace Officer Standards and Training, *Administrative Manual* (State of California: POST, 1990), p. c–5. Reprinted by permission.

Contrary to the media image, police officers are often afraid on the job, and far too many are injured or killed. Figure 6–5 identifies the dangerous circumstances in which officers find themselves and the frequency with which they are assaulted. The data reveal that disturbance calls (for example, a family quarrel or a man with a gun) and arrests of suspects are the most dangerous circumstances for police officers.

Each year, police officers are also killed while on duty. In 1996, for example, 55 officers were killed in the line of duty—19 fewer than the year before.[10] Accidents during the performance of official duties claimed the lives of an additional 45 officers, 12 fewer than in 1995.

From 1978 through 1996, 1475 law enforcement officers were killed in the line of duty; the most in any one year was 106 in 1979, while the least in any one year was 55 in 1996.[11]

FIGURE 6–5

Law Enforcement Officers Assaulted in the United States, 1995

Circumstances at Scene of Incident	Total
Total	56,686
Percent of Total	100%
Disturbance calls (family quarrel, man with gun, etc.)	18,709
	33%
Burglaries in progress or pursuit of burglary suspects	710
	1.0%
Robberies in progress or pursuit of robbery suspects	611
	1.0%
Other arrest attempts	10,023
	18%
Civil disorders (mass disobedience, riot, etc.)	661
	1.0%
Handling, transporting, custody of prisoners	6,628
	12%
Investigation of suspicious persons and circumstances	6,063
	11%
Ambush (no warning)	243
	0.4%
Mentally deranged	773
	0.1%
Traffic pursuits and stops	5,761
	10%
All other	6,504
	11%

Source: Kathleen Maguire and Ann L. Pastore (eds.), *Sourcebook of Criminal Justice Statistics 1996,* U.S. Department of Justice, Bureau of Justice Statistics (Washington: GPO, 1997), p. 357, Table 3.161.

FYI

Today, some 675,000 sworn officers put their lives on the line for our protection each day. The first known line-of-duty death was that of U.S. Marshal Robert Forsyth, who was shot and killed on January 11, 1794, while serving court papers in a civil suit. Wilmington, Delaware, police matron Mary T. Davis was the first female officer killed on duty. She was beaten to death in 1924 while guarding a prisoner in the city jail.

Operational Styles

Operational styles The different-ent overall approaches to the police job.

After police officers are trained and begin to gain experience and wisdom from their encounters with veteran police officers and citizens on the street, it is believed that they develop **operational styles** that characterize their overall approach to the police job. If these styles actually exist, it means that the effort of the police department to systematically train and deploy officers with the same philosophy and practical approach to policing in the community has not been entirely successful. The research on operational styles shows that they vary both between departments and among officers of the same department.

One of the earliest scholars to report on the existence of policing styles was James Q. Wilson, who found the following three styles in a study of eight police departments:

1. Legalistic style. The emphasis is on violations of law and the use of threats or actual arrests to solve disputes in the community. In theory, the more arrests that are made, the safer a community will be. This style is often found in large metropolitan areas.

2. Watchman style. The emphasis is on informal means of resolving disputes and problems in a community. Keeping the peace is the paramount concern, and arrest is used only as a last resort to resolve any kind of disturbance of the peace. This style of policing is most commonly found in economically poorer communities.

3. Service style. The emphasis is on helping in the community, as opposed to enforcing the law. Referrals and diversion to community treatment agencies are more common than arrest and formal court action. The service style is most likely to be found in wealthy communities.[12]

John Broderick classified police officers by their degree of commitment to maintaining order and their respect for due process:

1. Enforcers. The emphasis is on order, with little respect for due process.

2. Idealists. The emphasis is on both social order and due process.

3. Optimists. The emphasis is on due process, with little priority given to social order.

4. Realists. Little emphasis is given to due process or social order.[13]

Another classification is based on the way officers use their authority and power in street police work. The two key ingredients of this scheme are passion and perspective. Passion is the ability to use force or the recognition that force is a legitimate means of resolving conflict; perspective is the ability to understand human suffering and to use force ethically and morally. According to William Muir's styles of policing, police officers may be:

1. Professionals. Officers have the necessary passion and perspective to be valuable police officers.

2. Enforcers. Officers have passion in responding to human problems but do not recognize limits on their power to resolve them.

3. Reciprocators. Officers are too objective in that they have perspective but virtually no passion, resulting in a detachment from the suffering they encounter and often a failure to take action.

4. Avoiders. Officers have neither passion nor perspective, resulting in no recognition of people's problems and no action to resolve them.[14]

Are there identifiable styles of policing, and what value are they to us? In any area of human endeavor, classifications have been constructed. We have done it with leaders, prisoners, quarterbacks, and teachers. They give us a framework of analysis, a basis for discussion. But can they be substantiated when we go into a police agency to see if they actually exist? Ellen Hochstedler examined the issue of policing styles with 1134 Dallas, Texas, police officers and was not able to confirm the officer styles identified in the literature by Broderick, Muir, and others. Her conclusion was that it is not possible to "pigeonhole" officers into one style or another because the way officers think and react to street situations varies, depending on the particular situation, the time, and the officers themselves.[15]

Police Functions

The list of functions that police are expected to carry out is long and varies from place to place. In the following sections, we will look at the major operations of police departments and the services they provide.

Patrol

Police administrators have long referred to patrol as the backbone of the department. It is unquestionably the most time-consuming and resource-intensive task of any police agency. More than half of the sworn personnel in any police department are assigned to patrol. In Houston, Chicago, and New York, for example, patrol officers make up more than 65 percent of the sworn personnel in each department.

Patrol officers respond to burglar alarms, investigate traffic accidents, care for injured people, try to resolve domestic disputes, and engage in a host of other duties that keep them chasing radio calls across their own beats, and the entire city and county when no other cars are available to respond. Precisely how to conduct patrol activities, however, is a matter of much debate in the nation today. Indeed, it seems that there are many ways to police a city.

Street patrol is the most resource-intensive task of any police agency.

Preventive Patrol For decades, police officers patrolled the streets with little direction. Between their responses to radio calls, they were told to be "systematically unsystematic" and observant in an attempt to both prevent and ferret out crime on their beats. In many police departments, as much as 50 percent of an officer's time is uncommitted and available for patrolling the

189

Policing America: Culture, Conflict, and Decision Making

CHAPTER 6

Preventive patrol Patrolling the streets with little direction; between responses to radio calls, officers are "systematically unsystematic" and observant in an attempt to both prevent and ferret out crime. Also known as *random patrol.*

beats that make up a political jurisdiction. The simultaneous increases in crime and the size of police forces beginning in the 1960s caused police managers and academics to question the usefulness of what has come to be known as **preventive patrol** or random patrol. To test the usefulness of preventive patrol, the now famous Kansas City (Missouri) Preventive Patrol Experiment was conducted in 1972.

The Kansas City, Missouri, Police Department and the Police Foundation set up an experiment in which 15 patrol districts were divided into three matched groups according to size, record of calls for service, and demographic characteristics. In the first group, the "control beats," the police department operated the same level of patrol used previously in those beats. In the second group of districts, the "proactive beats," the police department doubled or even tripled the number of patrol officers normally deployed in the area. In the third group of districts, the "reactive beats," the police department deployed no officers at all on preventive patrol. Officers only responded to calls for service and did no patrolling on their own. At the end of the one-year study, the results showed no significant differences in crime rates among the three groups of patrol districts. In other words, a group of districts that had no officers on preventive patrol had the same crime rates as groups that had several times the normal level of staffing engaged in patrol activity. The number of officers made no difference in the number of burglaries, robberies, vehicle thefts, and other serious crimes experienced in the three groups of police districts. Perhaps even more important is that the citizens of Kansas City did not even notice that the levels of patrol in two of the three districts had been changed.[16]

The law enforcement community was astounded by the results of the study, which showed that it made no difference whether patrol officers conducted preventive, or random, patrol. The research was immediately attacked on both philosophical and methodological grounds. How could anyone say that having patrol officers on the street made no difference?

One of the criticisms of the study was that no one in the community was told that there were no officers on patrol in reactive districts. What might have happened to the crime rates had the community known no officers were on patrol? Moreover, during the course of the study, marked police cars from other departments and districts crossed the reactive districts to answer calls but then left when the work was completed. Thus, there appeared to be a police presence even in the so-called reactive districts.

This study has forced police executives and academics to reconsider the whole issue of how patrol is conducted, once considered a closed issue. Police administrators have begun to entertain the possibility of reducing the number of officers on patrol. Innovations in patrol methods have also been proposed.

MYTH   FACT

Adding more police officers will reduce crime.

Short of having a police officer on every corner, evidence indicates no relationship between the number of police officers and the crime rate.

Field interrogation has been found to reduce crime in targeted areas.

Directed Patrol In **directed patrol,** officers are given guidance or orders on how to use their patrol time. The guidance is often based on the results of crime analyses that identify problem areas. Evidence shows that directed patrol can reduce the incidence of targeted crimes such as thefts from autos and robberies.[17]

Directed patrol Patrolling under guidance or orders on how to use patrol time.

Aggressive Patrol In nearly all police departments, some patrol officers have used aggressive patrol tactics and have been rewarded as high performers because they made many arrests for both minor and serious offenses. When the entire patrol section is instructed to make numerous traffic stops and field interrogations, the practice is referred to as **aggressive patrol.** A **field interrogation** is a temporary detention in which officers stop and question pedestrians and motorists they find in suspicious circumstances. Such procedures have been found to reduce crime in targeted areas.[18]

Aggressive patrol The practice of having an entire patrol section make numerous traffic stops and field interrogations. **Field interrogation** A temporary detention in which officers stop and question pedestrians and motorists they find in suspicious circumstances.

At least two problems can occur as a result of aggressive patrol. First, random traffic stops and field interrogations inconvenience innocent citizens. To avoid conflict, the police must be certain that those tactics are necessary, and they must explain the necessity to the public. Second, it is often difficult to get all officers on each work shift and in each patrol division motivated to use aggressive patrol tactics. Many officers are reluctant to carry out their duties in an aggressive way. Nevertheless, with crime rates high and research confirming that aggressive patrol can reduce crime, aggressive patrol tactics are likely to continue.

Foot Patrol During the last few years, there has been renewed interest in having police officers patrol their beats on foot. Is there value in this practice, or is it just nostalgia for a more romantic period in law enforcement? The use of motorized patrols has allowed the police to respond rapidly to citizen calls and to cover large geographical areas. Yet, officers working a busy shift, perhaps responding to more than two dozen calls, come to feel as if they are seeing the world through a windshield. Moreover, it is now generally accepted that rapid response time is useful in only a small portion of the incidents and crimes to which the police are asked to respond.

Challenging conventional wisdom about rapid response, two cities—Flint, Michigan, and Newark, New Jersey—launched substantial programs in foot patrol. In Newark, the results of the foot patrol experiment showed that foot patrol had little or no effect on the level of crime. However, positive effects were identified:

1. Newark residents noticed whether foot patrol officers were present.
2. They were more satisfied with police service when foot patrol officers delivered it.
3. They were less afraid than citizens being served by motorized patrol.[19]

In Flint, Michigan, the extensive neighborhood foot patrol experiment also had positive results:

1. Flint residents had a decreased fear of crime.
2. Their satisfaction with police service increased.
3. There were moderate decreases in crime.
4. There were decreased numbers of calls for police service.

Citizens would wait to talk to their neighborhood foot patrol officer about a problem instead of calling the police department through 911 and speaking with an officer they were not likely to know. One astounding result of the Flint program was that the foot patrol officers became so popular that citizens saw them as real community leaders. They often became more influential than some elected officials. Evidence of the degree of satisfaction with the foot patrol program in Flint was that the community voted three times to continue and expand foot patrol at a time when the city was experiencing one of the nation's highest unemployment rates.[20] Perhaps even more important, the findings of foot patrol research provided the seeds of a much broader concept for law enforcement: community policing, which we will discuss later in this chapter.

MYTH

Shorter police response time contributes to more arrests.

FACT

For most crimes, police response time is irrelevant. Approximately two-thirds of crimes are "cold"; the offender is gone long before the crime is discovered. In cases where time counts, the critical delay often occurs in the time it takes the victim to call the police.

INVESTIGATION

The role of the detective has generally been glorified by media sources in both fiction and nonfiction accounts. Homicide investigation, in particular, has captured the imagination of fiction readers worldwide. Most police officers aspire to be investigative specialists by attaining the position of detective. But it should be noted that detectives represent only one unit in a police department that conducts investigations. Investigators work in a variety of capacities in a police agency:

1. Traffic homicide and hit-and-run accident investigators in the traffic section.

2. Undercover investigators in narcotics, vice, and violent gang cases.

3. Internal affairs investigators conducting investigations of alleged crimes by police personnel.

4. Investigators conducting background checks of applicants to the police department.

5. Uniformed patrol officers investigating the crimes they have been dispatched to or have encountered on their own while on patrol.

What Is Criminal Investigation? Berg and Horgan define criminal investigation as a lawful search for people and things to reconstruct the circumstances of an illegal act, apprehend or determine the guilty party, and aid in the state's prosecution of the offender.[21] The criminal investigation process is generally divided into two parts: the preliminary, or initial, investigation and the continuing, or follow-up, investigation. Most of the time the preliminary investigation in both felony and misdemeanor cases is conducted by patrol officers, although for homicides and other complex, time-consuming investigations, trained investigators are dispatched to the crime scene immediately. The continuing investigation in serious crimes is ordinarily conducted by plainclothes detectives, although small and medium-sized agencies may require patrol officers or a patrol supervisor to follow up on serious criminal offenses.

Investigative Functions In any type of investigation in a police agency, all investigators share responsibility for a number of critical functions. They must:

1. Locate witnesses and suspects.

2. Arrest criminals.

3. Collect, preserve, and analyze evidence.

4. Interview witnesses.

5. Interrogate suspects.

6. Write reports.

7. Recover stolen property.

8. Seize contraband.

9. Prepare cases and testify in court.

The specific application and context of those functions vary considerably, depending on whether the investigation is of the theft of expensive paintings, for example, or the rape of an elderly widow living alone.

Criminal investigation is a time-consuming task that requires much attention to detail.

The Role of the Detective At first glance, the role of the detective seems highly desirable. To a patrol officer who has been rotating work shifts for several years, seldom getting a weekend off, detectives in the police department seem to have a number of advantages:

1. They do not have to wear uniforms.

2. They have anonymity during work hours if they choose it.

3. They have steady work hours, often daytime hours with weekends off.

4. They have offices and desks.

5. They enjoy the prestige associated with the position.

6. In many agencies, detectives receive higher compensation and hold a higher rank.

7. Perhaps most important, they enjoy more freedom than patrol officers from the police radio, geographical boundaries, and close supervision.

All these advantages add up to a high-status position, both within the police department and in the eyes of the public.

Productivity Despite all the advantages of being a detective, investigators are often faced with insurmountable obstacles and stressful work conditions. Notifying the next of kin in a homicide is one of the worst tasks:

> Of all the dirty tasks that go with the dirty work of chasing a killer, notifying the next of kin is the job that homicide detectives hate most. It's worse than getting up at 3 a.m. on a February night to slog through a field of freezing mud toward a body that needed burying two days ago. Worse than staring into the flat cold eyes of a teenager who bragged about dragging a man through the streets to his death. Worse than visiting every sleazy dive in town until you finally find the one person who can put the murderer away and having that person say as cool as a debutante with a full dance card, "I don't want to get involved."[23]

Detectives have the cards stacked against them most of the time. Unless they discover, during the preliminary investigation, a named suspect or a description or other information that leads to a named suspect, the chances of solving the crime are low. Property crimes with no witnesses are particularly hard to solve. In 1996, for example, the clearance rates for crimes against persons were 67 percent for murder, 58 percent for aggravated assault, 52 percent for forcible rape, and 27 percent for robbery. In crimes against property, the clearance rates were 14 percent for burglary, 20 percent for larceny-theft, and 14 percent for motor vehicle theft. Clearances for crimes against persons are generally higher than for property crimes because crimes against persons receive more intensive investigative effort and because victims and witnesses frequently identify the perpetrators. Overall, the national clearance rate in 1996 was 22 percent.[24] Studies have found that much of what a detective does is not needed and that an investigator's technical knowledge often does little to help solve cases.[25] In one study, for example, fewer than 10 percent of all arrests for robbery were the result of investigative work by detectives.[26] Nevertheless, police agencies retain detectives and plainclothes investigators, for a number of reasons:

1. Detectives have interrogation and case presentation skills that assist in prosecution.

2. Technical knowledge, such as knowing about burglary tools, does help in some investigations and prosecutions.

3. Law enforcement executives can assign detectives to a major, high-profile case to demonstrate to the public that they are committing resources to the matter.

The major studies of investigative effectiveness emphasize the value of improving the suspect-identification process. Once a suspect is identified by name or some other clearly distinguishing characteristic, the chances of making an arrest are increased substantially.

MYTH

Improvements in detective work and criminal investigation will significantly raise clearance rates or lower the crime rate.

FACT

"Cleared" crimes generally solve themselves. The offender either is discovered at the scene or can be identified by the victim or a witness. Investigation rarely solves "cold" or "stranger" crimes.

Recent Identification Developments in Criminal Investigation

Two recent developments in scientific investigation have improved the likelihood of identifying suspects from evidence found at the crime scene or on the suspects themselves.

DNA profiling DNA (deoxyribonucleic acid) is a molecule present in all forms of life. A unique genetic profile can be derived from blood, hair, semen, or other bodily substances found at the scene of a crime or on a victim. Not only can bodily substances found at a crime scene be matched with DNA samples from a suspect to give an extremely high probability of identifying the perpetrator, but it is believed that soon DNA from a sample as small as a flake of dandruff will yield a positive, unique identification, with no need to consider mathematical probabilities.

Automated Fingerprint Identification System An expensive but invaluable tool in criminal investigation is the Automated Fingerprint Identification System (AFIS). This relatively new technology allows investigators to sort through thousands of sets of stored fingerprints for a match with those of a suspect in a crime. In fact, many of the current attempts to match prints would not have been made without AFIS, because the old process would have taken thousands of hours. Large metropolitan police agencies use it to identify 200–500 suspects a year who would have escaped apprehension before the implementation of AFIS. The initial and maintenance costs for an AFIS, however, are expensive.

In approximately one-third of DNA examinations, the suspect's DNA cannot be matched with biological evidence from the crime scene. Thus, potential suspects can be eliminated from consideration early in the investigative process, allowing investigators to focus their efforts more effectively on other suspects or cases.

Traffic

When loss of life, serious injury, suffering, and property damage are all considered, the regulation and control of vehicle and pedestrian traffic are important, if not the most important, police responsibilities. Each year, nearly twice as many people are killed in automobile accidents on the streets and highways of the nation as are murdered. A large percentage of this highway death and suffering is attributable to alcohol. Enforcement of DUI (driving under the influence) laws is critical to the safety of a community. In addition, automobile insurance rates are based to some degree on a community's level of traffic enforcement. Thus, if the police neglect traffic regulation and enforcement, they are likely to hear about it.

Some of the debate about traffic enforcement concerns whether the major enforcers of traffic regulations should be specialized personnel or uniformed patrol officers. Some traffic responsibilities are already delegated to specialized personnel, such as enforcement of parking regulations and investigation of hit-and-run accidents and traffic fatalities. In some agencies, special **traffic accident investigation crews** are assigned to all traffic accident investigations. Otherwise, patrol officers investigate accidents as a normal part of their workload.

Traffic units exist in nearly all medium-to-large police agencies. Some of their more important functions are:

- To educate motorists in a community about traffic safety and proper driving procedures.
- To enforce traffic laws, particularly when violations of those laws cause traffic accidents.
- To recommend traffic engineering changes that will enhance the flow of traffic and promote safety.

Enforcing traffic laws may also reduce criminal activity because stopping vehicles for traffic violations both day and night is likely to put police officers in contact with criminals.

Traffic accident investigation crews In some agencies, the special units assigned to all traffic accident investigations.

MYTH

*F*ingerprints are crucial in solving crimes.

FACT

*A*lthough fingerprints are useful in cases involving known suspects, they are rarely helpful in solving crimes where the suspect is unknown (the vast majority of criminal cases) because of the difficulty of obtaining usable prints at the crime scene.

Many veteran officers consider working in the traffic division "clean" police work because it does not normally involve responding to radio calls that take them to the scene of fights, domestic disturbances, or other distasteful incidents, such as those involving drunks. Traffic officers in large police agencies are usually well schooled in scientific accident investigation, a skill that makes them employable in the private sector, usually doing traffic reconstruction for insurance companies. The Traffic Institute at Northwestern University is one of the major schools that prepare officers for sophisticated accident investigation, although many state peace officer and highway patrol academies now have comparable training programs.

Policing America: Culture, Conflict, and Decision Making

Community Policing

For decades, police followed the professional model, which rested on three foundations: preventive patrol, quick response time, and follow-up investigation. Sensing that the professional model did not always operate as efficiently and effectively as it could, criminal justice researchers set out to review current procedures and evaluate alternative programs. One of the first and best-known of these studies was the Kansas City, Missouri, Preventive Patrol Experiment, discussed earlier in this chapter. That study's conclusion was that preventive patrol did not necessarily prevent crime or reassure citizens. Following the study, some police departments assigned police units to proactive patrol, giving them specific assignments rather than having them randomly cruise the streets.

Another study, again with the Kansas City Police Department, examined the effects of police response time. The study found that police response time was unrelated to the probability of making an arrest. Researchers discovered that the time it takes a citizen to report a crime—not the speed with which police respond—was the major determinant of whether an on-scene arrest took place or witnesses could be located. In 90 percent of crimes, citizens wait 5–10 minutes to call the police, precluding catching the criminal at the scene.

As preventive patrol and fast response time were being questioned, so too was follow-up investigation. A study by the Rand Corporation reviewed the criminal investigation process for effectiveness. The researchers concluded that the work of a criminal investigator alone rarely leads to an arrest and that the probability of arrest is determined largely by information that patrol officers obtain at the crime scene in their preliminary investigation.[27]

Criminal justice researchers continued their review of accepted police functions with the aim of making policing more effective by initiating new techniques and procedures. One of the interesting findings of the foot patrol research was that foot patrol officers were better able to deal with minor annoyances—such as rowdy youths, panhandlers, and abandoned cars—that irritate citizens. In a theory called "broken windows," James Q. Wilson and George Kelling proposed that those minor annoyances are "signs of crime" and that if they are not dealt with early, more serious problems are likely to occur.[28] Wilson and Kelling concluded that to help solve both minor and major problems in a neighborhood and to reduce crime and fear of crime, police officers must be in close, regular contact with citizens. That is, police and citizens should work cooperatively to build a strong sense of community and shared responsibility in the neighborhood to improve the overall quality of life.

The Philosophy and Components of Community Policing

With community policing, citizens share responsibility for their community's safety. Citizens and the police work collectively to identify problems, propose solutions, implement action, and evaluate the results in the community. A community policing perspective differs in a number of ways from a traditional policing perspective. For example, in community policing, the police must share power with residents of a community, and critical

The Violent Crime Control and Law Enforcement Act of 1994—popularly known as the Crime Act—authorized $8.8 billion over six years for grants to local policing agencies to add 100,000 officers and promote community policing in innovative ways. To implement the law, the Office of Community Oriented Policing Services (COPS) was created in the U.S. Department of Justice. COPS cuts red tape to make it easier for local police agencies to apply for and receive federal community policing grants.

decisions need to be made at the neighborhood level, not at a downtown police headquarters. Such decentralization of authority means that credit for bringing about a safer community must be shared with the people of the community, a tall order for any group of professionals to accept. Achieving the goals of community policing requires successful implementation of three essential and complementary components or operational strategies: community partnership, problem solving, and change management.[29] Figure 6–6 shows some of the varied aspects of community policing.

Community Partnership Establishing and maintaining mutual trust between citizens of a community and the police is the main goal of the first component of community policing. Police have always recognized the need for cooperation with the community and have encouraged members of the

FIGURE 6–6

Aspects of Community Policing

★ ★ ★

NEIGHBORHOOD SUBSTATIONS

CITIZEN BLOCK WATCHES

COMMUNITY POLICING SPECIALISTS

INCREASED OFFICER VISIBILITY

community to come forward with crime-fighting information. In addition, police have spoken to neighborhood groups, worked with local organizations, and provided special-unit services. How are those cooperative efforts different from the community partnership of community policing?

In community policing, the police become an integral part of the community culture, and the community, in turn, helps the police define future crime prevention strategies and allocate community protection services. Establishing a community partnership means adopting a policing perspective that exceeds the standard law enforcement emphasis. The police no longer view the community as a passive presence connected to the police by an isolated incident or series of incidents. The community's concerns with crime and disorder become the target of efforts by the police and the community working together.

INVOLVEMENT IN
NEIGHBORHOOD FUNCTIONS

MERCHANT ORGANIZING

INTERACTION WITH
COMMUNITY GROUPS

HOUSE VISITS

For patrol officers, building police-community partnerships entails such activities as talking to local business owners to identify their concerns, visiting residents in their homes to offer advice on security, and helping to organize and support neighborhood watch groups and regular community meetings. It also involves ongoing communication with residents. For example, a patrol officer might canvass a neighborhood for information about a string of burglaries and then revisit those residents to inform them when the burglar is caught.

Problem Solving Problem solving requires a lot more thought, energy, and action than traditional incident-based police responses to crime and disorder. In full partnership, the police and a community's residents and business owners identify core problems, propose solutions, and implement a solution. Thus, community members identify the concerns that they feel are most threatening to their safety and well-being. Those areas of concern then become priorities for joint police-community interventions.

For this problem-solving process to operate effectively, the police need to devote time and attention to discovering a community's concerns, and they need to recognize the validity of those concerns. Police and neighborhood groups may not always agree on the specific problems that deserve attention first. For example, the police may regard robberies as the biggest problem in a particular neighborhood, while residents find derelicts who sleep in doorways, break bottles on sidewalks, and pick through garbage cans the number one problem. In community policing, both problems should receive early attention from the police, other government agencies, and the community.

Some community policing advocates recommended a four-step problem-solving process referred to as SARA: *S*canning—identifying problems; *A*nalysis—understanding underlying conditions; *R*esponse—developing and implementing solutions; *A*ssessment—determining the solutions' effect. One useful tool in working toward a solution is known as the *crime triangle* (see Figure 6–7). The crime triangle is a view of crime and disorder as an interaction among three variables: a victim, an offender, and a location. Solutions can be developed that affect one or more of the three elements of the crime triangle. For example, suppose elderly residents are being jeopardized by speeding teenagers in automobiles as they walk across the streets of a suburban residential neighborhood. Using a crime triangle analysis might result in the following police-community solutions: using the juvenile court to alter the probation period of offending drivers (focus on the offender), installing speed bumps in the pavement or changing the cycles of traffic signals on opposite ends of the street so that motorists cannot build up speed (focus on the location), holding safety education classes at the senior center to educate elderly residents to use marked crosswalks (focus on the victim). More than likely, in community policing, a combination of those solutions would be used. Such a response to a community problem is much more thorough than merely having a squad car drive by the location when a citizen calls in a complaint.

Change Management Forging community policing partnerships and implementing problem-solving strategies necessitates assigning new responsibilities and adopting a flexible style of management. Traditionally, patrol officers have been accorded lower status in police organizations and have been dominated by the agency's command structure. Community policing, in

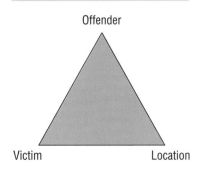

FIGURE 6–7

The Crime Triangle

Offender

Victim   Location

Policing America: Culture, Conflict, and Decision Making

contrast, emphasizes the value of the patrol function and the patrol officer as an individual. It requires the shifting of initiative, decision making, and responsibility downward within the police organization. The neighborhood police officer or deputy sheriff becomes responsible for managing the delivery of police services to the community or area to which he or she is permanently assigned. Patrol officers are the most familiar with the needs and concerns of their communities and are in the best position to forge the close ties with the community that lead to effective solutions to local problems.

Under community policing, police management must guide, rather than dominate, the actions of the patrol officer and must ensure that patrol officers have the necessary resources to solve the problems in their communities. Management must determine the guiding principles to convert the philosophy of the agency to community policing and then to evaluate the effectiveness of the strategies implemented.

Implementing Community Policing

Implementation plans for community policing vary from agency to agency and from community to community. The appropriate implementation strategy depends on conditions within the law enforcement agency and the community embarking on community policing. Successful implementation requires that the police and the members of the community understand the underlying philosophy of community policing and have a true commitment to the community policing strategy. Communication, cooperation, coordination, collaboration, and change are the keys to putting community policing into action.

Police Recruitment and Selection

Deciding whom to employ should be simple: hire the type of police officer that the citizens of the community want. Of course, that approach assumes that the citizens of a community have some idea of what it takes to be a police officer. Then there is the matter of which people to consult. Who should decide? The wealthy? The middle class? The politically conservative? The politically liberal? The young? The old? The business community? Some consensus is needed on the type of police officer desired. Seeking that consensus in metropolitan communities is filled with conflict. Police administrators need to be very careful in choosing police officers, who may well be with the agency for 20 years or more. The police department will never reach its full potential without selecting the best available personnel. Selection decisions have momentous long-term implications for a police department.[30]

Entering the World of Policing

Those entering a profession or an occupation will most likely be shaped by it if they spend any length of time on the job. Certainly the socialization process for new police officers has a permanent effect on their attitudes and behaviors. It may also manifest itself in a style of policing.

Entering the world of policing, which may include many experiences with hostility and violence, is not unlike entering the boxing ring. The personnel in policing and boxing are frequently told to "be careful out there" or to "defend yourselves at all times." No boxer would ever enter the ring without having properly trained for the fight. The same is true for police officers. Their training should be realistic, mental, physical, offensive, and defensive, just as it is for boxers. Boxers need to fight according to the rules to avoid being disqualified by the referee. Likewise, police officers must play by the rules of law, or cases will be lost and reputations ruined. At the end of a brutally contested fight, boxers often embrace each other, a rather odd occurrence when you think of what they have been trying to do to each other. The reason is that only a fighter can understand the preparation and pain that goes into being a boxer. Police officers are frequently criticized for socially isolating themselves, but putting their lives on the line every day brings a perspective to living and dying that only other officers can understand. Good police officers, like good boxers, need to keep training, "fight clean," stay close to their fellow officers, and console them when they need it.

Qualities of a Successful Police Officer

Given the complexity of the role of the police officer, it comes as no surprise that deciding what qualities the successful police officer needs is not easy. Indeed, police officers require a combination of qualities and abilities that is rare in any pool of applicants. Robert B. Mills, a pioneer in the psychological testing of police officers, believes that police applicants should possess the following psychological qualities:

- Motivation for a police career.
- Normal self-assertiveness.
- Emotional stability under stress.
- Sensitivity toward minority groups and social deviates.
- Collaborative leadership skills.
- A mature relationship with social authority.
- Flexibility.
- Integrity and honesty.
- An active and outgoing nature.[31]

The Berkeley, California, Police Department lists these qualities:

- Initiative.
- Ability to carry heavy responsibilities and handle emergencies alone.
- Social skills and ability to communicate effectively with persons of various cultural, economic, and ethnic backgrounds.
- Mental capacity to learn a wide variety of subjects quickly and correctly.
- Ability to adapt thinking to technological and social changes.
- Understanding of other human beings and the desire to help those in need.
- Emotional maturity to remain calm and objective and provide leadership in emotionally charged situations.
- Physical strength and endurance to perform these exacting duties.[32]

Policing America: Culture, Conflict, and Decision Making

Three qualities seem to be of paramount importance. One commentator refers to them as the **three I's of police selection:** intelligence, integrity, and interaction skills. In short, police officers need to be bright enough to complete rigorous training. They should be honest enough to resist—and have a lifestyle that allows them to resist—the temptation of corrupting influences in law enforcement. They should also be able to communicate clearly and get along with people of diverse backgrounds. Other qualities, such as physical strength, endurance, and appearance, seem less important. If you were the one who needed to be dragged from a burning automobile, however, the physical strength of the police officer might be important to you.

Three I's of police selection
Three qualities of the American police officer that seem to be of paramount importance: intelligence, integrity, and interaction skills.

The Police Recruitment and Selection Process

Few occupations have selection processes as elaborate as the ones used in choosing police officers in most departments of the nation. Before choices are made, a wide net must be cast in the recruiting effort to come up with enough potential applicants to fill the vacancies for an academy class. Police departments, often working with city personnel agencies, are generally guided in their selection decisions by civil service regulations. Those regulations are developed either locally or at the state level. They guarantee a merit employment system with equal opportunity for all.

Because employment qualifications are supposed to be based on perceived needs in policing, law enforcement agencies must be careful not to set unnecessary restrictions that have no bearing on an officer's ability to complete training and perform successfully on the job. The addition of just one seemingly minor qualification, such as requiring four pull-ups instead of three during physical ability testing, or making the eyesight requirement slightly more stringent, may eliminate thousands of men and women from the selection process in a large metropolitan area. It is difficult enough to find capable police candidates without needlessly eliminating them from the selection process.

Recruitment Most police agencies have finally realized that the kind of officers they desire will not gravitate naturally to the doors of the department. The search for top-notch applicants is very competitive, and many chiefs and sheriffs believe that they have to look at larger pools of applicants than in the past to find the same number of qualified officers. The reasons for the increased difficulty in finding good police candidates involve social maturity and lifestyle issues. Young police applicants today do not seem as mature as those of earlier eras. Problems with drugs and alcohol, sexually transmitted diseases, personal debt, and dependability have also reduced the number of qualified police applicants.

The major goal of the recruiting effort is to cast police work as an attractive and sustaining career, even to those who might initially be turned off by it. Research supports the allure of policing for many people who view a career in law enforcement as financially rewarding and status enhancing. In addition, the work itself is intrinsically satisfying because it is nonroutine, exciting, generally outdoors, and people oriented.[33]

Affirmative Action Since the passage of the Civil Rights Act of 1964 and the threat of court challenges to the fairness of the police selection

Increasing the number of female officers is a major concern in police selection and employment.

process, police agencies have struggled to find the best-qualified applicants and yet achieve satisfactory race and gender representation within the ranks of the department. Failure to seriously pursue equitable representation has led to expensive lawsuits, consent decrees, and court-ordered quotas to achieve the desired diversity. Consequently, affirmative action has become a major concern in police selection and employment. Now affirmative action programs are being questioned on several legal grounds. That questioning may lead to more difficulty in trying to achieve race and gender balance in police departments.

How successful has affirmative action been in accomplishing the desired goal of race and gender balance in police departments? Affirmative action *has* been relatively successful in increasing the percentage of minority members in policing. But it has been less successful in increasing the percentage of women. As noted previously, over 80 percent of the sworn officers in the nation's police departments are white males. However, as shown in Figure 6–8, the percentage of black and Hispanic officers in local departments is 11.3 and 6.2, respectively. Those figures closely approximate the percentage of blacks and Hispanics in the general population of the United States (11.3% for blacks and 9.2% for Hispanics). However, women, who compose over 50 percent of the United States population, represent less then 10 percent of the police officers in local police departments.[34]

FIGURE 6–8

Minority Representation in Local Police Departments in the United States, 1993

Race/Ethnicity	Police	Population
Black	11.3%	11.3%
Hispanic	6.2%	9.2%
White	81.5%	75.7%
Other	1.0%	3.8%

Source: Brian A. Reaves, *Local Police Departments, 1993* (Washington: Bureau of Justice Statistics, 1996).

Education Given the amount of discretion that law enforcement officers have and the kinds of sociological problems with which they deal, selecting reasonably intelligent, college-educated officers seems a wise practice. Many police agencies in the country currently require some college background. As a result, the average level of education in policing today is nearly two years of college. Among the advantages of hiring college-educated officers are the following:

1. Better written reports.

2. Enhanced communication with the public.

3. More effective job performance.

4. Fewer citizen complaints.

5. Wiser use of discretion.

6. Heightened sensitivity to racial and ethnic issues.

7. Fewer disciplinary actions.[35]

This list of advantages should impress police administrators and the public. Satisfied citizens, the savings of substantial amounts of money by avoiding lawsuits, and fewer disciplinary actions against officers are good reasons for law enforcement executives to search for police applicants with college backgrounds.

Recognition that college-educated police officers are generally better performers than officers without that level of education is long overdue. And the idea is catching on. Minnesota's Peace Officer Licensing Commission now requires a four-year college degree for licensing. The Peace Officer Council in Ohio now has more than one dozen **college academies,** where students pursue a program that integrates an associate's degree curriculum in law enforcement or criminal justice with the state's required peace officer training. Upon receipt of the associate's degree, students sit for the peace officer certification exam. If they receive a passing score on the exam, they are eligible to be hired by any police agency and to go to work without any additional academy training.

College academies Schools where students pursue a program that integrates an associate's degree curriculum in law enforcement or criminal justice with the state's required peace officer training.

Successful Recruiting Practices

Where do you find the best-qualified police applicants? Some of the more successful recruiting practices have included going to colleges, neighborhood centers, and schools in minority communities; using television, radio, and newspaper advertisements; and working with local employment offices. Demystifying the nature of police work and the selection process and shortening the time from application to final selection have also helped to attract and retain qualified candidates.

Public Safety Officers Another promising recruitment strategy has been the employment of 18-year-olds as **public safety officers** (sometimes called community service officers or public service aides), who perform many police service functions but do not have arrest powers. By the time they are 21, the department has had an excellent opportunity to assess their qualifications and potential to be sworn officers.

Public safety officers Police department employees who perform many police services but do not have arrest powers.

Police Cadets **Police cadet programs** have been around since the 1960s (Cincinnati Police), and as recently as the 1990s, the New York City Police launched a cadet program combining a college education with academy training and work experience in the police department. Upon graduation from the university, a cadet is promoted to police officer.

Police cadet program A program that combines a college education with agency work experience and academy training. Upon graduation, a cadet is promoted to police officer.

Tech prep (technical preparation) A program in which area community colleges and high schools team up to offer 6 to 9 hours of college law enforcement courses in the eleventh and twelfth grades, as well as one or two training certifications, such as police dispatcher or local corrections officer. Students who graduate are eligible for police employment at age 18.

Merit system A system of employment whereby an independent civil service commission, in cooperation with the city personnel section and the police department, sets employment qualifications, performance standards, and discipline procedures.

High School Tech Prep Programs A new idea is beginning to take hold that will attract capable police officers at an even earlier age. The program is known as **tech prep** or **technical preparation** for a criminal justice career. Area community colleges and high schools team up to offer 6 to 9 hours of college law enforcement courses in the eleventh and twelfth grades, as well as one or two training certifications, such as police dispatcher or local corrections officer. Students who graduate are eligible for employment at age 18. They become interested in law enforcement work early and are ideal police applicants when they become old enough to apply. Accurate law enforcement career information can be passed on to high school students through a tech prep program because the teachers are required to either currently work in law enforcement or have police experience in their backgrounds.

The Police Selection Process

In many communities, selection of police officers takes place through a merit system. A **merit system** of employment is established when an independent civil service commission, in cooperation with the city personnel section and the police department, sets employment qualifications, performance standards, and discipline procedures. Officers employed under such a system are hired and tenured, in theory, only if they meet and maintain the employment qualifications and performance standards set by the civil service commission. Officers in such a system cannot be fired without cause.

To find the best possible recruits to fill department vacancies, police agencies use a selection process that includes some or all of the following steps:

Short Application This brief form registers the interest of the applicant and allows the agency to screen for such things as minimum age, level of education, residency, and other easily discernible qualifications.

Detailed Application This document is a major source of information for the department and background investigators. The applicant is asked for complete education and work histories, military status, medical profile, references, a record of residence over many years, and other detailed information. Applicants are also asked to submit copies of credentials, military papers, and other certificates.

Medical Examination This exam determines if applicants are free of disease, structural abnormalities, and any other medical problems that would disqualify them for police work. This information is critical because retiring a young officer on a medical disability shortly after employment could cost the public hundreds of thousands of dollars.

Physical Ability Test Physical ability tests are common in police selection despite having been challenged in the courts as having an adverse effect on the hiring of female applicants. Physical ability tests were initially a direct response to the elimination of height and weight standards, which were also discriminatory against female applicants. The first tests required exceptional speed and strength, such as going over walls that were taller than any of the

Policing America: Culture, Conflict, and Decision Making

walls in the cities that had such tests. Those tests were struck down by the courts as not being job-related. Today, any physical ability tests must be based on a thorough analysis of the actual work of police officers.

Written Examination Police agencies once used intelligence tests in their selection process. Most agencies now use some type of aptitude, personality, general knowledge, reading comprehension, writing, or police skill exam. The courts have held that those tests must be true measures of the knowledge and abilities needed to perform police work successfully. Pre-employment tests have been the subject of much controversy in the courts.

Background Investigation Investigators in this process look for any factors in the backgrounds of applicants that would prevent them from performing successfully as police officers. Past drug use or excessive alcohol use, a poor driving record, employer problems, a bad credit history, criminal activity, and social immaturity are areas of concern in the background investigation. The investigator relies heavily on the detailed application, verifies its contents, explores any discrepancies, and develops additional leads to follow.

Psychological Testing Emotional stability and good mental health are critical to the ability to perform police work, which can be very stressful. Departments have been held liable for not screening their applicants for those psychological traits.[36]

Systematic psychological testing of police officers began in the 1950s. At first, the typical approach was to have the psychological evaluators look for disqualifying factors. The process included a pencil-and-paper test and a one-on-one interview with a psychologist. Today, the testing focus has generally shifted to a search for the positive psychological qualities required in police work. Current tests include multiple versions of both written and clinical evaluations.

The validity of psychological tests has been an issue for decades. Psychologists are often reluctant to rate with any specificity the police candidates they evaluate. Candidates considered "unacceptable" are sometimes classified as "uncertain" to avoid lawsuits. It is important to remember, however, that understanding and predicting human behavior is an inexact art. So it is easy to appreciate the reluctance of psychologists to be more specific.

Oral Interview/Oral Board This step is frequently the final one in the selection process. Members of the interview team have the results of the previous selection procedures, and they now have an opportunity to clear up inconsistencies and uncertainties that have been identified. The board normally restricts itself to evaluating the following qualities:

1. Appearance, poise, and bearing.
2. Ability to communicate orally and organize thoughts.
3. Attitude toward law enforcement and the job required of police officers.
4. Speech and the ability to articulate.
5. Attitude toward drug, narcotic, and alcohol use.
6. Sensitivity to racial and ethnic issues.[37]

At the end of many police academy training programs, there is a state licensing or certification examination.

Academy Training The police academy is part of the selection process. Virtually every academy class in any sophisticated police department loses up to 10 percent of its students. Thus, to survive academy training, students must be committed to the process. Students undergo from 400 to more than 1,000 hours of academic, skill, and physical training and are tested virtually every week of the process. At the end of many academy training programs, students must take a state licensing or certification examination.

Probation Under local or state civil service requirements, employers may keep a new police officer on probation for six months to a year. The probation period gives the new police officer a chance to learn policing under the guidance of a well-qualified field training officer. Formal field training is a wise investment, and it ensures that new officers get as much knowledge and experience as possible before an agency commits to them for their careers.

A problem is that with police academy training now often extending five or six months, a six-month probation period no longer seems logical. The agency is, in effect, offering the police officer tenure in a matter of weeks after graduation from the academy. This practice defeats the purpose of probation, which was designed to allow the employer to see whether the newly trained officer can successfully perform the job.

The Selection of a Law Enforcement Executive

No less important than the selection of operations-level officers is the choice of the chief executive of a police agency. This executive might be a chief of police, a sheriff, or the head of a state law enforcement organization. A crucial decision in the selection process is whether to allow people from outside the agency to apply. In some police agencies in the United States, civil service regulations prohibit the selection of outside candidates. The rationale for this rule is that there must be qualified internal candidates. In addition, it is discouraging to hard-working and talented police administrators to be denied a chance to lead the agency they have spent many years serving.

Actual hiring decisions are usually shared by members of a selection committee. Frequently, an executive search firm is also employed. The selection committee usually consists of representatives of the local government, the police department, the search firm, and the community. Applicants are put through a rigorous process that includes several visits to the city, written exams, interviews, and assessment center testing, in which candidates try to resolve "real-world" management problems. Once the interviews and testing have been completed, applicants are normally ranked, and the list is presented to the city manager, the mayor, or others so that a final selection can be made.

The pursuit of a police chief's job is very competitive. Often several hundred candidates contend for a position even in a small suburban community. A typical police chief rarely serves longer than ten years, and life in the chief's seat may not be very comfortable, particularly if a new chief intends to change things. Much of the political controversy and many of the social problems in major cities and counties end up at the door of the police department, so police chiefs must be politically savvy to survive. Many chiefs discover that they cannot please everybody, particularly if they are trying to change the department. Should police chiefs have protection under civil service? Most commentators say no, arguing that mayors and city managers ought to have the authority to pick the management teams that work immediately under their direction. A small number of cities give their police chiefs civil service protection to insulate them from unnecessary political interference.

The selection of a sheriff of one of the nation's counties is just as important as choosing a police chief. The difference in the two processes has to do with who does the selecting. In all but a few of the nation's counties, sheriffs are elected by the county's eligible voters. To be elected, sheriffs must be good politicians. They often have a much better idea of the priorities of a community and wield more influence with prosecutors and in the legislature than chiefs of police. Sheriffs who do not exhibit this political acumen are not likely to be reelected.

Issues in Policing

Our discussion of law enforcement thus far has made it clear that not all matters of policing in America are settled. In this final section of the chapter, we will study some of the issues that continue to be major topics of debate in law enforcement and have significant impact on the quality of life in neighborhoods and communities across the nation.

Discretion

Discretion is the exercise of individual judgment, instead of formal rules, in making decisions. No list of policies and procedures could possibly guide police officers in all of the situations in which they find themselves. Even the police officer writing a ticket for a parking meter violation exercises a considerable amount of discretion in deciding precisely what to do.[38] Police even have the discretion to ignore violations of the law when they deem it appropriate in the context of other priorities.

The issue of police discretion is very controversial. Some believe that the discretion of police officers should be reduced. The movement to limit the discretion of police officers is the result of abuses of that discretion, such as physical abuse of citizens or unequal application of the law in making arrests. Other people argue that we should acknowledge that officers operate with great discretion and not attempt to limit it. Advocates of this view believe that better education and training would help officers exercise their judgment more wisely.

Patrol Officer Discretion Patrol officers frequently find it necessary to exercise their discretion. Within the geographical limits of their beats, they have the discretion to decide precisely where they will patrol when they are not answering radio calls. They decide whom to stop and question. For example, they may tell some children playing ball in the street to move, while they ignore others. Patrol officers decide for themselves which traffic violators are worth chasing through busy traffic and which ones are not. They even have

Discretion The exercise of individual judgment, instead of formal rules, in making decisions.

the right not to arrest for a minor violation when, for example, they are on the way to investigate a more serious matter.

Some of the more critical situations involve decisions about stopping, searching, and arresting criminal suspects. Many citizens have been inconvenienced and some have been abused because of a police officer's poor use of discretion in those areas.

Police officers cannot make an arrest for every violation of law that comes to their attention—that is, they cannot provide **full enforcement.** The police do not have the resources to enforce the law fully, nor can they be everywhere at once. And even if full enforcement were possible, it may not be desirable. For example, persons intoxicated in front of their own homes may not need to be arrested, but only to be told to go inside. Motorists slightly exceeding the speed limit need not be arrested if they are moving with the flow of traffic. Prostitution may be widely practiced in large metropolitan areas, but police officers have little to gain by searching hotels and motels to stamp it out, particularly when judges will turn the prostitutes right back out on the street. Generally, only when such an activity becomes a clear nuisance, is the subject of a public outcry, or threatens health and safety do the police department and its officers choose to take formal action.

The practice of relying on the judgment of the police leadership and rank-and-file officers to decide which laws to enforce is referred to as **selective enforcement.** The practice allows street police officers to decide important matters about peacekeeping and enforcement of the law.

For most violations of the law, but not all felonies, a police officer can usually exercise a number of options:

1. Taking no action at all if the officer deems that appropriate for the situation.
2. Giving a verbal warning to stop the illegal action.
3. Issuing a written warning for the violation.
4. Issuing a citation to the perpetrator to appear in court.
5. Making a physical arrest in serious matters or in situations with repeat offenders.

Factors Affecting Discretion Dozens of studies have been conducted on the exercise of discretion by police patrol officers. A number of significant factors affect discretion:

- **The Nature of the Crime** The more serious the crime, the more likely it is that police officers will formally report it. In cases involving lesser felonies, misdemeanors, and petty offenses, police officers are more likely to handle the offenses informally. A minor squabble between over-the-fence neighbors is an example of a matter that would probably be handled informally.

- **Departmental Policies** If the leadership of a police department gives an order or issues a policy demanding that particular incidents be handled in a prescribed way, then an officer is not supposed to exercise discretion but is to do as the order or policy directs. Thus, if a city has

Full enforcement A practice in which the police make an arrest for every violation of law that comes to their attention.

Selective enforcement The practice of relying on the judgment of the police leadership and rank-and-file officers to decide which laws to enforce.

Policing America: Culture, Conflict, and Decision Making

had many complaints about dangerous jaywalking in a certain downtown area, the chief of police may insist that citations be issued to those found jaywalking, even though in the past citations had not been issued.

- **The Relationship Between the Victim and the Offender** Particularly for minor offenses, the closer the relationship between the victim of an alleged offense and the suspected perpetrator, the more discretion the officer is able to exercise. For example, police officers are not likely to deal formally with a petty theft between two lovers if they believe that the victim will not prosecute his or her partner.

- **The Amount of Evidence** If officers do not have enough evidence to substantiate an arrest or to gain a conviction in court, they are likely to handle the case in some way other than making an arrest.

- **The Preference of the Victim** Sometimes the victim of a crime may simply want to talk the matter over with someone, and the police are available on a 24-hour basis. Also, if the officer senses that the victim of a minor assault does not wish to prosecute the perpetrator of the offense, the patrol officer will not make a formal complaint, and the complainant will most likely never know that a report was not made.

- **The Demeanor of the Suspect** Suspects who are disrespectful and uncooperative may very well feel the full brunt of the law. Patrol officers often choose the most severe option possible in dealing with such suspects.

- **The Legitimacy of the Victim** Patrol officers are bound to pass some kind of judgment on the legitimacy of the victim. An assault victim who is belligerent and intoxicated, for instance, will not be viewed favorably by the investigating officer. Criminals victimized by other criminals are also seen as less then fully authentic victims, no matter what the offense.

- **Socioeconomic Status** The more affluent the complainant, the more likely a patrol officer is to use formal procedures to report and investigate a crime. Contrary to popular belief, the personal characteristics of an officer (such as race, gender, and education) do not seem to influence the exercise of discretion.

Factors Limiting Discretion Several methods are employed to control the amount of discretion exercised by police officers. One method is close supervision by a police agency's management. For example, a department may require that officers consult a sergeant before engaging in a particular kind of action. Department directives or policies also limit the options police officers have in particular situations. Decisions of the United States Supreme Court, such as one restricting the use of deadly force to stop a fleeing felon, limit the options available to officers on the street. Finally, the threat of civil liability suits has reduced the discretion an officer has, for example, in the use of deadly force or in the pursuit of fleeing suspects in an automobile.

The debate over how much control should be placed on the exercise of police discretion is ongoing. Few other professionals have experienced a comparable attack on their authority to make decisions for the good of the clients they serve. The continuing attempt to limit discretion also seems out of place at a time when community policing is being widely advocated. Remember that community policing decentralizes authority and places it in the hands of the local beat officers and their supervisors. Community policing is bound to fail if citizens see that the police they work with every day do not have the authority and discretion to make the decisions that will ultimately improve the quality of life in a community.

Use of Force

No issue in policing has caused as much controversy in recent decades as the use of force. In Los Angeles, Detroit, Miami, and many other cities, excessive-force charges against police officers have been made and documented and have resulted in the loss of public confidence in the police. Although the vast majority of police officers of this country go to work every day with no intention of using excessive force, far too many instances of brutality still occur.

A precise definition of brutality is not possible. However, the use of excessive physical force is undoubtedly a factor in everyone's definition. For many people, particularly members of racial and ethnic minorities, brutality also includes verbal abuse, profanity, harassment, threats of force, and unnecessary stopping, questioning, and searching of pedestrians or those in vehicles.

Excessive Force Why do the police have to use force as frequently as they do? A major responsibility of police officers is to arrest suspects so that they can answer criminal charges. No criminal suspect wants his or her liberty taken away, so some of them resist arrest. Invariably, a few suspects are armed with some kind of weapon, and some are prepared to use that weapon against the police to foil the arrest. The police need to establish their authority to control such conflicts. The disrespect and physical resistance that are frequently the result of those encounters have caused the police on occasion to use **excessive force,** which is a measure of coercion beyond that necessary to control participants in a conflict.

Research reveals that police brutality does not occur as often as some people might think. For example, in a recent study conducted in the state of Washington, only 4 percent of brutality complaints against the police could be substantiated, and most of the charges were of verbal abuse or insults.[39] Widespread media coverage of high-profile cases, such as the Los Angeles police officers' assault on Rodney King, can lead the public to believe that brutality is much more common than it really is. The Los Angeles police, however, had a higher rate of wounding and killing suspects than any other police department in the nation, according to the Christopher Commission, which investigated the assault on Rodney King.

Excessive force A measure of coercion beyond that necessary to control participants in a conflict.

Policing America: Culture, Conflict, and Decision Making

Deadly Force The greatest concern over the use of force by the police has to do with the infliction of death or serious injury on citizens and criminal suspects. Since the U.S. Supreme Court's 1985 decision in *Tennessee v. Garner*, the use of deadly force has been severely restricted, and police shootings of suspects and citizens have been reduced. In the *Garner* case, an unarmed teenage boy was shot as he fled a house burglary, failing to heed the warning to stop given by a Memphis police officer. The boy later died of a gunshot wound to the head. He was found with ten dollars in his pocket that he had stolen from the home. The Memphis officer was acting in compliance with his department's policy on the use of deadly force and with the law in Tennessee and in most other states in the nation. Giving law enforcement officers the authority to use deadly force to stop a fleeing felon, even when they know the suspect is unarmed and not likely to be a danger to another person, derives from the common law in England and the United States, which permitted such a practice. At the time the rule developed, however, unlike today, dozens of crimes were capital offenses, and the fleeing suspect, if apprehended and convicted, would have been executed. The *Garner* decision, no doubt, was long overdue, and it included a rule that many police agencies in the nation had adopted years earlier. The perspective that professional law enforcement agencies had already begun to adopt on deadly force was from the Model Penal Code, Section 307(2)(B). It reads as follows:

There is much debate on how much control should be placed on the decisions of police officers in arrest situations.

The use of deadly force is not justifiable under this section unless:

1. The arrest is for a felony.

2. The person effecting the arrest is authorized to act as a peace officer or is assisting a person whom he believes to be authorized to act as a peace officer.

3. The actor believes that the force employed creates no substantial risk of injury to innocent persons.

4. The actor believes that:
   a. The crime for which the arrest is made involved conduct including the use or threatened use of deadly force.
   b. There is substantial risk that the person to be arrested will cause death or serious bodily harm if his apprehension is delayed.

Even with explicit guidelines, the decision to use deadly force is seldom clear-cut for police officers, because of the violent and occasionally ambiguous situations in which they find themselves. For example, consider the confrontation a Dallas, Texas, police officer had in the summer of 1993. As a plainclothes officer, he responded to a call to an apartment complex where it was reported that a man had fired shots. It was nighttime, and when he arrived at the parking lot of the complex, he saw a man perhaps 50 feet from him with the butt end of a pistol sticking out of the waistband of his trousers.

Policing America: Culture, Conflict, and Decision Making   **CHAPTER 6**

The police officer told him to stop and put his hands in the air. Instead of doing what he was ordered to do, the man pulled the gun from his waistband and moved it toward the officer. The officer responded by firing his weapon several times at the man and killing him. Later, it was discovered that the man was a Mexican citizen who spoke no English.

Some members of the Hispanic community were enraged that the officer did not offer commands in Spanish, because Dallas officers were required to study 20 hours of the language in the police academy. After several months of investigation and the grand jury's ignoring the case, the officer was exonerated. However, the recently appointed chief of police assured the community that new police recruits would study three times the previously required amount of Spanish and that annual in-service training would also require the study of Spanish. In addition, the chief stated that in situations such as the one in question, undercover and plainclothes officers would be required, if possible, to put on jackets that would readily identify them as police officers. Some people argue that the man with the gun in this situation not only did not understand English, but also had no idea that the officer with drawn gun was a police officer.

It should not be forgotten that citizens and criminal suspects also attack the police. Mentally ill persons, parties to a family dispute, and suspects trying to avoid arrest feloniously assault between 50 and 100 officers each year. About two-thirds of those assaults are shootings. In response, police officers exercise caution by wearing protective vests, they proactively use what they learn in courses on self-defense (unarmed and armed), and they attempt to defuse hostile situations through peaceful techniques they learn in training.

Unfortunately, research on the police use of force, excessive force, and deadly force has not identified any specific procedures that would significantly reduce the injury or death of police officers and the citizens they confront. Only the number of deaths of citizens is decreasing, and violent regions of the nation with a high density of guns continue to be dangerous areas for police officers.[40]

Police Corruption

Almost from the beginning of formal policing in the United States, corruption of law enforcement officers has been a fact of life. Nothing is more distasteful to the public than a police officer or a whole department gone bad. Throughout history, police officers have bought their positions and promotions, sold protection, and ignored violations of the law for money.

Why is policing so susceptible to bribery and other forms of corruption? Perhaps it has to do with the combination of two critical features of the police role in society. On the one hand, the police have authority to enforce laws and to use power to make sure that those laws are obeyed. On the other hand, they also have the discretion *not* to enforce the law. The combination of those two features makes the police vulnerable to bribes and other forms of corruption. Other features of police work add to the potential for corruption: low pay in relation to important responsibilities, cynicism about the courts' soft handling of criminals that the police spend so much time trying to apprehend, society's ambivalence about vice (most citizens want the laws on the books, but many of them are willing participants), and the practice of recruiting officers from working-class and lower-class backgrounds, where skepticism about obeying the law might be more prevalent.

Types of Corruption In 1972, the Knapp Commission issued a report on corruption in the New York City Police Department. Two types of corrupt officers were identified: "grass eaters" and "meat eaters." **"Grass eaters"** were officers who occasionally engaged in illegal or unethical activities, such as accepting small favors, gifts, or money for ignoring violations of the law during the course of their duties. **"Meat eaters,"** on the other hand, actively sought ways to make money illegally while on duty. For example, they would solicit bribes, commit burglaries, or manufacture false evidence for a prosecution.[42]

A little over a quarter of a century ago, Ellwyn Stoddard identified a more complete list of types of police misconduct, with examples, in what he described as the "blue-coat code":

1. Bribery: accepting cash or gifts in exchange for nonenforcement of the law.
2. Chiseling: demanding discounts, free admission, and free food.
3. Extortion: the threat of enforcement and arrest if a bribe is not given.
4. Favoritism: giving breaks on law enforcement, such as for traffic violations committed by families and friends of the police.
5. Mooching: accepting free food, drinks, and admission to entertainment.
6. Perjury: lying for other officers apprehended in illegal activity.
7. Prejudice: unequal enforcement of the law with respect to racial and ethnic minorities.
8. Premeditated theft: planned burglaries and thefts.
9. Shakedown: taking items from the scene of a theft or a burglary the officer is investigating.
10. Shopping: taking small, inexpensive items from a crime scene or an unsecured business or home.[43]

Controlling Corruption Corruption in law enforcement strikes at the very core of the profession and takes a heavy toll. All peace officer positions in the United States are positions of honor and trust, and agencies have invested large sums of money and investigative time in selecting officers with integrity. To see this investment lost is disheartening. But more than anything else, public confidence and trust plummet after a widely publicized corruption case, such as the police drug-trafficking episode in Miami, which involved dozens of that department's officers. In the following list, some ways to control and reduce corruption in policing are described.

- **High Moral Standards** Selecting and maintaining officers with high moral standards is a step in the right direction. Some police agencies in the United States still hire convicted felons to do police work. In-depth academy and in-service training on ethical issues that officers are likely to face on the beat and in other assignments would prepare officers for the compromises they may be asked to make later in their careers.

"Grass eaters" Officers who occasionally engage in illegal and unethical activities, such as accepting small favors, gifts, or money for ignoring violations of the law during the course of their duties.

"Meat eaters" Officers who actively seek ways to make money illegally while on duty.

An eight-month investigation by the *Miami Herald* in 1997 documented a police scam involving hundreds of officers in thousands of cases in Dade County. Dubbed "collars for dollars," the scam works like this. Police officers list one another as witnesses in drunken-driving and misdemeanor cases even if they do little or no police work on the cases. They then go to court on overtime and receive pay they don't deserve. According to the newspaper report, "collars for dollars" happens often and costs Dade County tax payers millions of dollars.[41]

- **Police Policies and Discipline** A police department should develop rigid policies that cover the wide range of activities that corruption comprises. Drug testing of officers, particularly those in narcotics-sensitive positions, may be necessary, although unpopular. Policies mean nothing unless they are enforced. Discipline should be imposed and prosecutions should go forward when officers are found guilty of violating established policies and laws.

- **Proactive Internal Affairs Unit** The **internal affairs investigations unit** of a police department should ferret out illegal and unethical activity. Any internal affairs unit that sits back and waits for complaints probably is not going to receive many of them. First-line supervisors of a police department should also know whether their subordinates are engaging in unethical and illegal violations of the rules of the department and the laws of the state. They should also be held responsible for the actions of their subordinates.

- **Uniform Enforcement of the Law** If a police agency makes it clear that no group of citizens, no matter what their affiliation with the police department or its personnel, is going to receive special treatment from the police department, the incentive for offering bribes and other forms of corruption will be minimized. This process starts with clear policies and procedures and must be backed up with discipline when necessary.

- **Outside Review and Special Prosecutors** Heavily resisted by police leadership and police labor associations is any kind of outside review of their actions. However, both the Christopher Commission and the Knapp Commission are examples of outside reviews that brought about improvements in the agencies they investigated. Special prosecutors are recommended in serious cases to relieve the police department and the government of any accusations of a whitewash.

- **Court Review and Oversight** Criminal prosecutions or civil liability suits deriving from police corruption cases can be very costly to a police agency. Such visible forms of oversight often result in adverse media coverage, civil liability awards, and higher insurance rates—all of which should encourage police agencies to control corruption.[44]

Professionalizing Law Enforcement

Many people would argue that policing in America has already reached professional status. There is no question that law enforcement is a valued service. Its agents make important decisions daily that substantially affect the lives of people and the quality of life in a community. The police officer's position is one of honor and trust. There are academy programs consisting of hundreds of hours of instruction, as well as law enforcement degree programs. Now there are even signs that law enforcement is attempting to police its own profession. Professional accreditation for police agencies is a rite of passage that is needed if law enforcement is to join the list of the most respected professions. Nevertheless, resistance to it and the other developments is still widespread. Other professions, such as law, teaching, and medicine, have had similar experiences on their treks to professional status.

Not everyone has the qualities to be a police officer. We should have the courage to tell that to government leaders when they press to have the standards of the profession lowered. To allow into law enforcement those people with no desire to serve, low intelligence, a shady past, poor work habits, and no ability to communicate effectively is to court disaster for every department that does so—and for the entire profession.

Some police officers and their leaders resist 600 hours of initial training and do all they can to avoid continuing education and training. Real professionals seek advanced training.

Professionals in any field make mistakes, and a caring public should forgive most of them. In police work, there are incomplete interviews, evidence left at crime scenes, and bad reports written. In the long run, the consequences of such mistakes are generally insignificant as long as corrections are made. Mistakes can also be technological, such as the failure of a radar gun or the misfiring of a firearm. No one should blame the police for technological mishaps that are not the result of negligence.

One kind of mistake, however, stands out more than any other: the condoning of racist and brutal tactics like the Los Angeles police officers' beating of Rodney King. The findings of the Christopher Commission confirmed that such tactics were generally condoned and even encouraged. The videotaped replay of that performance will be an embarrassment to professional policing for years to come. Police departments need to search out officers who would participate in or overlook such violence and must remove them from the profession.

Many police officers go to work each day with a negative attitude, and some may take out their frustrations on the citizens they meet. Police officers need to treat their on-duty time as a professional performance and render the best service possible on any given day. If they treat the citizens they serve with respect and concern, officers will make great progress in improving the public's perception of law enforcement as a profession worthy of trust and admiration.

By the end of 1995, 375 police agencies in the United States were accredited by the Commission on Accreditation for Law Enforcement Agencies (CALEA).[45]

6 Review and Applications

SUMMARY BY CHAPTER OBJECTIVES

CHAPTER OBJECTIVE 1

According to surveys, the American public is generally satisfied with the quality of the service the police provide. The level of confidence varies across racial and ethnic groups. As with most services, the public believes there is room for improvement.

CHAPTER OBJECTIVE 2

The role of the police officer is complex and requires a combination of special characteristics, which involve quick decision making, invisible work, "dirty work," and danger.

CHAPTER OBJECTIVE 3

Wilson's three operational styles in policing are legalistic, watchman, and service.

CHAPTER OBJECTIVE 4

The three major functions of police departments in the United States are patrol, investigation, and traffic.

CHAPTER OBJECTIVE 5

The three main components of community policing are community partnership, problem solving, and change management.

CHAPTER OBJECTIVE 6

Community policing relies heavily on problem solving. The four steps in a community policing approach to problem solving are scanning, analysis, response, and assessment.

CHAPTER OBJECTIVE 7

Police applicants go through several different kinds of testing to become law enforcement officers. Steps in an effective police officer selection process include: recruitment, short application, detailed application, medical examination, physical ability test, written examination, background investigation, psychological testing, oral interview/oral board, academy training, and a probationary employment period.

CHAPTER OBJECTIVE 8

With so many police officers in the United States, at several levels of government, some critical issues concerning the police are still unresolved. These include proper limits on discretion, control of the police, elimination of corruption, and the qualities of successful police officers.

KEY TERMS

role, p. 184
role expectation, p. 184
role conflict, p. 184
operational styles, p. 188
preventive patrol, p. 190
directed patrol, p. 191
aggressive patrol, p. 191
field interrogation, p. 191

traffic accident investigation crews, p. 196
three I's of police selection, p. 203
college academies, p. 205
public safety officers, p. 205
police cadet program, p. 205
tech prep (technical preparation), p. 206

merit system, p. 206
discretion, p. 209
full enforcement, p. 210
selective enforcement, p. 210
excessive force, p. 212
"grass eaters," p. 215
"meat eaters," p. 215
internal affairs investigations unit, p. 216

1. In general, what is the attitude of the American public toward the police?

2. What is a common source of role conflict for the police?

3. Distinguish among the three sets of operational styles identified by criminal justice scholars.

4. How are *preventive patrol, directed patrol,* and *aggressive patrol* different?

5. What are some of the functions of a criminal investigator?

6. What is the philosophy of community policing?

7. What are the three complementary operational strategies of community policing?

8. Explain how the three I's of police selection (intelligence, integrity, and interaction skills) relate to the success of a police officer.

9. What factors affect a police officer's discretion?

10. What is meant by *excessive force*?

11. List some ways of controlling and reducing police corruption.

EXPERIENTIAL ACTIVITIES

1. In groups of three or four, select a local crime or disorder problem. Using the first three components of the SARA approach to problem solving, and considering the elements of the crime triangle, formulate some options to deal with the problem. Present your options to the class, and let the whole class vote to determine which option is the best to solve the problem.

2. Contact your local police department, and find out what it does to recruit police candidates. Compare your findings with those of others in the class.

3. Conduct a survey about the police in your neighborhood. Use the same survey questions and categories as in Figures 6–1, 6–2, and 6–3. Compare the results of your survey with the results in Figures 6–1, 6–2, and 6–3.

4. Look through several police periodicals, such as *Law and Order, Police Chief,* or other professional police magazines. What do the advertised products tell you about law enforcement? Write a brief summary of your findings.

5. **INTERNET** Access the Community Policing Consortium at **www.communitypolicing.org**. Find out which police organizations make up the consortium and who administers and funds the consortium. Then choose and read one of the topics offered, and write a summary of what you learn.

CRITICAL THINKING EXERCISES

1. You are the sheriff of one of 88 counties in a midwestern state. Your department has recently received a Community Oriented Policing Services (COPS) grant from the federal government. The money award resulted from your department's submitting a winning community policing plan to the Department of Justice. The grant of $150,000 will help put two additional officers on patrol. The money will fund 75 percent of the salaries and benefits for the new officers for three years. As part of the grant award agreement, your department must assume the total support of the two officers at the end of the three-year period. What should you do now to ensure that your department has the community's support to retain the officers when the federal money runs out?

2. You are the mayor of a midsized city. At a recent city council meeting, a council member criticized the police after the city agreed to pay another settlement for what had been called police misconduct. The police chief bristled at the criticism, blaming you and the council for not providing enough money to properly train police officers. The chief pointed out that the police had received only 15 percent of what they had requested for training. The complaining council member retorted that the chief needed to prioritize department requests. In response, the chief said that city council designates where much of the police department's budget is spent. As mayor, what should you do?

ADDITIONAL READING

Ahern, James. *Police in Trouble.* New York: Hawthorn Books, 1972.

Brown, Michael. *Working the Street.* New York: Russell Sage, 1981.

Cordner, Gary and Donna Hale (eds.). *What Works in Policing? Operations and Administration Examined.* Cincinnati: Anderson, 1992.

del Carmen, Rolando V. *Civil Liabilities in American Policing.* Englewood Cliffs, NJ: Prentice Hall, 1991.

Sparrow, Malcolm, Mark Moore, and David Kennedy. *Beyond 911, A New Era for Policing.* New York: Basic Books, 1990.

ENDNOTES

1. W.S. Wilson Huang and Michael S. Vaughn, "Support and Confidence: Public Attitudes Toward the Police," pp. 31-45 in Timothy J. Flanagan and Dennis R. Longmire (eds.), *Americans View Crime and Justice: A National Public Opinion Survey* (Thousand Oaks, CA: Sage, 1996), p. 44.

2. Kathleen Maguire and Ann L. Pastore (eds.), *Sourcebook of Criminal Justice Statistics 1996,* U.S. Department of Justice, Bureau of Justice Statistics (Washington: GPO, 1997), p. 129, Table 2.23.

3. Kathleen Maguire, Ann L. Pastore, and Timothy J. Flanagan (eds.), *Sourcebook of Criminal Justice Statistics 1992,* U.S. Department of Justice, Bureau of Justice Statistics (Washington: GPO, 1993), p. 171, Table 2.18.

4. Ibid., p. 172, Table 2.19.

5. Ibid., p. 173, Table 2.21.

6. Maguire and Pastore, op. cit., 1997, p. 125, Table 2.17.

7. Keith Haley, "Training," in Gary Cordner and Donna Hale (eds.), *What Works in Policing Operations and Administration Examined* (Cincinnati: Anderson, 1992).

8. Lee Rainwater, "The Revolt of the Dirty Workers," *Transaction* (November 1967), p. 2.

9. Jerome Skolnick, *Justice Without Trial* (New York: Wiley, 1966).

10. U.S. Department of Justice, Federal Bureau of Investigation, *Crime in the Unites States, 1996* (Washington: GPO, 1997), p. 285.

11. Maguire and Pastore, 1997, op. cit., p. 354, Table 3.154; *Crime in the United States, 1996*, op. cit.

12. James Q. Wilson, *Varieties of Police Behavior* (Cambridge, MA: Harvard University Press, 1968), pp. 140-227.

13. John Broderick, *Police in a Time of Change* (Morristown, NJ: General Learning Press, 1977), pp. 9–88.

14. William Muir, Jr., *Police: Streetcorner Politicians* (Chicago: University of Chicago Press, 1977).

15. Ellen Hochstedler, "Testing Types: A Review and Test of Police Types," *Journal of Criminal Justice*, Vol. 9 (1981), pp. 451–66.

16. G. Kelling, T. Pate, D. Dieckman, and C. Brown, *The Kansas City Preventive Patrol Experiment: A Summary Report* (Washington: Police Foundation, 1974).

17. Gary Cordner, "Patrol," in Gary Cordner and Donna Hale (eds.), op. cit.

18. James Q. Wilson and Barbara Boland, "The Effect of Police on Crime," *Law and Society Review*, Vol. 12 (1978), pp. 367–84.

19. George Kelling, *The Newark Foot Patrol Experiment* (Washington: Police Foundation, 1981).

20. Robert C. Trojanowicz, *The Neighborhood Foot Patrol Program in Flint, Michigan* (East Lansing, MI: National Neighborhood Foot Patrol Center, n.d.).

21. Bruce L. Berg and John J. Horgan, *Criminal Investigation*, 3d ed. (Westerville: Glencoe/McGraw-Hill, 1998).

22. Alfred Blumstein and Joan Petersilia, "NIJ and Its Research Program," *25 Years of Criminal Justice Research*, (Washington: The National Institute of Justice, 1994) p. 13.

23. Christine Wicker, "Death Beat," in Keith N. Haley and Mark A. Stallo, *Texas Crime, Texas Justice* (New York: McGraw-Hill, 1996).

24. *Crime in the United States, 1996* op. cit., p. 203.

25. Mark Willman and John Snortum, "Detective Work: The Criminal Investigation Process in a Medium-Size Police Department," *Criminal Justice Review*, Vol. 9 (1984), pp. 33–39; V. Williams and R. Sumrall, "Productivity Measures in the Criminal Investigation Function," *Journal of Criminal Justice*, Vol. 10 (1982), pp. 111–22; I. Greenberg and R. Wasserman, *Managing Criminal Investigations* (Washington: U.S. Department of Justice, 1979); P. Greenwood and J. Petersilia, *The Criminal Investigation Process*, Vol. I, *Summary and Policy Implications* (Washington: U.S. Department of Justice, 1975); B. Greenberg, C. Elliot, L. Kraft, and H. Procter, *Felony Investigation Decision Model: An Analysis of Investigative Elements of Information* (Washington: GPO, 1975).

26. John Conklin, *Robbery and the Criminal Justice System* (New York: J. B. Lippincott, 1972), p. 149.

27. Material on research studies based on information in Blumstein and Petersilia, op. cit., pp. 10–14.

28. James Q. Wilson and George L. Kelling, "Broken Windows: The Police and Neighborhood Safety," *Atlantic*, Vol. 256 (1982), pp. 29–38.

29. Material in this subsection is based on information in the following sources: Community Policing Consortium, *Understanding Community Policing: A Framework for Action*, monograph. www.communitypolicing.org/conpubs.html, January 1998; U.S. Department of Justice, National Institute of Corrections, *Community Justice: Striving for Safe, Secure, and Just Communities* (Louisville, KY: LIS, 1996).

30. Larry Gaines and Victor Kappeler, "Police Selection," in Gary Cordner and Donna Hale (eds.), op. cit.

31. Robert B. Mills, "Psychological, Psychiatric, Polygraph, and Stress Evaluation," in Calvin Swank and James Conser (eds.), *The Police Personnel System* (New York: Wiley, 1981).

32. O. W. Wilson and Roy McLaren, *Police Administration* (New York: McGraw-Hill, 1972), p. 261.

33. Albert Reiss, *The Police and the Public* (New Haven, CT: Yale University Press, 1971).

34. Brian A. Reaves, *Local Police Departments, 1996*, U.S. Department of Justice, Bureau of Justice Statistics (Washington: GPO, 1997) online update, 4/15/98.

35. David Carter, Allen Sapp, and Darrel Stephens, *The State of Police Education: Policy Direction for the 21st Century* (Washington: Police Executive Research Forum, 1989).

36. *Hild v. Bruner*, 1980; *Bonsignore v. City of New York*, 1981.

37. Jack Gregory, "The Background Investigation and Oral Interview," in Calvin Swank and James Conser (eds.), op. cit.

38. Skolnick, op. cit., p. 45.

39. John Dugan and Daniel Breda, "Complaints About Police Officers: A Comparison Among Types and Agencies," *Journal of Criminal Justice*, Vol. 19 (1991), pp. 165–71.

40. David Lester, "The Murder of Police Officers in American Cities," *Criminal Justice and Behavior*, Vol. 11 (1984), pp. 101–13.

41. Jeff Leen, Gail Epstein, and Lisa Getter, "Dade Cops Like to Plan Collars for Dollars, *The Orlando Sentinel*, July 20, 1997, p. B-1.

42. Knapp Commission, *Report on Police Corruption* (New York: George Braziller, 1972).

43. Ellwyn R. Stoddard, "The Informal 'Code' of Police Deviancy: A Group Approach to Blue-Coat Crime," *Journal of Criminal Law, Criminology, and Police Science*, Vol. 59 (1968), p. 204.

44. Candace McCloy, "Lawsuits Against Police: What Impact Do They Have?" *Criminal Law Bulletin*, Vol. 20 (1984), pp. 49–56.

45. "CALEA, Commission on Accreditation for Law Enforcement Agencies," pilot.wash.lib.md.us/hag/police/calea.html.

7 The Administration of Justice

The American Court Structure

Dual court system The court system in the United States, consisting of one system of state and local courts and another system of federal courts.

Jurisdiction The authority of a court to hear and decide cases.

Original jurisdiction The authority of a court to hear a case when it is first brought to court.

Appellate jurisdiction The power of a court to review a case for errors of law.

General jurisdiction The power of a court to hear any type of case.

Special jurisdiction The power of a court to hear only certain kinds of cases.

Subject matter jurisdiction The power of a court to hear a particular type of case.

Personal jurisdiction A court's authority over the parties to a lawsuit.

The United States has a **dual court system**—a separate judicial system for each of the states and a separate federal system. Figure 7–1 displays this dual court system and routes of appeal from the various courts. As can be seen in the figure, the only place where the two systems connect is the U.S. Supreme Court.

The authority of a court to hear and decide cases is called the court's **jurisdiction.** It is set by law and is limited by territory and type of case. A court of **original jurisdiction** has the authority to hear a case when it is first brought to court. Courts having the power to review a case for errors of law are courts of **appellate jurisdiction.** Courts having the power to hear any type of case are said to exercise **general jurisdiction.** Those with the power to hear only certain types of cases have **special jurisdiction. Subject matter jurisdiction** is the court's power to hear a particular type of case. **Personal jurisdiction** is the court's authority over the parties to a lawsuit.

The Federal Courts

The authority for the federal court system is the U.S. Constitution, Article III, Section 1, which states, "The judicial power of the United States shall be vested in one Supreme Court, and in such inferior courts as Congress may from time to time ordain and establish." The present federal court system includes the U.S. Supreme Court, the federal courts of appeals, and the federal district courts. The current federal court system is shown in Figure 7–2.

United States District Courts Forming the base of the federal court structure are the U.S. district courts. These are courts of *original jurisdiction,*

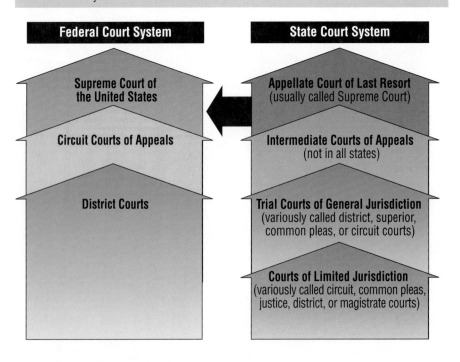

FIGURE 7–1

Dual Court System of the United States

Federal Court System	State Court System
Supreme Court of the United States	Appellate Court of Last Resort (usually called Supreme Court)
Circuit Courts of Appeals	Intermediate Courts of Appeals (not in all states)
District Courts	Trial Courts of General Jurisdiction (variously called district, superior, common pleas, or circuit courts)
	Courts of Limited Jurisdiction (variously called circuit, common pleas, justice, district, or magistrate courts)

FIGURE 7–2

The Federal Court Structure

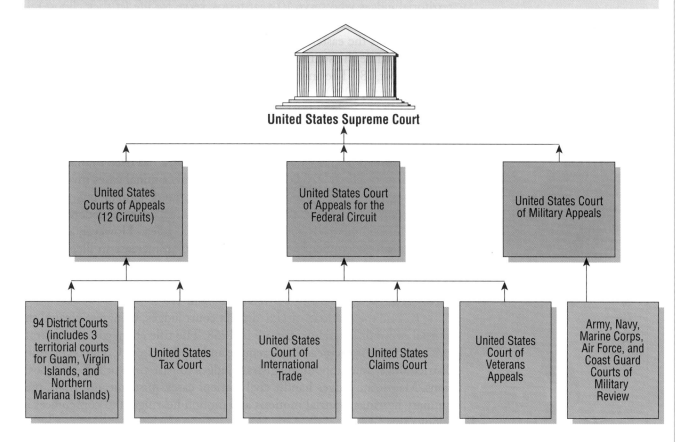

or courts where most violations of federal criminal and civil law are first adjudicated and where decisions of fact are made. Today, there are 94 district courts divided into 13 circuits, with at least one federal district court in each state, one each in the District of Columbia and the Commonwealths of Puerto Rico and the Northern Mariana Islands, and one each in the U.S. territories of the Virgin Islands and Guam. In some states, the courts are divided into districts geographically. New York, for example, has northern, eastern, southern, and western district courts.

Two factors determine the jurisdiction of federal district courts: the subject matter of a case and the parties to a case. Federal district courts have *subject matter jurisdiction* over cases that involve federal laws, treaties with foreign nations, or interpretations of the Constitution. Cases involving admiralty or maritime law—the law of the sea, including ships, their crews, and disputes over actions and rights at sea—also come under federal district court jurisdiction.

Federal district courts have *personal jurisdiction* in cases if certain parties or persons are involved. These include (1) ambassadors and other representatives of foreign governments, (2) two or more state governments, (3) the United States government or one of its offices and agencies, (4) citizens of different states, (5) a state and a citizen of a different state, (6) citizens of the same state claiming lands under grants of different states, and (7) a state or its citizens and a foreign country or its citizens.

Writ of *certiorari*

A written order, from the U.S. Supreme Court to a lower court whose decision is being appealed, to send the records of the case forward for review.

illegal search at the time of the arrest. The defendant may appeal to the U.S. Supreme Court on the constitutional issue only. The Supreme Court generally has no jurisdiction to rule on the state issue (whether the accused actually violated state law). The Court would decide only whether Fourth Amendment rights were violated. Decisions of the High Court are binding on all lower courts.

The U.S. Supreme Court is composed of a chief justice, officially known as the Chief Justice of the United States, and eight associate justices. They are appointed for life by the President with the consent of the Senate and, like other federal judges, can only be removed from office against their will by "impeachment for, and Conviction of, Treason, Bribery, or other high Crimes and Misdemeanors." The Chief Justice, who is specifically nominated by the President for the position, presides over the Court's public sessions and private conferences, assigns justices to write opinions (when the Chief Justice has voted with the majority), and supervises the entire federal judiciary. (When the Chief Justice has voted with the minority, the Associate Justice who has the greatest seniority, that is, has been on the Court the longest, assigns who writes the opinion.) The salary of the Chief Justice is $171,500; the salaries of the Associate Justices are $164,100 (as of January 1, 1998).

For a case to be heard by the Supreme Court, at least four of the nine justices must vote to hear the case (the "rule of four"). When the required number of votes has been achieved, the Court issues a **writ of *certiorari*** to the lower court whose decision is being appealed, ordering it to send the records of the case forward for review. The Court is limited by law and custom in the types of cases for which it issues writs of *certiorari*. The Court will issue a "writ" only if the defendant in the case has exhausted all other avenues of appeal and the case involves a susbstantial federal question as defined by the appellate court. A substantial federal question, as noted, is one in which there is an alleged violation of either the U.S. Constitution or federal law.

When the Supreme Court decides a case it has accepted on appeal, it can do one of the following:

1. Affirm the verdict or decision of the lower court and "let it stand";
2. Modify the verdict or decision of the lower court, without totally reversing it;
3. Reverse the verdict or decision of the lower court, requiring no further court action;

    or

4. Reverse the verdict or decision of the lower court and remand the case to the court of original jurisdiction, for either retrial or resentencing.

In some cases, the Supreme Court has ordered trial courts to resentence defendants whose original sentences violated the Eighth Amendment prohibition against cruel and unusual punishment. In other cases, prison authorities have been ordered to remedy unconstitutional conditions of imprisonment.

Appeals to the Supreme Court are heard at the discretion of the Court, in contrast to appeals to the U.S. circuit courts, which review cases as a matter of right. Generally, the High Court's refusal to hear a case ends the process of direct appeal. In fiscal year 1996, for example, the U.S. Supreme Court denied

Current U.S. Supreme Court Justices. Top row (L–R): Associate Justices Ruth Bader Ginsburg, David Souter, Clarence Thomas, and Stephen Breyer. Bottom row (L–R): Associate Justices Antonin Scalia and John Paul Stevens, Chief Justice William Rehnquist, Associate Justices Sandra Day O'Connor and Anthony Kennedy.

nearly 99 percent of the petitions for review on writ of *certiorari* in criminal proceedings.[10] Writs of *certiorari* in criminal proceedings accounted for 40 percent of such writs filed with the Court; the rest were either civil appeals or administrative appeals.[11] In certain circumstances, an imprisoned defendant whose appeal has been denied may still try to have the Supreme Court review his or her case on constitutional grounds by filing a writ of *habeas corpus*. A **writ of *habeas corpus*,** which is guaranteed by Article I, Section 9 of the U.S. Constitution, the Federal Habeas Corpus Act, and state *habeas corpus* laws, is a court order directing a law officer to produce a prisoner in court to determine if the prisoner is being legally detained or imprisoned. The *habeas corpus* proceeding does not test whether the prisoner is guilty or innocent.

The U.S. Supreme Court also has original jurisdiction. However, Article III, Section 2.2 of the Constitution limits the Court's original jurisdiction to two types of cases: (1) cases involving representatives of foreign governments; and (2) certain cases in which a state is a party. Many cases have involved two states and the federal government. When Maryland and Virginia argued over oyster fishing rights, and when a dispute broke out between California and Arizona over the control of water from the Colorado River, the Supreme Court had original jurisdiction in the matters. Original jurisdiction cases are a very small part of the Court's yearly workload. Most of the cases the Court decides fall under its appellate jurisdiction.

Writ of *habeas corpus* An order from a court to an officer of the law to produce a prisoner in court to determine if the prisoner is being legally detained or imprisoned.

The State Courts

The state courts have general power to decide nearly every type of case, subject only to the limitations of the U.S. Constitution, their own state constitutions, and state law. State and local courts are the courts with which citizens most often have contact. These courts handle most criminal matters and the majority of day-to-day legal matters. The laws of each state determine the organization, function, and even the names of its courts. Thus, no two state court systems are exactly alike. For discussion purposes, it is useful to distinguish four levels of state courts: trial courts of limited jurisdiction, trial courts of general jurisdiction, intermediate appellate courts, and state courts of last resort.[12]

Trial Courts of Limited Jurisdiction At the base of the state court structure (see Figure 7–1) are the approximately 13,000 trial courts of limited jurisdiction, sometimes referred to generally as "inferior trial courts" or simply as "lower courts." Depending on the jurisdiction, those courts are called city courts, municipal courts, county courts, circuit courts, courts of common pleas, justice-of-the-peace courts, district courts, or magistrate courts. (Technically, most of the lower courts are not really part of the state judicial structure because they are the creation of, and funded by, either city or county governments.) In several states, judges of the lower courts are not required to have any formal legal training.

The lower courts typically deal with minor cases, such as ordinance and traffic violations, some misdemeanors, and—in many jurisdictions—civil cases involving less than $1,000. For those types of offenses, the lower courts in many states are allowed to conduct **summary trials,** or trials without a jury. Typically, the greatest penalty that can be imposed is a fine of $1,000 and a maximum of 12 months in jail. Unlike trial courts of general jurisdiction, the lower courts are not courts of record, where detailed transcripts of the proceedings are made. Because they are not courts of record, an appeal from such a lower court requires a **trial *de novo*,** in which the entire case must be reheard by a trial court of general jurisdiction.

In addition to handling minor cases, the lower courts in most states hear the formal charges against persons accused of felonies, set bail, appoint counsel for indigent defendants, and conduct preliminary hearings for crimes that must be adjudicated at a higher level. The legal proceedings in these courts are typically less formal, and many cases are resolved without defense attorneys. Lower courts process and quickly dispose of large numbers of cases, approximately 70 million a year.

Trial Courts of General Jurisdiction Variously called district courts, superior courts, and circuit courts, depending on the jurisdiction, the more than 3,000 trial courts of general jurisdiction have the authority to try all civil and criminal cases and to hear appeals from lower courts. They are courts of record (formal transcripts of the proceedings are made), and judges and lawyers in those courts have formal legal training. Trial courts of general jurisdiction are funded by the state.

Some states have created specialty courts to deal with increases in certain types of crimes or chronic social problems. In the late 1980s, for instance, the first drug courts were established to (1) help handle the dramatic increase

Summary trial A trial without a jury.

Trial *de novo* A trial in which an entire case is reheard by a trial court of general jurisdiction because there is an appeal and there is no written transcript of the earlier proceeding.

The county courthouse is a familiar sight in many local areas.

in drug cases that resulted from the War on Drugs and was overwhelming the trial courts of general jurisdiction and (2) use the court's authority to reduce crime by changing defendants' drug-using behavior. In exchange for the possibility of dismissed charges or reduced sentences, defendants accept diversion to drug treatment programs during the judicial process. Drug court judges preside over drug court proceedings, monitor the progress of defendants by means of frequent status hearings, and prescribe sanctions and rewards as appropriate, in collaboration with prosecutors, defense attorneys, treatment providers, and others.[13]

In 1997, Broward County in south Florida instituted the first mental-health court in the nation. This court is charged with ensuring treatment for mentally ill or developmentally disabled individuals who have been charged with nonviolent misdemeanors and, at the same time, with protecting the public. Before the court was created, mentally disabled people often sat in jail for weeks or months for crimes that typically warranted no more than several days of confinement for other offenders. Mentally disabled arrestees often remained in jail for such long periods because they were unable to make a telephone call or post bond. The specialty court speeds up first appearances for those defendants and generally orders them to be hospitalized for evaluation.[15]

Intermediate Appellate Courts In some of the geographically smaller and less populous states, there is only one appellate court, the state court of last resort, usually called the state supreme court. Many states, however, have created intermediate appellate courts to reduce the overwhelming case burden of the state supreme court. As of January 1, 1996, 38 states had intermediate courts of appeal.[16]

As of March 31, 1997, there were 161 drug court programs operating in 38 states, the District of Columbia, and Puerto Rico. Forty percent of the programs were in California and Florida. Since 1989, the programs have admitted more than 65,000 offenders. The average completion rate for the programs is 48 percent (the range is from 8 percent to 95 percent).[14]

In 1966, it was estimated that about 5.5 percent of all criminal jury trials ended with a hung jury. Between 1992 and 1994, in contrast, the average hung-jury rate in the nine most ethnically diverse California counties, including Los Angeles, was 13 percent. Also, between 1992 and 1996, the hung-jury rate in all federal criminal trials in Washington, D.C., was 13 percent, compared with only 5 percent in 1991.[43]

then the judge can either direct the jury to acquit the defendant or "take the case from the jury" and grant the motion for dismissal.

If the defense does not seek a dismissal or a dismissal is not granted, the defense follows the prosecution with its witnesses and any contrary evidence. Then the prosecution and the defense take turns offering rebuttals to the other side's evidence, cross-examining witnesses, and reexamining their own witnesses. Following the rebuttal period, the prosecution summarizes its case. The defense then summarizes its case and makes its closing statement. The closing statement by the prosecution ends the adversarial portion of the trial.

Normally, after the closing statement by the prosecution, the judge instructs, or *charges*, the jury concerning the principles of law the jurors are to utilize in determining guilt or innocence. The judge also explains to the jury the charges, the rules of evidence, and the possible verdicts. In some jurisdictions, the judge summarizes the evidence presented from notes taken during the trial. The jury then retires to deliberate until it reaches a verdict. In a room where it has complete privacy, the jury elects from its members a foreperson to preside over the subsequent deliberations. Jurors are not allowed to discuss the case with anyone other than another juror. In some cases, a jury is sequestered at night in a hotel or motel to prevent any chance of outside influence.

Careers in Criminal Justice

JUDGE

Judges apply the law and oversee the legal process in courts of law. They ensure that trials and hearings are conducted fairly and that the court administers justice in a manner consistent with procedural safeguards. Juries usually decide the outcome of a case; however, judges decide cases when the law does not require a jury trial or where the defendant waives his or her right to a trial by jury.

In addition to time spent in the courtroom, judges also work in their chambers—reading documents, holding hearings with lawyers, researching legal issues, and writing opinions. Appellate-court judges rule on fewer cases than do trial-court judges, and appellate judges rarely have contact with the actual litigants in a case.

Most judges, but not all, have been lawyers first. All federal and state trial judges are required to be lawyers. Salaries for federal judges are generally higher than those at other levels. Salaries of state and local judges vary widely.

COURT REPORTER

Court reporters are responsible for recording everything that is said in a legal proceeding. Court reporters work in state and federal court systems. In smaller areas, a court reporter may work in several courts within the judicial system. Court reporters use special machines to take notes. After the proceedings, they dictate their notes into a machine for transcription at a later time. Every word said in the legal proceeding must be included in the official transcript.

To become a court reporter, a candidate must be able to take at least 160 words of dictation a minute. An associate's degree or certification from a preprofessional training program is preferred. In addition to being quick and accurate, court reporters must be able to concentrate on the task in a busy setting with many distractions. Salaries for court reporters vary with training and experience.

To find a defendant guilty as charged, the jury must be convinced "beyond a reasonable doubt" that the defendant has committed the crime. Some juries reach a verdict in a matter of minutes; some juries have taken weeks or more. If the jury finds the defendant guilty as charged, as it does in two-thirds of criminal cases, the judge begins to consider a sentence. In some jurisdictions, the jury participates to varying degrees in the sentencing process. If the jury finds the defendant not guilty, the defendant is released from the jurisdiction of the court and is a free person. After the verdict has been read in the courtroom, either the defense or the prosecution may ask that the jury be polled individually, with each juror stating publicly how he or she voted.

In the federal courts and in nearly every state, a unanimous verdict is required. If even one juror cannot agree with the others on a verdict, the result is a **hung jury.** In that case, the judge declares a mistrial, and the prosecutor must decide whether to retry the case. The only exceptions are Texas, Louisiana, Oklahoma, Oregon, and Montana, where majority verdicts are allowed in criminal cases heard by 12-member juries.

Hung jury The result when jurors cannot agree on a verdict. The judge declares a mistrial. The prosecutor must decide whether to retry the case.

7 Review and Applications

CHAPTER OBJECTIVE 1

The United States has a dual court system—a separate judicial system for each of the states and a separate federal system. The only place where the two systems "connect" is the United States Supreme Court. The federal court system is composed of U.S. district courts, U.S. circuit courts of appeals, and the U.S. Supreme Court. The state court system consists of trial courts of limited jurisdiction, trial courts of general jurisdiction, intermediate appellate courts (in most states), and state courts of last resort.

CHAPTER OBJECTIVE 2

The purposes of courts are (1) to do justice, (2) to appear to do justice, (3) to provide a forum where disputes between people can be resolved justly and peacefully, (4) to censure wrongdoing, (5) to incapacitate criminal offenders, (6) to punish offenders, (7) to rehabilitate offenders, (8) to deter people from committing crimes, (9) to determine legal status, and (10) to protect individual citizens against arbitrary government action.

CHAPTER OBJECTIVE 3

Prosecutors are the most powerful actors in the administration of justice because they conduct the final screening of all persons arrested for criminal offenses, deciding whether there is enough evidence to support a conviction, and because, in most jurisdictions, they have unreviewable discretion in deciding whether to charge a person with a crime and prosecute the case.

CHAPTER OBJECTIVE 4

People charged with crimes may have privately retained counsel, or if indigent, they may have court-appointed attorneys, public defenders, or "contract" lawyers, depending on which is provided by the jurisdiction.

CHAPTER OBJECTIVE 5

Judges have a variety of responsibilities in the criminal justice process. Among their nontrial duties are determining probable cause, signing warrants, informing suspects of their rights, setting and revoking bail, arraigning defendants, and accepting guilty pleas. Judges spend much of the workday in their chambers, negotiating procedures and dispositions with prosecutors and defense attorneys. The principal responsibility of judges in all of those duties is to ensure that suspects and defendants are treated fairly and in accordance with due process of law. In jury trials, judges are responsible for allowing the jury a fair chance to reach a verdict on the evidence presented. A judge must ensure that his or her behavior does not improperly affect the outcome of the case. Before juries retire to deliberate and reach a verdict, judges instruct them on the relevant law. Additionally, in jurisdictions without professional court administrators, each judge is responsible for the management of his or her own courthouse and its personnel, with the added duties of supervising building maintenance, budgets, and labor relations.

CHAPTER OBJECTIVE 6

At the initial appearance, the first pretrial stage, defendants are given formal notice of the charges against them and are advised of their constitutional rights (for example, the right to counsel). For a misdemeanor or an ordinance violation, a summary trial may be held. For a felony, a hearing is held to determine whether the suspect should be released or whether there is probable cause to hold the suspect for a preliminary hearing.

CHAPTER OBJECTIVE 7

Bail is usually a monetary guarantee deposited with the court that is supposed to ensure that the suspect or defendant will appear at a subsequent stage in the criminal justice process. Different pretrial release options include station-house bail, surety bonds, full cash bonds, deposit bonds, release on own recognizance (ROR), conditional release, and unsecured bonds.

CHAPTER OBJECTIVE 8

A grand jury is a group of 12 to 23 citizens who, for a specific period of time (generally three months), meet in closed sessions to investigate charges coming from preliminary hearings or to engage in other responsibilities. A primary purpose of the grand jury is to determine whether there is probable cause to believe that the accused committed the crime or crimes with which he or she is charged by the prosecutor. Other purposes of a grand jury are to protect citizens from unfounded government charges and to consider the misconduct of government officials.

CHAPTER OBJECTIVE 9

The primary purpose of arraignment is to hear the formal information or grand jury indictment and to allow defendants to enter a plea. Plea options include "guilty," "not guilty," and in some states and in the federal courts, *"nolo contendere."* In some states, defendants can also stand mute or can plead "not guilty by reason of insanity."

CHAPTER OBJECTIVE 10

Plea bargaining seemingly serves the interests of all the court participants by, among other things, reducing uncertainty about the length or outcome of trials. Plea bargains serve prosecutors by guaranteeing them high conviction rates; judges by reducing court caseloads; defense attorneys by allowing them to avoid trials and to spend less time on each case; and even some criminal offenders by enabling them to escape a prison sentence altogether, to receive a lesser sentence than they might have received if convicted at trial, or to escape conviction of socially stigmatizing crimes. Two types of criminal offenders are not served by plea bargaining: (1) innocent, indigent defendants who fear being found guilty of crimes they did not commit and receiving harsh sentences, and (2) habitual offenders.

CHAPTER OBJECTIVE 11

The stages in a criminal trial are as follows: (1) selection and swearing in of the jury, in jury trials; (2) opening statements by the prosecution and the defense; (3) presentation of the prosecution's case; (4) presentation of the defense's case; (5) rebuttals, cross-examination, and reexamination of witnesses; (6) closing arguments by the defense and the prosecution; (7) the judge's instructing, or charging, the jury; and (8) deliberation and verdict.

KEY TERMS

dual court system, p. 224
jurisdiction, p. 224
original jurisdiction, p. 224
appellate jurisdiction, p. 224
general jurisdiction, p. 224
special jurisdiction, p. 224
subject matter jurisdiction, p. 224
personal jurisdiction, p. 224
writ of *certiorari*, p. 228
writ of *habeas corpus*, p. 229
summary trial, p. 230
trial *de novo*, p. 230
due process of law, p. 232
incapacitation, p. 233
punishment, p. 233

rehabilitation, p. 233
general deterrence, p. 233
nolle prosequi (*nol. pros.*), p. 234
plea bargaining or negotiating, p. 236
rules of discovery, p. 236
probable cause, p. 244
booking, p. 244
complaint, p. 245
information, p. 245
grand jury indictment, p. 245
arrest warrant, p. 246
bail/bail bond, p. 246
preventive detention, p. 247
bench warrant or *capias*, p. 248

release on own recognizance (ROR), p. 249
conditional release, p. 249
unsecured bond, p. 249
preliminary hearing, p. 250
grand jury, p. 250
indictment, p. 250
subpoena, p. 251
arraignment, p. 251
nolo contendere, p. 251
bench trial, p. 255
venire, p. 257
voir dire, p. 257
hung jury, p. 261

1. What is the difference between *original* and *appellate jurisdiction*? Between *general* and *special jurisdiction*? Between *subject matter* and *personal jurisdiction*?

2. Under what circumstances will the U.S. Supreme Court issue a *writ of certiorari*?

3. Ideally, what are the three conditions that must be met before a prosecutor charges a person with a crime and prosecutes the case?

4. Why do prosecutors sometimes choose not to prosecute criminal cases?

5. In general, when does an individual accused of a crime have the right to counsel?

6. By what methods are judges selected?

7. Describe the "funneling" or screening process in the administration of justice.

8. When do suspects officially become defendants?

9. How long may suspects arrested without a warrant be held in jail before being brought before a judge for an initial appearance?

10. In what two ways are preliminary hearings similar to criminal trials, and in what two ways do preliminary hearings differ from criminal trials?

11. What is the primary purpose of a grand jury?

12. What are three basic types of plea bargains?

13. What are three principal purposes of jury trials?

14. What is *voir dire*, and what is its purpose?

EXPERIENTIAL ACTIVITIES

1. Visit the office of a local bail bonds person. It is generally near the courthouse and well marked, but bonds persons are also listed in the Yellow Pages of the phone book. When the bonds person is not busy, ask him or her to describe the job. Ask about major problems with the business and satisfactions of the job. Specific questions might include the following: (1) For what type of offender is it most risky to provide bail? (2) How does a bail transaction work? (3) Do bonds people actually have to give money to the court when they put up bail? (4) If a client does not appear, does the bonds person actually have to pay or forfeit the bond to the court? How does that work? (5) Have any of their clients absconded, never to be seen again? Summarize the visit in a short written or oral report.

2. Visit several different types of courts, such as a lower court, a trial court, and an appellate court, state courts and federal courts. Observe the proceedings, and describe how they differ from or are similar to those described in this chapter. Share your findings with the class.

3. Scan a local newspaper for a story of a criminal trial. Write a report that includes information about (1) the type of local, state, or federal court in which the trial is being held amd why that court has jurisdiction, (2) the type of case being tried (misdemeanor or felony), (3) the outcome of the case, and (4) your opinion of the verdict.

4. **INTERNET** Access the Federal Judiciary Homepage at **www.uscourts.gov**, and find the directory of district courts. Locate your home state. Then look up the number of districts your state is divided into, where the courts for the districts are located, and how many judgeships are authorized for each district.

1. As a defense attorney, what would you do under the following circumstances?

   a. Your client tells you that he committed the crime or crimes for which he is being prosecuted.

   b. Your client tells you about a serious crime that will be committed sometime next week.

   c. Your client tells you that if you lose the case, his friends will harm your family.

   d. You learn that your client, who has paid you nothing so far for your services, will not be able to pay your fee.

   e. Your client insists on testifying, even though you believe that it is not in his best interests to do so.

2. In John Grisham's *A Time To Kill,* the defendant, a black man whose young daughter was viciously raped by two white men, is on trial for gunning down the two men on the courthouse steps in full view of many bystanders. Even though it was obvious to all that the defendant had killed the two men, the jury in the case returned a not-guilty verdict, and the defendant was allowed to walk free. This is an example of *jury nullification,* the power of a jury in a criminal case to acquit a defendant despite overwhelming evidence. The jury can acquit for any reason or for no reason at all, and the decision of the jury cannot be appealed. Jury nullification is one of the problems cited by critics who call for the abolition of the present American jury system. Another complaint about the jury system is the inability of some jurors in some trials to understand legal arguments, the evidence presented, or the instructions of the judge. Critics of the jury system suggest replacing jury trials with bench trials or with trials before a panel of judges or substituting professionally trained jurors for the current "amateur" jurors.

   a. Should the American jury system be abolished? Why or why not?

   b. Do you believe that any of the alternatives suggested by jury critics would produce a better or more just system? Defend your answer.

ADDITIONAL READING

Eisenstein, James, Roy Flemming, and Peter Nadulli. *The Contours of Justice: Communities and Their Courts.* Boston: Little, Brown, 1988.

Feely, Malcolm. *The Process Is the Punishment: Handling Cases in Lower Criminal Court.* New York: Russell Sage Foundation, 1979.

Hans, Valerie P. and Neil Vidmar. *Judging the Jury.* New York: Plenum, 1986.

Heilbroner, David. *Rough Justice: Days and Nights of a Young D.A.* New York: Pantheon, 1990.

Kalven, Harry, Jr. and Hans Zeisel. *The American Jury.* Boston: Little, Brown, 1966.

Levine, James P. *Juries and Politics.* Pacific Grove, CA: Brooks/Cole, 1992.

Loftus, Elizabeth and E. Ketcham. *For the Defense.* New York: St. Martin's, 1991.

McIntyre, Lisa J. *The Public Defender: The Practice of Law in the Shadows of Repute.* Chicago: University of Chicago Press, 1987.

Neubauer, David W. *America's Courts and the Criminal Justice System,* 4th ed. Pacific Grove, CA: Brooks/Cole, 1992.

Neubauer, David W. *Judicial Process: Law, Courts and Politics in the United States.* Pacific Grove, CA: Brooks/Cole, 1991.

O'Brien, David M. *Storm Center: The Supreme Court in American Politics,* 3d ed. New York: W. W. Norton & Co., 1993.

Satter, Robert. *Doing Justice: A Trial Judge at Work.* New York: Simon & Schuster, 1990.

Smith, Christopher. *Courts, Politics, and the Judicial Process.* Chicago: Nelson-Hall, 1993.

Stumpf, Harry P. and John H. Culver. *The Politics of State Courts.* New York: Longman, 1992.

Wice, Paul. *Judges and Lawyers: The Human Side of Justice.* New York: Harper-Collins, 1991.

Wice, Paul. *Chaos in the Courthouse: The Inner Workings of the Urban Criminal Courts.* New York: Praeger, 1985.

Wishman, Seymour. *Confessions of a Criminal Lawyer.* New York: Penguin, 1982.

ENDNOTES

1. Administrative Office of the U.S. Courts, Federal Judiciary Homepage, "District Courts," www.uscourts.gov, February 1998.

2. Administrative Office of the U.S. Courts, Federal Judiciary Homepage, "1996 Year-End Report on the Federal Judiciary, www.uscourts.gov/cj96.htm, August 1997; *Sourcebook of Criminal Justice Statistics 1995,* Online, p. 467, Table 5.18; Kathleen Maguire, Ann L. Pastore, and Timothy J. Flanagan (eds.), *Sourcebook of Criminal Justice Statistics 1992,* U. S. Department of Justice, Bureau of Justice Statistics (Washington: GPO, 1993), p. 485, Table 5.14. The increase in drug offenses prosecuted was calculated from data in Maguire et al., Table 5.14, and *Sourcebook,* Online, Table 5.18.

3. Administrative Office of the U.S. Courts, Federal Judiciary Homepage, "U.S. Magistrate Judges," www.uscourts.gov, February 1998.

4. *Sourcebook of Criminal Justice Statistics 1995,* Online, op. cit., p. 518, Table 5.78; also Administrative Office of the U.S. Courts, Federal Judiciary Homepage, "1996 Year-End Report on the Federal Judiciary, " op. cit.

5. Administrative Office of the U.S. Courts, Federal Judiciary Homepage, "Courts of Appeal," www.uscourts.gov/understanding_courts/8996. htm; also "1996 Year-End Report on the Federal Judiciary," op. cit.

7. Ibid.

8. Administrative Office of the U.S. Courts, Federal Judiciary Homepage, "Judicial Councils & Conferences," www.uscourts.gov, February 1998.

9. Kathleen Maguire and Ann L. Pastore (eds.), *Sourcebook of Criminal Justice Statistics 1996,* U. S. Department of Justice, Bureau of Justice Statistics (Washington: GPO, 1997), p. 485, Table 5.72 (calculated from data in the tables).

10. Ibid.

11. Clerk of the Supreme Court; 28 U.S.C. §1911.

12. Material on the state courts is based on information from the following sources: David W. Neubauer, *America's Courts and the Criminal Justice System,* 4th ed. (Pacific Grove, CA: Brooks/Cole, 1992); Christopher Smith, *Courts, Politics, and the Judicial Process* (Chicago: Nelson-Hall, 1993); N. Gary Holten and Lawson L. Lamar, *The Criminal Courts: Structures, Personnel, and Processes* (New York: McGraw-Hill, 1991); Lawrence Baum, *American Courts,* 3d ed. (Boston:

Houghton Mifflin, 1994). U.S. Department of Justice, Bureau of Justice Statistics, *Report to the Nation on Crime and Justice,* 2d ed. (Washington: GPO, 1988); H. Ted Rubin, *The Courts: Fulcrum of the Justice System* (Santa Monica, CA: Goodyear, 1976); James Eisenstein, Roy Flemming, and Peter Nadulli, *The Contours of Justice: Communities and Their Courts* (Boston: Little, Brown, 1988); Malcolm Feeley, *The Process Is the Punishment: Handling Cases in Lower Criminal Court* (New York: Russell Sage, 1979); Harry P. Stumpf and John H. Culver, *The Politics of State Courts* (New York: Longman, 1992); Paul Wice, *Chaos in the Courthouse: The Inner Workings of the Urban Criminal Courts* (New York, Praeger, 1985).

13. Material in this section about drug courts is from "Drug Courts: Overview of Growth, Characteristics, and Results," GAO/GGD-97-106, www.ncjrs.org/txtfiles/dcourts.txt, July 31, 1997.

14. Ibid.

15. Maya Bell, "Mentally Ill Get Court of Their Own—and Help," *The Orlando Sentinel,* July 13, 1997, p. A−1.

16. *Sourcebook of Criminal Justice Statistics,* Online, Table 1.70.

17. Ibid.

18. Ibid.

19. Laura B. Myers, "Bringing the Offender to Heel: Views of the Criminal Courts," in Timothy J. Flanagan and Dennis R. Longmire (eds.), *Americans View Crime and Justice: A National Public Opinion Survey* (Thousand Oaks, CA: Sage, 1996), pp. 46–61.

20. Rubin, op. cit.

21. In addition to the other sources cited, material on the key actors in the court process is from Neubauer, op. cit.; David W. Neubauer, *Judicial Process: Law, Courts and Politics in the United States* (Pacific Grove, CA: Brooks/Cole, 1991); Smith, op. cit.; Holten and Lamar, op. cit.; Baum, op. cit.

22. Material about prosecutors is also taken from David Heilbroner, *Rough Justice: Days and Nights of a Young D.A.* (New York: Pantheon, 1990).

23. In addition to the other sources cited, material on defense attorneys is from Elizabeth Loftus and E. Ketcham, *For the Defense* (New York: St. Martin's, 1991); Paul Wice, *Judges and Lawyers: The Human Side of Justice* (New York: Harper-Collins, 1991); Paul Wice, *Criminal Lawyers: An Endangered Species* (Newbury Park, CA: Sage, 1978); Seymour Wishman,

Confessions of a Criminal Lawyer (New York: Penguin, 1982); Lisa J. McIntyre, *The Public Defender: The Practice of Law in the Shadows of Repute* (Chicago: University of Chicago Press, 1987).

24. Based on figures provided in C. Ronald Huff, Arye Rattner, and Edward Sagarin, "Guilty Until Proven Innocent: Wrongful Conviction and Public Policy," *Crime and Delinquency*, Vol. 32 (1986), pp. 518–44.

25. Steven K. Smith and Carol J. DeFrances, "Indigent Defense," U.S. Department of Justice, *Bureau of Justice Statistics Selected Findings*, (Washington), February 1996.

26. "Despite Gains, Women Lawyers Still Face Bias," *The Orlando Sentinel*, August 18, 1996, p. A–20.

27. In addition to the other sources cited, material on judges is from Paul Ryan, Allan Ashman, Bruce D. Sales, and Sandra Shane-DuBow, *American Trial Judges* (New York: Free Press, 1980); Robert Satter, *Doing Justice: A Trial Judge at Work* (New York: Simon & Schuster, 1990); Wice (1991), op. cit.; Wice (1985), op. cit.

28. Elisha P. Douglass, "Judges Were Suggested by Jethro," *The Anniston* (Alabama) *Star*, June 9, 1983.

29. Debbie Salamone and Gerald Shields, "Justice to ABA: Races Not Popularity Contests," *The Orlando Sentinel*, August 4, 1996, p. A–23.

30. *Sourcebook of Criminal Justice Statistics*, Online, Tables 1.73 and 1.75.

31. In addition to the other sources cited, material on pretrial stages is from Neubauer (1992), op. cit.; Holten and Lamar, op. cit.

32. In addition to the other sources cited, material on plea bargaining is from Neubauer (1992), op. cit.; Neubauer (1991), op. cit.; Holten and Lamar, op. cit.; Baum, op. cit.

33. Patrick A. Langan and Jodi M. Brown, "Felony Sentences in State Courts, 1994," U.S. Department of Justice, *Bureau of Justice Statistics Bulletin*. (Washington), January 1997, p. 9, Table 11.

34. Cited in *The Anniston* (Alabama) *Star*, June 3, 1985, p. 5A.

35. Ibid.

36. "Washington Court Deems '3 Strikes' Constitutional," *The Orlando Sentinel*, August 9, 1996, p. A–12.

37. In addition to the other sources cited, material on criminal trials is from Neubauer (1992), op. cit.; Neubauer (1991), op. cit.; Smith, op. cit.; Holten and Lamar, op. cit.

38. In addition to the other sources cited, material on juries is from Holten and Lamar, op. cit.; Valerie P. Hans and Neil Vidmar, *Judging the Jury* (New York: Plenum, 1986); Harry Kalvan, Jr. and Hans Zeisel, *The American Jury* (Boston: Little, Brown, 1996); James P. Levine, *Juries and Politics* (Pacific Grove, CA: Brooks/Cole, 1992).

39. "Court: Farmers Can Miss Jury Duty in Crop Seasons," *The Orlando Sentinel*, October 23, 1997, p. A–18.

40. "McVeigh's Jury Pool: Educated, Patriotic," *The Orlando Sentinel*, April 20, 1997, p. A–5.

41. In addition to the other sources cited, material on the trial process is from Satter (1990), op. cit.

42. "DuPont Must Pay Cost of Murder Trial: $742,000," *The Orlando Sentinel*, June 11, 1997, p. A–16.

43. Jeffrey Rosen, "One Angry Woman: Why Are Hung Juries on the Rise?" *The New Yorker*, February 24 & March 3, 1997, p. 55.

CHAPTER OUTLINE

8 Sentencing, Appeals, and the Death Penalty

CHAPTER OBJECTIVES

After completing this chapter, you should be able to:

1 Identify the general factors that influence a judge's sentencing decisions.

2 Describe how judges tailor sentences to fit the crime and the offender.

3 Distinguish between indeterminate and determinate sentences.

4 Explain the three basic types of determinate sentences.

5 List five rationales or justifications for criminal punishment.

6 Explain the purposes of presentence investigation reports.

7 List the legal bases for appeal.

8 Identify the type of crime for which death may be a punishment.

9 Summarize the three major procedural reforms the Supreme Court approved for death penalty cases in the *Gregg* decision.

Sentencing

If a criminal defendant pleads guilty or is found guilty by a judge or jury, then the judge must impose a sentence.[1] In a few jurisdictions, sentencing is the responsibility of the jury for certain types of offenses (for example, capital crimes). Figure 8–1 displays, by the most serious offense, the amount of time from conviction to sentencing for defendants in the 75 largest U.S. counties in 1992. As Figure 8–1 shows, for most offenses a majority of defendants are sentenced either on the day of conviction or the next day.

Sentencing is arguably a judge's most difficult responsibility. Judges cannot impose just any sentence. They are limited by statutory provisions and guided by prevailing philosophical rationales, organizational considerations, and presentence investigation reports. They are also influenced by their own personal characteristics.

FIGURE 8–1

Time From Conviction to Sentencing for Convicted Defendants, by Most Serious Offense, 1992

Most Serious Conviction Offense	Number of Defendants	Total	Percent of Convicted Defendants in the 75 Largest Counties Who Were Sentenced Within:			
			0–1 Day	2–30 Days	31–60 Days	61 Days or More
All offenses	31,234	100%	61%	18%	14%	7%
All felonies	24,729	100%	56%	21%	15%	7%
Violent offenses	4,721	100%	54%	20%	18%	8%
Property offenses	9,119	100%	62%	20%	12%	6%
Drug offenses	8,178	100%	50%	25%	17%	8%
Public-order offenses	2,589	100%	53%	20%	16%	11%
Misdemeanors	6,505	100%	83%	6%	7%	4%

Note: Data on time from conviction to sentencing were available for 96% of all cases that had reached sentencing.

Source: Felony Defendants in Large Urban Counties, 1992. U.S. Department of Justice, Bureau of Justice Statistics (Washington: GPO, 1995), p. 30, Table 25.

Statutory Provisions

As described in Chapter 4, state and federal legislative bodies enact penal codes that specify appropriate punishments for each statutory offense or class of offense, such as a class B felony or class C felony. Currently, five general types of punishment are in use in the United States: fines, probation, intermediate punishments (various punishments that are more restrictive than probation but less restrictive and costly than imprisonment), imprisonment, and death. As long as judges impose one or a combination of those five punishments, and the sentence type and length are within statutory limits, judges are free to set any sentence they want.

Thus, within limits, judges are free to tailor the punishment to fit the crime and the offender. As noted, judges can impose a combination sentence of, for example, imprisonment, probation, and a fine. They can suspend the imprisonment portion of a combination sentence, or they can suspend the entire sentence if the offender stays out of trouble, makes **restitution** (pays money or provides services to victims, their survivors, or the community to make up for the injury inflicted), or seeks medical treatment. If the offender has already spent weeks, months, or sometimes even years in jail awaiting trial, judges can give the offender credit for jail time and deduct that time from any prison sentence. When jail time is not deducted from the sentence, it is called "dead time." In some cases, the sentence that a judge intends to impose closely matches the time an offender has already spent in jail awaiting trial. In such cases, the judge may impose a sentence of "time served" and release the offender.

Restitution Money paid or services provided by a convicted offender to victims, their survivors, or the community to make up for the injury inflicted.

When an offender is convicted of two or more crimes, judges can order the prison sentences to run concurrently (together) or consecutively (one after the other). Judges can also delay sentencing and retain the right to impose a sentence at a later date if conditions warrant.

MYTH

*M*ost felons are street-wise and therefore able to manipulate the criminal justice process to their advantage.

FACT

*A*lthough many felony defendants act tough and knowledgeable about the justice process, they are generally as unsuccessful in evading punishment as they are in crime and in life generally.

Figure 8–2 on page 272 shows, by offense, the types of felony sentences imposed by state courts in 1994. (The figure also shows the percentages of all convictions for specific offenses. Note that nearly a third of all convictions are for property offenses, nearly a third are for drug offenses, nearly a fifth are for violent offenses, and the remainder are for other offenses.)

The sentence of death is generally limited to offenders convicted of "aggravated" murder, and because most criminal offenders are poor, fines are seldom imposed for serious crimes. (When they are, it is generally for symbolic reasons.) Thus, in practice, judges have three sentencing options—probation, intermediate punishments, and imprisonment. Later chapters in this text will cover those options. The death penalty will be discussed at the end of this chapter.

The type of sentence imposed on an offender can be a highly volatile issue. Also controversial is the length of the sentence imposed. Judges in states that have indeterminate sentencing statutes generally have more discretion in sentencing than do judges in states with determinate sentencing laws. An **indeterminate sentence** has a fixed minimum and maximum term of incarceration, rather than a set period. Sentences of 10 to 20 years in prison or of not less than 5 years and not more than 25 years in prison are examples of indeterminate sentences. The amount of the term that is actually served is determined by a parole board, which will be discussed in Chapter 11.

The first indeterminate sentence in the United States was imposed in 1924 in New York. Until then, determinate sentences had been used. In 1975, Maine became the first state to replace indeterminate sentencing with determinate sentencing. It abolished parole at the same time.

Indeterminate sentence A sentence with a fixed minimum and maximum term of incarceration, rather than a set period.

Sentencing, Appeals, and the Death Penalty   **CHAPTER 8**

On July 8, 1993, Charles Keating, Jr. was sentenced in federal court to 12.5 years in prison for "looting" Lincoln Savings and Loan and swindling small investors in what U.S. District Judge Mariana Pfaelzer called a crime "staggering in its proportion." Keating was convicted of 73 counts of fraud, racketeering, and conspiracy. The sentence runs concurrently with a 10-year state prison sentence he was already serving. Keating was also ordered to pay $122.4 million restitution to the government.[2]

FIGURE 8–2

Types of Felony Sentences Imposed by State Courts and Percentage of All Convictions in 1994, by Offense

Most Serious Conviction Offense	Percent of Felons Sentenced to— Incarceration		Probation	Percent of All Convictions
	Prison	Jail		
All Offenses	45%	26%	29%	100.0%
Violent Offenses	62%	20%	18%	18.9%
Murder[a]	95%	2%	3%	1.4%
Rape	71%	17%	12%	2.3%
Robbery	77%	11%	12%	5.3%
Aggravated Assault	48%	27%	25%	7.5%
Other Violent[b]	45%	30%	25%	2.4%
Property Offenses	42%	26%	32%	31.5%
Burglary	53%	22%	25%	11.2%
Larceny[c]	38%	28%	34%	13.0%
Fraud[d]	32%	28%	40%	7.3%
Drug Offenses	42%	27%	31%	31.5%
Possession	34%	32%	34%	12.5%
Trafficking	48%	23%	29%	19.0%
Weapons Offenses	42%	27%	31%	3.6%
Other Offenses[e]	36%	30%	34%	14.6%

Note: For persons receiving a combination of sentences, the sentence designation came from the most severe penalty imposed—prison being the most severe, followed by jail, then probation. Prison includes death sentences. Data on sentence type were available for 867,709 cases.
a. Includes nonnegligent manslaughter.
b. Includes offenses such as negligent manslaughter, sexual assault, and kidnapping.
c. Includes motor vehicle theft.
d. Includes forgery and embezzlement.
e. Composed of nonviolent offenses such as receiving stolen property and vandalism.

Source: Patrick A. Langan and Jodi M. Brown, "Felony Sentences in State Courts, 1994," U.S. Department of Justice, *Bureau of Justice Statistics Bulletin* (Washington: GPO, January 1997), p. 2, Tables 2 and 1 combined.

Indeterminate sentences have been a principal tool in the effort to rehabilitate offenders for much of the past 75 years. They are based on the idea that correctional personnel must be given the flexibility necessary to successfully treat offenders and return them to society as law-abiding members. The rationale underlying indeterminate sentencing is that the time needed for "correcting" different offenders varies so greatly that a range in sentence length provides a better opportunity to achieve successful rehabilitation.

Beginning in the early 1970s, social scientists and politicians began to question whether the rehabilitation of most criminal offenders was even possible. The skepticism about correcting offenders, a public outcry to do something about crime, and a general distrust of decisions made by parole boards continued to grow. By the mid-1970s, several state legislatures had abandoned or at least deemphasized the goal of rehabilitation and had begun to replace indeterminate sentencing with determinate sentencing.

A **determinate sentence** has a fixed period of incarceration, which eliminates the decision-making responsibility of parole boards. The hope of determinate sentencing is that it will at least get criminals off the street for longer periods of time. Some people also consider a determinate sentence more humane because prisoners know exactly when they will be released, something that they do not know with an indeterminate sentence. Several states and the federal government have developed guidelines for determinate sentencing; other states have established sentencing commissions to do so.

There are three basic types of determinate sentences: flat-time, mandatory, and presumptive. With **flat-time sentencing,** judges may choose between probation and imprisonment but have little discretion in setting the length of a prison sentence. Once an offender is imprisoned, there is no possibility of a reduction in the length of the sentence. Thus, parole and **good time** (the number of days deducted from a sentence by prison authorities for good behavior or for other reasons) are not options under flat-time sentencing.

With **mandatory sentencing,** a specified number of years of imprisonment, usually within a range, is provided for particular crimes. Mandatory sentencing usually allows credit for good time but does not allow release on parole.

Presumptive sentencing allows a judge to retain some sentencing discretion, subject to appellate review. In presumptive sentencing, the legislature determines a sentence range for each crime. The judge is expected to impose the normal sentence, specified by statute, unless mitigating or aggravating circumstances justify a sentence below or above the range set by the legislature. Any sentence that deviates from the norm, however, must be explained in writing and is subject to appellate review. Generally, with presumptive sentencing, credit is given for good time, but there is no opportunity for parole. Figure 8–3 on page 274 displays Minnesota's presumptive sentencing guidelines grid.

In today's "law and order" climate, state legislatures, as noted, are increasingly replacing indeterminate sentences with determinate ones. This trend, however, has not escaped criticism. For example, it has been argued that the consequences of determinate sentencing include longer prison sentences and overcrowded prisons. Whether it is the result of a shift in sentencing philosophy or some other factor or factors, there is no question that the United States has been experiencing a dramatic increase in the number of people sentenced to prison and in the length of terms of incarceration. A result has been a crisis of prison overcrowding. In recent years, the United States has had one of the highest imprisonment rates in the world. Furthermore, as of January 1, 1997, 333 prisons in 28 states, the District of Columbia, and the federal system were under court orders to alleviate crowding or other conditions of confinement.[4] As of June 30, 1996, the entire adult correctional departments of 15 states (Alabama, Alaska, Arizona, Connecticut, Indiana, Louisiana, Mississippi, New Hampshire, Ohio, Oklahoma, Rhode Island, South Carolina, Utah, and Virginia) and the

Determinate sentence A sentence with a fixed period of incarceration, which eliminates the decision-making responsibility of parole boards.

Flat-time sentencing Sentencing in which judges may choose between probation and imprisonment but have little discretion in setting the length of a prison sentence. Once an offender is imprisoned, there is no possibility of reduction in the length of the sentence.

Good time The number of days deducted from a sentence by prison authorities for good behavior or for other reasons.

Mandatory sentencing Sentencing in which a specified number of years of imprisonment (usually within a range) is provided for particular crimes.

Presumptive sentencing Sentencing that allows a judge to retain some sentencing discretion, subject to appellate review. The legislature determines a sentence range for each crime. The judge is expected to impose the normal sentence, specified by statute, unless mitigating or aggravating circumstances justify a sentence below or above the range set by the legislature.

FIGURE 8–3

Sample Sentencing Guidelines

MINNESOTA SENTENCING GUIDELINES GRID

Presumptive Prison Sentence Lengths in Months

LESS SERIOUS ◄─────────────────────► MORE SERIOUS

SEVERITY OF OFFENSE (Illustrative Offenses)	CRIMINAL HISTORY SCORE						
	0	1	2	3	4	5	6 or more
Sale of simulated controlled subsstance	12*	12*	12*	13	15	17	19 *18–20*
Theft Related Crimes ($2500 or less) Check Forgery ($200–$2500)	12*	12*	13	15	17	19	21 *20–22*
Theft Crimes ($2500 or less)	12*	13	15	17	19 *18–20*	22 *21–23*	25 *24–26*
Nonresidential Burglary Theft Crimes (over $2500)	12*	15	18	21	25 *24–26*	32 *30–34*	41 *37–45*
Residential Burglary Simple Robbery	18	23	27	30 *29–31*	38 *36–40*	46 *43–49*	54 *50–58*
Criminal Sexual Conduct 2nd Degree	21	26	30	34 *33–35*	44 *42–46*	54 *50–58*	65 *60–70*
Aggravated Robbery	48 *44–52*	58 *54–62*	68 *64–72*	78 *74–82*	88 *84–92*	98 *94–102*	108 *104–112*
Criminal Sexual Conduct, 1st Degree Assult, 1st Degree	86 *81–91*	98 *93–103*	110 *105–115*	122 *117–127*	134 *129–139*	146 *141–151*	158 *153–163*
Murder, 3rd Degree Murder, 2nd Degree (felony murder)	150 *144–156*	165 *159–171*	180 *174–186*	195 *189–201*	210 *204–216*	225 *219–231*	240 *234–246*
Murder, 2nd Degree (with intent)	306 *299–313*	326 *319–333*	346 *339–353*	366 *359–373*	386 *379–393*	406 *399–413*	426 *419–433*

☐ At the discretion of the judge, up to a year in jail and/or other non-jail sanctions can be imposed instead of prison sentences as conditions of probation for most of these offenses. If prison is imposed, the presumptive sentence is the number of months shown.

☐ Presumptive commitment to state prison for all offenses.

Notes: 1. Criminal history score is based on offender's prior record and seriousness of prior offenses. 2. Numbers in italics represent the range of months within which a judge may sentence without the sentence being deemed a departure from the guidelines. 3. First degree murder is excluded from the guidelines by law and carries a mandatory life sentence.

* One year and one day

Source: Minnesota Sentencing Guidelines Commission. Effective August 1, 1994; reprinted in *Seeking Justice: Crime and Punishment in America,* New York: The Edna McConnell Clark Foundation, 1995, p. 24.

Federal Bureau of Prisons were under court orders or consent decrees to reduce overcrowding or improve other conditions of confinement.[5]

A related criticism of determinate sentencing is that it produces an unusually harsh prison system. For example, because of prison overcrowding, many states have all but abandoned even the pretense of rehabilitating offenders. Prisons are increasingly becoming places where offenders are simply "warehoused." In addition, because of the abolition of good time and parole under some determinate sentencing schemes, prison authorities are having a more difficult time maintaining discipline and control of their institutions. Eliminating good time and parole removed two of the most important incentives that prison authorities use to get inmates to behave and to follow prison rules. Also, because of the perceived harshness of some of the determinate sentencing schemes, some judges simply ignore the guidelines. Other judges have ignored sentencing guidelines because they believe they are too lenient. For example, six months after Florida instituted new sentencing rules in 1983 to standardize punishments for felons, judges were ignoring the guidelines and deriding the new system as "justice by computer."

MYTH

Judges are "soft" on crime, allowing many dangerous criminals to escape imprisonment.

FACT

Whether or not an offender is imprisoned usually depends on the facts of the case. In cases of robbery and burglary, for example, judges are generally "hard" on robberies involving strangers and relatively "soft" on prior-relationship burglaries. According to a 1996 public opinion poll, 78 percent of Americans think that the courts are not harsh enough with criminals. In general, however, the "softness" or "hardness" of a judge's sentence depends on the seriousness of the offense, and only about 10 percent of all felonies reported to the police are violent.

FYI

I n the federal system, before implementation of determinate sentencing and the Sentencing Reform Act of 1984 (effective November 1, 1987), good time and parole reduced time actually served, on average, to about one-third of the sentence originally imposed.

In response to overcrowding, some states are erecting tents on prison grounds, as in this Huntsville, Texas, facility.

Sentencing, Appeals, and the Death Penalty   **CHAPTER 8**

A third criticism of determinate sentencing is that it merely shifts sentencing discretion from judges to legislatures and prosecutors (through plea bargaining). Whether or not this shift in sentencing responsibility is desirable is a matter of debate. On one hand, prosecutors generally exercise their discretion in secret, whereas judges exercise discretion in the open. Also, prosecutors and legislators are generally subject to more political influence than are judges.

Yet, on the other hand, one of the major criticisms of indeterminate sentencing and a principal reason for the adoption of determinate sentencing schemes by some states is judicial disparity in sentencing. Judges vary widely in the sentences they impose for similar crimes and offenders. For example, in one study, 41 New York State judges were asked to review files of actual cases and to indicate the sentences they would impose. Sentences for the same crime were quite different. In one case, an elderly man was robbed at gunpoint by a heroin addict. The assailant was unemployed, lived with his pregnant wife, and had a minor criminal record. He was convicted of first-degree robbery, and under New York's indeterminate sentencing statute, the actual sentence was between 0 and 5 years. When the 41 judges were asked what sentence they would impose in the case, 22 percent of them chose the actual sentence (between 0 and 5 years), 29 percent chose a sentence of 5 to 10 years, another 29 percent selected a sentence of 10 to 15 years, 12 percent opted for a sentence of 15 to 20 years, and 7 percent of them chose a sentence of 20 to 25 years.[7] Figure 8–4 displays the judges' choices. Obviously, differ-

FIGURE 8–4

Sentencing Choices of 41 New York State Judges

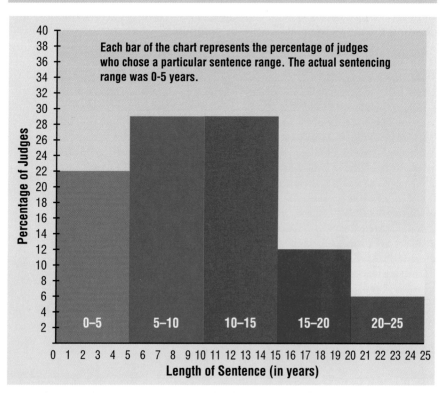

Each bar of the chart represents the percentage of judges who chose a particular sentence range. The actual sentencing range was 0-5 years.

Source: Adapted from "Sentence Disparity in New York: The Response of Forty-One Judges," *The New York Times,* March 30, 1979, p. B3.

ent judges view the same circumstances very differently. Critics have charged that disparity in sentencing has resulted in discrimination against minorities and the poor.

A fourth, related criticism of determinate sentencing in those jurisdictions that retain good time is that sentencing discretion, at least to some degree, actually shifts from legislators and prosecutors to correctional personnel. By charging inmates with violations of prison rules, correctional personnel can reduce (if the charges are upheld) the amount of good time earned by inmates and, by doing so, increase an inmate's time served.

A fifth criticism of determinate sentencing is that it is virtually impossible for legislatures or sentencing commissions to define in advance all of the factors that ought to be considered in determining a criminal sentence. You may recall from the discussion in Chapter 3 that this was a problem with one of the crime prevention implications of the classical school (equal punishment for equal crime) and the major reason for the neoclassical reforms.

MYTH   FACT

Determinate sentencing, especially mandatory sentencing, has a significant impact on serious crime.

In practice, this myth has at least two problems. First, "mandatory" aspects of the laws are easy to evade. Second, the basic assumption on which the myth rests is wrong: that "soft" judges release too many dangerous offenders on probation. A recent study indicates that a low of 66 percent of all convicted robbers in Los Angeles and a high of 91 percent of all convicted robbers in Indianapolis and New Orleans are imprisoned.

As a compromise between legislatively mandated determinate sentences and their indeterminate counterparts, several states and the federal courts in recent years have adopted sentencing guidelines as a different way of restricting the sentencing discretion of judges. **Sentencing guidelines** provide ranges of sentences for most offenses, based on the seriousness of the crime and the criminal history of the offender. In jurisdictions that have adopted them, judges must provide written explanations when they depart from the guidelines.

Philosophical Rationales

At the beginning of Chapter 2, the goals of criminal justice in the United States were identified as the prevention and the control of crime. Those are also the goals of **criminal sanctions** or **criminal punishment**—the penalties that are imposed for violating the criminal law. What has always been at issue, however, is how best to achieve those goals. This decision is the main problem faced by legislators who determine what the criminal sanctions will be in general and by judges who make sentencing decisions in individual cases. Historically, four major rationales or justifications have been given for the punishment imposed by the criminal courts: retribution, incapacitation, deterrence, and rehabilitation. A fifth rationale, restoration, has also been receiving greater attention.

Frequently, judges impose sentences for all five reasons, but at certain times in history, one or more of the reasons have been seen as less important than the others. Today, for example, punishment is imposed less for

Sentencing guidelines
Guidelines that provide ranges of sentences for most offenses, based on the seriousness of the crime and the criminal history of the offender.

Criminal sanctions or **criminal punishment** Penalties that are imposed for violating the criminal law.

Sentencing, Appeals, and the Death Penalty   **CHAPTER 8**

rehabilitative purposes than it once was, because of the prevalent view that we do not know how to change the behavior of criminal offenders. We will now examine each of the rationales for criminal punishment.

Retribution From biblical times through the eighteenth century, **retribution** was the dominant justification for punishment. Although it has probably always played some role in sentencing decisions, it is now increasingly popular with the public as a rationale for punishment. However, *retribution* is an imprecise term that has been defined in many ways.[8] Nevertheless, when people say that criminal punishment should be imposed for retribution, what most of them want is probably either *revenge* or *just deserts*. **Revenge** is the justification for punishment expressed by the biblical phrase, "An eye for an eye, and a tooth for a tooth." People who seek revenge want to pay offenders back by making them suffer for what they have done. **Just deserts** is another justification in which punishment is seen as a paying back, but one that is based on something more than vindictive revenge and supposedly does not contain the emotional element of vengeance. *Just deserts* draws part of its meaning from the idea, attributed to the German philosopher Immanuel Kant (1724–1797), that offenders should be punished automatically, simply because they have committed a crime—they "deserve" it. Another aspect of *just deserts* is proportionality of punishment. That is, a punishment should fit the crime and should not be more or less than the offender deserves.

Based on the assumption that the desire for revenge is a basic human emotion, retributivists generally believe that state-authorized punishment greatly reduces the likelihood that individual citizens will take it upon themselves to pay back offenders for what they have done. Vigilante justice is thereby avoided. Retributivists also believe that if offenders are not punished for their crimes, then other people will lose respect for the criminal law and will not obey it.

Finally, retribution is the only rationale for criminal punishment that specifically addresses what has happened in the past; that is, to pay back offenders for their crimes. All of the other rationales focus on the future and seek to influence it; for example, to restrain or prevent an offender from committing future crimes.

Incapacitation **Incapacitation** is the removal or restriction of the freedom of those found to have violated criminal laws. Incapacitation makes it virtually impossible for them to commit crimes during the period of restraint. Banishment or exile was once used to achieve incapacitation. Even today, foreign nationals are deported after conviction of certain crimes. Currently, incapacitation is achieved primarily through imprisonment, which restrains inmates from committing further crimes (at least outside the prison). Some states, as noted in the last chapter, have habitual-offender statutes or "three strikes and you're out" laws that are intended to incapacitate repeat felons for life. Capital punishment is the ultimate means of incapacitation. An executed offender can never commit a crime again.

Deterrence As described in Chapter 3, in keeping with their goal of achieving the "greatest happiness for the greatest number," Beccaria and other classical theorists believed that the only legitimate purpose for punishment is

---

Retribution A dominant justification for punishment.

Revenge The punishment rationale expressed by the biblical phrase, "An eye for an eye, and a tooth for a tooth." People who seek revenge want to pay offenders back by making them suffer for what they have done.

Just deserts The punishment rationale based on the idea that offenders should be punished automatically, simply because they have committed a crime—they "deserve" it—and the idea that the punishment should fit the crime.

Incapacitation The removal or restriction of the freedom of those found to have violated criminal laws.

Historically, many people have believed that public executions have a general deterrent effect.

Most Americans (53%) think the most important purpose in sentencing should be retribution, 21% think it should be rehabilitation, and 13% each choose deterrence or incapacitation. Retribution is chosen more frequently than rehabilitation even though three-fifths (61%) of Americans think that most or some offenders could be rehabilitated "given early intervention with the right program." Only 9% of Americans think that no offenders can be rehabilitated.[9]

the prevention or deterrence of crime. They generally viewed punishment for purely retributive reasons as a pointless exercise.

There are two forms of deterrence. **Special** or **specific deterrence** is the prevention of individuals from committing crime again by punishing them. **General deterrence** is the prevention of people in general from engaging in crime by punishing specific individuals and making examples of them.

One of the problems with general deterrence as a rationale for punishment is that even though it makes intuitive sense, social science is unable to measure its effects. Only those people who have not been deterred come to the attention of social scientists and criminal justice personnel.

Rehabilitation For the past 70 years or so, the primary rationale for punishing criminal offenders has been **rehabilitation,** which is the attempt to "correct" the personality and behavior of convicted offenders through educational, vocational, or therapeutic treatment. The goal has been to return them to society as law-abiding citizens. However, as mentioned earlier, the goal of rehabilitating offenders has been challenged on the grounds that we simply do not know how to correct or cure criminal offenders because the causes of crime are not fully understood. As was also mentioned before, beginning in the mid-1970s, the goal of rehabilitation was abandoned altogether in some states, or at least deemphasized in favor of the goals of retribution and incapacitation. In other states, attempts at rehabilitation continue in an institutional context that seems to favor retribution and incapacitation (as it probably always has). Some critics have suggested that

Special or **specific deterrence** The prevention of individuals from committing crime again by punishing them.

General deterrence The prevention of people in general from engaging in crime by punishing specific individuals and making examples of them.

Rehabilitation The attempt to "correct" the personality and behavior of convicted offenders through educational, vocational, or therapeutic treatment and to return them to society as law-abiding citizens.

Most defendants facing the death penalty receive competent legal representation.

According to a *National Law Journal* study, criminal defendants in six southern states—Alabama, Florida, Georgia, Louisiana, Mississippi, and Texas (states that account for nearly 60 percent of all post-*Furman* executions)—often wind up on death row after being represented by inexperienced, unskilled, or unprepared court-appointed lawyers. Many poor defendants sentenced to death had lawyers who had never handled a capital trial before, or lawyers who had been reprimanded or disciplined or were subsequently disbarred.[29]

FYI

For more than 20 years, Justice Harry A. Blackmun supported the administration of capital punishment in the United States. However, on February 22, 1994, in a dissent from the Court's refusal to hear the appeal of a Texas inmate scheduled to be executed the next day, Blackmun asserted that he had come to the conclusion that "the death penalty experiment has failed" and that it was time for the Court to abandon the "delusion" that capital punishment could be administered in a way that was consistent with the Constitution. He noted that "from this day forward, I no longer shall tinker with the machinery of death."

Some death penalty opponents believe that a principal reason for the continuing support of capital punishment is that most people know very little about the subject and what they think they know is based almost entirely on myths. It is assumed that if people were educated about capital punishment, most of them would oppose it. Unfortunately, research suggests that educating the public about the death penalty may not have the effect abolitionists desire.[30] Although information about the death penalty can reduce suppport for the sanction—sometimes significantly—rarely is the support reduced to less than a majority.

What, then, sustains the public's death penalty support? We believe that there are three major factors:

1. The desire for vindictive revenge.
2. The incapacitative power of the penalty.
3. The symbolic value it has for policitians and law enforcement officials.

In a recent Gallup poll on the subject, one-half of all respondents who favored the death penalty selected "a life for a life" as a reason.[31] Moreover, there were no racial differences, as 50 percent of whites and 48 percent of blacks selected "a life for a life." No other reason was selected by as many as 20 percent of death penalty proponents. The reason selected second most often (by only 19%) was incapacitation, to "keep them from killing again." The only other reasons selected by more than 10 percent of the death penalty proponents were general deterrence and the cost of imprisonment (both were selected by 13%).[32]

The choice of "a life for a life" indicates support of the penal purpose of retribution. Those who chose "a life for a life" want to repay the offender for what he or she has done. This response, moreover, has a strong emotional or visceral component and thus has been called "vindictive revenge."[33] That the public supports the death penalty primarily for vindictive revenge raises two important questions. First, is the satisfaction of the desire for vindictive revenge a legitimate penal purpose? And second, does pandering to or legitimizing this desire for vindictive revenge contribute to the violent social relationships that pervade our nation?

The second factor that sustains death penalty support is the unquestionable incapacitative power of the penalty: Once a capital offender has been executed, he or she can never kill again. Although this seems a persuasive reason, it is not a reason often given by the public. Only 19 percent of Gallup-polled death penalty proponents chose it.

Nevertheless, research confirms that a small percentage of capital offenders released from prison have killed again. The execution of all convicted capital offenders would have prevented those killings. However, a

The death row population in the United States has grown steadily in recent years.

FYI

n *Herrera v. Collins* (1993) the Supreme Court held that in the absence of constitutional grounds, new evidence of innocence is no reason for the Court to order a new trial. According to the majority opinion: "Where a defendant has been afforded a fair trial and convicted of the offense for which he was charged, the constitutional presumption of innocence disappears. . . . Thus, claims of actual innocence based on newly discovered evidence [are not] grounds for . . . relief absent an independent constitutional violation occuring in the course of the underlying state criminal proceedings." For some, the decision is a reasonable response to the Court's need to limit its jurisdiction in *habeas corpus* cases.

problem with simply executing all convicted capital offenders is that, inevitably, innocent people are executed. The possibility of executing an innocent person does not seem to be a crucial problem for a majority of Supreme Court justices, given the Court's recent ruling in this area (see the FYI on this page, about *Herrera v. Collins*, 1993). It might, however, be a problem for many Americans. In any event, to prevent capital offenders from killing again, doesn't it make sense simply to keep them imprisoned? At least then, when errors are made, they can be rectified to some degree.

The third factor that sustains death penalty suppport is the symbolic value it has for politicians and criminal justice officials. Politicians use support for the death penalty as a symbol of their toughness on crime. Opposition to capital punishment is invariably interpreted as symbolic of softness on crime. Criminal justice officials and much of the public often equate support for capital punishment with support for law enforcement in general. It is ironic that although capital punishment has virtually no effect on crime, the death penalty continues to be a favored political silver bullet—a simplistic solution to the crime problem used by aspiring politicians and law enforcement officials.

In short, the reasons provided for supporting capital punishment do not stand up well to critical scrutiny. But the American public has not been deterred from its enthusiastic support of the penalty. Together with the movement to replace indeterminate sentencing with determinate sentencing and to abolish parole, the death penalty is part of the "law and order" agenda popular in the United States since the mid-1970s. Whether this direction in criminal justice has run its course is anyone's guess. However, it appears that the effort to "get tough" with criminals has not produced the results desired by its advocates.

1. In addition to the other sources cited, material on sentencing and appeals is from David W. Neubauer, *America's Courts and the Criminal Justice System*, 5th ed. (Belmont, CA: Wadsworth, 1996); Christopher Smith, *Courts, Politics, and the Judicial Process* (Chicago: Nelson-Hall, 1993); N. Gary Holten and Lawson L. Lamar, *The Criminal Courts: Structures, Personnel, and Processes* (New York: McGraw-Hill, 1991); Lawrence Baum, *American Courts*, 3d ed. (Boston: Houghton Mifflin, 1994); David Garland, *Punishment and Modern Society: A Study in Social Theory* (Chicago: University of Chicago Press, 1990); Paul Wice, *Chaos in the Courthouse: The Inner Workings of the Urban Criminal Courts* (New York: Praeger, 1985); John Paul Ryan, Allan Ashman, Bruce D. Sales, and Sandra Shane-DuBow, *American Trial Judges* (New York: Free Press, 1980); Robert Satter, *Doing Justice: A Trial Judge at Work* (New ork: Simon & Schuster, 1990); Herbert Packer, *The Limits of the Criminal Sanction* (Stanford, CA: Stanford University Press, 1968).

2. E. Scott Reckard, "Keating Sentenced in 'Staggering' S & L Crime," *The Charlotte (NC) Observer*, July 9, 1993.

3. Jurg Gerber and Simone Engelhardt-Greer, "Just and Painful: Attitudes Toward Sentencing Criminals," pp. 62–74 in Timothy J. Flanagan and Dennis R. Longmire (eds.), *Americans View Crime and Justice: A National Public Opinion Survey* (Thousand Oaks, CA: Sage, 1996), p. 70, Table 5.2.

4. Camille Graham Camp and George M. Camp, *The Corrections Yearbook 1997* (South Salem, NY: Criminal Justice Institute, Inc., 1997), pp. 54–55.

5. *American Correctional Association 1997 Directory: Juvenile and Adult Correctional Departments, Institutions, Agencies and Paroling Authorities* (Lanham, MD: American Correctional Association, 1997), p. xx.

6. Laura B. Myers, "Bringing the Offender to Heel: Views of the Criminal Courts," pp. 46–61 in Timothy J. Flanagan and Dennis R. Longmire (eds.), *Americans View Crime and Justice: A National Public Opinion Survey* (Thousand Oaks, CA: Sage, 1996), p. 54.

7. "Sentence Disparity in New York: The Response of Forty-One Judges," *The New York Times*, March 30, 1979, p. B3.

8. See Robert M. Bohm, "Retribution and Capital Punishment: Toward a Better Understanding of Death Penalty Opinion," *Journal of Criminal Justice*, Vol. 20 (1992), pp. 227-35.

9. Timothy J. Flanagan, "Reform or Punish: Americans' Views of the Correctional System," pp. 75–92 in Timothy J. Flanagan and Dennis R. Longmire (eds.), *Americans View Crime and Justice: A National Public Opinion Survey* (Thousand Oaks, CA: Sage, 1996), p.69, Table 5.1 and p. 78.

10. "Restorative Justice: An Interview With Visiting Fellow Thomas Quinn," *National Institute of Justice Journal* (Issue No. 235, March 1998), p. 10.

11. Unless indicated otherwise, material about the death penalty is from James R. Acker, Robert M. Bohm, and Charles S. Lanier (eds.), *America's Experiment with Capital Punishment: Reflections on the Past, Present, and Future of the Ultimate Penal Sanction* (Durham, NC: Carolina Academic Press, 1998); Hugo Alan Bedau, *The Death Penalty in America; Current Controversies* (New York: Oxford University Press, 1997), Hugo Adam Bedau (ed.), *The Death Penalty in America*, 3d ed. (London: Oxford University Press, 1982); William J. Bowers, with Glenn L. Pierce and John McDevitt, *Legal Homicide: Death as Punishment in America, 1864–1982* (Boston: Northeastern University Press, 1984); Raymond Paternoster, *Capital Punishment in America* (New York: Lexington, 1991); Robert M. Bohm, "Humanism and the Death Penalty, with Special Emphasis on the Post-*Furman* Experience," *Justice Quarterly*, Vol. 6 (1989), pp. 173–95; Victoria Schneider and John Ortiz Smykla, "A Summary Analysis of Executions in the United States, 1608–1987: The Espy File," in R. M. Bohm (ed.), *The Death Penalty in America: Current Research* (Cincinnati: Anderson, 1991), pp. 1–19.

12. Ibid.

13. *Death Row, U.S.A.*, NAACP Legal Defense and Educational Fund (Spring 1998).

14. For a summary of those studies, see United States General Accounting Office, *Death Penalty Sentencing: Research Indicates Pattern of Racial Disparities*, Report to the Senate and House Committees on the Judiciary (Washington: GPO, 1990). For the view that the evidence does not show racial discrimination, see William Wilbanks, *The Myth of a Racist Criminal Justice System* (Monterey, CA: Brooks/Cole, 1987).

15. *Death Row, U.S.A.*, op. cit..

16. Ibid.

17. Ibid.

18. Ibid.

19. Hugo Adam Bedau and Michael L. Radelet, "Miscarriages of Justice in Potentially Capital Cases," *Stanford Law Review*, Vol. 40 (1987), pp. 21–179; Michael L. Radelet, Hugo Adam Bedau, and Constance E. Putnam, *In Spite of Innocence: Erroneous Convictions in Capital Cases* (Boston: Northeastern University Press, 1992).

20. Tracy L. Snell, *Capital Punishment 1996*, U.S. Department of Justice, Bureau of Justice Statistics Bulletin (Washington: GPO, 1997).

21. Snell, op. cit., p. 15, appendix table 3.
22. Ibid., Paternoster, op. cit., pp. 208–9.
23. Robert M. Bohm, "The Economic Costs of Capital Punishment: Past, Present, and Future," pp. 429-50 in James R. Acker, Robert M. Bohm, and Charles S. Lanier (eds.), *America's Experiment with Capital Punishment: Reflections on the Past, Present, and Future of the Ultimate Sanction* (Durham, NC: Carolina Academic Press, 1998).
24. The Death Penalty Information Center, op. cit.
25. *Death Row, U.S.A.*, op. cit.
26. David W. Moore, "Majority Advocate Death Penalty for Teenage Killers," *The Gallup Poll Monthly* (September 1994); Robert M. Bohm, "American Death Penalty Opinion, 1936–1986: A Critical Examination of the Gallup Polls," pp. 113–45 in R. M. Bohm (ed.), *The Death Penalty in America: Current Research* (Cincinnati: Anderson, 1991).
27. Ibid.
28. Alec Gallup and Frank Newport, "Death Penalty Support Remains Strong," *The Gallup Monthly Report* (June 1991); William J. Bowers, "Capital Punishment and Contemporary Values: People's Misgivings and the Court's Misperceptions," *Law and Society Review*, Vol. 27 (1993), pp. 157–75; Marla Sandys and Edmund F. McGarrell, "Attitudes Toward Capital Punishment: Preference for the Penalty or Mere Acceptance?" *Journal of Research in Crime and Delinquency*, Vol. 32 (1995), pp. 191–213; Edmund F. McGarrell and Marla Sandys, "The Misperception of Public Opinion Toward Capital Punishment: Examining the Spuriousness Explanation of Death Penalty Support," *American Behavioral Scientist*, Vol. 39 (1996), pp. 500–13.
29. Marcia Coyle, Fred Strasser, and Marianne Lavelle, "Fatal Defense," *The National Law Journal*, Vol. 12 (June 11, 1990), pp. 29–44.
30. Robert M. Bohm, Louse J. Clark, and Adrian F. Aveni, "Knowledge and Death Penalty Opinion: A Test of the Marshall Hypotheses," *Journal of Research in Crime and Delinquency*, Vol. 28 (1991), pp. 360–87; Robert M. Bohm and Ronald E. Vogel, "A Comparison of Factors Asssociated with Uninformed and Informed Death Penalty Opinions," *Journal of Criminal Justice*, Vol. 23 (1994), pp. 125–43; Robert M. Bohm, Ronald E. Vogel, and Albert A. Maisto, "Knowledge and Death Penalty Opinion: A Panel Study," *Journal of Criminal Justice*, Vol. 21 (1993), pp. 29–45.
31. Gallup and Newport, op. cit., p. 42.
32. Ibid.
33. Bohm, "Retribution and Capital Punishment," op. cit.; see also Bohm and Vogel, "A Comparison of Factors Associated with Uninformed and Informed Death Penalty Opinions," op. cit.

9 Institutional Corrections

CHAPTER OBJECTIVES

After completing this chapter, you should be able to:

1 Summarize the purposes of confinement in Europe before confinement became a major way of punishing criminals.

2 Describe how offenders were punished before the large-scale use of confinement.

3 Explain why confinement began to be used as a major way of punishing offenders in Europe.

4 Describe the recent trends in the use of incarceration in the United States.

5 List some of the characteristics of the incarcerated population in the United States.

6 Describe how incarceration facilities are structured, organized, and administered by the government in the United States.

7 Name some of the common types of correctional facilities in the United States.

8 Identify some of the procedures that institutions employ to maintain security and order.

9 List the services and programs that are commonly available to inmates in prison.

62   63   JANITOR

21   JANITOR

Historical Overview of Institutional Corrections

Students often wonder why they must learn about the history of institutional corrections. One reason is that it is impossible to fully understand (and improve) the present state of affairs without knowledge of the past; the present developed out of the past. People who fail to remember the past are destined to repeat its mistakes. Another reason is that nothing helps us see how institutional corrections is linked to our larger society and culture better than the study of history. Try to keep those two points in mind when studying history.

MYTH

Throughout history, imprisonment has been the primary sentence for lawbreakers, and it still is today.

FACT

Viewed historically, imprisonment is a relatively recent sentence for lawbreaking. Even today in the United States, the number of people in prison is small compared with the number on probation or under other types of supervision in the community.

European Background

In Europe, institutional confinement did not become a major punishment for criminals until the 1600s and 1700s. (In the United States, institutional confinement was not used extensively as a punishment until the 1800s.) As a practice, though, institutional confinement has existed since ancient times. Before the 1600s, however, it usually served functions other than punishment for criminal behavior. For example, confinement was used to:

1. Detain people before trial.
2. Hold prisoners awaiting other sanctions, such as death and corporal punishment.
3. Coerce payment of debts and fines.
4. Hold and punish slaves.
5. Achieve religious indoctrination and spiritual reformation (as during the Inquisition).
6. Quarantine disease (as during the bubonic plague).[1]

Forerunners of Modern Incarceration Unlike modern incarceration, which strives to change the offender's character and is carried out away from public view, popular early punishments for crime, which predated the large-scale use of imprisonment, were directed more at the offender's body and property; one basic goal was to inflict pain.[2] Furthermore, those punishments were commonly carried out in public to humiliate the offender and to deter onlookers from crime. Examples of such early punishments are fines, confiscation of property, and diverse methods of corporal and capital punishment. Some popular methods of corporal and capital punishment were beheading, stoning, hanging, crucifixion, boiling and burning, flogging, branding, or placement in the stocks or pillory.[3] As this brief list illustrates, the eventual shift to incarceration reduced the severity and violence of punishment.

Besides being painful, placement in the stocks or pillory was intended to humiliate and shame offenders.

Two additional forerunners of modern incarceration were banishment and transportation. In essence, they were alternatives to the more severe corporal punishments or capital punishment. Originating in ancient times, **banishment** required offenders to leave the community and live elsewhere, commonly in the wilderness. The modern version of banishment is long-term incarceration (for example, life imprisonment without opportunity for parole). As population and urban growth displaced frontiers across Europe and as demands for cheap labor increased with the rise of Western capitalism, **transportation** of offenders from their home nation to one of that nation's colonies gradually replaced banishment. England, for instance, was transporting hundreds of convicts a year to North America by the early 1600s.[5] Transportation fell into disuse as European colonies gained independence.

The closest European forerunners of the modern U.S. prison were known as **workhouses** or *houses of correction*. Offenders were sent to them to learn discipline and regular work habits. The fruits of inmate labor were also expected to pay for facility upkeep and even to yield a profit. One of the first and most famous workhouses, the London Bridewell, opened in the 1550s, and workhouses spread through other parts of Europe thereafter. Such facilities were used extensively throughout the next three centuries, coexisting with such responses to crime as transportation, corporal punishment, and capital punishment. In fact, crowding in workhouses was a major impetus for the development of transportation as a punishment.

Reform Initiatives As described in Chapter 3, the Enlightenment was a time of faith in science and reason as well as a period of humanistic reform. The Enlightenment thinkers and reformers of the 1700s and 1800s described the penal system of their day with such descriptors as *excessive, disorderly,*

Banishment A punishment, originating in ancient times, that required offenders to leave the community and live elsewhere, commonly in the wilderness.

Transportation A punishment in which offenders were transported from their home nation to one of that nation's colonies to work.

Workhouses European forerunners of the modern U.S. prison, where offenders were sent to learn discipline and regular work habits.

inefficient, arbitrary, capricious, discriminatory (against the poor), and *unjust*. Three reformers who were important to initiatives in corrections were Cesare Beccaria (1738–1794), John Howard (1726–1790), and Jeremy Bentham (1748–1832).

Graeme Newman and Pietro Marongiu contend that Beccaria's famous book, *On Crimes and Punishments* (1764), though often acclaimed for its originality, actually brought together the reformist principles espoused by other thinkers of the era, such as Montesquieu and Voltaire.[6] One of those principles concerned replacing the discretionary and arbitrary administration of justice with a system of detailed written laws describing the behaviors that constitute crime and the associated punishments. People need to know, Beccaria believed, exactly what punishments are prescribed for various offenses if the law is to deter criminal behavior. As part of his quest to deter crime, Beccaria declared that the punishment should fit the crime in two senses. First, the severity of punishment should parallel the severity of harm resulting from the crime. Second, the punishment should be severe enough to outweigh the pleasure obtainable from the crime. Furthermore, to deter crime, he believed, punishment needed to be certain and swift. Certainty implies that the likelihood of getting caught and punished is perceived as high. Swiftness implies that punishment will not be delayed after commission of the crime.

Beccaria did not ground his thinking firmly in empirical observations and did little to actively campaign for the reforms he advocated.[7] The work of John Howard, an English sheriff and social activist, presents an interesting contrast in that regard. Howard's 1777 book, *The State of the Prisons in England and Wales*, was based on his visits to penal institutions in various parts of Europe. Howard was appalled by the crowding, overall poor living conditions, and disorderly and abusive practices he observed in those facilities. He advocated that penal environments be made

MYTH

T*he reason punishment fails to adequately deter crime in the United States is that it is not severe enough.*

FACT

The United States has a higher rate of imprisonment and longer sentences than virtually any other nation. It is also one of the few advanced, industrialized nations to have retained the death penalty. It is hard indeed to support the argument that our punishment is not severe enough. Certainty and swiftness, however, are lacking, and that is the failure to which Beccaria would probably point.

safe, humane, and orderly. Howard's opinion was that incarceration should do more than punish—that it should also instill discipline and reform inmates. Toward that end, he proposed an orderly institutional routine of religious teaching, hard work, and solitary confinement to promote introspection and penance.[8] Howard's work inspired the growing popularity of the term *penitentiary* to refer to penal confinement facilities.

In **penology,** the study of prison management and the treatment of offenders, Jeremy Bentham is perhaps best remembered for his idea that order and reform could be achieved in a prison through architectural design. His **panopticon** ("all-seeing" or "inspection-house") prison design consisted of a round building with tiers of cells lining the circumference and facing a central

Penology The study of prison management and the treatment of offenders.

Panopticon A prison design consisting of a round building with tiers of cells lining the inner circumference and facing a central inspection tower.

Institutional Corrections

inspection tower so that prisoners could be watched by staff from the tower. Although no facilities completely true to Bentham's panopticon plan were ever constructed, structures similar in design were erected at Illinois's Stateville Penitentiary (now Stateville Correctional Center), which opened in 1925.

In sum, the historical roots of the modern prison lie in Europe. It was in America, however, that the penitentiary concept was first put into wide practice.

Developments in the United States

In colonial America, penal practice was loose, decentralized, and unsystematic, combining private retaliation against wrongdoing with fines, banishment, harsh corporal punishments, and capital punishment. Local jails were scattered about the colonies, but they were used primarily for temporary holding rather than for punishment.[9] Some people, such as William Penn, promoted incarceration as a humane alternative to the physically brutal punishments that were common. However, that idea was largely ignored because there was no stable central governmental authority to coordinate and finance (through tax revenue) the large-scale confinement of offenders.

The Penitentiary Movement In the aftermath of the American Revolution, it rapidly became apparent that the colonial system of justice would not suffice. Economic chaos and civil disorder followed the war. Combined with population growth and the transition from an agricultural society to an industrial one, they created the need for strong, centralized government to achieve political and economic stability. The rise of the penitentiary occurred in that context.[10] Philosophically, it was guided by Enlightenment principles. In 1790, the Walnut Street Jail in Philadelphia was converted from a simple holding facility to a prison to which offenders could be sentenced for their crimes. It is commonly regarded as the nation's first state prison. In a system consistent with Howard's plan, its inmates labored in solitary cells and received large doses of religious teaching. Later in the 1790s, New York opened Newgate Prison. Other states quickly followed suit, and the penitentiary movement was born. By 1830, Pennsylvania and New York had constructed additional prisons to supplement their original ones.

Pennsylvania and New York pioneered the penitentiary movement by developing two competing systems of confinement.[11] The **Pennsylvania system,** sometimes called the *separate system,* required that inmates be kept in solitary cells so that they could study religious writings, reflect on their misdeeds, and perform handicraft work. In the New York system, or the **Auburn system** (named after Auburn Penitentiary and also referred to as the *congregate* or *silent system*), inmates worked and ate together in silence during the day and were returned to solitary cells for the evening. Ultimately, the Auburn system prevailed over the Pennsylvania system as the model followed by other states. It avoided the harmful psychological effects of total solitary confinement and allowed more inmates to be housed in less space because cells could be smaller. In addition, the Auburn system's congregate work principle was more congruent with the system of factory production emerging in wider society than was the outdated craft principle of the separate system. If prison labor was to be profitable, it seemed that the Auburn plan was the one to use.

Pennsylvania system An early system of U.S. penology in which inmates were kept in solitary cells so that they could study religious writings, reflect on their misdeeds, and perform handicraft work.

Auburn system An early system of penology, originating at Auburn Penitentiary in New York, under which inmates worked and ate together in silence during the day and were placed in solitary cells for the evening.

It is interesting that although penitentiary construction flourished and the United States became the model nation in penology during the first half of the nineteenth century, there was serious discontent with the penitentiary by the end of the Civil War. There were few signs that penitentiaries were deterring crime, reforming offenders, or turning great profits from inmate labor. In fact, prisons were becoming increasingly expensive to maintain, and opposition was growing to the practice of selling prisoner-made goods on the open market. With faith in the penitentiary declining, the stage was set for a new movement—a movement that, rather than challenging the fundamental value of incarceration as a punishment, sought to improve the method of incarceration.

The Reformatory Movement The reformatory movement got its start at the 1870 meeting of the National Prison Association, in Cincinnati. The principles adopted at that meeting were championed by such leaders in the field as Enoch Wines (1806–1879) and Zebulon Brockway (1827–1920).[12] A new type of institution, the reformatory, was designed for younger, less hardened offenders, between 16 and 30 years of age. Based on a military model of regimentation, it emphasized academic and vocational training in addition to work. A classification system was introduced, in which inmates were rated according to their progress toward reformation. The sentences for determinate periods of time (for example, five years), typical of the older penitentiary, were replaced with indeterminate terms, in which inmates served sentences within given ranges (for example, between two and eight years). Parole or early release could be granted for favorable progress in reformation.

It has often been observed that indeterminate sentences and the possibility of parole facilitate greater control over inmates than is possible with determinate sentences. Many inmates are interested, above all else, in gaining their freedom. The message conveyed to inmates by indeterminate sentences and the possibility of parole is this: "Conform to institutional expectations or do more time."

The Elmira Reformatory, which opened in 1876 in Elmira, New York, was the first institution for men that was based on reformatory principles.

Institutions for Women Until the reformatory era, there was little effort to establish separate facilities for women. Women prisoners were usually confined in segregated areas of male prisons, and they generally received inferior treatment. The reformatory movement, reflecting its assumptions about differences between categories of inmates and its emphasis on classification, helped feminize punishment.[13] The first women's prison organized according to the reformatory model opened in Indiana in 1873. By the 1930s, several other women's reformatories were in operation, mainly in the Northeast and the Midwest. Most employed cottages or a campus and a family-style living plan, as distinguished from the cell-block plan of men's prisons. And most of them concentrated on molding inmates to fulfill stereotypical domestic roles, such as cleaning and cooking, upon release.

Developments in the Twentieth Century

John Irwin has provided a useful typology for summarizing imprisonment in the twentieth century.[14] According to Irwin, three types of institutions have been dominant. Each has dominated a different part of the century. The dominant type for about the first three decades was the "big house." In Irwin's words:

> The Big House was a walled prison with large cell blocks that contained stacks of three or more tiers of one- or two-man cells. On the average, it held 2,500 men. Sometimes a single cell block housed over 1,000 prisoners in six tiers of cells. Most of these prisons were built over many decades and had a mixture of old and new cell blocks. Some of the older cell blocks were quite primitive.[15]

Big-house prisons, which consisted of large cell blocks containing stacks of cells, were the dominant prison design of the early twentieth century.

It is important to realize that big houses were not new prisons, distinct from earlier penitentiaries and reformatories. They were the old penitentiaries and reformatories, expanded in size to accommodate larger inmate populations. Originally, big-house prisons exploited inmate labor through various links to the free market. Industrial prisons predominated in the North, while plantation prisons characterized much of the South. With the rise of organized labor and the coming of the Great Depression, free-market inmate labor systems fell into demise during the 1920s and 1930s. Big houses became warehouses oriented toward custody and repression of inmates.

Jail A facility, usually operated at the local level, that holds convicted offenders and unconvicted persons for relatively short periods.

by the police or the court. If there is cause, a suspect may be transferred from the lockup to the jail.

A **jail** is a facility that holds convicted offenders and unconvicted persons for relatively short periods. The modern term *jail* comes from the English term *gaol* (the pronunciation is identical), and English gaols have a history that dates to the 1100s. In contrast to prisons, most jails are administered at the county or city level of government. Excluding lockups, there are more jails (between 3,000 and 4,000) than any other kind of confinement facility in the United States. Although most jails in the United States are small (about half of them hold fewer than 50 people), some, such as those in Los Angeles and New York City, are very large (refer to Figure 9–2).

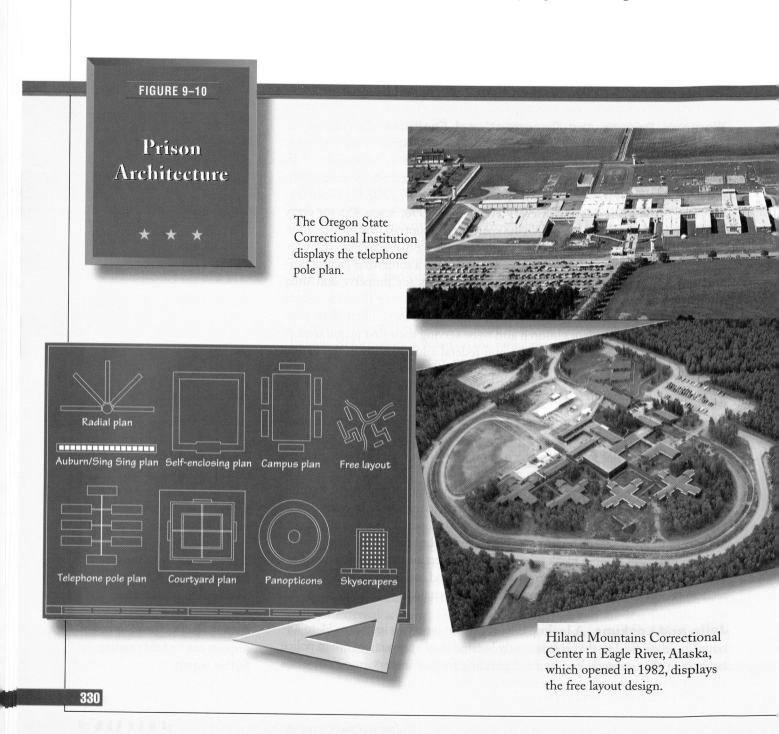

FIGURE 9–10

Prison Architecture

★ ★ ★

Radial plan

Auburn/Sing Sing plan   Self-enclosing plan   Campus plan   Free layout

Telephone pole plan   Courtyard plan   Panopticons   Skyscrapers

The Oregon State Correctional Institution displays the telephone pole plan.

Hiland Mountains Correctional Center in Eagle River, Alaska, which opened in 1982, displays the free layout design.

The number of people being held in local jails has risen dramatically in recent years. The U.S. local jail population increased from 209,582 in 1982 to 567,079 at midyear 1997, an increase of about 171 percent (see Figure 9–11). The jail incarceration rate was 96 inmates per 100,000 U.S. residents in 1983; by June 30, 1997, that number had climbed to 212 per 100,000, an increase of 121 percent.[66] Although just 1.6 percent of the jail population consisted of juveniles, that percentage amounts to 9,105 juveniles. The practice of holding juveniles in adult jails, where they are vulnerable to influence and victimization by adult criminals, is most common in rural areas, where there are no separate juvenile detention centers. That practice has been the target of much criticism and many policy initiatives for more than two

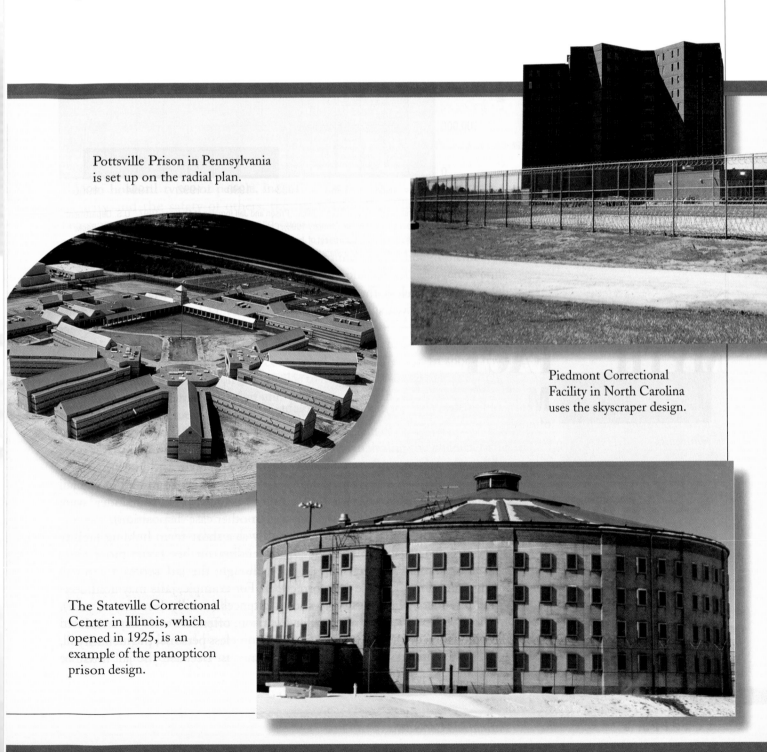

Pottsville Prison in Pennsylvania is set up on the radial plan.

Piedmont Correctional Facility in North Carolina uses the skyscraper design.

The Stateville Correctional Center in Illinois, which opened in 1925, is an example of the panopticon prison design.

10 Prison Life, Inmate Rights, Release, and Recidivism

CHAPTER OBJECTIVES

After completing this chapter, you should be able to:

1 Distinguish between the deprivation and importation models of inmate society.

2 Explain how today's inmate society differs from those of the past.

3 Identify some of the special features of life in women's prisons.

4 Describe the profile of correctional officers and explain some of the issues that they face.

5 Identify prisoners' rights and relate how they were achieved.

6 List the two most common ways that inmates are released from prison and compare those two ways in frequency of use.

7 Summarize what recidivism research reveals about the success of the prison in achieving deterrence and rehabilitation.

11 Community Corrections

One

offer
patio
years

petin
role:
This
tions,

probl
sion
descri
probl
help.
agenc
ple, a
couns
may
examp
to adv
comm

the du
tain th
that re
tion p
conflic
thing

A
their w
ing role
cate the
suggest

CHAPTER OBJECTIVES

After completing this chapter, you should be able to:

1 Define community corrections and identify the goals and responsibilities of community corrections agencies and their staffs.

2 Define probation and summarize the research findings on recidivisim rates.

3 Distinguish parole from probation.

4 Explain the functions of a parole board.

5 Describe how intermediate sanctions differ from traditional community corrections programs.

6 Explain two major concerns about intensive-supervision probation and parole (ISP).

7 Explain what day reporting centers and structured fines are.

8 Explain what home confinement and electronic monitoring are.

9 Identify the goal of halfway houses and compare them with other community corrections programs.

10 Summarize the purposes and outcomes of temporary-release programs.

How effective is probation in controlling recidivism? First, it should be noted that researchers attempting to address this question confront a variety of difficulties. One difficulty is deciding whether to define probationer recidivism in terms of technical violations, arrests for new crimes, new convictions, or revocations. The definition employed affects the amount of recidivism uncovered. Another important difficulty lies in accurately determining whether it is the probation experience or some additional factor that is responsible for the recidivism observed among a group of probationers. A simple finding that recidivism is low among a group of probationers does not necessarily mean that probation is containing recidivism. Other factors, such as improvements in the local economy or the selection of low-risk offenders for probation, may be responsible. To date, many studies of probation effectiveness have not been designed well enough to rule out the role of factors other than the probation experience. Difficulties like these must be kept in mind when reviewing studies on probation recidivism.

Research suggests that probation is less effective than many people would like in curtailing rearrests of felony offenders. In a well-known California study by Joan Petersilia and her colleagues, approximately 1,700 felony offenders placed on probation were tracked for a period of 40 months. During this period, about two-thirds of the probationers were rearrested, more than half were reconvicted, and about one-third were sent to jail or prison.[12] In a similar but larger-scale study by the U.S. Justice Department, 79,000 felons sentenced to probation in 1986 by state courts in 17 states were followed for three years. By 1989, 43 percent of those felons had been arrested for new felonies; 8.5 percent were rearrested for violent offenses, 14.8 percent for property crimes, 14.1 percent for drug offenses, and the remainder for other crimes.[13]

In general, the recidivism figures associated with probation do not seem substantially higher or lower than those associated with incarceration. (See Chapter 10 for data on recidivism following incarceration.) Accordingly, it can be argued that when feasible, probation should be the preferred sentence because probation costs less than imprisonment. Of course, this logic holds true only if probation does not culminate in revocation followed by incarceration. If revocation and subsequent incarceration occur, the combined costs of probation followed by incarceration may well exceed the cost of incarceration alone.

Parole

Recall that probation refers to the court-imposed sentence in which the offender, rather than being imprisoned, stays in the local community under the supervision of a probation officer. Two basic differences between probation and **parole** are that (1) parole is not a court-imposed sentence, and (2) parole is used with persons leaving prison. For purposes of definition, parole can be divided into two components. *Parole release* is one mechanism for releasing persons from prison. It involves releasing the inmate from prison, at the discretion of a parole board or similar paroling authority, before his or her sentence expires. *Parole supervision,* the aspect of parole that is often confused with probation, occurs after parole release. Essentially, parole supervision is a community-based continuation of the prison sentence. It

Parole A method of prison release whereby inmates are released at the discretion of a board or other authority before having completed their entire sentences; can also refer to the community supervision received upon release.

involves supervision of the released offender in the community, often for a period roughly equal to the time remaining in the prison sentence.

Probation and parole supervision have similar features, which is why the two are sometimes confused. For example, both involve specific rules and conditions that offenders must follow to avoid revocation, and both entail providing offenders with supervision and services. In some instances, one officer may supervise both probationers and parolees. However, *probationer* and *parolee* are two distinct legal statuses. It is not uncommon for parole rules and conditions to be somewhat stricter and for officers to be less tolerant of violations committed by parolees; revocation of parole may be sought quickly, even for a technical parole violation. In addition, parolees often face greater adjustment problems because of the stigma attached to their prison records and because of the time they have spent away from the free community.

Just as there are different types of probation (suspended-sentence probation, split-sentence probation, etc.), there are two general types of parole. In *straight parole,* offenders are released from prison directly into the community under the supervision of the parole agency. In *residential parole,* offenders serve part of the parole term in a community residential facility or halfway house. There are two variants of residential parole. In the first variant, offenders are released from prison into the residential facility, where they spend a temporary, transitional period before returning home. The idea is to make the release process a gradual one. In the second variant, a person who violates the conditions of parole is kept on parole and is placed in the residential facility for a period of structured living, rather than having parole revoked and being returned to prison.

Some offenders are released on parole before the end of their sentences, on the condition that they remain law-abiding and follow the rules designed to control their movement and to help them adjust to society.

There are four fundamental objectives of parole. Two of these are also objectives of probation and were discussed earlier in this chapter. As with probation, parole is meant to provide community safety and to promote offender betterment and reintegration into society. The other two objectives of parole are more subtle, often unstated, but no less important. They are to (1) relieve and contain prison crowding and (2) control the behavior of prison inmates.

Since its inception, parole has functioned as a "safety valve" for institutional corrections; crowding levels can be better contained if more inmates are granted early release. One of the clearest manifestations of this objective is the growing popularity of emergency release laws that permit executive authorities (usually governors) to accelerate parole eligibility for selected inmates when prison crowding reaches a particular level. Parole also gives prison officials some control over the behavior of inmates. The prospect of early release gives inmates an incentive to cooperate with prison officials and to avoid infractions of prison rules.

With respect to *program participation,* many halfway houses have a series of levels, or phases, through which residents must pass to receive a successful discharge. Typically, each level is associated with progressively more demanding goals and responsibilities for the resident to meet and also with more privileges and freedoms. For example, a requirement for an offender to move from the entry level to the second level may be the successful completion of a job skills class. Upon promotion to level two, the offender may receive one weekend furlough per month to spend with family and friends. Promotion to level three may carry additional furlough time and require that the offender obtain a job and complete a class on job retention skills.

As noted previously, halfway houses usually provide a variety of treatment services, such as employment counseling and training, life skills

FIGURE 11–10

Intermediate Sanctions

★ ★ ★

Intermediate sanctions lie between traditional probation and traditional imprisonment or, alternatively, between imprisonment and traditional parole.

Home confinement requires offenders to remain in their homes except for preapproved periods of absence. Most programs use electronic monitoring equipment to verify that offenders are at their designated locations at particular times.

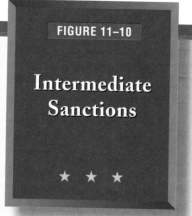

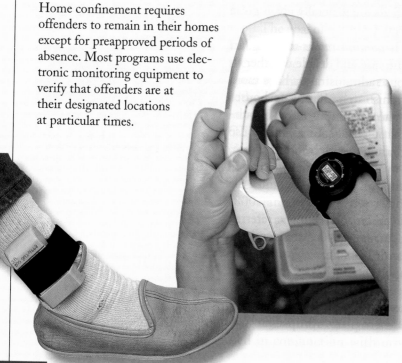

Community service sanctions require offenders to perform a specified number of hours for the community. Traditionally, the offender paid restitution directly to the victim. Community service is restitution to the community.

training, substance abuse intervention, and remedial education. Those services are provided either directly by house staff or indirectly through referrals to community agencies. To allow control and supervision, houses have a number of rules that govern both the in-house behavior of residents and residents' activities away from the facility. Those rules cover such matters as interaction between residents, care of facility property, curfews, and the use of alcohol. Progress through program levels requires completion of the goals and responsibilities associated with a particular level, participation in relevant treatment components, and compliance with house rules. Failure to achieve goals, to complete treatment components, or to abide by rules can result in the resident's staying at a given level or being demoted to a lower level.

Day reporting centers, which may be publicly or privately operated, are corrections centers where offenders must report regularly to comply with a sentence. Most day center programs include employment, counseling, education, and community service components.

Intensive-supervision probation and parole programs impose strict requirements for reporting to a probation or parole officer with a limited caseload. Often, mandatory curfews, employment, and restitution are part of the program.

Halfway houses may be operated by private for-profit or not-for-profit contractors or by public agencies. Some provide room, board, and help with employment. Others provide remedial education, individual or group counseling, and other types of life skills training.

A resident's behavior must be monitored and periodically reviewed throughout the term of program participation because, ultimately, the house administration must decide the resident's *termination,* or discharge, status. Residents who have satisfactorily completed all of the required levels are discharged into the community, frequently under probation or parole supervision. If a resident fails to make satisfactory progress through levels in a reasonable time, compiles an excessive number of less serious rule violations, or commits a serious rule infraction (such as another felony), the resident can also be discharged from the facility. An unsuccessful discharge can be granted at any point in a resident's stay and is frequently followed by incarceration.

Issues Several issues surround the use of halfway houses. Two of the most critical issues are (1) the relations between a halfway house and the local community of which it is a part and (2) recidivism among persons who have been discharged from the house.

For a halfway house to be established in a community and to operate effectively, cooperative relations between the staff of the house and members of the community are essential. Halfway house staff often depend on the surrounding community for such things as resident health care, counseling services, educational programming, and job placements. Furthermore, unfavorable reactions from community members toward residents will simply reinforce the sense of marginalization and alienation that many offenders already experience. To the extent that community members feel threatened by residents or have poor relations with staff, the halfway house program is in jeopardy.

Virtually all halfway houses must confront the issue of community resistance, and some must confront outright hostility from community members. There are at least two keys to doing this effectively. First, halfway house officials must actively cultivate support and assistance from community members by engaging in open, honest communication with them from the earliest possible stage of the halfway house's existence. Many fears that community members have of residents are founded on inaccurate, media-fueled stereotypes and can be reduced with realistic, factual information. Second, it is very helpful if community members can see that the halfway house is contributing something of value to the community, rather than simply consuming resources. For example, house residents can be involved in well-publicized and highly visible community service projects that save tax dollars. Also, in houses where a high proportion of residents are employed, community residents should be frequently reminded that residents are contributing to the tax base instead of consuming public revenue as jail or prison inmates. If community members can be convinced that the halfway house has a positive, contributing side, they are likely to be more accepting of the house.

Just as there are ways to facilitate cooperative community relations, there also are ways to create unfavorable relations. One way to almost ensure poor relations is for the halfway house to be sprung on the community without any notice of the desire of officials to establish the house and without community input in the early planning process. Another common mistake is for halfway house officials to be content with a low-profile image once the house is established. Believing that adequate community relations will exist as long as offenders are controlled and unfavorable media exposure is avoided, officials may try to minimize exposure of house operations to the public. The typical result is an atmosphere of secrecy, suspicion, and distrust. When the inevitable negative incident occurs, such as a crime by a resident against a community member, public outcry against the house is likely.

How many persons placed in halfway houses successfully complete their stays, and how high is recidivism among former residents after discharge? Those questions were addressed in a recent study of 156 probationers admitted to a halfway house in Michigan.[57] The study found that nearly 60 percent of all probationers received *unsuccessful* discharges. However, other studies have discovered *successful* discharge figures as high as 60 percent.[58] The Michigan study tracked former halfway house residents for seven years after their discharges. The researchers found that approximately 67 percent of the former residents were arrested at least once during the seven-year period for some type of criminal activity; about 60 percent were arrested at least once for felonies. However, persons who had successfully completed the halfway house program were significantly less likely to incur new arrests than the persons who had not done so. For instance, 44

MYTH

When an offender halfway house is established in a neighborhood, crime rates increase and property values fall.

FACT

Research on this subject has confirmed neither of those assumptions. Crime rates and property values tend to remain the same.

percent of the persons who had received successful discharges were arrested for new felonies, compared with 68.8 percent of those who had received unsuccessful discharges.

In another study, the recidivism of offenders who had been placed in halfway house programs was compared with the recidivism of those placed on regular probation supervision. Using a three-year follow-up period, the researchers found that 29.5 percent of the former halfway house residents and 30.7 percent of the regular probationers experienced new criminal convictions. Slightly more than 40 percent of the halfway house residents had failed to complete their programs successfully.[59]

Research clearly suggests that a large number of offenders placed in halfway houses do not successfully complete their programs. However, those who do receive successful discharges seem less likely to commit new crimes than those who do not. Yet, there is little reason to believe that halfway houses are associated with less recidivism than other types of community corrections programs.

Temporary-Release Programs

Temporary-release programs allow inmates in jail or prison to leave the facility for short periods to participate in approved community activities. Those programs are designed to permit inmates to establish or maintain community ties, thereby gradually preparing them for reentry into society. The programs also give institutional authorities a means of testing the readi-

Temporary-release programs
Programs that allow jail or prison inmates to leave the facility for short periods to participate in approved community activities.

ness of inmates for release as well as a means of controlling institutional behavior. Not surprisingly, opportunities for temporary release create a major incentive for inmates to engage in the conduct desired by officials.

Three of the most common temporary-release programs are work release, study release, and furloughs. The persons involved in such programs may be prison inmates, jail members or halfway house residents. As should be apparent from the previous section of this chapter, temporary release is an integral aspect of halfway houses. In prisons and jails, temporary release is reserved for inmates who have demonstrated, through their institutional behavior, that they are appropriate candidates to participate in community-based activities.

Organized temporary release programs are not new in American corrections. Although the programs date to the early 1900s, they did not gain widespread popularity until the 1960s, when the emphasis on community corrections began to grow. Today, almost all states offer temporary release.[60]

In work-release programs, inmates leave the facility for certain hours each day (for example, 8:00 A.M. to 5:00 P.M.) to work for their employers in the free community. Work-release inmates are paid prevailing wages, but they are usually required to submit their paychecks to corrections officials so that the officials can make deductions for such things as dependent support and restitution orders before placing the balance in inmates' accounts. Imates may withdraw some money to spend on themselves while in the facility but are usually required to save a certain amount for their ultimate release from incarceration. A major limitation of such programs is that most inmates must settle for low-skilled and low-paying jobs. This limitation exists because:

1. A large proportion of inmates lack the educational and vocational backgrounds needed to secure higher-paying employment.

2. There is more competition for higher-paying jobs.

3. Many employers are reluctant to hire work-release inmates, especially for positions that pay well and require considerable skill and responsibility.

Study-release inmates are able to leave jail or prison to participate in high school equivalency classes, vocational training, or college coursework. A major limitation of study release is that, unlike work release, it does not generate immediate financial resources. If inmates are unable to pay for their own educational programs or obtain some type of financial aid, study release must be funded by the jurisdiction. Even in the unlikely event that a jurisdiction has ample resources to fund study release, there may still be reluctance to do so because of the argument that inmates are getting free education at taxpayers' expense.

In furlough programs, inmates are granted leaves of absence from the facility for brief periods (for example, 48 hours) to accomplish specific things. Inmates may be granted furloughs to spend time with family members, to attend funerals, or to search for employment and housing just before release. Depending on the jurisdiction and the particular facility, furloughs may be granted at irregular or regular intervals during the sentence. Regular furlough intervals can be as short as two weeks or as long as a year.

One of the most commonly voiced fears about temporary-release programs is that many inmates will flee or will commit serious crimes while away from the facility. In fact, research shows that the vast majority of inmates neither flee nor commit serious offenses. The most frequent problems are late returns and the use of alcohol and illegal drugs.

As many readers will recall, temporary-release programs became a significant issue in the U.S. presidential election campaign of 1988. Massachusetts Governor Michael Dukakis, the Democratic presidential nominee, was heavily criticized by Vice President George Bush, the Republican nominee, for allowing temporary release of inmates with records of violence. Specifically, Willie Horton, a black man who had been serving a first-degree murder sentence at a Massachusetts institution, was convicted of committing violent crimes against a white couple during his tenth furlough from the institution. Bush made much of the "liberal" prison release policies of Massachusetts in an attempt to discredit Dukakis and brand him a liberal. Many people believe that Bush's strategy helped gain him the presidency.

It turns out that around the same time, an evaluation of temporary release in Massachusetts was being conducted. The evaluation was published in 1991.[61] The researchers studied persons released from Massachusetts facilities between 1973 and 1983. Offenders were tracked for one year after release, and recidivism was defined as return to prison. The recidivism of persons who had participated in furloughs, prerelease-center (halfway house) programs, and both furloughs and prerelease centers was compared with the recidivism of persons who had participated in neither. Using complex statistical controls for differences in offenders' background characteristics, the researchers concluded that "prerelease programs following prison furloughs, and prison furloughs alone, appear to reduce dramatically the risks to public safety after release." The implications of this study are that eliminating or significantly curtailing temporary-release programs is likely to result in a long-term decline in community safety from recidivism.

11 Review and Applications

CHAPTER OBJECTIVE 1

Although community corrections programs are very diverse across the nation, the common feature of those programs is that they provide supervision and treatment services for offenders outside jails and prisons. The dual emphasis on supervision and treatment creates a potential role conflict for community corrections staff. There is some indication, however, that the traditional focus on treatment has been declining relative to the growing emphasis on supervision.

CHAPTER OBJECTIVE 2

The most commonly used type of community sentence is probation. Offenders placed on probation are supervised and provided with various services in the community instead of being incarcerated. In return, they are required to abide by the rules of the probation sentence. Overall, studies indicate that probation is about as effective as incarceration in controlling recidivism. Available data indicate that recidivism is quite high among felons sentenced to probation. Furthermore, research has not found a strong association between probation officers' caseloads and the likelihood of probationer recidivism. If anything, reduced caseloads seem to increase the probability that instances of recidivism will be detected.

CHAPTER OBJECTIVE 3

Unlike probation, parole is not a court-imposed sentence. Parole is a mechanism of releasing persons from prison and a means of supervising them after release, instead of an alternative to an incarceration sentence. Parole supervision is often confused with probation because the two share many similarities. Four major objectives of parole agencies are to: (1) preserve community safety by supervising the behavior of parolees, (2) promote the betterment of parolees by responding to their treatment needs, (3) control prison crowding, and (4) control the behavior of prison inmates by providing early release opportunities in exchange for good prison conduct.

CHAPTER OBJECTIVE 4

In general, a parole board directs a jurisdiction's parole policies and manages the parole release and termination processes. Parole board members (or their representatives) conduct parole-grant hearings to determine which inmates should receive early release from prison. Boards also determine whether to revoke the parole of persons who have violated parole conditions. In most states, field service agencies are administratively independent of parole boards. A field service agency provides community supervision and treatment services for persons who have been granted parole release by the board and makes recommendations to the board concerning termination of parole.

CHAPTER OBJECTIVE 5

Compared with traditional programs in community corrections, intermediate sanctions are oriented less toward rehabilitation and more toward retribution, deterrence, and incapacitation. They are more punitive and more restrictive. The recent popularity of intermediate sanctions is attributable largely to the record high levels of prison crowding that plague many jurisdictions and a corresponding need to devise acceptable alternatives to imprisonment.

CHAPTER OBJECTIVE 6

Two major concerns about ISP are (1) the potential for net-widening and (2) the lack of demonstrated reduction of recidivism. Net-widening occurs when offenders placed in a novel program such as ISP are not the offenders for whom the program was intended. The consequence is that those in the program receive more severe sanctions than they would have received had the new program been unavailable. Studies show that ISP is associated with a substantially higher percentage of technical violations than alternative sanctions such as regular probation, prison, or regular parole.

CHAPTER OBJECTIVE 7

Day reporting centers allow offenders to live at home but require them to report to the center regularly to confer with center staff about supervision and treatment matters. Program components commonly focus on work, education, counseling, and community service. Structured fines, or day fines, differ fundamentally from the fines (called *tariff fines*) more typically imposed by American criminal courts. Whereas tariff fines require a single fixed amount of money, or an amount within a narrow range, to be paid by all defendants convicted of a particular crime, without regard to their financial circumstances, structured fines, or day fines, are based on defendants' ability to pay. The basic premise of structured fines is that punishment by a fine should be proportionate to the seriousness of the offense and should have a roughly similar economic impact on persons with differing financial resources who are convicted of the same offense.

CHAPTER OBJECTIVE 8

In home confinement programs (also known as home incarceration, home detention, and house arrest), offenders are required by the court to remain in their homes except for preapproved periods of absence. Electronic monitoring, which is generally coupled with home confinement, allows an offender's whereabouts to be gauged through the use of computer technology.

CHAPTER OBJECTIVE 9

The goal of halfway houses is to provide offenders with a temporary (for instance, six-month) period of highly structured and supportive living so that they will be better prepared to function independently in the community upon discharge. To this end, most programs place a heavy emphasis on addressing offenders' educational and employment deficits. Research clearly suggests that a large number of offenders placed in halfway houses do not successfully complete their programs. However, those who do receive successful discharges seem less likely to commit new crimes than those who do not. Yet, there is little reason to believe that halfway houses are associated with less recidivism than other community corrections programs.

CHAPTER OBJECTIVE 10

By allowing incarcerated persons to temporarily leave their facilities to participate in approved activities in the community, temporary release programs are intended to foster ties between inmates and their communities, thus gradually preparing inmates for return to society. These programs also give officials a way to judge the readiness of inmates for release, and since most inmates want to participate in temporary release, the programs give inmates an incentive to maintain good institutional behavior. Although the programs are often plagued by fear and other forms of resistance from community members, there is evidence that participation in temporary release is associated with a decreased likelihood of recidivism upon release from incarceration. Some common types of temporary release include work release, study release, and furlough.

KEY TERMS

community corrections, p. 376
probation, p. 379
diversion, p. 379
presentence investigation (PSI),
    p. 381
probation conditions, p. 385
restitution, p. 385
revocation, p. 387

technical violations, p. 387
recidivism, p. 389
parole, p. 390
parole guidelines, p. 393
reintegration, p. 399
intermediate sanctions, p. 401
intensive-supervision probation
    and parole (ISP), p. 401

net-widening, p. 402
day reporting centers, p. 404
structured fines, or day fines, p. 404
home confinement, p. 406
electronic monitoring, p. 406
halfway houses, p. 408
temporary release programs,
    p. 413

QUESTIONS FOR REVIEW

1. What are David Duffee's three varieties of community corrections, and how do they differ?

2. What are three aspects of the helping role of community corrections staff?

3. Why is community corrections important?

4. What are five types of probation?

5. What are three fundamental objectives of probation agencies?

6. What is a probation subsidy, and what is its goal?

7. What is the main task of the PSI?

8. What are two types of probation conditions, and how do they differ?

9. For what general types of violations can probation be revoked?

10. What two landmark Supreme Court cases define the procedural guidelines for revoking probation or parole?

11. What are two general types of parole, and what is their function?

12. According to a recent study, what are the four most important factors parole authorities consider before granting release on parole?

13. What are some criticisms of parole release?

14. What are two ways that halfway house officials might effectively confront community resistance?

EXPERIENTIAL ACTIVITIES

1. Take a guided tour of the probation or parole agency in your community. Ask the guide to explain the various activities of the agency. Also ask to speak with various officers about their work. Request sample copies of agency documents, such as risk-and-needs-assessment instruments.

2. Obtain a copy of the rules of behavior for a halfway house. Evaluate the rules, and decide whether you think they are too stringent, not stringent enough, or on target. Rewrite any rules that you think are deficient.

3. **INTERNET** Visit the Sedgwick County, Kansas, Department of Corrections, Community Corrections Division, web site at **www.sedgwick.ks.us/corrections/scas.html** or the North Carolina Department of Correction, Division of Adult Probation and Parole, web site at **www.doc.state.nc.us/dapp/welcome.htm**. Choose from the topics provided, and write a brief summary of the information you find and how it is related to community corrections.

CRITICAL THINKING EXERCISES

1. You are a probation or parole officer. Your caseload averages 100 clients.

   a. A client tells you that her boss is treating her unfairly at work because of her criminal record and probation or parole status. Your client is afraid of being fired and having her probation or parole revoked. What do you do?

   b. You discover that a client is using marijuana. You like the client, and other than the marijuana use, he has been doing well on probation or parole. What do you do?

c. You have a problem client who is using drugs (marijuana and cocaine), hanging out with a "bad" group of people, and probably (though you have no hard evidence) committing petty thefts to support her drug habit. You have warned the client to stop this behavior, but she has ignored your warnings. Furthermore, the client has threatened to harm you and your family should you revoke her probation or parole. What do you do?

d. You have a client who, as a condition of his probation or parole, is required to earn his GED. Although the client has been attending classes regularly and seems to be trying very hard, his teacher informs you that the client just does not have the intellectual capacity to earn the GED. What do you do?

2. As an employee of your state department of corrections, you have been asked to establish a halfway house for parolees, all of whom are former substance abuse offenders, in the nice, middle-class community where you live. Assuming that you take the job, how would you address the following questions?

   a. Would you communicate to the community your intention of establishing the halfway house? Why or why not?

   b. How would you address community resistance to the halfway house should it arise?

   c. Would you ask community residents to aid you in your efforts? Why or why not?

   d. Besides community resistance, what other problems might arise in your effort to establish the halfway house? How would you handle them?

   e. Would you be willing to remain a resident of the community after the halfway house is established (especially if you have a family with small children)? Why or why not?

ADDITIONAL READING

Allen, Harry E., Chris W. Eskridge, Edward J. Latessa, and Gennaro F. Vito. *Probation and Parole in America.* New York: Free Press, 1985.

Ball, Richard A., C. Ronald Huff, and J. Robert Lilly. *House Arrest and Correctional Policy: Doing Time at Home.* Beverly Hills, CA: Sage, 1988.

Byrne, James M. (ed.). *Smart Sentencing: The Emergence of Intermediate Sanctions.* Beverly Hills, CA: Sage, 1992.

Champion, Dean. *Probation, Parole and Community Corrections.* Upper Saddle River, NJ: Prentice Hall, 1996.

Clear, Todd R., Val B. Clear, and William D. Burrell. *Offender Assessment: The Presentence Investigation Report.* Cincinnati: Anderson, 1989.

Clear, Todd R. and Vincent O'Leary. *Controlling the Offender in the Community.* Lexington, MA: Lexington Books, 1983.

Cromwell, Paul F. and George G. Killinger. *Community-Based Corrections: Probation, Parole, and Intermediate Sanctions,* 3d ed. Minneapolis/St. Paul: West, 1994.

Dillingham, Steven D., Reid H. Montgomery, Jr., and Richard W. Tabor. *Probation and Parole in Practice,* 2d ed. Cincinnati: Anderson, 1990.

Duffee, David E. and Edmund F. McGarrell (eds.). *Community Corrections: A Community Field Approach.* Cincinnati: Anderson, 1990

Ellsworth, Thomas (ed.). *Contemporary Community Corrections.* Prospect Heights, IL: Waveland Press, 1992.

Galaway, Burt and Joe Hudson (eds.). *Criminal Justice, Restitution, and Reconciliation.* Monsey, NY: Criminal Justice Press, 1990.

Keller, Oliver J. Jr. and Benedict S. Alpert. *Halfway Houses.* Lexington, MA: Lexington Books, 1970.

Klein, Andrew R. *Alternative Sentencing: A Practitioner's Guide.* Cincinnati: Anderson, 1988.

McCarthy, Belinda R. (ed.). *Intermediate Punishments: Intensive Supervision, Home Confinement and Electronic Surveillance.* Monsey, NY: Criminal Justice Press, 1987.

McCarthy, Belinda Rodgers and Bernard J. McCarthy, Jr. *Community-Based Corrections,* 2d ed. Pacific Grove, CA: Brooks/Cole, 1991.

McCleary, Richard. *Dangerous Men: The Sociology of Parole.* Beverly Hills, CA: Sage, 1978.

McShane, Marilyn D. and Wesley Krause. *Community Corrections.* New York: Macmillan, 1993.

Morris, Norval and Michael Tonry. *Between Prison and Probation: Intermediate Punishments in a Rational Sentencing System.* New York: Oxford University Press, 1990.

Petersilia, Joan, Susan Turner, James Kahan, and Joyce Peterson. *Granting Felons Probation: Public Risks and Alternatives.* Santa Monica, CA: Rand, 1985.

Rothman, David J. *Conscience and Convenience: The Asylum and Its Alternatives in Progressive America.* Boston: Little, Brown, 1980.

Smykla, John Ortiz, and William L. Selke (eds.). *Intermediate Sanctions: Sentencing in the 1990s.* Cincinnati: Anderson, 1994.

Travis, Lawrence F., III (ed.). *Probation, Parole, and Community Corrections: A Reader.* Prospect Heights, IL: Waveland Press, 1985.

Walsh, Anthony. *Understanding, Assessing, and Counseling the Criminal Justice Client.* Pacific Grove, CA: Brooks/Cole, 1988.

Zvekic, Ugljesa (ed.). *Alternatives to Imprisonment in Comparative Perspective.* Chicago: Nelson-Hall, 1994.

ENDNOTES

1. David E. Duffee, "Community Corrections: Its Presumed Characteristics and an Argument for a New Approach," in D. E. Duffee and E. F. McGarrell (eds.), *Community Corrections: A Community Field Approach* (Cincinnati: Anderson, 1990), pp. 1–41.

2. Timothy J. Flanagan, "Reform or Punish: Americans' Views of the Correctional System," pp. 75–92 in T. J. Flanagan and D. R. Longmire (eds.), *Americans View Crime and Justice: A National Public Opinion Survey* (Thousand Oaks, CA: Sage, 1996), p. 87.

3. Patricia M. Harris, Todd R. Clear, and S. Christopher Baird, "Have Community Supervision Officers Changed Their Attitudes Toward Their Work?" *Justice Quarterly,* Vol. 6 (1989), pp. 233–46. And see Robert T. Sigler, "Role Conflict for Adult Probation and Parole Officers: Fact or Myth," *Journal of Criminal Justice,* Vol. 16 (1988), pp. 121–29.

4. Belinda Rodgers McCarthy and Bernard J. McCarthy, Jr., *Community Based Corrections,* 2d ed. (Pacific Grove, CA: Brooks/Cole, 1991); Harry E. Allen, Eric W. Carlson, and Evelyn C. Parks, *Critical Issues in Adult Probation: A Summary* (Washington: National Institute of Law Enforcement and Criminal Justice, 1979), p. 22.

5. Camille Graham Camp and George M. Camp, *The Corrections Yearbook 1997* (South Salem, NY: Criminal Justice Institute, 1997), p. 155.

6. John Rosecrance, "Maintaining the Myth of Individualized Justice: Probation Presentence Reports," *Justice Quarterly,* Vol. 5 (1988), pp. 235–56.

7. Rolando V. del Carmen, "Legal Issues and Liabilities in Community Corrections," in T. Ellsworth (ed.), *Contemporary Community Corrections* (Prospect Heights, IL: Waveland Press, 1992), pp. 383–407.

8. United States Department of Justice, National Institute of Justice Program Focus, *Making the Offender Foot the Bill: A Texas Program* (Washington: GPO, October 1992).

9. Jay S. Albanese, Bernadette A. Fiore, Jerie H. Powell, and Janet R. Storti, *Is Probation Working? A Guide for Managers and Methodologists* (New York: University Press of America, 1981), p. 65.

10. Ibid.

11. Camp and Camp, op. cit., p. 148.

12. Joan Petersilia, Susan Turner, James Kahan, and Joyce Peterson, *Granting Felons Probation: Public Risks and Alternatives* (Santa Monica, CA: Rand, 1985).

13. United States Department of Justice, Bureau of Justice Statistics Special Report, *Recidivism of Felons on Probation, 1986–89* (Washington: GPO, February 1992).

14. McCarthy and McCarthy, op. cit. Also see David J. Rothman, *Conscience and Convenience: The Asylum and Its Alternatives in Progressive America* (Boston: Little, Brown, 1980).

15. John C. Runda, Edward E. Rhine, and Robert E. Wetter, *The Practice of Parole Boards* (Lexington, KY: Host Communications Printing, 1994).

16. Ibid.

17. Ibid.

18. "Charles Manson Punished for Drug Deals in Prison," *The Orlando Sentinel* (June 11, 1997), p. A–16.

19. Runda et al., op. cit.

20. Ibid.

21. Ibid.

22. Ibid.

23. Ibid.

24. Ibid.

25. Ibid.

26. Ibid.

27. Richard McCleary, *Dangerous Men: The Sociology of Parole* (Beverly Hills, CA: Sage, 1978).

28. Flanagan, op. cit.

29. Peggy B. Burke, *Abolishing Parole: Why the Emperor Has No Clothes* (Lexington, KY: American Probation and Parole Association, 1995); Peggy B. Burke, "Issues in Parole Release Decision Making," in C. A. Hartjen and E. E. Rhine (eds.), *Correctional Theory and Practice* (Chicago: Nelson-Hall, 1992), pp. 213–32.

30. Burke, *Abolishing Parole*, p. 16.

31. Ibid.

32. Ibid.

33. John C. Watkins, Jr., "Probation and Parole Malpractice in a Noninstitutional Setting: A Contemporary Analysis," *Federal Probation*, Vol. 53 (1989), pp. 29–34 (quotations from p. 30). Also see Rolando V. del Carmen, op. cit.

34. "Probation and Parole Population Reaches Almost 3.8 Million," U.S. Department of Justice, Bureau of Justice Statistics (Washington: GPO, June 30, 1996).

35. Calculated from ibid, and Kathleen Maguire and Ann L. Pastore (eds.), *Sourcebook of Criminal Justice Statistics 1993*, U.S. Department of Justice, Bureau of Justice Statistics (Washington: GPO, 1994), p. 653, Table 6.93.

36. Camp and Camp, op. cit., p. 148.

37. Jeffrey K. Liker, "Wage and Status Effects of Employment on Affective Well-Being Among Ex-Felons," *American Sociological Review*, Vol. 47 (1982), pp. 264–83 (quotation from p. 282).

38. Richard A. Berk and David Rauma, "Capitalizing on Nonrandom Assignment to Treatments: A Regression-Discontinuity Evaluation of a Crime-Control Program," *Journal of the American Statistical Association*, Vol. 78 (1983), pp. 21–27. And see Peter H. Rossi, Richard A. Berk, and K. J. Lenihan, *Money, Work, and Crime: Experimental Evidence* (New York: Academic Press, 1980).

39. U.S. Department of Justice, Bureau of Justice Statistics Special Report, *Recidivism of Young Parolees* (Washington: GPO, May 1987).

40. Runda et al., op. cit. Also see United States G.A.O., *Intermediate Sanctions: Their Impacts on Prison Crowding, Costs, and Recidivism Are Still Unclear* (Washington: General Accounting Office, 1990).

41. Camp and Camp, op. cit., pp. 160–1 and 75.

42. Billie S. Erwin and Lawrence A. Bennett, *New Dimensions in Probation: Georgia's Experience With Intensive Probation Supervision*, United States Department of Justice, National Institute of Justice, Research in Brief (Washington: GPO, 1987), p. 4.

43. Joan Petersilia and Susan Turner, "Comparing Intensive and Regular Supervision for High-Risk Probationers: Early Results From an Experiment in California," *Crime and Delinquency*, Vol. 36 (1990), pp. 87–111.

44. Joan Petersilia and Susan Turner, *Evaluating Intensive Supervision Probation/Parole: Results of a Nationwide Experiment*, United States Department of Justice, National Institute of Justice, Research in Brief (Washington: GPO, 1993). For further detail see Joan Petersilia and Susan Turner, "Intensive Probation and Parole," in M. Tonry and A. J. Reiss (eds.), *Crime and Justice: A Review of Research*, Vol. 17 (Chicago: University of Chicago Press, 1993), pp. 281–335.

45. Ibid.

46. Dale G. Parent, *Day Reporting Centers for Criminal Offenders: A Descriptive Analysis of Existing Programs*, United States Department of Justice, National Institute of Justice, Issues and Practices (Washington: GPO, 1990).

47. Material in this section is from *How to Use Structured Fines (Day Fines) as an Intermediate Sanction*, U.S. Department of Justice, Bureau of Justice Assistance (November 1996).

48. Norval Morris and Michael Tonry (eds.), *Between Prisons and Probation: Intermediate Punishments in a Rational Sentencing System* (New York: Oxford University Press, 1990), p. 111.

49. *Tate v. Short* (1971).

50. *1997 Directory of Juvenile and Adult Correctional Departments, Institutions, Agencies and Paroling Authorities* (Lanham, MD: American Correctional Association, 1997), pp. xxviii–xxix.

51. Marc Renzema and David T. Skelton, "Use of Electronic Monitoring in the United States: 1989 Update," in T. Ellsworth (ed.), *Contemporary Community Corrections* (Prospect Heights, IL: Waveland Press, 1992), pp. 330–39. A successful termination rate of over 70 percent was also reported in a more recent study; see Roy Sudipto, "Adult Offenders in an Eletronic Home Detention Program: Factors Related to Failure," *Journal of Offender Monitoring*, Vol. 7 (1994), pp. 17–21.

52. James L. Beck, Jody Klein-Saffran, and Harold B. Wooten, "Home Confinement and the Use of Electronic Monitoring With Federal Parolees," *Federal Probation*, Vol. 54 (1990), pp. 22–33.

53. Rolando V. del Carmen and Joseph B. Vaughn, "Legal Issues in the Use of Electronic Surveillance in Probation," in T. Ellsworth (ed.), *Contemporary Community Corrections* (Prospect Heights, IL: Waveland Press, 1992), p. 426.

54. Camp and Camp, op. cit.

55. John P. Conrad, "Concluding Comments: VORP and the Correctional Future," in B. Galaway and J. Hudson (eds.), *Criminal Justice, Restitution, and Reconciliation* (Monsey, NY: Criminal Justice Press, 1990), p. 229.

56. Sherri M. Owens, "Neighbors Are Worried by Arrival of Rapist Who Drank Victim's Blood," *The Orlando Sentinel* (August 9, 1996), p. A–1.

57. David J. Hartmann, Paul C. Friday, and Kevin I. Minor, "Residential Probation: A Seven-Year Follow-Up Study of Halfway House Discharges," *Journal of Criminal Justice*, Vol. 22 (1994), pp. 503–15.

58. Patrick G. Donnelly and Brian E. Forschner, "Client Success or Failure in a Halfway House," *Federal Probation*, Vol. 48 (1984), pp. 38–44. Also see R. E. Seiter, H. Bowman Carlson, J. Grandfield, and N. Bernam, *Halfway Houses: National Evaluation Program: Phase I, Summary Report*, U.S. Department of Justice (Washington: GPO, 1977).

59. Edward J. Latessa and Lawrence F. Travis, "Halfway House or Probation: A Comparison of Alternative Dispositions," *Journal of Crime and Justice*, Vol. 14 (1991), pp. 53–75.

60. McCarthy and McCarthy, op. cit. Unless otherwise noted, the material in the remainder of this section draws on Chapter 6 of this source.

61. Daniel P. LeClair and Susan Guarino-Ghezzi, "Does Incapacitation Guarantee Public Safety? Lessons From the Massachusetts Furlough and Prerelease Programs," *Justice Quarterly*, Vol. 8 (1991), pp. 9–36 (quotation from p. 26).

12 Juvenile Justice

CHAPTER OBJECTIVES

After completing this chapter, you should be able to:

1 Describe some of the early institutions used to respond to wayward and criminal youths.

2 Explain the effects on juvenile justice of some landmark Supreme Court cases.

3 Identify and describe factors that influence the ways that police process juvenile cases.

4 Summarize the rationale for the use of diversion in juvenile justice.

5 Describe the adjudication hearing in juvenile justice.

6 Describe the disposition hearing and the types of dispositions available to the juvenile court.

7 Identify the types and describe the effectiveness of community-based correctional programs for juveniles.

8 Summarize recent trends in juvenile incarceration.

9 Identify the types and describe the effectiveness of institutional programs for juveniles.

Historical Development of Juvenile Justice

Juvenile delinquency A special category of offense created for youths—that is, in most U.S. jurisdictions, persons between the ages of 7 and 18.

From a historical perspective, juvenile delinquency and a separate justice process for juveniles are recent concepts. So are the ideas of childhood and adolescence. **Juvenile delinquency,** as you may recall from Chapter 2, is a special category of offense created for youths—that is, in most U.S. jurisdictions, persons between the ages of 7 and 18. Through most of recorded history, the young have not enjoyed the special statuses of childhood and adolescence as we now understand them: as special times during which the young need nurturing and guidance for their healthy development.

Before the sixteenth century, the young were viewed either as property or as miniature adults who, by the ages of five or six, were expected to assume the responsibilities of adults. They were also subject to the same criminal sanctions as adults. However, in the sixteenth and seventeenth centuries, a different view of the young emerged that recognized childhood as a distinct period of life, and children as corruptible but worth correcting.[1] Youths began to be viewed, not as miniature adults or as property, but rather as persons who required molding and guidance to become moral and productive members of the community. American colonists brought with them those new ideas about childhood as well as European mechanisms for responding to violators of social and legal rules.

During the colonial period, the family was the basic unit of economic production and the primary mechanism through which social control was exerted. Survival depended on the family's ability to produce what it needed, rather than relying on the production of others. Consequently, a primary responsibility of the family was overseeing the moral training and discipline of the young. During this period, two age-old mechanisms were employed to teach children a trade or to allow them an opportunity to earn a livelihood. One of those mechanisms was the **apprenticeship system,** which served as a primary means for teaching skilled trades to the children of the middle and upper classes. The other tradition was the *binding-out system,* which was reserved for poor children. Under the **binding-out system,** children who were difficult to handle or needed supervision were bound over to masters for care. However, under this system, masters were not required to teach the youths a trade. As a result, boys were often given farming tasks, while girls were assigned to domestic duties.[2]

Apprenticeship system The method by which middle- and upper-class children were taught skilled trades by a master.

Binding-out system Practice in which children who were difficult to handle or who needed supervision were "bound over" to masters for care. However, under the binding-out system, masters were not required to teach youths a trade.

Religion, particularly in New England, was another powerful force that shaped social life in the colonies. Regular church attendance was expected, and religious beliefs dominated ideas about appropriate behavior. Present-day concerns about the separation of church and state were nonexistent. What was believed to be immoral was also unlawful and subject to punishment by the authorities. Punishments such as fines, whipping, branding, and the use of stocks and the pillory served as reminders to both young and old that violations of community norms would not go unpunished.[3]

By the early 1800s, the social organization of colonial life began to change as a result of economic and social developments. The family-based production unit that had characterized colonial social life was giving way to a

Until the early 1900s, children were subject to the same punishments as adults.

factory-based system in the growing towns. As parents—particularly fathers—and children began to leave the home for work in a factory, fundamental changes occurred in the relationships between family members and in the role of the family in controlling the behavior of children. Further, as industry developed and as towns grew, communities became more diverse and experienced problems on a scale unheard of during earlier periods.

The Development of Institutions for Youths

At the time of the American Revolution, Philadelphia had fewer than 20,000 residents, and other large towns, such as New York, Boston, Newport, and Charleston, had fewer than 15,000 inhabitants. However, by 1820, the population of New York City was about 120,000 and was growing rapidly as a result of immigration. Immigration, in turn, was changing the composition of communities, which had been more homogeneous during colonial times.

The Houses of Refuge Accompanying those changes in the social and economic life of the growing cities were a host of social problems, such as poverty, vagrancy, drunkenness, and crime, including crimes committed by children. In response to those conditions, the first correctional institutions specifically for youths developed. Those institutions were called **houses of refuge.** The first was established in New York City in 1825, and houses of refuge soon spread to other cities such as Boston and Philadelphia.[5]

A primary goal of the houses of refuge was to prevent pauperism and to respond to youths who were ignored by the courts. Houses of refuge were meant to be institutions where children could be reformed and turned into hard-working members of the community. To accomplish this mission, youths were placed in houses of refuge for indeterminate periods or until their 18th or 21st birthdays. Placement, moreover, did not require a court hearing. A child could be committed to a house of refuge by a constable, by a parent, or on the order of a city alderman.[6]

Houses of refuge The first specialized correctional institutions for youths in the United States.

While there, children engaged in a daily regimen of hard work, military drill, and enforced silence, as well as religious and academic training. It was also common practice for outside contractors to operate shops within the houses of refuge. In those shops, children produced goods such as shoes or furniture, and in return, the houses of refuge were paid 10 to 15 cents per youth each day. This arrangement allowed houses of refuge to pay a substantial percentage of their daily operating expenses.[7] When the youthful inmates failed to meet production quotas, they were often punished. After "reformation," boys were frequently indentured to masters on farms or to tradesmen, and girls were placed in domestic service.[8]

Placing Out Soon after the establishment of houses of refuge, reformers began to recognize the inability of those institutions to accommodate the large numbers of children needing placement and to either reform or control youths. One early response to those problems was the development of *placing out*. **Placing out,** which involved the placing of children on farms in the West and Midwest, was believed to have several advantages over the houses of refuge. First, placing out was seen as a way of removing children from the supposedly corrupting influences of their parents, who frequently were immigrants, and especially of the cities, which reformers viewed as breeding grounds for idleness and crime. Second, many reformers recognized that the conditions in the houses of refuge were counterproductive to the goal of reform. Third, rural areas were assumed to be an ideal environment for instilling in children the values the reformers cherished—values that stressed discipline, hard work, and piety.

Agents hired by charitable organizations would take children west by train and place them with farm families. Although some children were placed in caring homes and were treated as members of the family, others were not so lucky. Many of the children who were placed out were required to work hard for their keep, were abused, were not accepted as members of the family, and never saw their own families again.

Probation Another effort to deal with troubled children was initiated by a Boston shoemaker, John Augustus. As described in Chapter 11, Augustus spent considerable time observing the court and became convinced that many minor offenders could be salvaged. As a result of his concern and his willingness to work with offenders, Augustus was permitted to provide bail for his first probation client in 1841.

Augustus's first client was a drunkard who showed remarkable improvement during the period in which he was supervised. The court was impressed with Augustus's work and permitted him to stand bail for other minor offenders, including children.

After Augustus died, the Boston Children's Aid Society and other volunteers carried on his work. Then, in 1869, the state of Massachusetts formalized the existing volunteer probation system by authorizing visiting probation agents, who were to work with both adult and child offenders who showed promise. Under this arrangement, youths were allowed to return home to their parents, provided they obeyed the law.[9] In 1878, an additional law was passed in Boston that provided for paid probation officers.[10] Subsequently, several other states authorized the appointment of probation officers. However, it was

Placing out The practice of placing children on farms in the Midwest and West to remove them from the supposedly corrupting influences of their parents and the cities.

Juveniles incarcerated at the turn of the century were put into job training programs that would help them when they were released. Typically, male offenders learned industrial trades; female offenders learned ironing, laundry work, and cooking.

not until after the turn of the century and the development of the first juvenile court that probation gained widespread acceptance.[11]

Reform Schools, Industrial Schools, and Training Schools By the late 1800s, the failure of houses of refuge was well known. Dislocations produced by the Civil War placed tremendous strain on houses of refuge and the placing-out system. Perhaps most disappointing, the number of problem youths was growing. In response, state and city governments took over the administration of institutions for juvenile delinquents. Another response was the establishment of **reform**, **industrial**, or **training schools**, correctional facilities that focused on custody.[12] Those institutions were of two types: cottage reformatories and institutional reformatories.

Cottage reformatories were usually located in rural areas to avoid the negative influences of the urban environment. They were intended to closely parallel family life. Each cottage contained 20 to 40 youths, who were supervised by cottage parents charged with the task of overseeing residents' training and education.[13]

In addition to cottage reformatories, larger, more institutional reformatories were developed in many states. Like the cottage reformatories, the institutional reformatories were usually located in rural areas in an effort to remove youths from the negative influences of city life. However, the institutions were frequently large and overcrowded.

Another development, in the late 1800s, was the establishment of separate institutions for females. Previously, girls had been committed to the same institutions as boys, although there was strict gender segregation in those institutions. Moreover, girls were often committed by parents or relatives for moral, as opposed to criminal, offenses. Those moral offenses consisted of such actions as "vagrancy, beggary, stubbornness, deceitfulness, idle and vicious behavior, wanton and lewd conduct, and running away."[14] The expressed goal of those institutions was to prepare girls to be good housewives and mothers. Yet, the institutions, like those for boys, were little different from the prisons of the day.

Reform, industrial, or training schools Correctional facilities for youths, first developed in the late 1800s, that focused on custody. Today, those institutions are often called training schools and although they may place more emphasis on treatment, they still rely on custody and control.

Cottage reformatories Correctional facilities for youths, first developed in the late 1800s, that were intended to closely parallel family life and remove children from the negative influences of the urban environment. Children in those facilities lived with surrogate parents, who were responsible for the youths' training and education.

427

The reform, industrial, and training schools placed more emphasis on formal education than did the houses of refuge, but in many other respects there was little difference. Indeed, those institutions confronted many of the same problems as the houses of refuge had. Moreover, the conditions in the reformatories were certainly no better than those in the houses of refuge, and in many cases they were worse.

The Development of the Juvenile Court

By the end of the 1800s, a variety of institutions and mechanisms had been developed in response to problem children. Yet, the problems presented by children who were believed to be in need of correctional treatment—problems such as homelessness, neglect, abuse, waywardness, and criminal behavior—proved difficult to solve. Consequently, during the late 1800s a new group of reformers, the *child savers,* began to advocate a new institution to deal with youth problems. This new institution was the juvenile court.

The Social Context of the Juvenile Court The period from 1880 to 1920, a period historians refer to as the Progressive Era, was a time of major change in the United States. Although industrialization and urbanization were well under way, and previous waves of immigrants had added to the population of the country, the pace of industrialization, urbanization, and immigration quickened.

In an effort to respond to the problem of youth crime and waywardness, reformers again sought to save children from the crime-inducing conditions of the cities. Supported by important philanthropic and civic organizations, the child savers worked to improve jail and reformatory conditions. However, the primary outcome of the child-saving movement was the extension of governmental control over children's lives. The child savers argued for stricter supervision of children, and they improved legal mechanisms designed to regulate children's activities.[16] In short, the child savers felt that children needed to be protected and that the best institutions for protecting them were government agencies such as the police and the courts, as well as local charitable organizations.

The Legal Context of the Juvenile Court By the late 1800s, legal mechanisms for treating children differently and separately from adults had existed for some time. For example, jurisdictions had set the minimum age at which a child could be considered legally responsible for criminal behavior. Minimum ages for placement in adult penitentiaries were also enacted during the first half of the 1800s.[17] Moreover, special institutions for dealing with youths had been in existence since 1825, when the first house of refuge was established in New York City. Yet, cases involving juveniles were still heard in criminal courts. Many of the child savers believed that criminal courts failed to respond adequately to many of the transgressions of the young.

The legal philosophy justifying state intervention in the lives of children, the doctrine of **parens patriae** (the state as parent), was given judicial endorsement in the case *Ex parte Crouse* (1838). Mary Ann Crouse had been committed to the Philadelphia House of Refuge by her mother against her father's wishes. Mary Ann's father contested his daughter's placement, arguing that she was being punished even though she had committed no criminal

The city of Chicago provides a good example of the changes experienced during the Progressive Era. Between 1890 and 1910, Chicago's population grew from 1 million to 2 million. Between 1880 and 1890, the number of factories nearly tripled. By 1889, nearly 70 percent of the inhabitants of the city were immigrants.[15]

Parens patriae The legal philosophy justifying state intervention in the lives of children when their parents are unable or unwilling to protect them.

offense. However, the Pennsylvania Supreme Court ruled that Mary Ann's placement was legal because (1) the purpose of the Philadelphia House of Refuge was to reform youths, not to punish them, (2) formal due-process protections provided to adults in criminal trials were unnecessary because Mary Ann was not being punished, and (3) when parents were unwilling or unable to protect their children, the state had a legal obligation to do so.[18]

However, the right of the state to intervene in the lives of children did not go unchallenged. In *People v. Turner* (1870), for example, the Illinois Supreme Court ruled that Daniel O'Connell, who was committed to the Chicago House of Refuge against both his parents' wishes, was being punished and not helped by his placement. The court also decided that because placement in the house of refuge actually was punishment, due-process protections were necessary.[19] The ruling, together with increasing concern over the willingness or ability of the criminal courts to protect or control youths, led reformers in Chicago to consider other mechanisms by which their aims might be achieved. The mechanism they created was the first juvenile court, which was established in Chicago in 1899 by passage of the Juvenile Court Act in Illinois.[20] Some scholars argue that the Juvenile Court Act was a means for the child savers, intent on salvaging poor and especially poor immigrant children, to get around the *Turner* decision's requirement of due-process protections for youths.

The Operation of Early Juvenile Courts The Juvenile Court Act of 1899 gave the Chicago juvenile court broad jurisdiction over persons under the age of 16 who were delinquent, dependent, or neglected. In addition, the act required:

1. The court to be overseen by a special judge.
2. Hearings to be held in a separate courtroom.
3. Separate records to be kept of juvenile hearings.[21]

It also made probation a major component of the juvenile court's response to offenders and emphasized the use of informal procedures at each stage of the juvenile court process. Indeed, this informality has been a hallmark of the juvenile court since its beginning, a key feature distinguishing it from criminal court proceedings. The major reason for this informality is that the juvenile court has traditionally focused, not on the act, but on the "whole child."

In practice, the informality of the juvenile court allowed complaints against children to be made by almost anyone in the community. It also allowed juvenile court hearings to be held in offices, instead of in traditional courtrooms, and to be closed to the public, unlike criminal trials, which were open to the public. In the typical juvenile court hearing, the only persons present were the judge, the parents, the child, and the probation officer, who met and discussed the case. Also, few if any records were kept of hearings, proof of guilt was not necessary for the court to intervene in children's lives, and little or no concern for due process existed. Finally, judges exercised wide discretion in how they dealt with children, ranging from a warning to placement in an institution.[22]

The idea of a juvenile court spread rapidly after the passage of the Illinois legislation. Within a decade, ten states had established special courts for children, and by 1925 all but two states had juvenile courts.[23] Moreover,

FYI

Like Mary Ann Crouse, who was committed by her mother against her father's wishes, Daniel O'Connell was institutionalized even though he had committed no criminal offense. He was placed in the house of refuge because he was perceived to be in danger of becoming a pauper or a criminal. However, Daniel's case differed from Mary Ann's because both his parents objected to his placement and, even more important, because the court ruled that Daniel's placement was harmful, not helpful.

The use of informal procedures is characteristic of the juvenile court system.

those juvenile courts followed closely the model developed in Chicago of an informal court intended to "serve the best interests of children."

Despite the growing popularity of the new courts, they did not go completely unchallenged. In the case *Commonwealth v. Fisher* (1905), for example, the Pennsylvania Supreme Court again examined the juvenile court's mission, the right to intervene, and the due-process protections owed to children. In this case, Frank Fisher, a 14-year-old male, was indicted for larceny and committed to the house of refuge until his 21st birthday. Frank's father objected to his placement, claiming that Frank's seven-year sentence for a minor offense was more severe than he would have received in criminal court.[24]

In its ruling, the Pennsylvania Supreme Court upheld the idea of the juvenile court, and in many respects repeated the arguments it had made in the *Crouse* decision. The court found that the state may intervene in families when parents are unable or unwilling to prevent their children from engaging in crime, and that Frank was being helped by his placement in the house of refuge. It further ruled that due-process protections were unnecessary when the state acted under its *parens patriae* powers.[25]

The *Fisher* case set the legal tone for the juvenile court from its beginnings until the mid-1960s, when new legal challenges began to be mounted. Those legal challenges attempted primarily to expand juveniles' due-process protections. Critics of the juvenile courts recognized that despite their expressed goal of "serving the best interests of children," the established institutions of juvenile justice often did the opposite.

The Legal Reform Years: The Juvenile Court After *Gault* The 1960s and 1970s provided the social context for a more critical assessment of American institutions, including juvenile justice. Beginning in the mid-1960s and continuing though the mid-1970s, a number of cases decided by the U.S. Supreme Court altered the operation of the juvenile court. The most important of those cases was *In re Gault*, which expanded the number of due-process protections afforded juveniles within the juvenile court. However, a number of other cases also helped define juveniles' rights within juvenile justice and contributed to the legal structure found in juvenile courts today. The first of those cases was *Kent v. United States* (1966).

Morris Kent was a 16-year-old juvenile on probation who was transferred to criminal court to stand trial on charges of robbery and rape. Although the juvenile court judge received several motions from Kent's attorney opposing the transfer, he made no ruling on them. Further, after indicating that a "full investigation" had been completed, the juvenile court judge transferred Kent to criminal court for trial.[26] Thus, an important decision had been made, the decision to try Kent as an adult, even though no hearing had been held. Kent's attorney had no opportunity to see or to question material that had been used to make the decision to transfer jurisdiction, and no reasons for the court's decision were given.

The *Kent* case is important for several reasons. It was the first major ruling by the U.S. Supreme Court that closely examined the operation of the juvenile courts. It also made clear the need for due-process protections for juveniles who were being transferred to criminal court for trial. The Court noted that even though a hearing to consider transfer to criminal court is far less formal than a trial, juveniles are still entitled to some due-process protections. Specifically, the Court ruled that before a juvenile court could transfer a case to criminal court, there must be a hearing to consider the transfer, the defendant must have the assistance of defense counsel if requested, defense counsel must have access to social records kept by the juvenile court, and the reasons for the juvenile court's decision to transfer must be stated.[27]

Having given notice that it would review the operations of the juvenile court, the Supreme Court, within a year of the *Kent* decision, heard another landmark case. This case, *In re Gault* (1967), went far beyond the ruling in *Kent* in its examination of juvenile court practices. The *Gault* case is important because it extended a variety of due-process protections to juveniles. In addition, the facts of the case clearly demonstrate the potential for abuse in the informal practices of the traditional juvenile court.

Gerald Gault was 15 years old when he, along with a friend, was taken into custody by the Gila County, Arizona, sheriff's department for allegedly making an obscene phone call to a neighbor, Ms. Cook. At the time of his arrest, Gerald was on six months' probation as a result of his presence when another friend had stolen a wallet from a woman's purse. Without notifying his mother, a deputy took Gerald into custody on the oral complaint of Ms. Cook and transported him to the local detention unit.

When Ms. Gault heard Gerald was in custody, she went to the detention facility. The superintendent of the facility told her that a juvenile court hearing would be held the next day. On the following day, Gerald, his mother, and the deputy who had taken Gerald into custody appeared before the juvenile court judge in chambers. The deputy had filed a petition alleging that Gerald was delinquent. Ms. Cook, the complainant, was not present. Without being informed that he did not have to testify, Gerald was questioned by the judge about the telephone call and was sent back to detention. No record was made of this hearing, no one was sworn, and no specific charge was made, other than an allegation that Gerald was delinquent. At the end of the hearing, the judge said he would "think about it." Gerald was released a few days later, although no reasons were given for his detention or release.

On the day of Gerald's release, Ms. Gault received a letter indicating that another hearing would be held a few days later about Gerald's delinquency. The hearing was held and, again, the complainant was not present. Again, there was no transcript or recording of the proceedings, and what was said was disputed by the parties. Neither Gerald nor his parent was advised of a right to remain silent, a right to be represented by counsel, or any other constitutional rights. At the conclusion of the hearing, Gerald was found delinquent and was committed to the state industrial school until he was 21 years old, unless released earlier by the court. This meant that Gerald received a sentence of up to six years for an offense that if committed by an adult, would probably have been punished with a much less severe sentence.

The Latin phrase *in re* in the description of court cases (for example, *In re Gault*) means, literally, "in the matter of" or "concerning." It is used when a case does not involve adversarial parties.

When the case finally reached the Supreme Court, the Court held that a youth has procedural rights in delinquency hearings where there is the possibility of confinement in a state institution. Specifically, the Court ruled that juveniles have a right against self-incrimination, a right to adequate notice of charges against them, a right to confront and to cross-examine their accusers, and a right to assistance of counsel. In addition, the Court's ruling implied that juveniles also have the rights to sworn testimony and appeal.

The landmark *Gault* decision was not the last Supreme Court decision to influence juvenile court procedures. The Supreme Court further expanded protections for juveniles three years after *Gault*. In a 1970 case, *In re Winship*, the Court ruled that delinquency charges must be proven beyond a reasonable doubt where there was a possibility that a youth could be confined in a locked facility. Until the *Winship* ruling, the standard of proof typically employed at the adjudication stage of the juvenile justice process was a preponderance of the evidence, the level of proof employed in civil proceedings. **Adjudication** is the juvenile court equivalent of a trial in criminal court, or the process of rendering a judicial decision regarding the truth of the facts alleged in a petition. Under the preponderance-of-the-evidence standard of proof, juveniles could be adjudicated delinquent (found guilty) if the weight of the evidence was slightly against them, a much lower standard of proof than the standard required in criminal courts.

It is important to note that both the *Gault* and *Winship* decisions not only increased procedural formality in juvenile court cases, but also shifted the traditional focus from the "whole child" to the child's act. Once this shift occurred, it was only a short step to offense-based sentencing and the more punitive orientation characteristic of the juvenile justice system today.

The Supreme Court's extension of due-process protections to juveniles slowed in the year following the *Winship* decision, however. In a 1971 ruling, *McKeiver v. Pennsylvania*, the Court held that juveniles were not entitled to a trial by jury. The Court cited several reasons for the decision:

1. The Court did not want to turn the juvenile court into a fully adversarial process.

2. The Court determined that bench trials could produce accurate determinations.

3. The Court felt that it was too early to completely abandon the philosophy of the juvenile court and its treatment mission.

To grant juveniles all of the protections granted adults, the Court surmised, would make the juvenile court indistinguishable from the criminal court.

The continued informality of the juvenile court may explain why very few youths contest charges against them and why a surprising number of youths who are not adjudicated delinquent (found guilty) are placed on probation. Indeed, most youths who appear before the juvenile court admit to the charges against them.[28] Moreover, data collected by the National Center for Juvenile Justice indicate that in 1994, 22 percent of youths who were *not* adjudicated delinquent in juvenile courts were still placed on some form of probation (see Figure 12–3 on page 441).[29]

Today, juveniles have been granted many, but not all, of the due-process protections given adults in criminal trials. However, the daily operation of

---

Adjudication The juvenile court equivalent of a trial in criminal court or the process of rendering a judicial decision regarding the truth of the facts alleged in a petition.

Many states have required more due-process protections for juveniles than have been mandated by the Supreme Court. For example, many state laws specify that juveniles have a right to trial (adjudication) by a jury. In fact, at least one state, Texas, requires that all adjudications be heard by a jury. Nevertheless, jury trials are rare in states that have this right, including Texas. This is because the right must be exercised or, as in Texas, the automatic right to a trial by jury can be waived. In practice, jury trials are often discouraged because they are time-consuming and costly.

juvenile courts calls into question the extent to which court-mandated changes in juvenile justice procedures have influenced the traditional informality of the juvenile court. Juvenile court procedures are still characterized by an informality that most people would find unacceptable if it were applied to adults in criminal court.

The Processing of Juvenile Offenders

Juvenile delinquency in the United States is widespread, and people respond to it both formally and informally. Informal responses consist of actions taken by members of the public that do not rely on official agencies of juvenile justice. Formal responses, on the other hand, rely on official agencies of juvenile justice such as the police and juvenile court. Figure 12–1 depicts the stages in the formal juvenile justice process. Before we provide a detailed examination of the formal juvenile justice process, however, we will first briefly discuss the informal juvenile justice process.

The Informal Juvenile Justice Process

An examination of the juvenile justice process usually begins with the police, and the police do play a critical role in juvenile justice. However, any discussion of the juvenile justice process should really begin with the public, because police involvement with juveniles is typically the result of citizen complaints.

The informal actions taken by citizens to respond to delinquency constitute an **informal juvenile justice** process that operates outside the official agencies of juvenile justice. Many illegal behaviors by juveniles are handled informally by neighbors, business owners, teachers, and others who are not part of the formal juvenile justice apparatus. The informal processing of juveniles is important because it is one of the mechanisms that operate to control youths' behavior, and the more citizens rely on informal control and the more effective they are, the less necessary the formal processing of juveniles becomes.

Although many delinquent actions are handled informally, in other instances members of the public decide to call the police or the juvenile court and to request action from the formal agencies of juvenile justice. Thus, most youths become involved in the formal juvenile justice process when the people who make up the informal process decide, in their discretion, to involve the police or the juvenile court. This means that some combination of the public and the police plays a major role in determining who the clientele of juvenile justice will be.

Informal juvenile justice The actions taken by citizens to respond to juvenile offenders without involving the official agencies of juvenile justice.

Teachers are an important part of the informal juvenile justice process.

FIGURE 12–1

The Juvenile Justice System

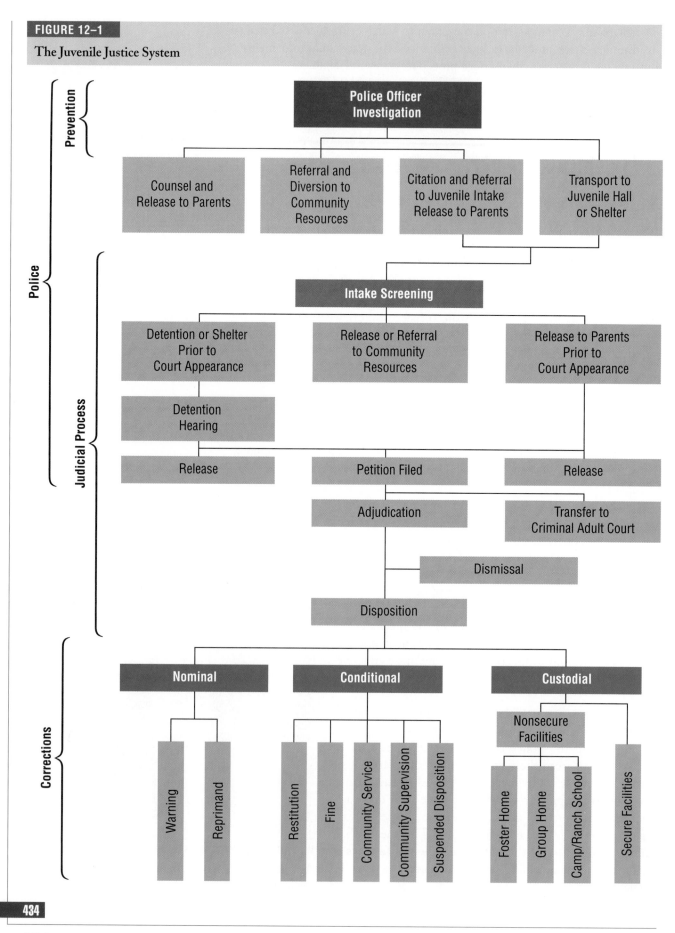

The Formal Juvenile Justice Process

The police represent the primary gatekeepers to the formal juvenile justice process. For example, in 1994, 86 percent of delinquency cases referred to the juvenile courts came from police agencies,[31] while about one-half of the cases referred for status offenses typically came from police agencies. **Status offenses,** as you may recall, are acts that are not crimes when committed by adults but are illegal for children. They include such offenses as truancy and running away from home.

MYTH

The commission of serious, violent crime by juveniles is widespread.

FACT

In 1996, for example, there were 465 arrests for every 100,000 juveniles 10 to 17 years of age for murder and nonnegligent manslaughter, forcible rape, robbery, and aggravated assault. If each of those arrests involved a different juvenile (which is very unlikely), then fewer than one-half of 1 percent of all persons aged 10 to 17 in the United States were arrested for one of those four crimes in 1996. Although many juveniles who commit crimes are not arrested, the fact remains that the vast majority of juveniles do not commit serious, violent crime.[32]

The Police Response to Juveniles Like citizens, the police exercise discretion in handling juvenile cases. Typical responses that police officers may employ are to:

1. Warn and release.
2. Refer to parents.
3. Refer to a diversionary program operated by the police or another community agency.
4. Refer to court.

In some communities, an officer may have a variety of options, while in other communities available options are more limited.

Describing the typical police response to juveniles in trouble is difficult because there is considerable variation in the ways individual officers approach juvenile offenders. A number of factors influence the ways police officers handle juvenile suspects. Among those factors are:

1. The seriousness of the offense.
2. The police organization.
3. The community.
4. The wishes of the complainant.
5. The demeanor of the youth.
6. The gender of the offender.
7. The race and social class of the offender.

Offense Seriousness The most important factor in the decision to arrest is the seriousness of the offense. Regardless of the subject's demeanor or other factors, as the seriousness of the offense increases, so does the likelihood of arrest. Most police-juvenile encounters involving felony offenses result in an

Status offenses Acts that are not crimes when committed by adults but are illegal for children (for example, truancy or running away from home).

arrest. However, most police-juvenile encounters involve minor offenses. When offenses are minor, a number of other factors have been found to influence police decision making.

The Police Organization As described in Chapter 6, police departments develop their own particular styles of operation. Those styles, in turn, help structure the way officers respond to juvenile offenders. For example, in one study that categorized police departments by the extent to which they employed a legalistic style of policing, characterized by a high degree of professionalism and bureaucratic structure, it was discovered that officers in most legalistic departments were more likely to arrest juvenile suspects than were officers in less legalistic departments.[33] Thus, the ways that police departmental personnel respond to juvenile offenders is to some extent a product of the organizational characteristics and policies developed by police departments. However, police departments do not operate in a political and social vacuum. They are also influenced by the communities in which they operate.

The Community Communities influence policing in a variety of ways. Through their interactions with residents of a community, police develop assumptions about the communities they police, the people who live in those communities, and the ability and willingness of community residents to respond to crime and delinquency. Research suggests that police operate differently in lower-class communities than in wealthier communities. Police expect lower-class communities to have higher levels of crime and delinquency because more arrests are made in those communities and because they know that lower-class communities have fewer resources with which to respond informally to the array of problems experienced there. Consequently, when police have contact with juveniles in lower-class communities, formal responses become more likely because informal responses are believed to be ineffective in most cases. Indeed, research that has examined the effect of neighborhood socioeconomic status has found that as the socioeconomic status of the neighborhood increases, the likelihood that a police-juvenile encounter will end in arrest declines.[34]

The Wishes of the Complainant As noted earlier, many police-juvenile interactions occur because of a citizen complaint to the police. What police do in those situations often depends on whether the complainant is present, what the complainant would like the police to do, and, perhaps, who the complainant is.

The Demeanor of the Youth As one might expect, how youths behave toward the police can influence whether an arrest is made. Interestingly, youths who are either unusually antagonistic or unusually polite are more likely to be arrested. In contrast, youths who are moderately respectful to the police are less likely to be arrested—as long as the offense is not serious.[35]

The Gender of the Offender Gender also appears to influence the decision to arrest, particularly when status offenses are involved. A number of studies have found that female status offenders are more likely to be formally processed than male status offenders.[36]

A juvenile's demeanor can influence arrest decisions.

The National Center for Juvenile Justice estimates that almost one-third of all juveniles will have arrest records by the time they reach 18 years of age.[37]

When it comes to criminal offenses, however, research results are mixed. Some of the research shows that girls are less likely than boys to be arrested for criminal offenses, even when prior record and seriousness of offense are taken into account.[38] Other research suggests that any gender bias that existed in the past has diminished or disappeared.[39]

The Race and Social Class of the Offender There is strong evidence that a juvenile's race and social class influence police decision making. The evidence is clear that minority and poor youths are represented disproportionately in arrest statistics. For example, according to 1996 UCR data, white youths accounted for 70 percent of all arrests of persons under 18 years of age. They accounted for 70 percent of arrests for index property offenses and about 50 percent of arrests for index violent offenses. In contrast, African-American youths accounted for about 27 percent of all arrests of persons under 18 years of age, 26.4 percent of index property-crime arrests, and approximately 47 percent of index violent-crime arrests. Other racial groups accounted for the remainder of arrests of persons under 18 years of age.[40] Thus, although white youths account for the majority of juvenile arrests, African-American youths are arrested in disproportionate numbers; they compose only 15.6 percent of the U.S. population under 18 years of age.[41]

The UCR does not report arrests by social class. However, self-report data reveal that the prevalence of delinquency (that is, the proportion of the youth population involved in delinquency) does not differ significantly between social classes when all types of offenses are considered. In other words, the proportions of middle-class and lower-class youths who engage in delinquency are similar. However, when different types of offenses are examined, significant social class differences appear. Middle-class youths have higher rates of involvement in such offenses as stealing from their families, cheating on tests, cutting classes, disorderly conduct, and drunkenness. Lower-class youths, on the other hand, have higher rates of involvement in more serious offenses, such as felony assault and robbery.[42]

Police Processing of Juvenile Offenders When a police officer encounters a juvenile who has committed an illegal act, the officer must decide what to do. One option is to make an arrest. (In some jurisdictions, this is referred to as "taking into custody.") For practical purposes, an arrest takes place whenever a youth is not free to walk away.

As a general rule, the basis for arresting a juvenile is the same as for arresting an adult. An officer needs to have probable cause. There are, however, several differences between arrests of adults and juveniles. First, the police can arrest juveniles for a wider range of behaviors. For example, juveniles, but not adults, can be arrested for status offenses. (Technically, juveniles are not "arrested" for status offenses, because such offenses are not crimes. Also, because status offenses are not crimes, the apprehension of juveniles for status offenses does not require probable cause.) Second, at least in some jurisdictions, juveniles are "Mirandized" in the presence of a parent, guardian, or attorney. This is not necessary, however, because the Supreme Court, in *Fare v. Michael C.* (1979), ruled that parents or attorneys do not have to be present for juveniles to waive their rights. Third, in many jurisdictions, juveniles are more likely than adults who have committed similar offenses to be detained pending adjudication. In *Schall v. Martin* (1984), the Supreme Court ruled that preventive detention of juveniles is acceptable.

Concern about the detention of juveniles generally focuses on the use of preventive detention. Some critics argue that it amounts to punishment before a youth has been found guilty of an offense. The conditions juveniles are sometimes exposed to in detention units and adult jails raise additional concerns.

The exact procedures that the police must follow when taking a juvenile into custody vary from state to state and are specified in state juvenile codes. However, those codes typically require officers to notify a juvenile's parents that the juvenile is in custody. Police often ask parents to come to the police station. Sometimes, an officer transports a youth home prior to any questioning. When an officer feels that detention of a juvenile is appropriate, the juvenile is transported to a juvenile detention facility. If such facilities are not available, the youth may be taken to an adult jail in some jurisdictions. In cases where a juvenile is released to his or her parents, the juvenile and the parents are informed that they will be contacted by the court at a later date about the case. After a juvenile is released, an officer completes the complaint, collecting any additional information needed, and then forwards it to the next stage of the juvenile justice process for further action. When a juvenile is detained in a juvenile detention facility or an adult jail, the processing of the complaint is expedited because juvenile codes require a detention hearing to determine the appropriateness of detention and the complaint is needed at the hearing.

Trends in Police Processing of Juveniles In 1995, approximately 66 percent of all juveniles taken into police custody were referred to juvenile court, about 28 percent were handled within the police department and released, and 3.3 percent were referred to adult or criminal courts.[45] However, an examination of such data over time reveals a trend toward increased formal processing of cases (referral to court) by police agencies. For example, in 1972, approximately 51 percent of youths taken into custody by the police were referred to the juvenile court, 45 percent were handled

FIGURE 12-2

Percentage Distribution of Juveniles Taken Into Police Custody, by Method of Disposition

	Referred to Juvenile Court Jurisdiction	Handled Within Department and Released	Referred to Criminal or Adult Court	Referred to Other Police Agency	Referred to Welfare Agency
1972	50.8%	45.0%	1.3%	1.6%	1.3%
1973	49.5	45.2	1.5	2.3	1.4
1974	47.0	44.4	3.7	2.4	2.5
1975	52.7	41.6	2.3	1.9	1.4
1976	53.4	39.0	4.4	1.7	1.6
1977	53.2	38.1	3.9	1.8	3.0
1978	55.9	36.6	3.8	1.8	1.9
1979	57.3	34.6	4.8	1.7	1.6
1980	58.1	33.8	4.8	1.7	1.6
1981	58.0	33.8	5.1	1.6	1.5
1982	58.9	32.5	5.4	1.5	1.6
1983	57.5	32.8	4.8	1.7	3.1
1984	60.0	31.5	5.2	1.3	2.0
1985	61.8	30.7	4.4	1.2	1.9
1986	61.7	29.9	5.5	1.1	1.8
1987	62.0	30.3	5.2	1.0	1.4
1988	63.1	29.1	4.7	1.1	1.9
1989	63.9	28.7	4.5	1.2	1.7
1990	64.5	28.3	4.5	1.1	1.6
1991	64.2	28.1	5.0	1.0	1.7
1992	62.5	30.1	4.7	1.1	1.7
1993	67.3	25.6	4.8	0.9	1.5
1994	63.2	29.5	4.7	1.0	1.7
1995	65.7	28.4	3.3	0.9	1.7

Note: Because of rounding, percentages may not add to 100.

Source: Kathleen Maguire and Ann L. Pastore (eds.), *Sourcebook of Criminal Justice Statistics 1996,* U.S. Department of Justice, Bureau of Justice Statistics (Washington: GPO, 1997), p. 404, Table 4.26.

within the police department and released, and only about 1 percent were referred to criminal courts (see Figure 12–2). Figure 12–2 shows that there has been a trend toward:

1. Referring more youths to juvenile court.
2. Handling fewer cases within police departments.
3. Referring more cases to criminal courts.

Diversion The goal of juvenile diversion programs is to respond to youths in ways that avoid formal juvenile justice processing. Diversion can occur at any stage of the juvenile justice process, but it is most often employed before adjudication.

Diversion programs are based on the understanding that formal responses to youths who violate the law, such as arrest and adjudication, do not always protect the best interests of children or the community. Consequently, efforts to divert youths *from* the juvenile justice process by warning and releasing them, as well as efforts to divert youths *to* specific diversionary programs, such as counseling, have long been a part of juvenile justice practice. This is especially true for status offenders. Since the enactment of the Juvenile Justice and Delinquency Act of 1974, which stipulated that status offenders not be placed in secure detention facilities or secure correctional facilities, the number of status offenders diverted from formal juvenile justice processing has increased dramatically.

Today, diversion strategies are of two basic types. Some diversion strategies are based on the idea of *radical nonintervention*. Other strategies are designed to involve youths, and possibly parents, in a diversionary program. **Radical nonintervention** is based on the idea that youths should be left alone if at all possible, instead of being formally processed. The police practice of warning and releasing some juvenile offenders is an example of radical nonintervention. The practice of referring juveniles to community agencies for services such as individual or family counseling is an example of a strategy that involves youths in a diversionary program.

Contemporary diversion programs are operated by both juvenile justice and community agencies. Interventions employed in those programs include providing basic casework services to youths; providing individual, family, and group counseling; requiring restitution; and imposing community service.

Detention Sometimes a youth is held in a secure detention facility during processing. There are three primary reasons for this practice: (1) to protect the community from the juvenile, (2) to ensure that the juvenile appears at a subsequent stage of processing, and (3) to secure the juvenile's own safety. In 1994, juveniles were held in detention facilities at some point between referral to court and case disposition in 21 percent of all delinquency cases disposed. The percentage of juveniles detained during processing has not changed very much since 1985.[46]

Intake Screening When the decision to arrest a youth is made, or a social agency such as a school alleges that an offense has occurred, the next step in the juvenile justice process is **intake screening.** The purpose of intake screening is to make decisions about the continued processing of cases. Those decisions and others made during juvenile court processing of delinquency cases in 1994 are shown in Figure 12–3 on page 441.

The location of the intake screening and the educational background and training of the person who conducts it vary from jurisdiction to jurisdiction. Traditionally, intake screening has been performed by probation officers. However, in recent years there has been a move toward involving the prosecuting attorney in the intake process. In fact, in some jurisdictions, such as Colorado and Washington, intake screening is now the responsibility of the prosecuting attorney's office.[47] In other states, such as Michigan, intake screening is done by an intake officer (probation officer) who works for the

---

Radical nonintervention A practice based on the idea that youths should be left alone if at all possible, instead of being formally processed.

Even though diversion programs are frequently touted as a way to reduce the number of youths involved in juvenile justice, some diversionary strategies contribute to net-widening. Net-widening occurs when a program handles youths who would have been left alone in the absence of the new program.

Intake screening The process by which decisions are made about the continued processing of juvenile cases. Decisions might include dismissing the case, referring the youth to a diversion program, or filing a petition.

FIGURE 12-3

Juvenile Court Processing of Delinquency Cases, 1994

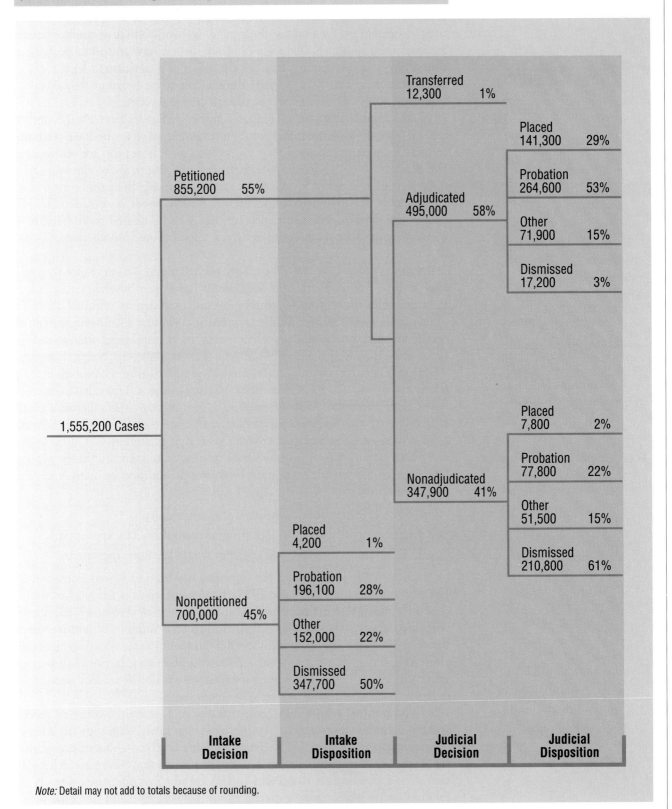

Transferred
12,300   1%

Placed
141,300   29%

Probation
264,600   53%

Petitioned
855,200   55%

Adjudicated
495,000   58%

Other
71,900   15%

Dismissed
17,200   3%

Placed
7,800   2%

Probation
77,800   22%

1,555,200 Cases

Nonadjudicated
347,900   41%

Other
51,500   15%

Dismissed
210,800   61%

Placed
4,200   1%

Probation
196,100   28%

Nonpetitioned
700,000   45%

Other
152,000   22%

Dismissed
347,700   50%

| Intake Decision | Intake Disposition | Judicial Decision | Judicial Disposition |

Note: Detail may not add to totals because of rounding.

Source: Jeffrey A. Butts, Howard N. Snyder, Terrence A. Finnegan, Anne L. Aughenbaugh, and Rowen S. Poole, *Juvenile Court Statistics 1994* (Washington: National Center for Juvenile Justice, Office of Juvenile Justice and Delinquency Prevention, December 1996), p. 9.

juvenile court, although the prosecuting attorney's office reviews most complaints for legal sufficiency.

Possible intake decisions might include dismissing the case or having youths and parents in for a conference or an informal hearing to collect additional information for making the intake decision. Other decisions include referral of the youth to a diversion program (for example, informal probation, counseling at a community agency), the filing of a **petition** (a legal form of the police complaint that specifies the charges to be heard at the adjudication), and waiver or transfer of the case to criminal court.

As in police decision making, a number of factors have been found to influence intake screening decisions. For example, youths who have committed serious offenses, those with prior records, and those who are uncooperative are more likely to have petitions filed. In addition, lower-class minority males, at least in some jurisdictions, are more likely than other groups to receive more formal responses at intake. Finally, there is considerable evidence that females status offenders are likely to be treated more harshly at intake than are their male counterparts, at least in some jurisdictions.[48]

Transfer, Waiver, or Certification to Criminal Court

Since the early days of the juvenile court, state legislatures have given juvenile court judges statutory authority to transfer certain juvenile offenders to criminal court. In some jurisdictions, transfer is called *waiver* or *certification*. **Transfer, waiver,** or **certification** may occur in cases where youths meet certain age, offense, and (in some jurisdictions) prior-record criteria. For example, in North Carolina, waiver may occur if a youth has reached 13 years of age and has committed a felony. In Michigan, a juvenile must be 14 years of age and must have committed one of a number of felonies specified by law. In many states, before a youth is transferred to an adult criminal court, a separate transfer or waiver hearing must be conducted to determine the waiver's appropriateness.

The judicial waiver process varies from state to state, but at the typical waiver hearing, probable cause must be shown. In addition, in many states the prosecutor must show that:

1. The youth presents a threat to the community.
2. Existing juvenile treatment programs would not be appropriate.
3. Programs within the adult system would be more appropriate.

Historically, judicial transfer authority has been exercised infrequently. For example, between 1985 and 1995, the percentage of petition cases transferred to criminal court remained around 1.4 percent. However, consistent with the increase of nearly 70 percent in the total number of petition cases between 1985 and 1995, the number of delinquency cases waived by juvenile court judges rose 71 percent from 7,200 to 12,300 cases. In the 12,300 cases waived in 1994, 96 percent of the juveniles were male, 88 percent were 16 or older, and 49 percent were white (48 percent were black).[50]

The number of juvenile cases transferred to criminal court in recent years is actually much larger than the aforementioned data suggest. This is because there are no national statistics available on the number of prosecutorial transfers. Prosecutorial transfers occur in states that have passed legislation giving prosecutors discretion to file certain juvenile cases directly in criminal court when a youth meets certain age, offense, and (in some jurisdictions) prior-record criteria. In Florida alone, more than 7,000 juvenile cases were transferred to criminal court in fiscal year 1995–1996 through

---

Petition A legal form of the police complaint that specifies the charges to be heard at the adjudication.

Among the American public, 62% agree that a juvenile charged with a serious property crime should be tried as an adult, 69% agree that a juvenile charged with selling illegal drugs should be tried as an adult, and 87% agree that a juvenile charged with a serious violent crime should be tried as an adult.[49]

Transfer, waiver, or **certification** The act or process by which juveniles who meet specific age, offense, and (in some jurisdictions) prior-record criteria are transferred to criminal court for trial.

prosecutorial transfer. Today, because of the availability of prosecutorial transfer, judicial waiver is almost never used in Florida.[51]

Besides the increasing number (though not rate) of juvenile cases transferred, additional developments in this area include (1) an expansion of the number of transfer mechanisms, (2) simplification of the transfer process in some states, (3) pending federal legislation that would reward states for transferring youths to criminal court, and (4) the lowering by some states of the maximum age for juvenile court jurisdiction.

MYTH

Greater use of transfer or expansion of transfer criteria will reduce crime because of the adult sanctions that will be applied.

FACT

Youths transferred to criminal court are more likely to commit further crimes than similar youths retained in the juvenile justice system. Also, there is no evidence that transfer has any general deterrent effect.[52]

As part of that last development, since 1995, all 17-year-olds in at least eight states (Georgia, Illinois, Louisiana, Massachusetts, Michigan, Missouri, South Carolina, and Texas) and all 16- and 17-year olds in at least three states (Connecticut, New York, and North Carolina) have been subject only to criminal court jurisdiction. Those developments reflect a shift in many jurisdictions toward a more punitive orientation toward juvenile offenders.[53]

The Adjudication Hearing When a petition is filed at intake and the case is not transferred to criminal court, the next step is adjudication. As noted previously, adjudication is the juvenile court equivalent of a trial in criminal court. In some states, such as Michigan, adjudication is now called a trial. It is at adjudication, moreover, that a juvenile begins to develop an official court record.

Before adjudication can take place, several preliminary actions are necessary. A petition must be filed, a hearing date must be set, and the necessary parties (such as the youth, the parents, and witnesses) must be given notice of the hearing. Notice is typically given through a summons or subpoena. A summons, an order to appear in court, is issued to the youth, with copies to the parents or guardians. The summons specifies the charges and the date, time, and location of the hearing, and it may list the youth's rights, such as a right to an attorney. Subpoenas are issued to witnesses, instructing them to appear on a certain day, time, and place to provide testimony or records.

When charges specified in the petition are contested by a juvenile and the juvenile is represented by an attorney, another critical event often takes place before adjudication—a plea bargain. Plea bargaining, including its problems, was discussed in detail in Chapter 7. Although the extent of plea bargaining in juvenile justice is unknown, it is believed to be a common practice in many juvenile courts.

There are two types of adjudications: contested ones (in which juveniles dispute the charges) and uncontested ones. Contested adjudications are similar to trials in criminal courts, which were described in Chapter 7. They typically employ the same rules of evidence and procedure. Most contested adjudications are bench adjudications, in which the *hearing officer*—a judge, referee, court master, or commissioner—makes a finding of fact based on the evidence presented. A **hearing officer** is a lawyer, empowered by the juvenile court to hear juvenile cases. In some jurisdictions, contested adjudications are jury trials. However, as noted earlier in this chapter, juveniles do not have a

Hearing officer A lawyer empowered by the juvenile court to hear juvenile cases.

Uncontested adjudications are generally brief. At the end, the youth or the youth's attorney admits the charges.

constitutional right to a jury trial, and even in states that give juveniles the right to a jury trial, jury trials are rare.

Like their criminal court counterparts, the vast majority of juvenile court adjudications are uncontested. Uncontested adjudications are generally brief and consist of a reading of the charges, advice of rights, and possibly brief testimony by the youth or other parties, such as a probation officer. After this, the youth, or frequently the youth's attorney, admits the charges. In some states, an uncontested adjudication is called an arraignment.

The majority of cases that are not adjudicated are dismissed. Suprisingly, however, many juveniles whose cases are neither adjudicated nor dismissed are still placed on informal probation or treated in some other way. For example, of the estimated 347,900 delinquency cases filed but not adjudicated in 1994, 61 percent were dismissed. In 22 percent, the juvenile was placed on informal probation, and the remaining 17 percent were disposed of in other ways (see Figure 12–3). However, the majority of cases in which petitions are filed are adjudicated. In 1994, for example, 58 percent of the delinquency cases in juvenile courts were adjudicated (see Figure 12–3). Although 58 percent may not seem like a large percentage, keep in mind that many cases not adjudicated still receive some court supervision, such as informal probation.

Disposition An order of the court specifying what is to be done with a juvenile who has been adjudicated delinquent. A disposition hearing is similar to a sentencing hearing in criminal court.

Disposition **Disposition** is the juvenile court equivalent of sentencing in criminal court. At the disposition hearing, the court makes its final determination of what to do with the juvenile officially labeled delinquent. Some of the options available to juvenile courts are probation, placement in a diversion program, restitution, community service, detention, placement in foster care, placement in a long-term or short-term residential treatment program, placement with a relative, and placement with the state for commitment to a state facility. In addition, the court may order some combination of those dispositions, such as placement on probation, restitution, and a short stay in detention. However, disposition possibilities are limited by the available options in a particular jurisdiction. In a few jurisdictions, they are also limited by statutory sentencing guidelines. In practice, the disposition options available to most juvenile courts are quite narrow, consisting of probation or incarceration. When incarceration is used, an indeterminate period of commitment or incarceration is the norm.[55]

As part of the disposition, the court also enters various orders regarding the youth's behavior. Those orders consist of rules the youth must follow. Also, the court may enter orders regarding parents, relatives, or other people who live in the home. For example, the court may order parents to attend counseling or a substance abuse treatment program, a boyfriend to move out of the house, or parents to clean up their house and pay for court costs or services provided, such as counseling caseworker services. If parents fail to follow those orders, at least in some jurisdictions, they may be held in contempt of court and placed in jail.

In making the disposition, the hearing officer usually relies heavily on a presentence investigation report (sometimes called a predisposition report), which is completed by a probation officer or an investigator before the disposition. Presentence investigation reports were described in detail in Chapter 8.

The most frequently used disposition in juvenile courts is probation, followed by placement. In 1994, for example, approximately 53 percent of the youths adjudicated delinquent were placed on probation. Twenty-nine percent of the youths adjudicated delinquent received some type of commitment. Relatively few delinquency cases received other dispositions or were dismissed after adjudication (see Figure 12–3).

Because of recent heightened concerns about violent juvenile offenders, many states have legislatively redefined the juvenile court's mission by deemphasizing the goal of rehabilitation and stressing the need for public safety, punishment, and accountability in the juvenile justice system. Along with this change in purpose has been a fundamental philosophical change in the focus of juvenile justice, from offender-based dispositions to offense-based dispositions, which emphasize punishment or incapacitation instead of rehabilitation. These changes are reflected in new disposition or sentencing practices, including (1) the use of *blended sentences,* which combine both juvenile and adult sanctions, (2) the use of mandatory minimum sentences for specific types of offenders or offense categories, and (3) the extension of juvenile court dispositions beyond the offender's age of majority, that is, lengthening the time an offender is held accountable in juvenile court.[57]

Correctional Programs for Juveniles

As noted above, when youths are adjudicated, a number of disposition options are available to juvenile courts, although the options typically used in any one jurisdiction are fairly narrow. Three general types of dispositions are:

1. Dismissal of the case, which is used in a small percentage of cases.
2. The use of a community-based program.
3. The use of an institutional program.

According to a recent study by the Office of Juvenile Justice and Delinquency Prevention (OJJDP), the number of juvenile court cases increased 41 percent between 1985 and 1995, to more than 1.5 million cases. The increase for homicides between 1985 and 1995 was 144 percent (3,000 cases in 1995); for forcible rape, 25 percent (5,400 cases in 1995); for aggravated assault, 134 percent (85,300 cases in 1995); and for robbery, 53 percent (37,000 cases in 1995).[56]

Although some research has failed to find evidence that extralegal factors, such as race or social class, influence disposition, the bulk of the research indicates that extralegal factors often play a role in disposition. For example, a number of studies have found that minority and lower-class youths are more likely to receive the most severe dispositions, even when seriousness of offense and prior record are taken into account.[58]

445

Because both community-based and institutional correctional programs for adults were the subjects of previous chapters of this book, only the features of those programs that are unique to juveniles will be discussed in the following sections.

Careers in Criminal Justice

JUVENILE PROBATION OFFICER

Juvenile probation officers conduct intake assessments (investigating juveniles' treatment needs; family, school, and social backgrounds; and delinquency histories) and supervise youths and their participation in programs. Although juvenile probation officers work to direct youths away from further criminal or status offenses, much of their time is also spent making referrals to community programs and agencies that can assist youths in remaining law-abiding. Referrals are made not only for the juvenile, but also for family services and assistance.

To be qualified to work as a juvenile probation officer, it is generally necessary to hold a bachelor's degree in criminal justice, social work, psychology, or a related field and to have at least two years of experience in some type of counseling work. The qualities generally looked for in candidates for jobs as juvenile probation officers are an ability to effectively manage a large caseload and the skills to work with a manipulative, often hostile, population. Salaries vary according to experience and education.

SUBSTANCE ABUSE COUNSELOR

Substance abuse counselors help juveniles who are physiologically or psychologically dependent on alcohol or drugs deal with the disease of chemical dependency. The substance abuse counselor also helps family members, former addicts, and persons who are afraid that they might become addicts. Substance abuse counselors interview their clients to identify abuse problems. Then they use their knowledge of counseling and of drug and alcohol abuse to set up programs for treatment and rehabilitation of those clients. A substance abuse counselor may counsel a client individually or in a group session in the methods of overcoming drug and alcohol dependency. The counselor also counsels family members in methods of dealing with and supporting the individual.

Substance abuse counselors are employed in rehabilitation centers, halfway houses, clinics, schools, government agencies, and private practice. Educational requirements for a substance abuse counselor vary greatly among employers. An associate's or a bachelor's degree may be the minimum for some employers; others may require a master's degree in substance abuse counseling. Salaries of substance abuse counselors vary with experience, education, and place of employment.

Community-Based Correctional Programs for Juveniles

Among the community-based correctional programs for juvenile offenders are diversion, pretrial release, probation, foster care, group home placement, and parole. Some of those programs are designed to provide services to youths in their own homes, while others provide services to youths who have been removed from their homes, at least for short periods of time. Moreover, although all community-based programs are intended to control offenders and provide sanctions for their behavior, they are also designed to accomplish a variety of additional objectives. Those objectives include allowing youths to maintain existing ties with the community, helping youths restore ties and develop new and positive ones with the community (reintegration), avoiding the negative consequences of institutional placement, providing a more cost-effective response to offenders, and reducing the likelihood of recidivism. We will examine some of the community-based correctional programs for juveniles in the following sections.

Probation Probation is the most frequently used correctional response for youths who are adjudicated delinquent in juvenile courts. Although the actual practice of juvenile probation varies from one jurisdiction to the next, probation officers usually perform four important roles in the juvenile justice process:

1. They perform intake screening.
2. They conduct presentence investigations.
3. They supervise offenders.
4. They provide assistance to youths placed on probation.

In some jurisdictions, all of those roles are performed by the same individual. In other jurisdictions, each probation officer specializes in only one of the roles.

A recent trend in juvenile probation is the development of intensive-supervision (probation) programs, which in some jurisdictions involve home confinement. Intensive-supervision programs are intended to ensure regular contact between probationers and probation officers. They are also intended to serve as an intermediate response that is more restrictive than standard probation but less restrictive than incarceration. However, like standard probation programs, the frequency of contact between probation officers and probationers varies considerably between intensive-supervision programs.[59]

Although there is wide variation in the meaning of intensive supervision, there is some indication that programs that provide frequent supervision of offenders, as well as services, are as effective as incarceration at reducing recidivism.[60] The same research also suggests that intensive-supervision programs are more cost-effective than incarceration, provided they actually divert a sizable number of youths from institutions.

A recent trend in intensive supervision of juveniles is the use of home confinement, which began to be used with juvenile offenders in the 1970s[61] and has grown in popularity since that time. Today, home confinement programs use two mechanisms to monitor youths: frequent probation officer contacts and electronic monitoring. Electronic monitoring requires an offender to wear a tamper-resistant electronic device that automatically notifies the probation department if the juvenile leaves home or another designated location.

The use of home confinement employing electronic monitoring of juvenile offenders began in the 1980s and has grown substantially.[62] However, because electronic monitoring technology is diverse, rapidly developing, and relatively new, little evidence of its effectiveness exists. Still, there are good reasons that some jurisdictions find electronic monitoring attractive:

1. It eases the problem of detention overcrowding.
2. It allows youths to participate in counseling, education, or vocational programs without endangering public safety.

3. It allows youths to live with supervision in a more natural environment than an institution.

4. It allows court workers to better assess the ability of youths to live in the community under standard probation after they leave the program.[63]

Besides probation, juvenile courts in some jurisdictions employ several other types of community-based interventions with juvenile offenders, such as restitution or community service programs, wilderness probation programs, and day treatment programs. In practice, probation is often combined with one of those other community-based interventions.

Restitution Restitution programs, as you may recall, require offenders to compensate victims for damages to property or for physical injuries. The primary goal of restitution programs is to hold youths accountable for their actions. In practice, there are three types of restitution:

1. *Monetary restitution,* a cash payment to the victim for harm done.

2. *Victim-service restitution,* in which the youth provides some service to the victim.

3. *Community-service restitution,* in which the youth provides assistance to a community organization.

Despite the growing popularity of juvenile restitution programs, as well as some programs' effective reduction of recidivism, there are potential problems with some of those programs. Problems include poorly managed, informal programs with low compliance rates; high recidivism rates in some programs; and hearing officers' ordering restitution that it is unrealistic to expect juveniles to complete. There is also a potential for net-widening, and restitution requirements can be subject to discretionary abuse. (Some jurisdictions have established restitution guidelines to remedy this problem.) Thus, rather than achieving the goals of accountability, offender treatment, and

Some juvenile treatment programs strive to provide physically and emotionally challenging experiences to help youthful offenders gain confidence and learn responsibility for their actions.

victim compensation, restitution programs may fail to protect community safety. Moreover, they are likely to produce negative perceptions of juvenile justice by both offenders and victims.

Wilderness Probation (Outdoor Adventure) Programs Wilderness probation or outdoor adventure programs for juvenile offenders are based, in part, on ideas derived from programs such as Outward Bound. A basic assumption of those programs is that learning is best accomplished by acting in an environment where there are consequences for one's actions. Consequently, the programs involve youths in a physically and sometimes emotionally challenging outdoor experience intended to help them develop confidence in themselves, learn to accept responsibility for themselves and others, and develop a relationship of trust with program staff. This is done by engaging youths in a variety of activities, such as camping, backpacking, rock climbing, canoeing, sailing, negotiating rope courses, and a solo experience (spending one or more nights alone in the wilderness).[64]

Evaluations of several wilderness probation programs have shown that they can produce positive effects, such as increases in self-esteem and a decrease in criminal activity both during and after the program.[65] However, research also indicates that the positive effects of the programs may diminish over time or may be no greater than the effects produced by probation programs that provide regular and meaningful contacts between probation officers and probationers.[66]

Day Treatment Programs Day treatment programs for juvenile offenders are operated in a number of jurisdictions around the United States. The programs often target serious offenders who would otherwise be candidates for institutionalization. They provide treatment or services to youths during the day and allow them to return home at night. Because they are viewed as alternatives to incarceration, they are believed to be cost-effective. Because they provide highly structured programs for youths during the day, it is assumed that they protect community safety as well. The range of services or treatments can be quite varied and may include academic remediation, individual and group counseling, job skills training, job placement, and social-skills training. Although some evidence suggests that day treatment programs are as effective as or more effective than institutional placement, some programs may be no more effective at reducing recidivism than standard probation.[67]

Foster Homes Foster homes are out-of-home placements intended to resemble, as much as possible, a family setting. Foster parents are licensed to provide care for one or more youths (usually one to three) and are paid a daily rate for the costs of care. Foster placement is often used by a court when a youth's home life has been particularly chaotic or harmful. In such a case, foster care is used to temporarily separate the youth from the parents or guardian in an effort to resolve the problems that resulted in the youth's removal. Foster homes are also used to remove youths from particular neighborhoods and for some nonviolent offenders instead of more restrictive placements, such as institutionalization. When used in those ways, they are considered "halfway-in programs." In other instances, foster homes are used as transitions to home and are considered "halfway-out programs."

Although group homes are used extensively in juvenile justice, relatively little sound recent research has examined their effectiveness. One well-known, but older, study of a group home program, the Silverlake Experiment, found that youths placed in the program for approximately six months were no more likely to commit further crimes than similar youths who were randomly assigned to an institutional placement. In other words, placement in the program was neither more nor less effective than institutionalization at reducing recidivism.

Although foster homes are widely used by juvenile courts in some jurisdictions, there are few sound evaluations of their effectiveness. The limited research that exists indicates that foster care is generally not effective and may even be counterproductive.

Group Homes Similar to foster homes, group homes are open, nonsecure community-based facilities used in both "halfway-in programs" and "halfway-out programs." However, they are somewhat larger and frequently less family-like than foster homes. The purpose of many group homes is to avoid requiring youths to accept "substitute parents," because many youths are in the process of developing emotional independence from parental figures. Nevertheless, group homes are generally less impersonal than institutions and are less expensive than institutional placements. In addition, their location allows residents to take advantage of community services. Youths who live in group homes usually go to school in the home or in the community or work in the community. Treatment typically consists of group or individual counseling provided by group-home staff or outside counselors.

Aftercare Programs Aftercare involves the provision of services to assist youths in successfully making the transition from juvenile institutions to life back in the community. The services are the same as those provided by other types of community-based programs and may include foster care, shelter or group-home placement, home placement, or efforts to help youths live on their own. Parole, too, is one form of aftercare.

Unfortunately, the quality of many aftercare programs is questionable, and in some cases, youths fail to receive any services after institutional release. As in probation, parole supervision, in practice, may involve very little contact between parole officers and parolees. Moreover, large caseloads carried by aftercare workers may prevent the provision of meaningful services.

Institutional Programs for Juveniles

A variety of correctional institutions house juveniles within the United States, including detention centers, adult jails, shelter facilities (some of them more community-based), reception and diagnostic centers, ranches, forestry camps, farms, and training schools. These institutions hold a variety of youths, including those who are status offenders as well as those who have committed violent offenses against others. They are administered by either state or local governments or by private agencies.

MYTH

Most of the youths housed in juvenile correctional institutions pose an immediate threat to public safety.

FACT

As Jerome Miller notes in his book, *Last One Over the Wall: The Massachusetts Experiment in Closing Reform Schools* (1991), in Massachusetts only about 25 percent of youths committed to state correctional facilities had committed offenses against persons. Many of those offenses against persons did not actually involve physical violence or the threat of physical violence. Consequently, many youths placed in correctional facilities, including many of those placed for "violent offenses," do not pose a grave threat to public safety.

Juvenile Correctional Institutions What distinguishes institutional programs from their community-based counterparts is that institutional programs typically restrict youths' access to the community more than community-based programs do. Indeed, institutional programs are the most restrictive placements available to juvenile courts. However, juvenile institutions vary in the extent to which they focus on custody and control. For example, some juvenile institutions employ a variety of security hardware: perimeter fencing or walls, barbed or razor wire, and surveillance and detection devices, such as motion detectors, sound monitors, and security cameras. Those juvenile institutions, classified as secure facilities, closely monitor residents' movement within the facility and restrict residents' access to the community. Most public and private detention centers, reception and diagnostic centers, and state training schools are secure facilities. In contrast, other juvenile institutions rely much less on security

MYTH

T*he increasing use of incarceration for juvenile offenders during the past 15 to 20 years is a response to the growing juvenile crime rate, particularly the growing rate of violent juvenile crime.*

FACT

The overall juvenile crime rate has been quite stable over time, and the violent juvenile crime rate, as measured by index arrest rates (see Figure 12–4), did not show a significant increase for 15 years, until 1989, well after the trend toward increased incarceration began. Moreover, from 1994 to 1996, serious violent crimes by juveniles dropped 12 percent; there was a 31 percent decline in murders by juveniles during the same period. This suggests that the increase in juvenile incarceration is not simply a product of the extent or the seriousness of juvenile crime.

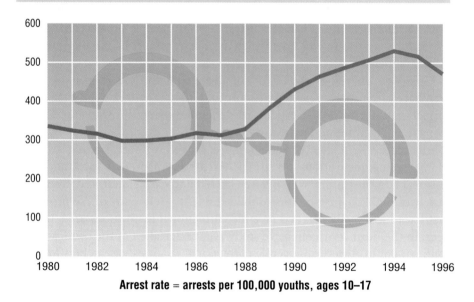

FIGURE 12–4

Violent Crime Index Rates of Juveniles, 1980–1996

Arrest rate = arrests per 100,000 youths, ages 10–17

Source: Howard N. Snyder, "Juvenile Arrests 1996," *Juvenile Justice Bulletin* (Washington: U.S. Department of Justice, Office of Juvenile Justice and Delinquency Prevention, November 1997), p. 4.

devices. Those facilities have no perimeter fencing, and some do not lock entrances or exits at night. Classified as open institutions, they rely more heavily on staff than on physical security. Most private facilities, as well as most public shelters, ranches, forestry camps, and farms, are open institutions.[68]

In addition to differences in the use of security hardware, juvenile correctional institutions also differ in a number of other ways. Some of the institutions are privately operated institutions, although the majority are public institutions. The majority of both private and public institutions are small, housing 40 or fewer residents, although some large, state-operated institutions have a legal capacity of 800 or more. Some institutions are coed; others are single-gender institutions.

Institutions also differ in the average length of time that residents stay in the facility. Typically, youths stay longer in private facilities than in public facilities. However, some private and public facilities are for short-term placements, while others are for long-term placements. Institutions such as detention centers and diagnostic and reception centers are typically for short-term placements. Detention centers usually house youths awaiting adjudication or those who have been adjudicated and are awaiting disposition. In some cases, youths are placed in those institutions for a period of time as a disposition. Other institutions, such as ranches, forestry camps, farms, and training schools, are generally for long-term placements. Youths are placed in them as a result of disposition and possibly assessment at a reception and diagnostic center.

Juvenile institutions also differ in types of programming and quality of care. Almost all juvenile correctional institutions offer basic educational and counseling programs for their residents. Moreover, more than half of all institutions offer family counseling, employment counseling, peer group meetings, a point system, or behavioral contracts. However, there is considerable variability in the extent to which institutions offer more specialized educational or counseling programs for clients and the extent to which residents participate in the programs. For example, fewer than half of all institutions offer vocational training, GED courses, tutoring, suicide prevention, or programs for special offender types, such as violent offenders, sex offenders, or drug offenders.[70]

An examination of the history of juvenile institutions reveals that children have often been subjected to abuse and inhumane treatment in juvenile correctional institutions. Certainly, the overall quality of institutional life in correctional facilities today is vastly improved over that experienced by most youths placed in houses of refuge and early reform and training schools. Many juvenile institutions are administered by competent, caring, and professional administrators, who oversee skilled and caring staff in delivering a variety of high-quality services to their residents. Yet, many of the problems that have historically plagued juvenile correctional institutions are still evident. In the most comprehensive study ever undertaken of the conditions of confinement in American juvenile correctional facilities, researchers found a number of widespread problems. Conducted between 1990 and 1992, this study found overcrowding that resulted in the following substantial deficiencies: a lack of adequate living space, security practices that resulted in

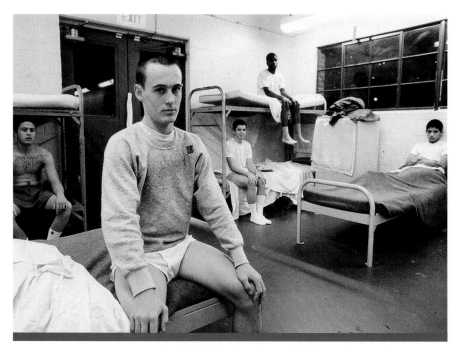

Historically, large juvenile institutions have proven ineffective at preventing subsequent offending.

FYI

There is considerable variation between the average time youths spend in public facilities and the average time they spend in private facilities. There is also variation by status. For example, for juveniles released in 1994, the average stays in public facilities were 147 days for committed youths, 15 days for detained youths, and 91 days for voluntarily committed youths. The average stay in private facilities, in contrast, was 109 days. (Specific categories were not provided for private facilities.)[71]

injuries to residents and escapes, inadequate health care for residents, and inadequate mechanisms for controlling suicidal behavior. In addition, the study discovered that such "deficiencies were distributed widely across facilities."[72]

Despite the long history of juvenile correctional institutions, there is surprisingly little information on the effectiveness of this response to juvenile offenders. Moreover, what is known is not encouraging. Although there is some indication that effective institutional programs for juveniles exist,[73] the bulk of the evidence indicates that many juvenile institutions have little effect on recidivism. For example, a recent review of the rearrest rates of youths released in states that rely heavily on institutions found that the percentage of youths rearrested ranged from 51 percent to more than 70 percent.[75] The results may not be surprising, considering the quality of life in many juvenile institutions.

MYTH

Most youths who are incarcerated in juvenile correctional facilities have committed serious crimes against persons.

FACT

In 1995, only 31 percent of youths placed in juvenile correctional facilities had committed crimes against persons. Further, only 17 percent had committed serious property crimes. Of the remaining youths incarcerated, 9 percent had committed nonserious property crimes, 8.5 percent had committed alcohol- and drug-related crimes, 5 percent had committed public order offenses, 6 percent had committed technical violations, and 23.5 percent had committed other violations or status offenses or were nonoffenders (e.g., youths referred for abuse, neglect, emotional disturbance, or mental retardation).[74]

Recent Trends in Juvenile Incarceration Incarceration has become an increasingly popular response to delinquency. According to the Office of Juvenile Justice and Delinquency Prevention's *Children in Custody Census,* which is an estimate of the number of children in juvenile facilities on a specific day during a particular year, the number of youths in public and private juvenile facilities increased from approximately 93,732 in 1991 to 108,746 in 1995 (the latest year for which data are available), an increase of 16 percent.[76] However, the juvenile incarceration rate (the number of juveniles incarcerated in relation to the size of the juvenile population) increased only about 7 percent during the same period, from 357 (per 100,000 youths aged 10–17) in 1991 to approximately 382 in 1995.[77]

In addition to the increase in both the number and the rate of juveniles incarcerated, other interesting trends in juvenile incarceration have been noted in recent years. One important trend has been the increasing privatization of juvenile corrections. For example, in 1995, nearly 40 percent of juveniles in custody were held in private facilities. Of juveniles held in private facilities, 45 percent were incarcerated for criminal offenses and 14 percent for status offenses. The remainder were being held for nonoffenses, such as abuse, neglect, emotional disturbance, or mental retardation (including voluntary admissions). Private facilities held more than 90 percent of such nonoffenders in 1995.[78]

Another recent trend in juvenile incarceration—a trend that partly accounts for the increase in the use of private facilities—is the crowding in public institutions. In 1995, for example, 40 percent of public juvenile custody facilities were operating above their design capacity—an increase of 4 percent since 1991. Only 8 percent of private facilities were operating above design capacity that year. Design capacity is "the number of residents a facility is constructed to hold without double bunking in single rooms and without using areas not designated as sleeping quarters."[79]

A third trend in juvenile incarceration is the disproportionate numbers of minorities who are institutionalized. In 1995, for example, minorities (that is, nonwhites) comprised 32 percent of the U.S. population aged 10–17. Yet, minorities accounted for 63 percent of all juveniles in custody in 1995. More than two-thirds (68 percent) of all juveniles in public facilities and nearly half (47 percent) of all juveniles in private facilities in 1995 were members of minority groups. Figure 12–5 illustrates the racial and ethnic composition of public and private juvenile incarceration facilities in 1995. Whites are underrepresented in both public and private facilities, blacks are overrepresented in both, Hispanics are overrepresented in public facilities and are underrepresented in private facilities, Asians and Pacific islanders are underrepresented in both, and Native Americans are overrepresented in private facilities and represented proportionally in public facilities. The Juvenile Justice and Delinquency Prevention Act of 1974, as amended, requires states to determine whether minorities are disproportionately represented in confinement. If overrepresentation is found, the state must reduce it.[80]

In conclusion, as juvenile justice in the United States enters the 21st century, several important problems remain unresolved. Many of the problems are the same ones that have plagued juvenile justice since the first specialized institutions for children were established in the early 1800s.

A recent survey of 984 detention centers, training schools, ranches, farms, and camps holding 65,000 juveniles found that only 20 to 26 percent had adequate bed space, health care, security, or suicide control. The survey discovered that more than 11,000 juveniles committed 18,000 acts of attempted suicide, suicidal gestures, or self-mutilation, and that institutions frequently failed to provide appropriate housing for suicidal juveniles. Nearly half the facilities exceeded their design capacity, and only 24 percent of detained youths were in places that met all living-space standards. Larger facilities tended to be the most crowded and had higher juvenile and staff injury rates.[81]

FIGURE 12–5

Racial and Ethnic Composition of Inmate Population of Public and Private Juvenile Incarceration Facilities, 1995

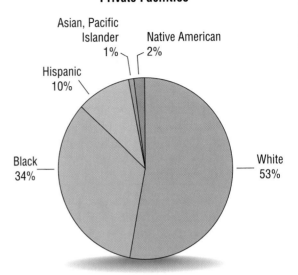

Public Facilities

Private Facilities

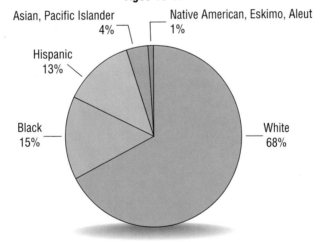

Racial and Ethnic Distribution of 1995 U.S. Population Ages 10-17

Sources: Melissa Sickmund, Howard N. Snyder, and Eileen Poe-Yamagata, *Juvenile Offenders and Victims: 1997 Update on Violence* (Washington: U.S. Department of Justice, Office of Juvenile Justice and Delinquency Prevention, 1997), p. 42; *Statistical Abstract of the United States* (1996), p. 22, Table 22.

Unresolved juvenile justice issues include the following:

1. Providing adequate due-process protections to youths at all stages of the juvenile justice process.

2. Continuing to build on knowledge of effective correctional interventions and developing a range of effective and humane correctional responses, from diversion to institutional aftercare programs.

3. Eliminating the abusive treatment of youths in correctional programs.

4. Working out the appropriate balance between community based and institutional correctional programs.

Review and Applications

SUMMARY BY CHAPTER OBJECTIVES

CHAPTER OBJECTIVE 1

Among the early institutions used to respond to wayward and criminal youths were houses of refuge, placing out, reform schools, industrial schools, and training schools.

CHAPTER OBJECTIVE 2

Landmark Supreme Court cases on juvenile justice (include *Ex parte Crouse, People v. Turner, Commonwealth v. Fisher, Kent v. United States, In re Gault, In re Winship,* and *McKeiver v. Pennsylvania.* Some of the effects of those cases on juvenile justice are the right to adequate notice of charges, protection against compelled self-incrimination, the right to confront and to cross-examine accusers, and the right to the assistance of counsel.

CHAPTER OBJECTIVE 3

Among the factors that influence the ways that police process juvenile cases are (1) the seriousness of the offense, (2) the community, (3) the wishes of the complainant, (4) the demeanor of the youth, (5) the gender of the offender, (6) the race and social class of the offender, and (7) the police organization.

CHAPTER OBJECTIVE 4

Diversion programs in juvenile justice are based on the understanding that formal responses to youths who violate the law, such as arrest and adjudication, do not always protect the best interests of children or the community. Indeed, some formal responses may be harmful to many youths and may increase the likelihood of future delinquent behavior. This is because formal processing may cause youths to develop negative or delinquent self-images, may stigmatize youths in the eyes of significant others, or may subject youths to inhumane treatment.

CHAPTER OBJECTIVE 5

There are two types of adjudications: contested ones (in which juveniles dispute the charges) and uncon-

tested ones. Contested adjudications are similar to trials in criminal courts. Most contested adjudications are bench adjudications, in which the hearing officer makes a finding of fact based on the evidence presented. In some jurisdictions, contested adjudications are jury trials. The vast majority of juvenile court adjudications are uncontested. At an uncontested adjudication hearing, the youth, or frequently the youth's attorney, admits the charges.

CHAPTER OBJECTIVE 6

The disposition is the juvenile court equivalent of sentencing in criminal court. At the disposition hearing, the court makes its final determination of what to do with the youth officially labeled delinquent. At the disposition, the court also enters various orders regarding the youth's behavior. Those orders consist of various rules the youth must follow. Also, the court may enter orders regarding parents, relatives, or other people who live in the home.

CHAPTER OBJECTIVE 7

Community-based correctional programs include diversion, pretrial release, probation, foster care, group home placements, and parole. Evaluations of some programs indicate that they are effective at reducing recidivism or that they are as effective as institutional placement. In contrast, evaluations of other community-based programs indicate that they have little effect on subsequent offending.

CHAPTER OBJECTIVE 8

One recent trend in juvenile incarceration is the increasing popularity of incarceration as a response to delinquency. A second trend has been the increasing privatization of juvenile corrections. Finally, a third trend has been the increased proportion of minority youths incarcerated and the decreased proportion of white youths being held.

CHAPTER OBJECTIVE 9

A variety of correctional institutions house juveniles in the United States, including detention centers, adult jails, shelter facilities, reception and diagnostic centers, ranches, forestry camps, farms, and training schools. There is some evidence that small, secure treatment facilities for violent or chronic offenders are effective at reducing recidivism. However, many institutions, particularly large state institutions, have often been found to have little positive effect on youths' subsequent delinquent behaviors. In fact, they may increase the likelihood that youths will commit further offenses.

KEY TERMS

juvenile delinquency, p. 424
apprenticeship system, p. 424
binding-out system, p. 424
houses of refuge, p. 425
placing out, p. 426
reform, industrial, or training schools, p. 427

cottage reformatories, p. 427
parens patriae, p. 428
adjudication, p. 432
informal juvenile justice, p. 433
status offenses, p. 435
radical nonintervention, p. 440
intake screening, p. 440

petition, p. 442
transfer, waiver, or certification p. 442
hearing officer, p. 443
disposition, p. 444

QUESTIONS FOR REVIEW

1. What changes occurred in the sixteenth and seventeenth centuries in the ways the young were viewed?

2. What were the purposes of houses of refuge?

3. What is *parens patriae,* and what was the legal context in which it arose?

4. What was the social and historical context in which the juvenile court was created?

5. Historically, what has been the fundamental difference between the procedures used in juvenile courts and those employed in criminal courts?

6. What is the informal juvenile justice process, and why is it important?

7. What are four typical responses that police officers employ when handling juvenile cases?

8. What are three recent trends in police processing of juveniles?

9. What are five possible intake decisions that might be made in the juvenile justice process?

10. What are five recent trends in the practice of transferring juvenile cases to criminal court, and what do they suggest about the current orientation of juvenile justice?

11. In practice, what two dispositions are typically available to juvenile court judges in most jurisdictions, and which one is most frequently used?

12. What are three new dispositional or sentencing practices employed by juvenile court judges?

13. What are six objectives of community-based correctional programs for juveniles?

14. In the most comprehensive study ever undertaken of the conditions of confinement in juvenile correctional facilities in the United States, what four problems were found to be most widespread?

15. What are some important problems that remain unresolved as juvenile justice in the United States enters the 21st century?

1. With fellow students, family members, or friends, debate whether the juvenile justice system ought to be abolished and juvenile offenders treated as adults.

2. Visit different juvenile correctional facilities in your community, both community-based facilities and institutional facilities. Compare what you see with the descriptions in this chapter.

3. **INTERNET** Access the Justice Information Center web site at **www.ncjrs.org**. Click on Juvenile Justice and then on Delinquency Prevention under Documents. Choose one of the documents (for example, "What Works: Promising Interventions in Juvenile Justice"). Read the document and then write a brief summary of it.

CRITICAL THINKING EXERCISES

1. Paul, a 15-year-old, sexually assaulted, robbed, and killed Billy, an 11-year-old. Billy was missing for two days. He was last seen selling candy door-to-door to raise money for his school. Paul hid Billy's body for those two days in a suitcase in his family's garage before dumping it in a wooded area near the house. Neighbors describe Paul as quiet and introverted. His parents state that he grew increasingly violent after they tried to keep him from a 43-year-old man named Smith. Paul had met Smith in a computer chat room. Smith was subsequently charged with sexually assaulting Paul. The two apparently had sex in motels five times during the previous four months.

   a. Should Paul be handled by the justice system (either juvenile or adult) or be diverted, perhaps to a mental health facility? Why?

   b. Should he be charged with first-degree murder (as well as the other crimes)? Why or why not?

   c. Should he be transferred to criminal court and tried as an adult? Why or why not?

   d. If tried as an adult, should he enter a plea of not guilty by reason of insanity? A plea of guilty but insane? Why or why not?

   e. If Paul is convicted of any of the charges, what sentence should be imposed? Why?

   f. If convicted of first-degree murder, should he be sentenced to death? Why or why not?

2. Seventeen-year-old James lives in a nice lower-middle-class neighborhood in central Florida. On his home's living room wall are scriptures and family photographs. His 53-year-old father is unemployed because of health problems, and his mother works in a dry-cleaning business. James's father is afraid of him. He caught James with drugs and suspects he is a dealer.

A few years ago, when James began running around with a bad crowd, his parents tried a variety of punishments, to no avail. James was eventually arrested and charged with burglary, theft, and other crimes. A juvenile court judge placed him on probation and ordered him to receive counseling. James violated probation, stopped going to counseling sessions, and began committing crimes again. After a subsequent arrest, James was ordered into a residential rehabilitation program for several months. After finishing the program, he was placed in a special school, from which he soon ran away. He was next placed in another residential program, one designed for youths "needing more structure." He ran away. After he was caught, a juvenile court judge returned him to the residential program for about six months.

James's father states that the rehabilitation programs are a waste of time and money; that they are disorganized and ineffectual. He complains that when James violated curfew and was truant from school, no one did anything. He is afraid that James will kill or be killed, and he would like for James to be locked up until the age of 19. A problem is that space is limited in the most secure juvenile institutions that hold youths from six months to three years. In central Florida, youths must commit, on average, 12 crimes before they are placed in such institutions.

a. Should James be handled by the justice system (either juvenile or adult) or be diverted? Why?

b. If he is diverted, what type of program would benefit him most? Why?

c. Should he be transferred to criminal court and tried as an adult? Why or why not?

d. If James is retained in the juvenile justice system, what disposition would be most appropriate and beneficial for him?

e. If he is transferred to criminal court, what sentence should be imposed?

ADDITIONAL READING

Bartollas, Clemens and Stuart J. Miller, *Juvenile Justice in America*, 2d ed. Upper Saddle River, NJ: Prentice Hall, 1997.

Bernard, Thomas J. *The Cycle of Juvenile Justice.* New York: Oxford University Press, 1992.

Feld, Barry C. "Criminalizing the American Juvenile Court." In Michael Tonry (ed.). *Crime and Justice: A Review of Research,* Vol. 17. Chicago: University of Chicago Press, 1993, pp. 197–280.

Jacobs, Mark D. *Screwing the System and Making It Work: Juvenile Justice in the No-Fault Society.* Chicago: University of Chicago Press, 1990.

Krisberg, Barry and James F. Austin. *Reinventing Juvenile Justice,* 2d ed. Newbury Park, CA: Sage, 1993.

Miller, Jerome G. *Last One Over the Wall: The Massachusetts Experiment in Closing Reform Schools.* Columbus, OH: The Ohio State University Press, 1991.

Platt, Anthony M. *The Child Savers: The Invention of Delinquency.* Chicago: University of Chicago Press, 1969.

Rothman, David J. *The Discovery of the Asylum: Social Order and Disorder in the New Republic.* Boston: Little, Brown, 1971.

Schwartz, Ira M. *(In)Justice for Juveniles: Rethinking the Best Interests of the Child.* Lexington, MA: Lexington Books, 1989.

Whitehead, John T. and Steven P. Lab. *Juvenile Justice: An Introduction,* 2d ed. Cincinnati: Anderson, 1996.

1. Philippe Aries, *Centuries of Childhood: A Social History of Family Life*, translated by Robert Baldick (New York: Random House, 1962).
2. Barry Krisberg and James F. Austin, *Reinventing Juvenile Justice* (Newbury Park, CA: Sage, 1993), p. 9.
3. Harry Elmer Barnes, *The Story of Punishment*, 2d ed. (Montclair, NJ: Patterson Smith, 1972).
4. Thomas J. Bernard, *The Cycle of Juvenile Justice* (New York: Oxford University Press, 1992).
5. David J. Rothman, *The Discovery of the Asylum* (Boston: Little, Brown, 1971).
6. Bernard, op. cit., p. 63; Rothman, op. cit., p. 207.
7. Robert M. Mennel, *Thorns and Thistles* (Hanover, NH: University Press of New England, 1973); Steven L. Schlossman, *Love and the American Delinquent* (Chicago: University of Chicago Press, 1977).
8. Alexander Pisciotta, "Treatment on Trial: The Rhetoric and Reality of the New York House of Refuge, 1857–1935," *The American Journal of Legal History*, Vol. 29 (1985), pp. 151–81; Rothman, op. cit., p. 231.
9. Clemens Bartollas and Stuart J. Miller, *Juvenile Justice in America* (Englewood Cliffs, NJ: Regents/Prentice Hall, 1994), p. 136.
10. LaMar T. Empey and Mark C. Stafford, *American Delinquency: Its Meaning and Construction*, 3d ed. (Belmont, CA: Wadsworth, 1991), p. 368.
11. Belinda R. McCarthy and Bernard J. McCarthy, *Community-Based Corrections*, 2d ed. (Pacific Grove, CA: Brooks/Cole, 1991), p. 98.
12. Krisberg and Austin, op. cit., pp. 23–24; Hastings Hart, *Preventive Treatment of Neglected Children* (New York: Russell Sage, 1910), p. 70.
13. Bartollas and Miller, op. cit., p. 209; John T. Whitehead and Steven P. Lab, *Juvenile Justice: An Introduction* (Cincinnati: Anderson, 1990), p. 47.
14. Cited in Meda Chesney-Lind and Randall G. Shelden, *Girls, Delinquency, and Juvenile Justice* (Pacific Grove, CA: Brooks/Cole, 1992), p. 111.
15. Harold Finestone, *Victims of Change* (Westport, CT: Greenwood Press, 1976).
16. Anthony M. Platt, *The Child Savers: The Invention of Delinquency* (Chicago: University of Chicago Press, 1969), p. 99.
17. Ibid., pp. 101–2.
18. See Bernard, op. cit., pp. 68–69.
19. Ibid., pp. 70–71.
20. Platt, op. cit., pp. 134–36; Bernard, op. cit., p. 73.
21. Empey and Stafford, op. cit, pp. 58–59.
22. Bartollas and Miller, op. cit., p. 92; Empey and Stafford, op. cit., p. 59.
23. Krisberg and Austin, op. cit., p. 30.
24. Bernard, op. cit., p. 96.
25. Ibid., pp. 96–97.
26. Walter Wadlington, Charles H. Whitebread, and Samuel M. Davis, *Cases and Materials on Children in the Legal System* (Mineola, NY: Foundation Press, 1983), p. 202; Bernard, op. cit., p. 110.
27. M. A. Bortner, *Delinquency and Justice: An Age of Crisis* (New York: McGraw-Hill, 1988), p. 60.
28. See Bernard, op. cit., p. 141.
29. Jeffrey A. Butts, Howard N. Snyder, Terrence A Finnegan, Anne L. Aughenbaugh, and Rowen S. Poole, *Juvenile Court Statistics 1994* (Washington: U.S. Department of Justice, Office of Juvenile Justice and Delinquency Prevention, December 1996).
30. Kathleen Maguire and Ann L. Pastore (eds.), *Sourcebook of Criminal Justice Statistics 1996*. U.S. Department of Justice, Bureau of Justice Statistics (Washington: GPO, 1997), p. 258, Table 3.58.
31. Butts et al., op. cit., p. 7.
32. Howard N. Snyder, *Juvenile Arrests 1996*, Juvenile Justice Bulletin (Washington: U.S. Department of Justice, Office of Justice and Delinquency Prevention, November 1997), p. 4.
33. Douglas A. Smith, "The Organizational Context of Legal Control," *Criminology*, Vol. 22 (1984), pp. 19–38.
34. Robert J. Sampson, "Effects of Socioeconomic Context on Official Reaction to Juvenile Delinquency," *American Sociological Review*, Vol. 51 (1986), pp. 876–85; also see A. Cicourel, *The Social Organization of Juvenile Justice* (New York: Wiley, 1968).
35. Donald Black and Albert J. Reiss, "Police Control of Juveniles," *American Sociological Review*, Vol. 35 (1970), pp. 63–77; Richard J. Lundman, Richard E. Sykes, and John P. Clark, "Police Control of Juveniles: A Replication," in Ralph Weisheit and Robert G. Culbertson (eds.), *Juvenile Delinquency: A Justice Perspective* (Prospect Heights, IL: Waveland Press, 1978), pp. 107–15; Irving Piliavin and Scott Briar, "Police Encounters With Juveniles," *American Journal of Sociology*, Vol. 70 (1964), pp. 206–14.
36. Marvin D. Krohn, James P. Curry, and Shirley Nelson-Kilger, "Is Chivalry Dead? An Analysis of Changes in Police Dispositions of Males and Females," *Criminology*, Vol. 21 (1983), pp. 417–37; Katherine Teilmann and Pierre H. Landry, "Gender Bias in Juvenile Justice," *Journal of Research in Crime and Delinquency*, Vol. 18 (1981), pp. 47–80; see also William G. Staples, "Law and Social Control in Juvenile Justice Dispositions," *Journal of Research in Crime and Delinquency*, Vol. 24 (1987), pp. 7–22; Meda Chesney-Lind, "Judicial Paternalism and the Female Status Offender: Training Women to Know Their Place," *Crime and Delinquency*, Vol. 23 (1977), pp. 121–30.
37. Gary F. Jensen and Dean Rojek, *Delinquency and Youth Crime*, 2d ed. (Prospect Heights, IL: Waveland Press, 1992), p. 5.
38. Robert J. Sampson, "Sex Differences in Self-Reported Delinquency and Official Records: A Multiple-Group Structural Modeling Approach," *Journal of Quantitative Criminology*, Vol. 1 (1985), pp. 345–67; Dale Dannefer and Russell K. Schutt, "Race and Juvenile Justice Processing in Court and Police Agencies," *American Journal of Sociology*, Vol. 87 (1982), pp. 1113–32.
39. Merry Morash, "Establishment of a Juvenile Police Record: The Influence of Individual and Peer Group Characteristics," *Criminology*, Vol. 22 (1984), pp. 97–111; Krohn et al., op. cit.; D. Elliott and H. L. Voss, *Delinquency and Dropout* (Lexington, MA: Lexington Brooks, 1974).
40. Federal Bureau of Investigation, *Crime in the United States 1996*, U.S. Department of Justice (Washington: GPO, 1997), p. 233, Table 43.
41. *Statistical Abstract of the United States* (1996), p. 22, Table No. 22.
42. Delbert S. Elliott and David Huizinga, "Social Class and Delinquent Behavior in a National Youth Panel," *Criminology*, Vol. 21 (1983), pp. 149–77.
43. Maguire and Pastore, op. cit., p. 511, Table 6.13.
44. Community Research Center, *An Assessment of the National Incidence of Juvenile Suicide in Adult Jails, Lockups, and Juvenile Detention Centers* (Champaign, IL: Community Research Center, 1980).
45. Maguire and Pastore, op. cit., p. 404, Table 4.26.
46. Butts et al., op. cit., p. 7.
47. Ted Rubin, "The Emerging Prosecutor Dominance of the Juvenile Court Intake Process," *Crime and Delinquency*, Vol. 26 (1980), pp. 299–318.
48. For a review of this literature, see Chesney-Lind and Shelden, op. cit., pp. 137–39.
49. Ruth Triplett, "The Growing Threat: Gangs and Juvenile Offenders," in Timothy J. Flanagan and Dennis R. Longmire (eds.), *Americans View Crime and Justice: A National Public Opinion Survey* (Thousand Oaks, CA: Sage, 1996), pp. 137–50, Table 10–1.
50. Jeffrey A. Butts, "Delinquency Cases Waived to Criminal Court, 1985–1994," U.S. Department of Justice, Office of Juvenile Justice and Delinquency Prevention, Fact Sheet #52 (Washington: GPO, February 1997); Carol J. DeFrances and Kevin J. Strom, *Juveniles Prosecuted in State Criminal Courts*, U.S. Department of Justice, Bureau of Justice Statistics Selected Findings (Washington: GPO, March 1997).
51. Florida Department of Juvenile Justice, Bureau of Data and Research, *Florida's Profile of Delinquency and Youths Referred: FY 1991–92 Through FY 1995–96* (Tallahassee: Florida Department of Juvenile Justice, November 1996).
52. Donna M. Bishop, Charles E. Frazier, Lonn Lanza-Daduce, and Lawrence Winner, "The Transfer of Juveniles to Criminal Court: Does It Make a Difference?" *Crime and Delinquency*, Vol. 42 (1996), pp. 171–91; Jeffrey Fagan, "Separating the Men From the Boys: The Comparative Advantage of Juvenile Versus Criminal Court Sanctions

on Recidivism Among Adolescent Felony Offenders," in James C. Howell, Barry Krisberg, J. David Hawkins, and John Wilson, eds., *A Sourcebook: Serious, Violent, and Chronic Juvenile Offenders* (Thousand Oaks, CA: Sage, 1995), pp. 213–37; Eric Jensen and Linda Metsger, "A Test of the Deterrent Effect of Legislative Waiver on Violent Juvenile Crime," *Crime and Delinquency,* Vol. 40 (1994), pp. 96–104.

53. Unless indicated otherwise, material in this section is from the following sources: Barry C. Feld, "Criminalizing the American Juvenile Court," in Michael Tonry (ed.), *Crime and Justice: A Review of Research,* Vol. 17 (Chicago: University of Chicago Press, 1993), pp. 197–280; Joseph B. Sanborn, Jr., "Policies Regarding the Prosecution of Juvenile Murderers: Which System and Who Should Decide," *Law & Policy,* Vol. 18 (1996), pp. 151–78; Joseph B Sanborn, Jr., "Certification to Criminal Court: The Important Policy Questions of How, When, and Why," *Crime and Delinquency,* Vol. 40 (1994), pp. 262–81; Howard N. Snyder, *Juvenile Arrests 1995,* U.S. Department of Justice, Office of Juvenile Justice and Delinquency Prevention, Juvenile Justice Bulletin (Washington: GPO, February 1997), p. 12; Barry C. Feld, "The Juvenile Court Meets the Principle of the Offense: Legislative Changes in Juvenile Waiver Statutes," *Journal of Criminal Law and Criminology,* Vol. 78 (1987), pp. 471–533; Barry Krisberg, Ira M. Schwartz, Paul Litsky, and James Austin, "The Watershed of Juvenile Justice Reform," *Crime and Delinquency,* Vol. 32 (1986), pp. 5–38; Donna Hamparian, Linda Estep, Susan M. Muntean, Ramon R. Prestino, Robert G. Swisher, Paul L. Wallace, and Joseph L. White, *Youth in Adult Court: Between Two Worlds* (Washington: OJJDP, 1982); and personal communications from Donna M. Bishop and Joseph B. Sanborn, Jr.

54. Joseph B. Sanborn, Jr., "Pleading Guilty in Juvenile Court," *Justice Quarterly,* Vol. 9 (1992), pp. 127–50.

55. Martin L. Forst, Bruce A. Fisher, and Robert B. Coates, "Indeterminate and Determinate Sentencing of Juvenile Delinquents: A National Survey of Approaches to Commitment and Release Decision-Making," *Juvenile and Family Court Journal* (Summer 1985), pp. 1–12.

56. Butts et al., op. cit., p. 5, Table 1.

57. Patricia Torbert, Richard Gable, Hunter Hurst IV, Imogene Montgomery, Linda Szymanski, and Douglas Thomas, *State Responses to Serious and Violent Juvenile Crime,* U.S. Department of Justice, Office of Juvenile Justice and Delinquency Prevention (Washington: GPO, July 1996), Chap. 3.

58. Jeffrey Fagan, Ellen Slaughter, and Richard Hartstone, "Blind Justice: The Impact of Race on the Juvenile Justice Process, *Crime and Delinquency,* Vol. 33 (1987), pp. 244–58; Belinda R. McCarthy and Brent L. Smith, "The Conceptualization of Discrimination in the Juvenile Justice Process," *Criminology,* Vol. 24 (1986), pp. 41–64.

59. Troy L. Armstrong, "National Survey of Juvenile Intensive Supervision" (Parts I and II), *Criminal Justice Abstracts,* Vol. 20 (1988), pp. 342–48 (Part I) and 497–523 (Part II).

60. Richard G. Wiebush, "Juvenile Intensive Supervision: The Impact on Felony Offenders Diverted From Institutional Placement," *Crime and Delinquency,* Vol. 39 (1993), pp. 68–89; William H. Barton and Jeffrey A. Butts, "Viable Options: Intensive Supervision Programs for Juvenile Delinquents," *Crime and Delinquency,* Vol. 36 (1990), pp. 238–56.

61. Richard A. Ball, Ronald Huff, and Robert Lilly, *House Arrest and Correctional Policy: Doing Time at Home* (Newbury Park, CA: Sage, 1988).

62. See Marc Renzema and David T. Skelton, "Use of Electronic Monitoring in the United States: 1989 Update," National Institute of Justice, Research in Brief (Washington: National Institute of Justice, 1990); Daniel Ford and Annesley K. Schmidt, "Electronically Monitored Home Confinement," National Institute of Justice, Research in Action (Washington: National Institute of Justice, 1985).

63. Joseph B. Vaughn, "A Survey of Juvenile Electronic Monitoring and Home Confinement Programs," *Juvenile and Family Court Journal,* Vol. 40 (1989), pp. 1–36.

64. Kevin I. Minor and Preston Elrod, "The Effects of a Probation Intervention on Juvenile Offenders' Self-Concepts, Loci of Control, and Perceptions of Juvenile Justice," *Youth and Society,* Vol. 25 (1994), pp. 490–511; Gerald L. Golins, *Utilizing Adventure Education to Rehabilitate Juvenile Delinquents* (Las Cruces, NM: Educational Resources Information Center, Clearinghouse on Rural Education and Small Schools, 1980).

65. See, for example, R. Callahan, "Wilderness Probation: A Decade Later," *Juvenile and Family Court Journal,* Vol. 36 (1985), pp. 31–51; John Winterdyk and Ronald Roesch, "A Wilderness Experiential Program as an Alternative for Probationers: An Evaluation," *Canadian Journal of Criminology,* Vol. 24 (1982), pp. 39–49.

66. H. Preston Elrod and Kevin I. Minor, "Second Wave Evaluation of a Multi-Faceted Intervention for Juvenile Court Probationers," *International Journal of Offender Therapy and Comparative Criminology,* Vol. 36 (1992), pp. 247–62; John Winterdyk and Curt Griffiths, "Wilderness Experience Programs: Reforming Delinquents or Beating Around the Bush? *Juvenile and Family Court Journal,* Vol. 35 (1984), pp. 35–44; Winterdyk and Roesch, op. cit.

67. Ted Palmer, *The Re-Emergence of Correctional Intervention* (Newbury Park, CA: Sage, 1992); Office of Juvenile Justice and Delinquency Prevention, *Project New Pride: Replication* (Washington: OJJDP, 1979); LaMar T. Empey and Maynard L. Erickson, *The Provo Experiment: Evaluating Community Control of Delinquency* (Lexington, MA: Lexington Books, 1972).

68. Terrence P. Thornberry, Stewart E. Tolnay, Timothy J. Flanagan, and Patty Glynn, *Office of Juvenile Justice and Delinquency Prevention Report on Children in Custody 1987: A Comparison of Public and Private Juvenile Custody Facilities* (Washington: OJJDP, 1991).

69. Eric Peterson, "Juvenile Boot Camps: Lessons Learned," U.S. Department of Justice, Office of Juvenile Justice and Delinquency Prevention, Fact Sheet #36 (Washington: GPO, June 1996).

70. Thornberry et al. (1991), op. cit.

71. Melissa Sickmund, Howard N. Snyder, and Eileen Poe-Yamagata, *Juvenile Offenders and Victims: 1997 Update on Violence,* U.S. Department of Justice, Office of Juvenile Justice and Delinquency Prevention (Washington: GPO, 1997), p. 39.

72. Dale G. Parent, Valerie Leiter, Stephen Kennedy, Lisa Livens, Daniel Wentworth, and Sarah Wilcox, *Conditions of Confinement: Juvenile Detention and Corrections Facilities Research Summary* (Washington: OJJDP, 1994), p. 5.

73. See, for example, Barry Krisberg, "Juvenile Justice: Improving the Quality of Care," *National Council on Crime and Delinquency* (San Francisco: NCCD, 1992); Carol J. Garrett, "Effects of Residential Treatment on Adjudicated Delinquents," *Journal of Research in Crime and Delinquency,* Vol. 22 (1985), pp. 287–308.

74. Percentages calculated from data in Sickmund et al., op. cit., p. 38, unnumbered table.

75. Barry Krisberg, Robert DeComo, and Norma C. Herrera, *National Juvenile Custody Trends 1978–1989* (Washington: OJJDP, 1992), p. 2; Also see Steven Lab and John T. Whitehead, "A Meta-Analysis of Juvenile Correctional Treatment," *Journal of Research in Crime and Delinquency,* Vol. 26 (1989), pp. 276–95.

76. Calculated from data in Robert DeComo, Sandra Tunis, Barry Krisberg, Norma C. Herrera, Sonya Rudenstine, and Dominic Del Rosario, *Juveniles Taken Into Custody: Fiscal Year 1992,* U.S. Department of Justice, Office of Juvenile Justice and Delinquency Prevention (Washington: GPO, 1995); Sickmund et al., op. cit., p. 38.

77. Calculated from data in same sources cited in endnote 81.

78. Sickmund et al., op. cit., pp. 38–39.

79. Ibid., p. 41.

80. Ibid., p. 42.

81. Parent et al., op. cit.

13 Understanding and Predicting the Future of Criminal Justice

CHAPTER OBJECTIVES

After completing this chapter, you should be able to:

1 Point out major differences between Packer's crime control and due process models.

2 Identify the factor that will probably most influence which of Packer's two models dominates criminal justice policy in the United States at any particular time in the future.

3 Describe the possible future of law enforcement if the crime control model dominates, and the possible future if the due process model dominates.

4 Describe the possible future of the administration of justice if the crime control model dominates, and the possible future if the due process model dominates.

5 Identify perhaps the most divisive issue that will confront correctional policy makers in the future.

6 Describe the possible future of corrections.

7 List some of the cost reduction strategies likely to be advocated in corrections in the future.

A Framework for Understanding the Future of Criminal Justice

In the preceding chapters of this book, we have described in detail the nature of crime and its consequences in the United States, theories of crime and delinquency causation, criminal law and its application, and the historical development of criminal and juvenile justice. We have also provided a comprehensive examination of the current operation of criminal and juvenile justice and have discussed problems associated with each. In this last chapter, we will describe the directions that criminal and juvenile justice in the United States might take in the future and will offer some predictions. We have excluded from this chapter predictions about future trends in crime and delinquency. That subject would take us too far afield. However, we do believe that crime and delinquency, in whatever new forms they take, are likely to remain pervasive social problems in the United States for the foreseeable future.

The principal guide that informs our predictions of the future directions of criminal and juvenile justice is Herbert Packer's model of the U.S. criminal justice process.[1] For us, Packer's model has had considerable explanatory power for about 30 years, and we have no reason to believe that its explanatory power will diminish greatly in the future. However, in making our predictions we will not limit ourselves to Packer's vision of possible criminal and juvenile justice futures but will, instead, peer into our own crystal ball—and those of others—and venture some predictions in areas where Packer's model is silent.

In his influential 1968 book entitled *The Limits of the Criminal Sanction*, legal scholar Herbert Packer describes the criminal justice process in the United States as the outcome of competition between two value systems. Those two value systems, which represent two ends of a value continuum, are the basis for two models of the operation of criminal justice—the crime control model and the due process model. Figure 13–1 depicts this continuum. From a political standpoint, the **crime control model** reflects traditional conservative values, while the **due process model** embodies traditional liberal values.[2] Consequently, when politically conservative values are dominant in society, as they are currently, the principles and policies of the crime control

Crime control model One of Packer's two models of the criminal justice process. It reflects traditional politically conservative values. In this model, the control of criminal behavior is the most important function of criminal justice.

Due process model One of Packer's two models of the criminal justice process. It embodies traditional politically liberal values. In this model, the principal goal of criminal justice is at least as much to protect the innocent as it is to convict the guilty.

FIGURE 13–1

Two Models of the Criminal Justice Process

Due Process Model	**Crime Control Model**
Traditional liberal values	Traditional conservative values

464

model seem to dominate the operation of criminal justice. During more politically liberal periods, such as the 1960s and early 1970s, on the other hand, the principles and policies of the due process model seem to dominate criminal justice activity.

The models are ideal types, neither of which corresponds exactly to the actual day-to-day practice of criminal justice. Rather, the two models provide a convenient way to understand and discuss both the current and the future operation of criminal justice in the United States. In practice, the criminal justice process represents a series of conflicts and compromises between the value systems of the two models. In the following sections, we will describe Packer's two models in detail.

The Crime Control Model

In the crime control model, the control of criminal behavior is by far the most important function of criminal justice. Although the means by which crime is controlled are important in this view (illegal means are not advocated), they are less important than the ultimate goal of control. Consequently, the primary focus of this model is on efficiency in the operation of the criminal justice process. Advocates of the crime control model want to make the process more efficient—to move cases through the process as quickly as possible and to bring them to a close. Packer characterizes the crime control model as "assembly-line justice." To achieve "quick closure" in the processing of cases, a premium is placed on speed and finality. Speed requires that cases be handled informally and uniformly; finality depends on minimizing occasions for challenge, that is, appeals.

To appreciate the assembly-line metaphor used by Packer and to understand how treating cases uniformly speeds up the process and makes it more efficient, consider the way that the McDonald's Corporation sells billions of hamburgers. When you order a Big Mac from McDonald's, you know exactly what you are going to get. All Big Macs are the same; they are made uniformly. Moreover, you can get a Big Mac in a matter of seconds most of the time. However, what happens when you order something different, or something not already prepared, such as a hamburger with ketchup only? Your order is taken, and you are asked to stand to the side because your special order will take a few minutes. Your special order has slowed down the assembly line and reduced efficiency. This happens in criminal justice, too! If defendants ask for something special, such as a trial, the assembly line is slowed and efficiency is reduced.

As described in Chapter 7 ("The Administration of Justice"), even when criminal justice is operating at its best, it is a slow process. The time from arrest to final case disposition can typically be measured in weeks or months. If defendants opt for a jury trial, as is their right in most felony cases, the cases are handled formally and are treated as unique; no two cases are the same either in their circumstances or in the way they are handled. If defendants are not satisfied with the outcome of their trials, then they have the right to appeal. Appeals may delay by years the final resolution of cases.

To increase efficiency—meaning speed and finality—crime control advocates prefer plea bargaining. As described in Chapter 7, plea bargaining is an informal process that is used instead of trial. Bargains can be offered and accepted in a relatively short time. Also, cases are handled uniformly because the mechanics of a plea bargain are basically the same; only the substance of the deals differs. Additionally, with successful plea bargains, there is no opportunity for challenge; there are no appeals. Thus, plea bargaining is the perfect mechanism for achieving the primary focus of the crime control model—efficiency.

The key to the operation of the crime control model is "a presumption of guilt." In other words, advocates of this model assume that if the police have expended the time and effort to arrest a suspect and the prosecutor has formally charged the suspect with a crime, then the suspect must be guilty. Why else would police arrest and prosecutors charge? Although the answers to that question are many (see the discussions in Chapters 6 and 7 of the extralegal factors that influence police and prosecutorial behavior), the fact is that a presumption of guilt is accurate most of the time. That is, most people who are arrested and charged with a crime or crimes are, in fact, guilty. A problem—but not a significant one for crime control advocates—is that a presumption of guilt is not accurate all of the time; miscarriages of justice do occur (see the discussion in Chapter 4, "The Rule of Law"). Another problem is that a presumption of guilt goes against one of the oldest and most cherished principles of American criminal justice—that a person is considered innocent until proven guilty.

Reduced to its barest essentials and operating at its highest level of efficiency, the crime control model consists of an administrative fact-finding process with two possible outcomes: a suspect's exoneration or the suspect's guilty plea.

The Due Process Model

Advocates of the due process model, by contrast, reject the informal fact-finding process as definitive of factual guilt. They insist, instead, on formal, adjudicative fact-finding processes in which cases against suspects are heard publicly by impartial trial courts. In the due process model, moreover, the factual guilt of suspects is not determined until the suspects have had a full opportunity to discredit the charges against them. For those reasons, Packer characterizes the due process model as "obstacle-course justice."

Legal guilt results when factual guilt is determined at a fair trial.

What motivates this careful and deliberate approach to the administration of justice is the realization that human beings sometimes make mistakes. The police sometimes arrest the wrong person, and prosecutors sometimes charge the wrong person. Thus, contrary to the crime control model, the demand for finality is low in the due process model, and the goal is at least as much to protect the innocent as it is to convict the guilty. Indeed, for due process model advocates, it is better to let a guilty person go free than it is to wrongly convict and punish an innocent person.

The due process model is based on the doctrine of legal guilt and the presumption of innocence. According to the **doctrine of legal guilt,** people are not to be held guilty of crimes merely on a showing, based on reliable evidence, that in all probability they did in fact do what they are accused of doing. In other words, it is not enough that people are factually guilty in the due process model; they must also be legally guilty. Legal guilt results only when factual guilt is determined in a procedurally regular fashion, as in a criminal trial, and when the procedural rules, or due-process rights, designed to protect suspects and defendants and to safeguard the integrity of the process are employed. Many of the conditions of legal guilt—that is, procedural, or due-process, rights—were described in Chapter 4. They include:

- Freedom from unreasonable searches and seizures.

- Protection against double jeopardy.

- Protection against compelled self-incrimination.

- A speedy and public trial.

- An impartial jury of the state and district where the crime occurred.

- Notice of the nature and cause of the accusation.

- The right to confront opposing witnesses.

- Compulsory process for obtaining favorable witnesses.

- The right to counsel.

- The prohibition of cruel and unusual punishment.

In short, in the due process model, factual guilt is not enough. For people to be found guilty of crimes, they must be found *both* factually and legally guilty.

This obstacle course model of justice is championed by due process advocates because they are skeptical about the ideal of equality on which American criminal justice is supposedly based. They recognize that there can be no equal justice where the kind of trial a person gets, or whether he or she gets a trial at all, depends substantially on how much money that person has. It is assumed that in an adversary system of justice (as described in Chapter 7 and employed in the United States), an effective defense is largely a function of the resources that can be mustered on behalf of the accused. It is also assumed that there are gross inequalities in the financial means of criminal defendants. Most criminal defendants are indigent, and because of their indigence, they are frequently denied an effective defense. Although procedural safeguards, or conditions of legal guilt, cannot by themselves correct the inequity in resources, they do provide indigent defendants, at least theoretically, with a better chance for justice than they would receive without them.

Doctrine of legal guilt The principle that people are not to be held guilty of crimes merely on a showing, based on reliable evidence, that in all probability they did in fact do what they are accused of doing. Legal guilt results only when factual guilt is determined in a procedurally regular fashion, as in a criminal trial, and when the procedural rules designed to protect suspects and defendants and to safeguard the integrity of the process are employed.

Fundamentally, the due process model defends the ideal of personal freedom and its protection. The model rests on the assumption that preventing tyranny by the government and its agents is the most important function of the criminal justice process.

Crime Control vs. Due Process

As noted earlier, which model dominates criminal justice policy in the United States at any particular time depends on the political climate. Currently, we are in the midst of a prolonged period—beginning in the mid-1970s—in which traditional politically conservative values have dominated the practice of criminal and juvenile justice. Thus, it should come as no surprise that the crime control model of criminal justice more closely resembles the actual practice of criminal and juvenile justice in the United States today. At the time Packer wrote and published his book, however, politically liberal values and, thus, the principles and policies of the due process model dominated the operation of criminal and juvenile justice. In any event, neither model is likely to completely control criminal justice. Even though the current operation of criminal and juvenile justice reflects the dominance of the crime control model, elements of the due process model remain evident. How long this trend will continue is anybody's guess. We suspect that the American people will eventually get tired of seeing their tax dollars spent on programs and a process that is not providing them with the safety from criminal behavior that they so desperately desire. However, if Packer's model of criminal justice is correct, a shift in criminal justice practice will come only after a shift in the values held by our political leaders and, of course, the citizens of the United States.

Using Packer's model as a guide, and barring any radical or fundamental changes, we will make our predictions about the future of criminal and juvenile justice in three sections: law enforcement, the administration of justice, and corrections. We will consider future directions in juvenile justice in the section on the administration of justice.

The Future of Law Enforcement

If the future of law enforcement increasingly reflects the principles and policies of the crime control model, then we might expect fewer limitations on how the police attempt to combat crime. For example, the practice of detaining and arresting suspects for investigation without probable cause is likely to increase, as is the length of time a suspect may be held before being charged. The Supreme Court may augment those practices by granting good-faith exceptions to the Fifth Amendment protection against compelled self-incrimination. If the crime control model is fully embraced, it is possible that the Court's decision in *Miranda v. Arizona* could be overturned and that coerced confessions would be admissible at trial.

The investigative abilities of the police should be improved and made easier by the expansion of community policing. Although, currently, the meaning of community policing remains vague (see Chapter 6), it will ultimately be defined by the way it is actually employed. If it is employed according to crime control principles, we should expect greater intrusion into the lives of citizens. Privacy will be sacrificed for efficiency in crime control.

Greater intrusion into people's lives will be facilitated by advances in electronic surveillance. For example, advances in **bionics** (the replacing of human body parts with mechanical parts) may someday produce bionic eyes powerful enough for law enforcement officers to see for miles or through walls, and bionic ears sensitive enough to enable law enforcement officers, from a considerable distance, to clearly hear conversations held behind closed doors.[4] Already, computer-controlled supersensitive listening and video devices are able to accomplish the same things.[5] To the extent that the crime control model is followed, there may be fewer or, perhaps, no limitations on the future uses of electronic surveillance. According to this scenario, George Orwell's vision of a society monitored totally by Big Brother (the state and its agents) may become a reality in the United States, as it did to varying degrees in the totalitarian nations of Eastern Europe, Communist China, and the former Soviet Union. In other words, to facilitate efficient crime control, according to the logic of the crime control model, it is conceivable that every move we make, every word we say and, possibly, every thought we think will be recorded for future incrimination, if the need arises.

Moreover, advanced electronic surveillance devices and other new technologies in law enforcement (to be discussed in more detail later in this chapter) should be available sooner than might normally be expected, because of the end of the Cold War. Billions of tax dollars that would have been spent on military hardware during the Cold War will probably be shifted to defense conversion programs. A primary beneficiary of the new programs will undoubtedly be domestic law enforcement.

On the other hand, if we see a shift to the principles and policies of the due process model, we should expect existing limitations on how the police combat crime to remain intact or even be expanded. Certainly, the practice of detaining and arresting suspects for investigation without probable cause will end or, at least, be decreased substantially. The present 48-hour limitation—with certain exceptions—on the length of time a suspect may be held before being charged will be standard operating procedure. Good-faith exceptions to protections against compelled self-incrimination will not be allowed, and current good-faith exceptions to the exclusionary rule may be eliminated. Adherence to the *Miranda* requirements will become even more routine among police officers than it is currently. Perhaps suspects will no longer be allowed to waive their rights.

Regardless of which of Packer's two models dominates in the future, community policing is likely to become standard practice throughout the country, as police officers become known as *public service officers*.[7] Community policing will at least make citizens feel much safer in their homes and communities (and, perhaps, reduce the likelihood of victimization by predatory criminal behavior) than did previous forms of policing. However, if community policing adheres to principles of the due process model, it will not in any way violate the privacy of citizens unless there is probable cause (strictly defined) to do so. Instead, for citizens and communities that seek help, community policing will help reduce the incidence of criminal victimization and, by doing so, improve the conditions of life—while respecting the privacy of citizens who do not want help.

Bionics The replacing of human body parts with mechanical parts.

FYI

Future technology will enhance crime prevention. It is likely that houses and vehicles will be made "smarter" in an effort to foil criminals. For example, "smart" houses and vehicles will be equipped to deny access and even to take defensive action against unauthorized intruders, by calling police, and releasing knockout gas into the home or vehicle.[6]

As described more fully in Chapter 6, a recent development in criminal investigation is DNA profiling. Although this new technology is still controversial, it will probably become a routine law enforcement tool in the near future. Perhaps the most thorny issue with this new technology is how the DNA database will be collected and used. If the principles of the due process model prevail in the future, then the DNA database will probably comprise DNA samples taken only from booked suspects (and criminal justice personnel upon hiring), as is the current practice with fingerprints. Such a policy is unlikely to be very controversial or to attract much public resistance. On the other hand, if policy reflects the principles of the crime control model, then the DNA database may comprise DNA samples taken shortly after birth from all infants born in the United States. This latter strategy would clearly make the DNA database more complete and, therefore, a more efficient tool in the effort to solve crimes. It would also be much more controversial and would probably be resisted by a large segment of the population.

To the extent that the due process model informs future law enforcement practice, electronic surveillance will not be allowed under any circumstances or will at least be strictly limited to a few types of crimes (for example, crimes that threaten national security, such as treason and espionage).

Advances in law enforcement technology are inevitable, but technology employed according to due process principles will be used to protect citizens and law enforcement personnel. For example, robots will be employed with greater frequency to perform a variety of law enforcement duties. Robots have been used by law enforcement personnel since the mid-1970s for handling bombs, and they are currently being used in other law enforcement situations, usually in SWAT or other dangerous circumstances.[9] In the future, they may be used routinely in hostage situations and in the arrest of dangerous suspects. Some of the ideas currently on drawing boards are:

- A pocket-sized, voice-activated voice-stress analyzer that police officers could use to determine whether suspects or witnesses experienced stress during questioning, indicating possible dishonest answers (used like current polygraph machines).

- An ultrasmall, two-way cellular phone (like a Dick Tracy wrist communicator), possibly implanted in officers' larynxes, that would allow police officers to be in constant contact with headquarters, fellow officers, or anyone around the world.

- A universal translator (that is, an ultrasmall computer) that could instantly translate speech from one language to another, allowing police officers to question suspects, witnesses, or crime victims without the language barrier they frequently confront today.[10]

- A "smart" gun that would electronically disable itself if taken away from a police officer during a struggle.

- A microwave device to shut off a car's ignition, stopping fleeing suspects without risk of a high-speed chase.

Law enforcement agencies use robots to handle bombs and other dangerous assignments.

- A supersticky foam that could be sprayed on armed suspects, neutralizing them by temporarily gluing their arms to their bodies.
- Spikes embedded in retractable panels beneath roads that could be raised by remote control to blow out a getaway car's tires.[11]
- Jet packs that officers could wear on their backs so that they could patrol by air.[12]

The future of law enforcement in the United States is likely to be very different from law enforcement today. New styles of policing, such as community policing, will be embraced and new technologies employed. The form that the change ultimately takes, however, will depend substantially on whether there is a dramatic shift toward the principles and policies of the crime control model or toward the principles and policies of its due process counterpart. In the next section, we will consider possible future developments in the administration of justice.

The Future of the Administration of Justice

If, in the future, the administration of justice in the United States is more in line with the crime control model, then the right to legal counsel (both court-appointed and privately retained) at critical pre- and posttrial stages may be scaled back significantly. Advocates of the crime control model consider legal representation at any stage, other than perhaps at trial, a luxury and an unnecessary impediment to the efficient operation of the process. Advocates of the crime control model argue that prior to trial (for example, during interrogation), providing counsel to a suspect only hampers the ability of police to investigate a case. After trial, during the appellate process, the availability of legal counsel further reduces the speed with which a case can be brought to closure. Crime control model supporters maintain that in both situations, a crafty lawyer may be able to win the freedom of a factually guilty client by means of a legal technicality.

If the principles and policies of the due process model dominate the future of the administration of justice, however, then it is likely that the current right to counsel at a variety of critical stages in the process will be retained and, perhaps, even extended somewhat (for example, to appeals beyond the first one). Advocates of the due process model believe that legal counsel is crucial throughout the process and must be made available immediately after

FIGURE 13-2

Technology and Criminal Justice

With document-imaging systems, attorneys do not have to go to the courthouse to see a document and can file lawsuits and other legal documents electronically.

Criminologists are using emission tomography to peer into the brains of violent offenders and try to determine whether those brains are fundamentally different.

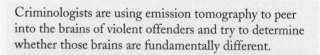

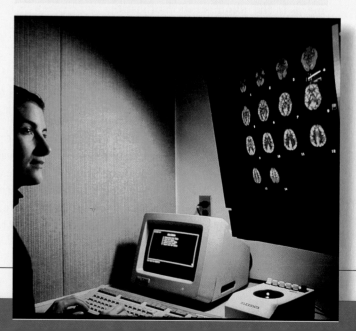

Forensic scientists can map DNA patterns in samples of skin, blood, semen, or other body tissues or fluids. The DNA patterns can then be stored, analyzed, and compared.

arrest. Otherwise, the likelihood that innocent people will be subject to harassment, or worse, by agents of the state (police officers and prosecutors) is increased to an intolerable level.

Along with a greatly reduced role for legal counsel in the administration of justice, crime control model enthusiasts advocate the abolition of the preliminary hearing. They argue that it is a waste of time and money to conduct a preliminary testing of the evidence and the charges imposed, because prosecutors have no reason to pursue cases that are unlikely to lead to conviction. Recall from the discussion in Chapter 7 that prosecutors' reputations and chances of achieving higher political office depend at least partially on the proportion of convictions they are able to obtain. Besides, for several reasons, including the sheer volume of cases that must be handled in the lower

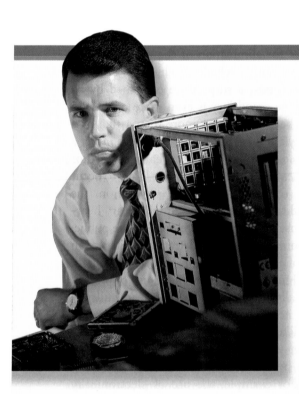

Special telephone units with alcohol sensors in the mouthpiece are being used by probation and parole departments to monitor offenders sentenced to home detention.

Criminal investigators use computer-evidence recovery techniques to uncover evidence from computers that have been used in criminal activities.

Infrared devices allow through-the-wall surveillance of a room in a building.

1. After briefly describing Packer's crime control and due process models to fellow students, family members, or friends, discuss with them whether the crime control model or the due process model ought to dominate criminal justice in the future.

2. There are numerous science fiction movies or videos that depict criminal justice in the future. Examples are *Blue Thunder, Escape From New York, Demolition Man,* and the *RoboCop* series. Watch one or more of those movies or videos, and consider how plausible they seem in light of what you have read in this chapter.

3. **INTERNET** Go to the Justice Technology Information Network (JUSTNET) at **www.nlectc.org**, and click on Law Enforcement, Corrections, or Forensics. Survey the new technologies available or on the drawing board in the area you have chosen. Following the format used in this chapter, write a two- or three-page scenario of how law enforcement, corrections, or forensics will change in the future if and when the new technology is implemented.

1. It is the year 2028, and you have been asked to serve on a citizens' committee charged with providing input about the creation of a new super-maximum-security federal prison. The prison will be built either several hundred feet beneath the ocean's surface off the east coast of the United States or on the moon. The rationale for these locations is to better isolate prisoners from the law-abiding population and to take advantage of prison labor for the high-risk jobs of either marine farming or the mining of new and useful materials in space. The technology and the resources to build the prison, though expensive, are available.

    a. Which location would be preferable? Why?

    b. Should public tax dollars be used to fund the project, or should a private corporation be allowed to build and operate the facility at its own expense and keep any profits from the farming or mining business?

    c. What special problems might arise because of the location of the prison?

2. It is the year 2028 in Washington, D.C., and public service officers, formerly called police officers, are flying routine patrol with the aid of their new jet packs. While flying over a condo near the city center, two of the officers, using their bionic eyes and ears, detect what appear to be a half dozen men plotting to bomb the White House. Surveying the condo from their sky perch, the officers see, stored in a bedroom closet, enough of a new, illegal, and largely undetectable hydrogen-based

explosive to do the job. The officers, using the ultrasmall two-way communication devices implanted in their larynxes, communicate to headquarters what they have seen. They await further orders.

a. Do the officers have probable cause to obtain a search warrant from a magistrate or to make an arrest? If you were a proponent of Packer's crime control model, what would your answer be? If you were a proponent of Packer's due process model, what would your answer be?

b. How might the legal issues of the right to privacy, the admissibility of evidence, the exclusionary rule, and the plain-view doctrine affect the use of this new technology by law enforcement officers?

c. What restraints, if any, should be imposed on the use of this new technology by law enforcement officers? If you were a proponent of Packer's crime control model, what would your answer be? If you were a proponent of Packer's due process model, what would your answer be?

ADDITIONAL READING

Dilulio, John J. Jr., *No Escape: The Future of American Corrections.* New York: Basic Books, 1991.

Klofas, John and Stan Stojkovic (eds.). *Crime and Justice in the Year 2010.* Belmont, CA: Wadsworth, 1995.

Maguire, Brendan and Polly Radosh (eds.). *The Past, Present, and Future of American Criminal Justice.* New York: General Hall, 1995.

Packer, Herbert. *The Limits of the Criminal Sanction.* Stanford, CA: Stanford University Press, 1968.

ENDNOTES

1. Herbert Packer, *The Limits of the Criminal Sanction* (Stanford, CA: Stanford University Press, 1968).
2. See, for example, Walter B. Miller, "Ideology and Criminal Justice Policy: Some Current Issues," *Journal of Criminal Law and Criminology,* Vol. 64 (1973), pp. 141–62.
3. Gene Stephens, "Drugs and Crime in the Twenty-First Century," *The Futurist* (May–June 1992), pp. 19–22.
4. Gene Stephens, "High-Tech Crime: The Threat to Civil Liberties," *The Futurist* (July–August 1990), pp. 20–25.
5. Gene Stephens, "Law Enforcement," in G. T. Kurian and G. T. T. Molitor (eds.), *Encyclopedia of the Future* (New York: Simon & Schuster, Macmillan, 1996), p. 538.
6. "Forensics Revolution Not Far Off," *The Orlando Sentinel* (October 9, 1997), p. A-13.
7. Jack Cheevers, "Beyond 'RoboCop': Concern for Officer Safety Fuels Innovation," *The Charlotte Observer* (August 26, 1994), p. 14A.
8. Robert S. Boyd, "Leaps in Technology Create a Roboboom," *The Charlotte Observer* (October 9, 1994), p. 1A.
9. Stephens (1992), op. cit.
10. Stephens (1996), op. cit., p. 539.
11. Cheevers, op. cit.
12. Stephens (1996), op. cit., p. 539.
13. See Stephens (1990), op. cit.
14. Anita Neuberger Blowers, "The Future of American Courts," in B. Maguire and P. Radosh (eds.), *The Past, Present, and Future of American Criminal Justice* (New York: General Hall, 1995).
15. Ibid.
16. Ibid.
17. Gene Stephens, "Crime and Punishment: Forces Shaping the Future," *The Futurist* (January–February 1987), pp. 18–26.
18. Ibid.
19. Stephens (1987), op. cit., p. 22.
20. Blowers, op. cit.
21. Stephens (1990), op. cit.
22. Ibid.
23. Blowers, op. cit.
24. Malcolm M. Feeley and Jonathan Simon, "The New Penology: Notes on the Emerging Strategy of Corrections and Its Implications," *Criminology,* Vol. 30 (1992), pp. 449–74.
25. Ibid.

26. Francis X. Clines, "A Futuristic Prison Awaits the Hard-Core 400," *The New York Times,* national ed. (October 17, 1994), p. 1A.
27. John J. Dilulio, Jr., *No Escape: The Future of American Corrections* (New York: Basic Books, 1991), pp. 3–4.
28. Ibid., p. 4.
29. Ibid.
30. Ibid.
31. Gene Stephens, "Prisons," in G. T. Kurian and G. T. T. Molitor (eds.), *Encyclopedia of the Future* (New York: Simon & Schuster, Macmillan, 1996), p. 751.
32. Feeley and Simon, op. cit., p. 470.
33. Stephens, "Prisons," op. cit.
34. Jim Mitchell, "Private Prisons Say They Hold Key," *The Dallas Morning News* (September 21, 1997).
35. See Francis T. Cullen and John P. Wright, "The Future of Corrections," in B. Maguire and P. Radosh (eds.), *The Past, Present, and Future of American Criminal Justice* (New York: General Hall, 1995).
36. Stephens (1990), op. cit.
37. Ibid.
38. Stephens, "Prisons," op. cit., p. 751.
39. Stephens (1990), op. cit.
40. Ibid.
41. Cullen and Wright, op. cit.
42. Ibid.

CHAPTER 13   *Understanding and Predicting the Future of Criminal Justice*

Glossary

Numbers in parentheses indicate the chapters in which the terms are defined.

A

Actus reus Criminal conduct—specifically, intentional or criminally negligent (reckless) action or inaction that causes harm. (2)

Adjudication The juvenile court equivalent of a trial in criminal court or the process of rendering a judicial decision regarding the truth of the facts alleged in a petition or charge. (12)

Administrative segregation The keeping of inmates in secure isolation so that they cannot harm others. (9)

Aggravating factors In death sentencing, circumstances that make a crime worse than usual. (8)

Aggressive patrol The practice of having an entire patrol section make numerous traffic stops and field interrogations. (6)

Allocution The practice at a sentencing hearing in which the convicted defendant has the right to address the court before the sentence is imposed. During allocution, a defendant is identified as the person found guilty and has a right to deny or explain information contained in the PSI if his or her sentence is based on it. (8)

Anomie For Durkheim, the dissociation of the individual from the collective conscience. For Merton, the contradiction between the cultural goal of achieving wealth and the social structure's inability to provide legitimate institutional means for achieving the goal. For Cohen, the inability of juveniles to achieve status among peers by socially acceptable means. (3)

Appellate jurisdiction The power of a court to review a case for errors of law. (7)

Apprenticeship system The method by which middle- and upper-class children were taught skilled trades by a master. (12)

Arbitration A dispute resolution process that brings disputants together with a third party (an arbitrator) who has the skills to listen objectively to evidence presented by both sides to a conflict, to ask probing and relevant questions of each side, and to arrive at an equitable solution to the dispute. (13)

Arraignment A pretrial stage; its primary purpose is to hear the formal information or indictment and to allow the defendant to enter a plea. (1) (7)

Arrest The seizure of a person or the taking of a person into custody, either actual physical custody (such as when a suspect is handcuffed by a police officer) or constructive custody (such as when a person peacefully submits to a police officer's control). (1) (4)

Arrest warrant A written order directing law enforcement officers to arrest a person. The charge or charges against a suspect are specified on the warrant. (1) (7)

Atavism A reversion to a savage type. (3)

Auburn system An early system of penology, originating at Auburn Penitentiary in New York, under which inmates worked and ate together in silence during the day and were placed in solitary cells for the evening. (9)

B

Bail/bail bond Usually, a monetary guarantee deposited with the court that is supposed to ensure that the suspect or defendant will appear at a later stage in the criminal justice process. (1) (7)

Banishment A punishment, originating in ancient times, required that offenders leave the community and live elsewhere, commonly in the wilderness. (9)

Bench trial A trial before a judge without a jury. (1) (7)

Bench warrant/capias A document that authorizes a suspect's or defendant's arrest for not appearing in court as required. (7)

Beyond a reasonable doubt The standard of proof necessary to find a defendant guilty in a criminal trial. Reasonable doubt refers to the amount of doubt about a defendant's guilt that a reasonable person might have after carefully examining all the evidence. (4)

Bifurcated trial A two-stage trial used in death penalty cases, consisting of separate "guilty" and "penalty" phases. (8)

Binding-out system Practice in which children who were difficult to handle or who needed supervision were "bound over" to masters for care. However, under the binding-out system, masters were not required to teach the youth a trade. (12)

Biological inferiority According to biological theories, a criminal's physiological makeup, which is assumed to produce certain physical or genetic characteristics that distinguish criminals from noncriminals. (3)

Bionics The replacing of human body parts with mechanical parts. (13)

Booking The administrative recording of an arrest. Typically, the suspect's name, the charge, and perhaps his or her fingerprints or photograph are entered on the police blotter. (1)

C

Chicago School A group of sociologists at the University of Chicago who assumed in their research that delinquent behavior is a product of social disorganization. (3)

Civil law One of two general types of law practiced in the United States (the other is criminal law); a means of resolving conflicts between individuals. It includes personal injury claims (torts), the law of contracts and property, and subjects such as administrative law and the regulation of public utilities. (4)

Class struggle For radical criminologists, the competition among wealthy people and among poor people and between rich people and poor people, which causes crime. (3)

Classical theory A product of the Enlightenment, based on the assumption that people exercise free will and are thus completely responsible for their actions. In classical theory, human behavior, including criminal behavior, is motivated by a hedonistic rationality, in which actors weigh the potential pleasure of an action against the possible pain associated with it. (3)

Classification facility A facility to which newly sentenced offenders are taken so that their security risks and needs can be assessed and they can be assigned to a permanent institution. (9)

Clear and convincing evidence The standard of proof required in some civil cases; and in federal courts, the standard of proof necessary for a defendant to make a successful claim of insanity. (4)

Cocorrectional facilities Usually small, minimum-security institutions that house both men and women with the goal of normalizing the prison environment by integrating the daytime activities of the sexes. (9)

Collective conscience The general sense of morality of the times. (3)

College academies Schools where students pursue a program that integrates an associate degree curriculum in law enforcement or criminal justice with the state's required peace officer training. (6)

Community corrections The subfield of corrections in which offenders are supervised and provided services outside jail or prison. (11)

Community policing A contemporary approach to policing that actively involves the community in a working partnership to control and to reduce crime. (5)

Commutations Reductions in sentences, given by a state's governor. (8) (10)

Complaint A charging document specifying that an offense has been committed by a person or persons named or described; usually used for misdemeanors and ordinance violations. (1) (7)

Confession An admission by a person accused of a crime that he or she committed the offense charged. (4)

Conflict theory A theory that assumes that society is based primarily on conflict between competing interest groups and that criminal law and the justice system are used to control subordinate groups. Crime is caused by relative powerlessness. (3)

Conjugal visits An arrangement whereby inmates are permitted to visit in private with their spouses or significant others to maintain their personal relationship. (9)

Constable The peacekeeper in charge of early English towns, responsible for organizing the watch and maintaining weapons for protection. (5)

Constable-Watch System A system of protection in early England in which citizens, under the direction of a constable, or chief peacekeeper, were required to guard the city and pursue criminals. (5)

Contraband An illegal substance or object. (4)

Contract security Protective services that a private security firm provides to people, agencies, and companies that do not employ their own security personnel or that need extra protection. Contract security employees are not peace officers. (5)

Control theory A view in which people are expected to commit crime and delinquency unless they are prevented from doing so. (3)

Convict code A constellation of values, norms, and roles that regulate the way inmates interact with one another and with prison staff. (10)

Cottage reformatories Correctional facilities for youths, first developed in the late 1800s, that were intended to closely parallel family life and remove children from the negative influences of the urban environment. Children in those facilities lived with surrogate parents, who were responsible for the youths' training and education. (12)

Crime control model One of Packer's two models of the criminal justice process. It reflects traditional politically conservative values. In this model, the control of criminal behavior is the most important function of criminal justice. (13)

Crime index An estimate of crimes committed. (2)

Crime index offenses cleared The number of offenses for which at least one person has been arrested, charged with the commission of the offense, and turned over to the court for prosecution. (2)

Crime rate A measure of the incidence of crime expressed as the number of crimes per unit of population or some other base. (2)

Criminal anthropology The study of "criminal" human beings. (3)

Criminal law One of two general types of law practiced in the United States (the other is civil law); "a formal means of social control [that uses] rules . . . interpreted [and enforced] by the courts . . . to set limits to the conduct of the citizens, to guide the officials, and to define . . . unacceptable behavior." (4)

Criminal sanctions or **punishment** Penalties that are imposed for violating the criminal law. (8)

Criminalization process The way people are defined as criminal. (3)

Criminological theory The explanation of criminal behavior, as well as the behavior of police, attorneys, prosecutors, judges, correctional personnel, victims, and other actors in the criminal justice process, as well as the behavior of criminal offenders. (3)

Crisis intervention A counselor's efforts to address some crisis in an inmate's life and to calm the inmate. (9)

Cryonics A process of human hibernation that involves freezing the body. (13)

Custody level The classification assigned to an inmate to indicate the degree of precaution that needs to be taken when working with that inmate. (9)

D

Dark figure of crime The number of crimes not officially recorded by the police. (2)

Day reporting centers Facilities that are designed for offenders who would otherwise be in prison or in jail and that require offenders to report regularly to confer with staff about supervision and treatment matters. (11)

Defendant A person against whom a legal action is brought, a warrant is issued, or an indictment is found. (1)

Deprivation model A theory that the inmate society arises as a response to the prison environment and the painful conditions of confinement. (10)

Determinate sentence A sentence with a fixed period of incarceration, which eliminates the decision-making responsibility of parole boards. (8)

Deterrence (general) The attempt to prevent people in general from engaging in crime by punishing specific individuals and making examples of them. (8)

Deterrence (special or **specific)** The prevention of individuals from committing crime again by punishing them. (8)

Differential association Sutherland's theory that persons who become criminal do so because of contacts with criminal patterns and isolation from anticriminal patterns. (3)

Directed patrol Patrolling under guidance or orders on how to use patrol time. (6)

Discretion The exercise of individual judgment, instead of formal rules, in making judgments. (6)

Disposition An order of the court specifying what is to be done with a juvenile who has been adjudicated delinquent. A disposition hearing is similar to a sentencing hearing in criminal court. (12)

Diversion Organized, systematic efforts to remove individuals from further processing in criminal justice by placing them in alternative programs; diversion may be pre- or posttrial in nature. (11)

Doctrine of fundamental fairness The rule that makes confessions inadmissible in criminal trials if they were obtained by means of either psychological manipulation or "third-degree" methods—for example, by beating suspects, by subjecting them to unreasonably long periods of questioning, or by using other physical tactics. (4)

Doctrine of legal guilt The principle that people are not to be held guilty of crimes merely on a showing based on reliable evidence, that in all probability, they did in fact do what they are accused of doing. Legal guilt results only when factual guilt is determined in a procedurally regular fashion, as in a criminal trial, and when the procedural rules designed to protect suspects and defendants and to safeguard the integrity of the process are employed. (13)

Double jeopardy The trying of a defendant a second time for the same offense when jeopardy attached in the first trial, and a mistrial was declared. (4)

Dual court system The court structure in the United States, consisting of one system of state and local courts and another system of federal courts. (7)

Due process model One of Packer's two models of the criminal justice process. It embodies traditional politically liberal values. In this model, the principal goal of criminal justice is at least as much to protect the innocent as it is to convict the guilty. (13)

Due process of law The rights of people suspected of or charged with crimes. (4) The procedures followed by courts to ensure that a defendant's constitutional rights are not violated. (7)

Duress Force or coercion as an excuse for committing a crime. (2)

E

Eight index crimes The part I offenses in the FBI's uniform crime reports. They are (1) murder and non-negligent manslaughter, (2) forcible rape, (3) robbery, (4) aggravated assault, (5) burglary, (6) larceny-theft, (7) motor vehicle theft, and (8) arson, which was added in 1979. (2)

Electronic monitoring An arrangement that allows an offender's whereabouts to be gauged through the use of computer technology. (11)

Entrapment A legal defense against criminal responsibility when a law enforcement officer, or his or her agent, has induced to commit a crime someone who was not already predisposed to committing it. (2)

Excessive force A measure of coercion beyond that necessary to control participants in a conflict. (6)

Exclusionary rule The rule that illegally seized evidence must be excluded from trials in federal courts. (4)

Ex post facto **law** A law that (1) declares an act criminal that was not illegal when it was committed, (2) increases the punishment for a crime after it is committed, or (3) alters the rules of evidence in a particular case after the crime is committed. (2)

Extinction A process in which behavior that previously was postively reinforced is no longer reinforced. (3)

F

Felony A relatively serious offense punishable by death or by confinement in a state or federal prison for more than one year. (1)

Feminist theory A perspective on criminality that focuses on women's experiences and seeks to abolish men's control over women' labor and sexuality. (3)

Field interrogation A temporary detention in which officers stop and question pedestrians and motorists they find in suspicious circumstances. (6)

Flat-time sentencing Sentencing in which judges may choose between probation and imprisonment but have little discretion in setting the length of a prison sentence. Once an offender is imprisoned, there is no possibility of a reduction in the length of the sentence. (8)

Frisking Conducting a search for weapons by lightly patting the outside of a suspect's clothing, feeling for hard objects that might be weapons. (4)

Full enforcement A practice in which the police make an arrest for every violation of law that comes to their attention. (6)

G

General deterrence The prevention of people in general or society at large from engaging in crime by punishing specific individuals and making examples of them. (3) (7) (8)

General jurisdiction The power of a court to hear any type of a case. (7)

Good time Time subtracted from a sentence by prison authorities for good behavior or for other reasons. (8) (10)

Grand jury A group of 12 to 23 citizens who, for a specific period of time, meet in closed sessions to, among other responsibilities, investigate charges coming from preliminary hearings. The grand jury's primary purpose is to determine whether there is probable cause to believe that the accused committed the crime or crimes charged by the prosecutor. (1) (7)

Grand jury indictment A written accusation by a grand jury that one or more persons have committed a crime. (1) (7)

"Grass eaters" Officers who occasionally engage in illegal and unethical activities (accepting small favors, gifts, or money for ignoring violations of the law) during the course of their duties. (6)

H

Habeas corpus A court order mandating that an incarcerated person be brought to court so that his or her claims may be heard. (7) (10)

Halfway houses Community-based residential facilities that are less secure and restrictive than prison or jail but provide a more controlled environment than other community correctional programs. (11)

Hands-off philosophy A philosophy under which courts are reluctant to hear prisoners' claims regarding their rights while incarcerated. (10)

Harm The external consequence required to make an action or inaction a crime. (2)

Hearing officer A lawyer, empowered by the juvenile court to hear juvenile cases. (12)

Hedonistic rationality The weighing of the potential pleasure of an action against the possible pain associated with it. (3)

Highway patrol model A model of state law enforcement services in which officers focus on highway traffic safety, enforcment of the state's traffic laws, and investigation of accidents on the state's roads and highways as well as crimes committed on state property. (5)

Home confinement A program that requires offenders to remain in their homes except for approved periods of absence; commonly used in combination with electronic monitoring. (11)

House of refuge The first specialized correctional institutions for youths in the United States. (12)

Hue and cry In medieval England, a process whereby citizens noting trouble in the community were obligated to call for help, and others were required to come to their assistance. (5)

Hundred A group of one hundred families in medieval England that had the responsiblity of keeping the peace and trying certain minor offenses. (5)

Hung jury The result when jurors cannot agree on a verdict. The judge declares a mistrial. The prosecutor must decide whether to retry the case. (7)

I

Illegitimate opportunity structure For Cloward and Ohlin, a structure that determines the type of delinquent adaptation available to juveniles. They identified three delinquent subcultures: the criminal, the violent, and the retreatist. (3)

Imitation or **modeling** A means by which a person can learn new responses by observing others without performing any overt act or receiving direct reinforcement or reward. (3)

Importation model A theory that the inmate society is shaped by the attributes inmates bring with them when they enter prison. (10)

Incapacitation The removal or restriction of the freedom of those found to have violated criminal laws. (7) (8)

Incarceration rate A figure derived by dividing the number of people incarcerated by the population of the area and multiplying the result by 100,000; used to compare incarceration levels of units with different population sizes. (9)

Indeterminate sentence A sentence with a fixed minimum and maximum term of incarceration, rather than a set period. (8)

Indictment A document that outlines the charge or charges against a defendant. (7)

Informal juvenile justice The actions taken by citizens to respond to juvenile offenders without involving the official agencies of juvenile justice. (12)

Information A document that outlines the formal charge or charges, the law or laws that have been violated, and the evidence to support the charge or charges. Used instead of a grand jury indictment. (1) (7)

Initial appearance A pretrial stage where defendants are brought before a lower-court judge to be given formal notice of the charge or charges against them and advised of their constitutional rights. In the case of a misdemeanor or an ordinance violation, a summary trial may be held. In the case of a felony, a hearing is held to determine whether there is probable cause to hold the defendant for a preliminary hearing. (1)

Insanity Mental or psychological impairment or retardation. A legal excuse or defense against a criminal charge. (2)

Institution of social control An organization that tries to persuade people, through subtle and not-so-subtle means, to abide by the dominant values of society. (1)

Intake screening The process by which decisions are made about the continued processing of juvenile cases. Decisions might include dismissing the case, referring the youth to a diversion program, or filing a petition. (12)

Intensive-supervision probation and parole (ISP) An alternative to incarceration that provides stricter conditions, closer supervision, and more treatment services than traditional probation and parole. (11)

Intermediate sanctions Sanctions that, in their restrictiveness and punitiveness, lie between traditional probation and traditional imprisonment or, alternatively, between imprisonment and traditional parole. (11)

Internal affairs investigations units The police unit that ferrets out illegal and unethical activity engaged in by the police. (6)

Interrogation The direct questioning of a criminal suspect, or the use of other methods, such as staging a lineup, minimizing the moral seriousness of the crime, or casting the blame on the victim or society to obtain incriminating information. (6)

J

Jail A facility, usually operated at the local level, that holds convicted offenders and unconvicted persons for relatively short periods. (9)

Jailhouse lawyer An inmate skilled in legal matters. (10)

Jurisdiction The right or authority of a justice agency to act in regard to a particular subject matter, territory, or persons; a politically defined geographical area; the authority of a court to hear and decide cases. (1) (5) (7)

Just deserts The punishment rationale based on the idea that offenders should be punished automatically, simply because they have committed a crime—they "deserve" it—and the idea that the punishment should fit the crime. (8)

Juvenile delinquency A special category of offense created for young offenders, usually those between 7 and 18 years of age. (2) (12)

K

Kansas City Police Patrol Experiment An experiment in 1972 that studied whether a group of patrol districts had less crime as a result of the number of officers on preventive patrol. (6)

L

Labeling theory A theory that emphasizes the criminalization process as the cause of some crime. (3)

Law Enforcement Education Program (LEEP) A program that provided federal funds in the 1970s to criminal justice personnel for college tuition. (5)

Learning theory A theory that explains criminal behavior and its prevention with the concepts of positive reinforcement, extinction, punishment, and modeling or imitation. (3)

Left realists A group of social scientists who argue that critical criminologists need to redirect their attention to the fear and the very real victimization experienced by working-class people. (3)

Legal definition of crime According to a typical legal definition, crime is an intentional violation of the criminal law or penal code, committed without defense or excuse and penalized by the state. (2)

Legality The requirement (1) that a harm must be legally forbidden for the behavior to be a crime and (2) that the law must not be retroactive. (2)

Legislative transfer (or **waiver)** Statutory process that requires that juveniles who meet specific age and offense criteria be waived to criminal court for trial. (12)

Less-eligibility principle The position that prisoners should receive no service or program superior to the services and programs available to free citizens without charge. (9)

Libel The writing of something false about another individual that dishonors or injures that person. (2)

Limbic system A structure surrounding the brain stem that, in part, controls the life functions of heartbeat, breathing, and sleep. It also is believed to moderate expressions of violence and other emotions such as anger, rage, fear, and sexual responses. (3)

Lockup A very short-term holding facility, that is frequently located in or very near an urban police agency so that suspects can be held pending further inquiry. (9)

M

Mala in se Wrong in themselves. A description applied to crimes that are characterized by universality and timelessness. (2)

Mala prohibita Offenses that are illegal because laws define them as such. They lack universality and timelessness. (2)

Mandatory release A method of prison release under which an inmate is released after serving a legally required portion of his or her sentence, minus good-time credits. (10)

Mandatory sentencing Sentencing in which a specified number of years of imprisonment (usually within a range) provided for particular crimes. Mandatory sentencing generally allows credit for good time but does not allow release on parole. (8)

"Meat eaters" Police officers who actively seek ways to make money illegally while on duty. (6)

Mediation A dispute resolution process that brings disputants together with a third party (a mediator) who is trained in the art of helping people resolve disputes to everyone's satisfaction. The agreed-upon resolution is then formalized into a binding consent agreement. (13)

Medical model A theory of institutional corrections, popular during the 1940s and 1950s, in which crime was seen as symptomatic of personal illness in need of treatment. (9)

Mens rea Criminal intent, a guilty state of mind. (2)

Mere supicion A standard of proof with the least certainty; a "gut feeling." With mere suspicion, law enforcement officers cannot legally even stop a suspect. (4)

Merit system A system of employment whereby an independent civil service commission in cooperation with the city personnel section and the police department, sets employment qualifications, performance standards, and discipline procedures. (6)

Milieu therapy A variant of group therapy that encompasses the total living environment so that the environment continually encourages positive behavioral changes. (9)

Misdemeanor Any less serious crime generally punishable by a fine or by incarceration for not more than one year. (1)

Mitigating factors In death sentencing, circumstances that make a crime less severe than usual. (8)

Myths Beliefs based on emotion rather than analysis. (1)

N

National Crime Information Center (NCIC) A national computer network that provides information storage and retrieval for law enforcement purposes. (5)

National crime victimization surveys A source of crime statistics based on interviews, in which respondents are asked whether they have been victims of any of the FBI's index offenses (except murder and nonnegligent manslaughter and arson) or other crimes during the past six months. If they have, they are asked to provide information about the experience. (2)

Necessity defense A legal defense against criminal responsibility that is used when a crime has been committed to prevent a greater or more serious crime. (2)

Need hierarchy In Maslow's theory, the source of human motivation, consisting of five basic levels of needs: physiological safety, belongingness and love, esteem, and self-actualization. (3)

Negative reinforcement The removal or reduction of a stimulus whose removal or reduction increases or maintains a response. (3)

Negligence The failure to take reasonable precautions to prevent harm. (2)

Neoclassical theory A modification of classical theory in which it was conceded that certain factors (such as insanity) might inhibit the exercise of free will. (3)

Net-widening A phenomenon that occurs when the offenders placed in a novel program are not the offenders for whom the program was designed. The consequence is that those in the program receive more severe sanctions than they would have received had the new program remained unavailable. (11)

New-generation jail A replacement for traditional jails that features architectural and programming innovations. (9)

Nolle prosequi (nol. pros.) The notation placed on the official record of a case when prosecutors elect not to prosecute. (7)

Nolo contendere Latin for "no contest." When defendatns plead "nolo," they do not admit guilt but are willing to accept punishment anyway. (7)

Nonenforcement The failure to reoutinely enforce prohibitions against certain behaviors. (2)

Norm Any standard or rule regarding what human beings should or should not think, say, or do under given circumstances. (2)

O

Offenses known to the police A crime index reported in the FBI's uniform crime reports, composed of crimes that are both reported to and recorded by the police. (2)

Operational styles The different overall approaches to the police job. (6)

Ordinance violation Usually, the violation of a law of a city or town. (1)

Original jurisdiction The authority of a court to hear a case when it is first brought to court. (7)

Overcriminalization The prohibition by the criminal law of some behaviors that arguably should not be prohibited. (2)

P

Panopticon A prison design consisting of a round building with tiers of cells lining the inner circumference and facing a central inspection tower. (9)

Pardon A "forgiveness" for the crime committed that stops further criminal processing. (8)

Parens patriae The legal philosophy justifying state intervention in the lives of children when their parents are unable or unwilling to protect them. (12)

Parole The conditional release of prisoners at the discretion of a board or other authority before they have served their full sentences. (1) (10) Also can refer to the community supervision received upon release. (11)

Parole guidelines Structured instruments used to estimate the probability of parole recidivism and to direct the release decisions of parole boards. (11)

Patriarchy Men's control over women's labor and sexuality. (3)

Peacemaking criminology An approach that suggests that the solution to all social problems, including crime, is the transformation of human beings, mutual dependence, reduction of class structures, the creation of communities of caring people, and universal social justice. (3)

Peel's Principles of Policing A dozen standards proposed by Robert Peel, the author of the legislation resulting in the formation of the London Metropolitan Police Department. The standards are still applicable to today's law enforcement. (5)

Penal code The criminal law of a political jurisdiction. (4)

Penal sanction An ideal characteristic of criminal law: the principle that violators will be punished or at least threatened with punishment by the state. (4)

Pennsylvania system An early system of U.S. penology in which inmates were kept in solitary cells so that they could study religious writings, reflect on their misdeeds, and perform handicraft work. (9)

Penology The study of prison management. (9)

Percent cleared by arrest Same as crime index offenses cleared. (2)

Personal jurisdiction A court's authority over the parties to a lawsuit. (7)

Petition A legal form of the police complaint that specifies the charges to be heard at the adjudication. (12)

Phrenology The estimation of character and intelligence based on an examination of the shape of the skull. (3)

Physiognomy The practice of judging character from facial features. (3)

Placing out The practice of placing children on farms in the Midwest and West to remove them from the supposedly corrupting influences of their parents and the cities. (12)

Plea bargaining/negotiating The practice whereby the prosecutor, the defense attorney, the defendant, and, in many jurisdictions, the judge agree on a specific sentence to be imposed if the accused pleads guilty to an agreed-upon charge or charges instead of going to trial. (1) (7)

Police boards and commissions Legislatively mandated bodies formed in the nineteenth century to govern the police in an attempt to minimize the influence of local corruption and meddling politicians. (6)

Police cadet program A program that combines a college education with agency work experience and academy training. Upon graduation, a cadet is promoted to police officer. (6)

Politicality An ideal characteristic of criminal law, referring to its legitimate source. Only violations of rules made by the state, the political jurisdiction that enacted the laws, are crimes. (4)

Positive reinforcement The presentation of a stimulus that increases or maintains a response. (3)

Posses Groups of able-bodied citizens of a community called into service by a sheriff or constable to chase and apprehend offenders. (5)

POST commissions Peace officer standards and training commissions, state law enforcement commissions that set personnel, education, and training standards for a variety of police and sheriffs' personnel. (6)

Power The force or capacity to gain compliance; the production of intended results; getting what you want; the lack of identifiable routine or detail in one's job. (6)

Power differentials The ability of some groups to dominate other groups in a society. (3)

Precedent A case that forms a potential basis for deciding the outcomes of similar cases in the future; a by-product of decisions made by trial and appellate court judges, who produce case law whenever they render a decision in a particular case. (4)

Preliminary hearing Pretrial stage used in about one-half of all states and only in felony cases. Its purpose is for a judge to determine whether there is probable cause to support the charge or charges imposed by the prosecutor. (1)

Preponderance of evidence Evidence that outweighs the opposing evidence, or sufficient evidence to overcome doubt or speculation. It is the standard of proof necessary to find a defendant liable in a civil lawsuit; the standard used in determining a good-faith exception to the exclusionary rule; and the standard of proof necessary for the state in criminal proceedings to show that the right to counsel has been waived "knowingly and intelligently." (4)

Presentence investigation (PSI) An investigation conducted by a probation agency or other designated authority at the request of a court into the past behavior, family circumstances, and personality of an adult who has been convicted of a crime, to assist the court in determining the most appropriate sentence. (11)

Presentence investigation reports Reports, often called PSIs or PSIRs, that are used in the federal system and the majority of states to help judges determine appropriate sentences. They also are used in classifying probationers, parolees, and prisoners according to their treatment needs and security risk. (8)

Presumptive sentencing Sentencing that allows a judge to retain some sentencing discretion, subject to appellate review. The legislature determines a sentence range for each crime. The judge is expected to impose the normal sentence specified by statute, unless mitigating or aggravating circumstances justify a sentence below or above the range set by the legislature. (8)

Preventive detention Holding suspects or defendants in jail without giving them an opportunity to post bail, because of the threat they pose to society. (7)

Preventive patrol Patrolling the streets with little direction; between responses to radio calls, officers are "systematically unsystematic" and observant in an attempt to both prevent and ferret out crime. Also known as *random patrol.* (6)

Prisonization The process by which an inmate becomes socialized into the customs and principles of the inmate society. (10)

Privatization The involvement of the private sector in the construction and the operation of confinement facilities. (9)

Probable cause An abstract term that basically means that a law enforcement officer or a judge has trustworthy evidence that, more likely than not, the proposed action (such as an arrest) is justified. Amount of proof necessary for a reasonably intelligent person to susptect that a crime has been committed or that items connected with criminal activity can be located in a particular place. Standard of proof necessary to conduct a search or to make an arrest. (1) (4) (7)

Probation A sentence in which the offender, rather than being incarcerated, is retained in the community under the supervision of a probation agency and required to abide by certain rules and conditions to avoid incarceration. (11)

Probation conditions Rules that specify what an offender is and is not to do during the course of a probation sentence. (11)

Problem-oriented policing Procedure that requires officers, in conjunction with community leaders, to identify problems in the neighborhood, to list possible solutions—even those that go far beyond the resources of the police department—and then to put the best solution into practice to resolve the problem or condition. (6)

Procedural law The body of law that governs the ways in which the substantive laws are to be administered, somtimes called *adjective* or *remedial* law. (4)

Proportionality review In some states, a review in which the appellate court compares the sentence in the case it is reviewing with penalties imposed in similar cases in the state. The object is to reduce, as much as possible, disparity in death penalty sentencing. (8)

Proprietary security In-house protective services that a security staff, not classified as sworn peace officers, provide for the entity that employs them. (5)

Prosecutorial transfer (or **waiver)** Statutory process that allows the prosecuting attorney to file juvenile cases in criminal court when youths meet certain age and offense criteria. (12)

Protective custody The segregation of inmates for their own safety. (9)

Psychopaths, sociopaths, or **antisocial personalities** Persons characterized by no sense of guilt, no subjective conscience, and no sense of right and wrong. They have difficulty in forming relationships with other people; they cannot empathize with other people. (3)

Public safety officers Police department employees who perform many police services but do not have arrest powers. (6)

Punishment In learning theory, the presentation of an aversive stimulus to reduce a response. (3) The imposition of a penalty for criminal wrongdoing. (7) A penal sanction used to prevent undesired conduct and to provide retribution ("an eye for an eye") for perceived wrongdoing. (8)

R

Radical nonintervention A practice based on the idea that youths should be left alone if at all possible, instead of being formally processed. (12)

Radical theories Theories of crime causation generally based on Marxist theory. (3)

Reasonable suspicion A standard of proof that is more than just a "gut feeling." It includes the ability to articulate reasons for the suspicion. With reasonable suspicion, a law enforcement officer is legally permitted to stop and frisk a suspect. (4)

Recidivism The return of probationers to illegal activity after release from incarceration. (10) (11)

Reform, industrial, or **training schools** Correctional facilities for youths, first developed in the late 1800s, that focused on custody. Today, those institutions are often called *training schools* and, although they may place more emphasis on treatement, they still rely on custody and control. (12)

Regularity An ideal characteristic of criminal law: the applicability of the law to all persons, regardless of social status. (4)

Regulation A penal sanction used to control future conduct for the best interests of the entire community. (8)

Rehabilitation The attempt to "correct" the personality and behavior of criminal offenders through educational, vocational, or therapeutic treatment and to return them to society as law-abiding citizens. (7) (8)

Reintegration The process of rebuilding former ties to the community and establishing new ties after release from prison. (11)

Relative powerlessness In conflict theory, the inability to dominate other groups in society. *See* power differentials. (3)

Release on own recognizance (ROR) A suspect's written promise to appear in court. (7)

Restitution Money paid or services provided by a convicted offender to victims, their survivors, or to the community to make up for the injury inflicted. (8) (11)

Retribution A dominant justification for punishment. (8) See *revenge* and *just deserts.*

Revenge The punishment rationale expressed by the Biblical phrase "An eye for an eye, a tooth for a tooth." People who seek revenge want to pay offenders back by making them suffer for what they have done. (8)

Revocation The repeal of a probation sentence or parole, and substitution of a more restrictive sentence, because of violation of probation or parole conditions. (11)

Reward In learning theory, a stimulus that increases or maintains a response. (3)

Role The rights and responsibilities associated with a particular position in society. (6)

Role conflict The psychological stress and frustration that results from trying to perform seemingly incompatible duties such as being a helping agent in the community and also having to control behavior through arresting law violators. (6)

Role expectation The behavior and actions that people expect from a person in a particular role. (6)

Rules of discovery Rules that mandate that a prosecutor provide defense counsel with any exculpatory evidence (evidence favorable to the accused that has an effect on guilt or punishment) in the prosecutor's possession. (7)

S

Searches Explorations or inspections by law enforcement officers of homes, premises, vehicles, or persons, for the purpose of discovering evidence of crimes or persons who are accused of crimes. (4)

Secondary deviance The commission of crime subsequent to the first criminal act, with the acceptance of a criminal label. (3)

Security level A designation applied to a facility to describe the measures taken, both inside and outside, to preserve security and custody. (9)

Seizures The taking of persons or property into custody in response to violations of the criminal law. (4)

Selective enforcement The practice of relying on the judgment of the police leadership and rank-and-file officers to decide which laws to enforce. (6)

Self-incrimination Being a witness against oneself. If forced, it is a violation of the Fifth Amendment. (4)

Self-report crime surveys Surveys in which subjects are asked whether they have committed crimes. (2)

Sentencing guidelines Guidelines that provide ranges of sentences for most offenses, based on the seriousness of the crime and the criminal history of the offender. (8)

Shire A territorial area in medieval England, approximately the size of a contemporary American country, that was composed of several hundreds and was governed by a sheriff in the employ of the English crown. (5)

Shire reeve In medieval England, the chief law enforcement officer in a territorial area called a *shire;* later called the *sheriff.* (5)

Shock incarceration The placement of offenders in facilities patterned after military boot camps. (9)

Slander The spoken equivalent of libel. (2)

Slave codes Laws enacted in the South to protect the slaveholders' rights of property in human beings. (5)

Slave patrols The earliest form of policing in the South. They were a product of the slave codes. (5)

Snitch system A system in which staff learn from inmate informants about the presence of contraband, the potential for disruptions, and other threats to security. (9)

Social contract An imaginary agreement entered into by persons who have sacrificed the minimum amount of their liberty necessary to prevent anarchy and chaos. (3)

Social disorganization The condition in which the usual controls over delinquents are largely absent, delinquent behavior is often approved of by parents and neighbors, there are many opportunities for delinquent behavior, and there is little encouragement, training, or opportunity for legitimate employment. (3)

Special deterrence The prevention of individuals from commiting crime again by punishing them. (3) (8)

Special jurisdiction The power of a court to hear only certain kinds of cases. (7)

Specificity An ideal characteristic of criminal law, referring to its scope. Although civil law may be general in scope, criminal law should provide strict definitions of specific acts. (4)

Stare decisis The principle of using precedents to guide future decisions in court cases; Latin for "to stand by decided cases." (4)

State police model A model of state law enforcement services in which the agency and its officers have the same law enforcement powers as local police, anywhere within the state. (5)

Status offense An act that is illegal for a juvenile but would not be a crime if committed by an adult (for example, truency or running away from home). (2) (12)

Statute of Winchester The codified law mandating service on the watch, response to the hue and cry, and maintenance of weapons to answer the call to arms for community protection. (5)

Stigmatized Negatively labeled. (3)

Strain *See* anomie (for Merton and Cohen).

Structured fines, or day fines Fines that are based on defendants' ability to pay. (11)

Subject matter jurisdiction The power of a court to hear a particular type of case. (7)

Subpoena A written order issued by a court that requires a person to appear at a certain time and place. It can also require that documents and objects be made available for examination by the court. (4) (7)

Sub-rosa economy The secret exchange of goods and services that, though often illicit, are in high demand among inmates; the black market of the prison. (10)

Substantive law The body of law that defines criminal offenses and their penalties. (4)

Summary trial An immediate trial without a jury. (1) (7)

Suppression hearing Procedure in which defense attorneys claim that incriminating evidence was obtained through an illegal search and seizure, a confession was obtained without the required warnings, an identification was made as a result of an invalid police lineup, or that evidence was in some other way illegally obtained, thus violating the Fourth Amendment. (8)

System A smoothly operating set of arrangements and institutions directed toward the achievement of common goals. (1)

T

Tech Prep (technical preparation) A program in which area community colleges and high schools team up to offer 6 to 9 hours of college law enforcement courses in the eleventh and twelfth grades, as well as one or two training certifications, such as police dispatcher or local corrections officer. Students who graduate are eligible for police employment at age 18. (6)

Technical violations Failure to abide by the technical rules or conditions of probation or parole (for example, not reporting regularly to the probation officer), as distinct from commission of a new criminal act. (11)

Temporary-release programs Programs that allow jail or prison inmates to leave their facility for short periods of time to participate in approved community activities. (11)

Theory An explaination that tells why or how things are related to each other. (3)

Three "I's" of police selection Three qualities of the American police officer that seem to be of paramount importance: intellignece, integrity, and interaction skills. (6)

Tithing system A private self-help protection system in early medieval England in which a group of ten families, or a *tithing,* agreed to follow the law, keep the peace in their areas, and bring law violators to justice. (5)

Tort A violation of the civil law. (4)

Total institution An institutional setting in which persons sharing some characteristic are cut off from the wider society and expected to live according to institutional rules and procedures. (10)

Traffic accident investigation crews In some agencies, special units assigned to all traffic accident investigations. (6)

Training schools *See* reform schools.

Transfer *See* waiver.

Transportation A punishment in which offenders were transported from their home nation to one of that nation's colonies to work. (9)

Treatment or rehabilitation A penal sanction that focuses on the criminal offender with the goal of changing the offender's behavior and, perhaps, his or her personality. (8)

Trial *de novo* A trial in which an entire case is reheard by a trial court of general jurisdiction because there is an appeal and there is no written transcript of the earlier proceeding. (7)

U

Undercriminalization The failure to prohibit some behaviors that arguably should be prohibited. (2)

Uniform crime reports A collection of crime statistics and other law enforcement information gathered under a voluntary national program administered by the FBI. (2)

Uniformity An ideal characteristic of criminal law: the enforcement of the laws against anyone who violates them regardless of social status. (4)

Unsecured bond Bail is set but no money is paid to the court. (7)

Utility In classical criminological thought, the principle that a policy should provide "the greatest happiness shared by the greatest number." (3)

V

Venire The pool from which jurors are selected. (7)

Venue The place of the trial. It must be geographically appropriate. (4)

Victim-impact statements Descriptions of the harm and suffering that a crime has caused victims and their survivors. (8)

Voir dire The process in which potential jurors who might be biased or unable to render a fair verdict are screened out. (7)

W

Waiver or **transfer** The act or process by which juveniles who meet specific age, offense, and (in some jurisdictions) prior-record criteria are transferred to criminal court for trial. (12)

Warrant A written order from a court directing law enforcement officers to conduct a search or to arrest a person. (4)

Workhouses European forerunners of the modern U.S. prison, where offenders were sent to learn discipline and regular work habits. (9)

Writ of *certiorari* A written order, from the U.S. Supreme Court to a lower court whose decision is being appealed, to send the records of the case forward for review. (7)

Writ of *habeas corpus* An order from a court to an officer of the law to produce a prisoner in court to determine if the prisoner is being legally detained or imprisoned. Post conviction remedies are collectively referred to as *habeas corpus* relief. (7)

Case Index

Subject Index

A

ABA. *See* American Bar Association (ABA)

Absolute certainty, as standard of proof, 123, 124

Accusation, right to be informed of nature and cause of, 130

actus reus, as element of crime, 27–28

Adjective law. *See* Procedural law

Adjudication, 432, 443–444

Adjustment, of prison inmates, 354–355
  life after prison and, 368–369, 399–400

Administrative agency decisions, as source of criminal law, 113, 114

Administrative Office of the Courts, 380, 392

Administrative screening, for halfway houses, 409

Administrative segregation, 335

Adoption studies, 73–74

Affidavit, 118

Affidavit of errors, 283

Affirmative action, police selection process and, 203–204

AFIS (Automated Fingerprint Identification System), 195

African Americans. *See* Race/ethnicity

Aftercare programs, for juvenile offenders, 450

Age. *See also* Elderly *entries;* Juvenile *entries*
  as defense against *mens rea,* 29
  legal responsibility and, 28–29

Aggravating factors, in capital cases, 293–295

Aggressive patrol, 191

AIDS (acquired immunodeficiency syndrome), in prison populations, 338

Akers, Ronald L., 86–87

Albanese, Jay S., 389

Allen, Linda, 361

Allocution, 282

Alternative dispute resolution, 477–478

American Bar Association (ABA)
  death penalty and, 295
  Standards Relating to Urban Police Function, 156

American Law Institute Model Penal Code
  on deadly force, 213
  substantial-capacity test of, 30

Anglo-Saxon law, 110–111

Anomie, 81, 83

Anomie theory, 67, 83–85

Antidrug efforts, costs of, 49

Antisocial personalities, 77

Appeals, 282–283
  automatic, in death penalty cases, 295–297
  future of, 475–476

Appellate courts
  federal
    U.S. circuit courts of appeal, 226–227
    U.S. Supreme Court. *See* U.S. Supreme Court
  state
    death penalty review function of, 295–296
    intermediate appellate courts, 231–232
    judge selection for, 243
    of last resort, 232

Appellate jurisdiction, 224

Application forms, for police officer applicants, 206

Apprenticeship system, 424

Arbitration, 477

Architecture
  jail, new-generation, 334
  prison, 310–311, 330–331

Arraignment, 11, 251–252
  standing mute at, 251

Arrests, 6, 117–118
  searches incident to, 119–121
  warrantless, 121–122, 246
  with warrants, 119

Arrest warrants, 7, 117, 119, 120, 246

Assistant district attorneys, 237

Asylums (Goffman), 350

Atavism, 72

Attica riot, 352

Attorneys. *See* Counsel; Lawyers; Legal profession; Prosecutors

Auburn plan, 328

Auburn system, 311

Augustus, John, 380, 426

Automated Fingerprint Identification System (AFIS), 195

Aversive stimuli, 87

Avoiders, police officers as, 189

B

Babylonian civilization, laws of, 109–110

Background investigations, of police officer applicants, 207

Bail (bail bond), 7, 246–249
  excessive, 249
    protection against, 133
  future of, 474–475
  setting amount of, 247
    recommendations for, 236

Bail bonds people, 247–248

Bailey, F. Lee, 239

Baldwin, Lola, 162

Bandura, Albert, 86

Banishment, 309

Barfield, Velma, 283

Barrett, Jackie, 167

Beccaria, Cesare, 65–68, 278–279, 310

Bedau, Hugh, 136

Behavior modification, 86

Bench trial, 11, 255

Bench warrants, 248

Bennett, Lawrence, 402

Bentham, Jeremy, 310–311

Beyond a reasonable doubt proof, 123, 124

Bible, idea of judges in, 242

Bifurcated trials, 293

Big-house prisons, 313

Bill of Rights, 114, 115
  Eighth Amendment and. *See* Eighth Amendment
  Fifth Amendment and. *See* Fifth Amendment
  Fourteenth Amendment and, 115–117
  Fourth Amendment and. *See* Fourth Amendment
  Sixth Amendment and. *See* Sixth Amendment
  as source of criminal law, 114–115

Bills of attainder, 134

Binding-out system, 424

Biological inferiority, 71

Biological theories, 66, 71–76
  body-type, 72, 73
  criminal anthropology and, 71–72
  heredity studies, 73–74

Bionics, 469

BJS (Bureau of Justice Statistics), National Incident-Based Reporting System and, 40–43

Black, Hugo, 116

Black market, in prisons, 353

Blackmun, Harry A., 298

Blended sentences, 445

Blue laws, 26, 235

Blumberg, Mark, 338

Bobbies, 148

Bobbitt, Lorena, 30

M

Prison(s). *See* Correctional facilities
Prisoners. *See* Inmates
Prisonization, 350
Prison terms, constancy of, 322
Privacy, probation and, 389
Private security, 170–173
  citizen contact with, 172
  diminished public responsibility and, 173
  officers' legal status and authority, 172
  police officers moonlighting in, 172–173
  qualifications and training in, 173
  reasons for growth, 171–172
Privatization, of prisons, 314–315, 481
Probable cause, 7, 122–123, 244
  search and arrest warrants and, 118
Probation, 379–390. *See also* Intensive-supervision probation and parole
  administration of, 380
  caseload size and, 389, 402
  confidentiality and privacy and, 389
  definition of, 379
  fees for, 388–389
  historical background of, 380
  for juveniles, 426–427, 447–448
    wilderness programs, 449
  parole vs., 390–391
  placement on, 381–385
    presentence investigation and, 381–383
    probation order and, 383–385
  recidivism during, 389–390
  stages of, 381
  supervision and service delivery and, 385–387
  termination of, 387–388
  types of, 379
Probation conditions, 385
Probation officers
  juvenile, employment as, 446
  liability of, 398
  matching probationers to, 385
Probation order, 383–385
Probation period, for new police officers, 208
Probation subsidy, 380
Problem solving, in community policing, 200
Pro bono representation, 240
Procedural law, 114–134
  Bill of Rights and, 114–115
  definition of, 106–107
  Eighth Amendment and. *See* Eighth Amendment
  Fifth Amendment and. *See* Fifth Amendment
  Fourteenth Amendment and, 115–117

Fourth Amendment and. *See* Fourth Amendment
  miscarriages of justice and, 134–137
  Sixth Amendment and. *See* Sixth Amendment
Professional(s)
  corrections officers as, 360–361
  police officers as, 188, 216–217
Professional model of policing, 154
Progesterone, 74, 75
Program participation, in halfway houses, 410–412
Proof, standards of, 122–124
Property crimes, 33
  percentage of inmates serving time for, 324
  rates of, 53, 54
  victims of, 55
Proportionality review, 295
Proprietary security, 170–171
Prosecutors, 233–237
  assistant district attorneys, 237
  decision to charge and prosecute and, 234–235
  decision to plea bargain and, 236
  employment as, 132
  grand juries and, 250–251
  plea bargaining and, 252, 253
  recommendation of amount of bail and, 236
  rules of discovery and, 236–237
  selection and career prospects of, 237
  special, police corruption and, 216
Pro se defense, 132
Prostitution, in prisons, 353
Protective custody, 335
Protective sweeps, 121
Pseudofamilies, of female inmates, 356–357
PSIRs (presentence investigation reports), 281–282, 381–383
Psychoanalytic theories, 66, 77–78
Psychological qualities, of successful police officers, 202–203
Psychological testing, for police officer applicants, 207
Psychological theories, 66, 76–81
  humanistic, 66, 78–81
  intelligence and, 66, 76
  psychoanalytic, 66, 77–78
Psychological victimization, in prisons, 353
Psychopaths, 77
Public. *See also* Community
  confidence in police, 180–183
    honesty and ethical standards and, 183
    prevention of crime and, 181, 182
    protection from crime and, 180–182

solution of crime and, 181, 182
    treatment of citizens and, 182–183
  support for death penalty, 297–299
Public defenders, 240–241
Public order offenses, 33
Public safety officers, recruitment of, 205
Public service officers, 469
Public trial, right to, 128, 129
Punishment. *See also* Incarceration
  capital. *See* Death penalty
  criminal, 277
  cruel and unusual, protection against, 133–134
  effective, 87–88
  as element of crime, 32
  future of, 480
  historical, 308–309
  as penal sanction, 108
  philosophical rationales for, 277–281
    deterrence as, 278–279
    incapacitation as, 278
    rehabilitation as, 279–280
    restoration as, 280–281
    retribution as, 278
  as purpose of court, 233

Q

Quakers, 284
Quinney, Richard, 93

R

"Rabble" class, 333
Race/ethnicity
  and confidence in police, 180–183
  death penalty and, 287–288, 289, 290, 297
  and fear of crime, 51
  inmate society and, 351, 352, 353, 354
  of juvenile offenders, 437
    incarcerated, 455
  of local police officers, 162, 204
  of prison inmates, 322–323, 324
  of sheriffs' department personnel, 166
Radelet, Michael, 136
Radical nonintervention, 90, 440
Radical theory, 67, 93–95
Random patrols, 155, 190
Rape, victims of, 53
Rational choice theory, 69
Realists, police officers as, 188
Reasonable doubt, proof beyond, 123, 124
Reasonable suspicion, 122, 123
Recidivism, 367–368
  halfway houses and, 413
  parole and, 399–400